Steve Cooper's AUSTRALIAN FISHING Guide

EDITION 2

EXPLORE AUSTRALIA

For Robert and Hilary, who encouraged me to write

CONTENTS

INTRODUCTION

Nobody I have met can truthfully say they have fished everywhere in Australia. It is too vast a continent with far too many angling opportunities to experience in one lifetime. When historian Professor Geoffrey Blainey coined the phrase the 'tyranny of distance' about geography's role in shaping Australia, he could have been writing about fishing in this great land.

I will never be able to fish all the places I would like to visit. But I will have fun trying.

I have been lucky, though, enjoying a variety of fishing destinations in every state and territory, and so I've packed this book with hundreds of my favourite places. It includes descriptions of destinations and facilities, lists of species found at each spot, tips and techniques, tackle advice and, of course, some great fishing yarns.

Fishing success at many of these destinations was achieved with the help of local knowledge. If you are heading to an area you know little about, consider spending a day on the water with a fishing guide – the investment will set you up for the rest of your stay.

Many places I have visited are not listed. Some were left out because I am not yet prepared to write about them – in several instances, this comes down to promising not to reveal the details. You'll have to discover them on your own.

According to the Australian Bureau of Statistics, there are more than five million anglers in Australia. The recreational fishing industry employs more than 100,000 people, providing significant numbers of jobs in coastal and regional areas, in the tackle, boating, tourism, fishing charter and associated industries.

Despite the size of the recreational fishing industry, the bureau says most angling effort takes place along the coast and estuaries of Queensland, NSW and Victoria, reflecting both the excellent fishing areas and the geographic spread of Australia's population.

Steve with the catch of the day

So, the good news is that beyond the east coast and the estuaries, our country has vast areas with little fishing pressure, and the adventurous angler has a wealth of opportunities to explore.

Why aren't you out there already?

Travel safely,
Steve Cooper

As well as all my fellow anglers mentioned throughout the book, I'd particularly like to thank Rod Harrison, Rod Mackenzie, Emma George, Al McGlashan, Roger Butler, Cam Whittam, Dom Domagala, Bob Hart, Bob McPherson, Michael Cooper, Gary Fitzgerald, Mick Fletorides, Alex Julius, Mike Baxter and Brendan Wing for their photographs and information. I also received assistance from tourism operators and some fishing guides. I would like to thank Vic McCristal's and Dick Eussen's invaluable fishing advice too.

Steve caught this barramundi in the Daly River, NT

Before YOU DROP A LINE

FISH NAME DIRECTORY

A non-angler listening to anglers converse could be forgiven for not understanding what was being said. 'Angler speak' is a different language from English. It comprises vernacular names for just about everything that swims, including anglers!

Australians have a habit of changing names, sometimes with a twist. Fish names like pillies, grubs, snotties, goodoo or jewie are vernacular names that are not understood outside of the fishing fraternity.

In 2001, the Fisheries Research and Development Corporation (FRDC) established an Australian Fish Names Committee to put some conformity into fish nomenclature. In 2007 the FRDC adopted the Australian Fish Names Standard, which includes 4500 Australian and imported species.

When I interviewed the Fish Names Committee chairman Roy Palmer, he said the committee's aim was to end more than 200 years of confusion by standardising Australian fish names. He said a dedicated group of seafood experts had taken six years to produce a standard name for 4500 varieties of seafood, both local and imported.

'We pulled together a committee of seafood catchers and sellers, scientists, and fisheries managers; then we talked to industry people and consumers from one end of the country to the other,' Mr Palmer said.

'It wasn't always an easy task convincing people they needed to let go of local names, no matter how quaint, in favour of a single name across the nation. I guess it was easy for something like the snotnose trevalla, but a bit harder with the tommy ruff.

'We had to make the changes to stop the purchasers' confusion, and, in some cases, to stop deliberate substitution of cheaper fish under false names.'

The outcome is a standard enforceable through Standards Australia Australian Standard® AS SSA 5300 – 2007: Australian Fish Names Standards.

A database of all species listed in the Australian Fish Names Standard is available at **www.fishnames.com.au**. When you look up snapper, for instance, the database comes up with 45 variations on the name; all of them different fish, and many of these names have other names as well.

In Victoria, small snapper are pinkies, then become reds or snapper. West Australians prefer to call snapper pinkies or pink snapper. In SA, small snapper are referred to as rugger, larger fish as cobs; in NSW and Queensland, small snapper are squire then snapper. Other names include cockney bream, squire, red bream, reddies and knobbies. Phew, confusing, isn't it?

One of Victoria's more confusing species is the trevalla. This species regularly enters our bays in good numbers. The correct name for trevalla is warehou. It comes with a list of vernacular names including: snotties, snotgall trevalla, silver or sea bream, the Lord's fish, slimeys and haddock.

Moreover, the appropriate vernacular depends on where you are fishing. At Portland and Apollo Bay, haddock is the popular nomenclature; Corio Bay anglers call these same fish snotties, while along the eastern seaboard of Port Phillip, trevalla is preferred. Silver trevally are called silvers down south, and blurters in southern NSW.

Across the Top End, fingermark bream in Queensland become golden snapper in the NT. Yellowtail kingfish are called kingies, yellowtail, hoodlums and bandits, from southern Queensland to SA. Moreover, herein lies one of the problems: in NSW, a yellowtail is a small baitfish, and kingfish is the more common term. Queen snapper is also called blue morwong from Victoria to WA, and saddletail snapper is called large mouth nannygai or ruby emperor, depending on where it is caught across northern Australia.

Victorian anglers refer to mulloway as just that. Go to NSW or parts further north though, and you will find yourself fishing for jewfish. Small mulloway are called soapies in Victoria and SA. The dropping from print of vernacular names due to political correctness is to be expected. Jewfish is rarely used in Victoria for that reason. Another fish name that has rightly disappeared altogether is 'nigger', a previously popular name for luderick or blackfish.

Marlin can be billfish or beakies; tuna come under different names as well. Yellowfin tuna are commonly called fin; mackerel tuna are also known as mack tuna, and to avoid confusion with southern bluefin, northern bluefin are now called longtail.

Mako sharks are also blue pointers, great whites are also white sharks, and white pointers while school sharks are sometimes called snapper sharks. The one that gets me is the elephant fish, also known as elephant shark, but is halfway between being a shark and a stingray.

Weather is not a problem for dedicated anglers, and when fish like bream are on the bite, conditions such as rain are not relevant

Multiple names aren't limited to fish. There are variations in bait nomenclature too. Pilchards are pillies, pipis can be cockles, depending on where you are, and grubs are also known as bardis and bardi grubs.

In the freshwater, Mr Palmer pointed out that yellowbelly swimming down the Murray River would undergo several name changes. It may start out as a yellowbelly, then change to golden perch, Murray perch and callop, depending on where it happens to be at the time. Even the mighty Murray cod goes under other names, like greenfish and goodoo.

He said that Australia's top-selling seafood was 'basa', a freshwater catfish imported from Vietnam. It has variously been sold as Pacific dory, shark catfish and freshwater fillet.

Take squid for example. Bay squid are commonly called southern calamari, and the variety caught offshore in Bass Strait is Gould's squid even though most anglers call them either arrow or aero squid.

There are many species of flathead, and the most common generic term for them is frog. There are variations within the species group. Dusky flathead are duskies, southern blue spotted or yank flathead are yanks while the small sand flathead caught in Port Phillip are commonly called channel rats.

One of the classic seafood names is flake, a name not found on the fish names website. However, go into a Victorian fish and chip shop and flake is on the list. The problem with flake is that most of us believe it is another name for gummy shark, but this is not always the case.

Mr Palmer said all shark meat tended to be categorised as flake, and while gummy shark was more expensive than most other sharks, shops were able to sell cheaper cuts as flake.

Vernacular fish names have been in common practise for as long as anyone can remember. As the angler travels about, names will change but the fish will stay the same.

TYPES OF FISHING

BAY FISHING

Bays are the most popular destination for saltwater anglers. Most bays are an estuary extension and may be broad, like Port Phillip, but they attract a host of similar species. When the wind blows, unlike being offshore, you can usually find somewhere to fish in the lee, out of the rough water. Many anglers take comfort knowing that the water is relatively calm and the shore isn't so far away. Such conditions are ideal for parents wanting to introduce children to fishing.

Bay fishing popularity can best be judged on weekends, holidays or during major fish migrations. During these times boat ramps and piers can become crowded. Boat ramps sometimes have long queues of cars and boat trailers, and on piers it can be standing room only when word is out of a hot bite. Although a boat gives more options, because it allows anglers to cover more water, it is not a prerequisite for success – there are times when boats are not as good as piers, breakwalls or beaches. Regardless of platform, you still have to catch the fish.

Like many southerners, I was always under the belief that anglers in the northern half of the country spent most of their fishing time chasing blue-water pelagics. However, when you go north you find most anglers fish for bottom species using similar methods to southern anglers. I have been to areas noted for their mackerel, GTs (giant trevally) and golden trevally, and even marlin, yet the fishing scene is dominated by small boats anchored up near channels and reefs. Many are fishing for southern mainstays like flathead, squid, whiting and snapper. There is no doubt that the sizzle of fresh fish fillets rates more highly with most anglers than the adrenalin rush of a high-speed pelagic.

Bay fishing is dominated by bread and butter species. In temperate waters fish such as bream snapper, flathead, mullet, whiting and squid are popular. As you head north, you find more anglers bottom bouncing for sand whiting, fingermark, dusky flathead and yellowfin bream than seeking out pelagic species like tuna or mackerel. You find anglers hooking a mix of pelagic and estuary fish because bays are estuary extensions. In Sydney Harbour, anglers catch good numbers of yellowtail kingfish and bonito, as well as bream; Hervey Bay has runs of mackerel and tuna, as well as whiting and squid; Trinity Inlet at Cairns produces bream, giant trevally and barramundi. In Port Phillip Bay, yellowtail kingfish are caught at the southern end of the bay during summer, while snapper, whiting and bream are caught in good numbers elsewhere in the bay.

Water depth and terrain are the controlling factors for species. When fishing for browsers like whiting and bream in Port Hacking, much of the fishing took place in water less than 3m deep, and sometimes as shallow as 1m. In deeper parts of the same bay, more than 5m, squid, mulloway and dusky flathead were caught.

Fish such as whiting are best targeted over ground where weed is interspersed with clear sand patches or holes. On the same ground in NSW you can expect to catch sand whiting, leatherjackets, squid, yellowfin bream and dusky flathead; in Victoria or SA, it would more likely be King George whiting, garfish, southern blue spotted (Yank) flathead, squid and mullet. Where there are pier structures, you will find the main angling target to be the likes of yellowtail scad, slimy mackerel, silver trevally, yelloweye mullet, luderick, garfish and black bream.

Rod Harrison with a giant trevally that was caught on a lure off Hervey Bay, Queensland

The best time to fish depends on the species. Whiting feed best when there is some current running and most bottom browsers are responsive to a berley trail. King George whiting school in large numbers and bite best when there is tidal flow. In terms of size, a 45–50cm whiting is a big fish while 30–35cm is common. The rig consists of a running sinker, 3–4kg breaking-strain line and hooks from No. 4 to No. 6. Top whiting baits include mussels, pipis, squid and sandworm.

Snapper often come on the bite around the change of tide. When the sun is up, snapper are more likely to be found in the deeper water, say 10–20m. After sunset, snapper often move into water as shallow as 3–5m to feed. Snapper can be caught from rocky headlands, bays and inlets and over reefs. Water turbulence can directly influence results. For example, immediately after an onshore blow – when the bottom is stirred up and the water turbid – snapper may work inshore during the day using the discoloured water as cover. At this time, shore-based anglers can expect to do well. Top baits include fish strips, garfish, squid, pilchards and octopus. Use a running sinker rig with size 4/0 Suicide pattern hooks.

Australian salmon are an excellent species to catch on lures, either trolling or spinning. Halco Twisty lures do well when spinning, while trolling from a boat, and when trolling generally you can't go past small white-skirted jigs. Use a 3kg outfit. For bait fishing, the paternoster rig with hook size about 3/0 does well. Best baits include pilchard pieces, squid, and bluebait.

Tailor are fun on light tackle and spinning for them with unweighted soft plastics seems to bring out the best in them. Sadly, the nickname 'chopper' isn't by chance and using plastics can be an expensive exercise. Better to use hard body or metal lures as these will last. A favourite bait among tailor anglers (on ganged hooks) is a whole fish, usually a pilchard, and then cast and retrieve.

Jim Harris got 'inked' by this squid

Squid range over inshore weed beds and under the lights of piers. Prawn imitation jigs or baited jigs are used in conjunction with a handline. The jig should be allowed to sink and then be retrieved slowly. Squid are attracted to the lights of piers at night and during daylight; you will catch them in water depths ranging from 1–7m.

Garfish love the shallows and are most commonly caught in water less than 2m deep, although this is not set in concrete as schools of beakies will venture into deeper water. Use a quill float and a No. 10 to No. 12 hook. Set bait should be about 1m below the float with some split shot on the line to keep the bait down. Berley is essential. Best baits include dough, sandworms and maggots. A similar set-up is used for mullet around the piers.

Black bream are much sought after in southern waters and can be found around most major pier complexes. Most of those caught weigh less than 1kg. Use a running sinker rig and a hook size about No. 4 to No. 6 with bait such as sandworms, freshwater yabbies, prawns, pipi or mussels. Lures used include metal vibes, soft plastics and small hard body types.

Yellowfin bream, which overlap with black bream in distribution terms, are often found over the same grounds as sand whiting mentioned earlier. Both species can be caught on small minnow and popper lures, soft plastics and bait including pipi and sandworm.

Many anglers carry too much gear, or they take the wrong type. Two basic outfits will cover most situations. For small species such as whiting, bream, yelloweye mullet and the like, a 3kg outfit will suffice. For bigger species such as snapper, mulloway or gummy sharks, use a heavier 7–9kg outfit. It can pay to pack away a handline with a squid jig as well.

If you intend specialising in either lure or bait, give some thought to rod choices. Many bait anglers fishing for bream or whiting prefer to employ a longer, quiver-tip style of rod – one of the best products that I have seen on the market over the past 30 years. To the best of my recollection, these rods appeared sometime during the mid-1980s and proved very popular. Little mention is made of quiver-tip rods these days, but they are still popular among anglers working bait for small, finicky fish.

For the uninitiated, a quiver-tip rod is essentially a normal tubular fibreglass rod that has been shortened by about a quarter of its length and the tubular glass tip section replaced with a thin, solid fibreglass tip extension; most tackle companies have variations. These soft-tip rods are light and ultra sensitive when it comes to bite detection. Most are about 2–2.7m long and rated for lines from 1–4kg breaking strain. The action is always classed as light due to the tip, but you can load them up and fight a good fish, once it is hooked, through the tubular glass section.

Apart from bite detection, another advantage in using these rods is when fishing in the wind. You can cast your bait, and then tighten the line. As you do so, the tip will bend under the load. Unlike other rods, the line stays tight in the wind and you can easily detect a bite – either by the rod straightening as the line goes slack, or else by the small twitches on the rod tip. If you fish bait, enjoy fishing light, and have never used a quiver tip, then perhaps you should try one – they are not expensive.

Ultra-light lure fishers use small threadline outfits in the 2–3kg ranges. The rods may feel light but have heaps of tip recovery, which gives accuracy and distance for casting. Lures are retrieved slowly, with a lift and tug on the line. As you stop pulling the line, the rod tip is lowered and, in the case of hard body minnows, the lure rises in the water column – a likely time for a strike. When soft plastics are used, the retrieving technique is the same except that instead of rising, the soft plastic drops, a time when many fish are hooked.

The first thing I do when fishing the bay, whether it is shore-based or from a boat, is to establish a berley trail. All the species listed, and more, will be attracted to a properly set up berley trail. Small plastic berley pots are available from most tackle stores. Berley is cheap and easy to make. A good base for berley usually consists of chook pellets, fish scraps, bread and tuna oil. The value of the bread is that it soaks up the oil so more of it sinks down to the fish, rather than floating away on the surface.

The trick to working berley is not to feed the fish. To that end try to establish a fine mist trail. If you put large chunks of berley in the water, the chances are the fish will feed on this and won't take your bait.

Tailor is one of Australia's most popular sport fish

Steve's

FAVOURITE FIVE DESTINATIONS FOR BAY FISHING

Fitzgerald Bay/Point Lowly, SA (p. 255)
Main fish species: *snapper*

Hervey Bay, Queensland (p. 326)
Main fish species: *golden trevally*, *mackerel tuna*, *longtail*

Port Hacking, NSW (p. 102)
Main fish species: *bream*, *flathead*, *squid*

Port Phillip, Victoria (p. 180)
Main fish species: *snapper*, *King George whiting*

Sydney Harbour, NSW (p. 96)
Main fish species: *yellowtail kingfish*, *tailor*, *salmon*, *bonito*

Western Port, Victoria (p. 167)
Main fish species: *snapper*, *King George whiting*, *gummy sharks*

Above: Life can be tough while waiting for a bite in the Coorong, SA
Below: Salmon are the mainstay of southern surf fishing

BEACH FISHING

There was a time when surf fishing was the major land-based saltwater fishing pursuit, supported by competitions that involved hundreds of competitors, and resulting in truckloads of fish being caught. Product names like Alvey (sidecast reels), Platypus (line) and Butterworth (rods) were the big end of the retail market.

The biggest beach fishing competitions were held in northern NSW and southern Queensland and the species caught was tailor. Champion anglers using long rods coupled with sidecast reels caught hundreds of tailor, becoming household names in the 1960s and 1970s through publications like *Outdoors* and *Anglers Digest*. In Queensland, there was Lester Guard, Len Thompson and Jack Alvey; the Garven brothers, John and Ross, and Harry Fuller dominated the NSW surf fishing competition scene.

These were huge events. It was in the days before mass pilchard harvesting and garfish was the main tailor bait, rigged on ganged hooks, three or four, depending on bait size. Garfish usually require four hooks, pilchards three. Even the size of the hook being ganged can alter the number of hooks required for this method. The competitions were so fierce that anglers brought boxes of ready-rigged garfish; some even had a back-up team to keep up the supply of rigged baits. Beach fishing was the big time. Sadly, many of those fish were picked up with the bucket of a front end loader, tipped into the back of a truck and taken away to a tip. We didn't think anything of this at the time – conservation wasn't the big issue it is today and anyway, there seemed to be an infinite supply of fish waiting to be caught.

The combination of beach-hauling nets that reduced catches and the ever-expanding development of boat fishing resulted in a decline in beach fishing. And besides, the public didn't want to see any more mass slaughters, even if all the fish went to a hospital or charity.

After being in the doldrums for many years, beach fishing is undergoing a resurgence in popularity (due in part to reduced netting pressures), which has seen fish like salmon and tailor more plentiful. In Victoria, for example, the numbers of Australian salmon – and the size of the fish – have grown consistently in recent years, presenting exciting opportunities for anglers who had never previously fished the surf. There was a time when fly fishers would exchange their six-weight rods for surf rods in winter. History has a habit of repeating – the decade-long drought that began around the turn of the millennium encouraged many freshwater anglers to seek a saltwater solution to their fishing addiction.

There is no in-between in surf fishing – you either love it or hate it. The rewards are there for anglers who are willing to put in time and effort. There is no shortage of beaches to fish – Australia is blessed with hundreds of surf beaches, many of them unnamed. The mainstay of southern surf anglers is Australian salmon; in the northern rivers and southern Queensland, tailor is the dominant fish. When solid reports of good schools of fish hitting a beach come in, you can guarantee the long rods and star sinkers will emerge. Many other species are available to beach anglers including flathead, mulloway, bream, snapper, shark, mullet, trevally and whiting.

READING A BEACH

Any beach angler worth their salt knows that the secret to successful fishing is primarily the ability to read a beach by water action, colour and current. This is best achieved from a high vantage point with a pair of polarising sunglasses on, before venturing down to commence fishing.

As you look at a beach, you will discern darker shades in the water where the waves do not break. These are an indication of holes or gutters where larger predators like mulloway are likely to be hunting, waiting for smaller fish to be swept past by the current or wash caused by a breaking wave.

A wave breaking offshore is often due to a shallow point, sandbar or reef. There will sometimes be calm areas on these bars where small fish seek the shelter of shallows, and flathead lie in wait along the drop offs. Rips can be found where waves change direction and the water flattens or swirls.

Tailor like to hunt along the edges of white water. Australian salmon are different. Although fast, and just as keen on a feed, salmon schools are most often found hunting along the back of breakers, or the edges of rips, for the same reason. Bigger fish – less concerned about shelter – are in the clean water away from the zones where the sand is being stirred up as it may agitate their gills.

Peak times on beaches are controlled by tide and daylight. At dusk or dawn, regardless of tide, there is often some action. A high tide with either of these times is the perfect arrangement for fish to feed. Other than dusk or dawn the optimum fishing period often occurs during a change of tide. Most anglers prefer the change at the top of the tide – although there are beaches that are most productive during low tide, especially when it brings the gutters close to shore, forcing small fish into them and into the waiting jaws of a predator.

Steve's

FAVOURITE FIVE DESTINATIONS FOR BEACH FISHING

Aire River, Victoria (p. 205)
Main fish species: *salmon, gummy sharks*

The Coorong, SA (p. 244)
Main fish species: *salmon, mulloway, gummy shark*

Fraser Island, Queensland (p. 329)
Main fish species: *tailor, flathead, dart*

Haycock Point, Merimbula, NSW (p. 109)
Main fish species: *salmon*

Venus Bay, Victoria (p. 164)
Main fish species: *salmon*

TACKLE

The best style of tackle to use on a beach depends on where you happen to be. In the northern rivers and southern Queensland, Australian-owned Alvey sidecast reels and long rods dominate the bait-fishing scene. Australian fishing tackle has a history of family-owned companies synonymous with quality products and Alvey has stood the test of time. The unique Alvey reel is accepted throughout Australia as being a reliable, efficient product.

Alvey reels owe its origins to Charles Alvey, an English migrant who in 1920 saw the need for a fishing reel that was easy to use, easy to cast, simple to maintain, and solidly constructed to give years of trouble free angling. His design – working on the basic principle of the Scottish Mallock reel – allowed the body of the reel to be turned sideways when casting, so the line stripped freely from the edge of a specially shaped spool. This took away the problem of backlash and overrun, common to users of the multiplying type of reel. When the reel was returned to the fishing position, it had the best positive direct rewind of a centrepin reel. The Alvey sidecast reel's simple design, and lack of moving parts that can be fouled by grit or water, make it a truly durable product. Despite its efficiency and durability, the sidecast reel is not as popular in southern states where beach fishing is dominated by the threadline reel.

Most surf rods are about 3.5m long and in two-piece configuration. The average surf rod can be used to cast sinkers up to 100g, which is adequate for most fishing situations. When the surf is light and side drift limited, it is preferable to use a lighter sinker. My advice is to go for a rod that you can handle in terms of its weight and power. Rod blank taper and construction determine distance, not the actual weight of the rod. How far you should aim to cast on a beach depends on where the channels or gutters are; some days they will be almost at your feet.

You must also decide whether you intend using a sidecast, overhead or threadline reel, as rod runners and reel seat locations are different. Threadline and sidecast rods have fewer guides and these are mounted higher than those bound on rods for overhead reels. The reel seat on a sidecast reel is closer to the butt end of the rod.

If you are new to beach fishing then the easiest way to start is a threadline reel, which is virtually trouble free. Overhead reels can be a problem in terms of getting an overrun when casting. The advantage of an overhead reel is that an experienced angler will cast further and maintain better control in a battle with a big fish. The rod and reel should be balanced to suit each other and the line weight. An 8–10kg outfit is a good starting point. Braid lines are all the go at present, but I recommend monofilament as the line of first choice. Braid is thinner than monofilament but it also tangles into impossible birds' nests, and doesn't have the same degree of abrasion resistance as the thicker monofilament lines.

RIGS

Australian salmon is the mainstay species of southern surf anglers. In this case there is no special leader requirement. Most anglers fish a simple two-dropper paternoster rig. The top dropper has a surf popper or saltwater fly instead of bait, the bottom dropper a 3–4/0 long shank, or Suicide pattern hook.

If you are chasing larger fish, mulloway for example, then a leader of about 25–30kg breaking strain is used. The rig is a running sinker variation of the paternoster, and hook size should be about a 6/0 in a Suicide pattern.

Star or grapnel sinkers are the most popular in the surf because they drive into the sand and become buried, making them less likely to be dislodged by wave action. The best way to attach a star sinker is with a clip swivel as this allows you a fast and easy way of changing sinker weights to suit conditions.

When fishing tailor, the rig is a short piece of piano wire attached to a set of ganged hooks, which are inserted into a garfish or pilchard. Bream, dart and flathead are caught using a running sinker – a small ball sinker allowed to run down to a No. 2 or No. 3 hook. Preferred bait is beachworm or whitebait.

Rod holders are used with threadline or overhead rods. No need to buy them, you can make your own simply by purchasing about a metre of 50mm diameter PVC tubing and cutting a 45-degree angle on one end. In the case of the sidecast, the angler generally holds his rod in a rod bucket at his waist.

Spinning is popular, and despite the advances in soft plastic lures, many of the old-fashioned chrome metal lures – such as slices and Twisties – still produce results.

BAIT

Pilchards, garfish, bluebait, whitebait, squid, pipi, beachworm and sandworm are commonly used baits. Anglers wanting to hook bigger fish prefer big baits like salmon fillets, fish heads and squid heads.

A small nylon bait board is one of the handiest items you can take, as it can be difficult filleting a fish or cutting a squid strip on sand.

Gus Storer shows off a gummy shark that was caught in the surf on squid

BOAT FISHING

The golden rule of boat ownership is to understand that it does not guarantee fishing success, a fact soon discovered by first-time boat owners. A boat can be a bonus or a liability; it depends on how and where you use it, and how well it is maintained.

Prospective boat buyers need to consider the type of fishing (bay, offshore, estuary and lake) they want to do and the number of passengers they will have. The size and type of hull will depend on where you will do most of your fishing. If you fish relatively calm waters such as rivers, lakes or estuaries, and want a stable casting platform, then look at a flat-bottomed hull – vee-shaped hulls are more suited to chop or the swell of bay and offshore waters. A deep vee hull will handle choppy conditions better than a moderate vee hull, but the latter is a more stable fishing platform. A 4.5–5m boat will cover most bay fishing; however, in my opinion, this is too small to be used several kilometres offshore. Deck space needs consideration too – a large cabin is a luxury in a fishing boat when a cuddly cabin, or even a canopy, will offer enough protection from rain and sun.

For registration purposes, the law requires powered boats to carry basic safety items such as flares and life jackets, a bailing bucket, an anchor with about 50m of rope, compass and, in some cases, a marine radio (27MHz or VHF). It is just as important to ensure that you teach whoever is on board, child or adult, how to drive the boat and use the radio – you never know when it might come in handy. If you intend going offshore more than two nautical miles (excluding bays) then an EPIRB (emergency position indicating radio beacon) is also required. If you don't have a marine radio then take out a mobile phone, these have proven good value for a number of boaters in difficulty. When the mobile phone says it has no signal, try sending an SMS, or SOS if you are in trouble, and the text message will often get through.

Ever wondered what to do when you come across a scene on the water that is a potential emergency? This is what happened in a main shipping channel of Port Phillip offshoot, Corio Bay. With two companions, we spotted an upturned catamaran yacht in the channel at about 7pm. A life jacket was attached to a rope and trailing off the stern. What do you do? Had someone fallen in without their lifejacket?

We tried calling the Coast Guard on the radio but there was no response, so out came the mobile phone and 000 was dialled. The woman who answered was pleasant enough and asked, 'where are you calling from?'

'Corio Bay, about 1km east of Point Henry in the shipping channel and close to Buoy No. 1,' I said.

'Where's Corio Bay?' she asked.

'Geelong,' I said.

'I'm from Melbourne and I've never heard of Corio Bay; I've found Corio Bay but I can't find Point Henry – but I have found Corio Quay,' she said.

The Quay is at the western end of the bay, several kilometres from our position. A number of minutes passed and the yacht continued drifting north until it was out of the channel, but then the mast was snagged on the bottom. In frustration, I asked the operator if she could put me through to the water police: 'No, I'm not allowed to do that until I establish a location.'

Finally, she took our telephone number. Meanwhile, one of the crew rang the Coast Guard: 'We'll be out there in about 20 minutes,' was the response. 'Can you stay with the boat?' An hour later, the southerly was blowing about 25 knots and still there was no sign of anybody. A couple more phone calls, during which time we were assured the Coast Guard was coming ... soon.

Finally, the truth came out. No-one was missing and the Coast Guard was at Point Henry waiting to pick up the yacht's owner so he could jump in the water and attach a rope: 'We are not worried if you leave the boat, it's private property and no-one is in danger.' And that's exactly what we did. That's when we spotted the Coast Guard boat heading down the

This boat ramp in the Bay of Fishes near Port Campbell is the longest and steepest in Victoria

channel – past our boat, and another boat that was also standing by, and past Buoy No. 1, where we had been standing by with the yacht.

As we headed into Stingray Bay, to catch what was left of the tide, I wondered where they were going. I'd had enough. I wondered if they found the yacht? Life was a lot less complicated when you could ring the police direct. At least the local coppers know how to find Corio Bay – and had we had a Global Positioning System (GPS) on board, we would have been able to relay our exact position through latitude and longitude.

NAVIGATION

In any sort of serious fishing boat, on-board equipment should include a sonar and GPS unit. Many boat-makers offer sonar–GPS combination units and these are excellent, especially those that come with charts. A good sonar–GPS unit will have navigational charts, digital compass, water temperature, boat speed, tide and lunar phase information, as well as tracking and distance-travelled features.

GPS technology works by receiving signals from satellites that are then interpreted to give you a position on the water calculated as latitude and longitude, which is a measure of distance, not time. In that regard, one degree equals 60 nautical miles or 111km; one minute equals one nautical mile; and one second equals one-sixtieth of a nautical mile. The value of a GPS is manifold. These units have removed the need for triangulation – that is, sighting up three fixed objects on land to find a mark. Moreover, the map facility shows your location, which can be handy in the middle of the night or in a fog. As for accuracy, if you can get within casting distance of a mark I reckon you are close enough.

Being able to position your boat on a waypoint or mark is fine; however, even better is being able to see the bottom and whether or not there are any fish. A good sonar–GPS will show clear definitions that the angler can easily decipher including the type of bottom, structure and weed. On some sonar–GPS, fish come up as arches or boomerangs and the bigger the arch, the bigger the fish.

Ancillary equipment to consider includes a bait board, set at about waist level. Bait fishers will appreciate multi-directional rod holders set on each

Cairns, in northern Queensland, is famous for its big gamefishing, which is why there are so many game boats in the harbour

side of a boat, which result in fewer tangles and give scope to use more lines and therefore achieve a broader coverage.

Noise can be a critical factor. Many species, mainly in calm conditions, are highly susceptible to noise over shallow grounds where they are more exposed and tend to be flighty. It is a problem that is compounded by noise amplified through water when there isn't the depth to muffle it. In this regard, the size and the materials a boat is constructed from come into play. Aluminium boats are not called tinnies without good reason. The clang of a sinker dropping onto bare metal resonates loudly enough to frighten fish away. One way of muffling sharp noises is to cover the metal floor with a material like carpet.

MAINTENANCE

The flat battery, or maybe a loose battery terminal connection, is the cause of much heartache for anglers starting a new fishing season after a few months off the water. Many anglers put their boats away for winter and then, come spring, wonder why the outboard won't start. There may be many reasons, but all reasons come down to one: maintenance, an essential part of boat ownership. When your boat doesn't start at the boat ramp, you take it home; however, when you are a few kilometres from a boat ramp and your outboard doesn't start, you have a problem. It is a basic fact of outboard motors that when they are left idle for long periods they should be serviced. It's the same with a boat trailer. At the very least, tyre pressure and wheel bearings need checking.

PLANNING

The first thing to do before you go boat fishing is to check the weather forecast, paying attention to the direction and strength of the wind and the influence that it may have on conditions. The weather bureau can be accessed online for the latest reports, radar and synoptic charts. In some waters, the Coast Guard issues regular weather updates and warnings that can be heard on Channel 88 on your marine radio. Before you head out, be sure to tell someone where you are going and when you expect to be back. Your most valuable asset is a means of communication – this is more important than an auxiliary motor, which can be useless unless conditions are calm.

RAMP ETIQUETTE

Every weekend thousands of boats are launched from boat ramps and every weekend there are problems like arguments, rubbish and a few comic performances. Most problems at boat ramps come down to etiquette and competence, or rather the lack of these attributes. There always seems to be queue jumpers, slow coaches and people who simply don't have enough experience. There are a few basic rules that should be followed to reduce stress and make life easy for everyone.

New boat owners often have trouble – sometimes this is because they are unsure of what they are doing. It only takes a couple of minutes to extend a little courtesy and give them some assistance. Backing a boat trailer isn't difficult; it's more a matter of doing it often enough to get a feel for it. If you decide to practise, do so using your door mirrors. The trick with mirrors is that you always steer towards the boat. When the boat appears in one of the mirrors, pull the steering wheel towards it. Therefore, in your right hand mirror with the boat appearing, you pull your steering wheel to the right to straighten the boat up.

When you arrive at a boat ramp, prepare your boat before moving into the lead lanes for launching. This means taking any ties off, putting in the bungs, unlocking the engine tilt and priming the fuel bowl. When launching at night turn your lights off when reversing. Other people trying to reverse won't be able to see what they're doing if they are looking into the glare of your headlights. Turning off your headlights will also improve your own night vision. Some anglers leave the running lights on their boats switched on to act as a guide at ramps with no lighting. Another good ploy is to place a torch on the side of the ramp at the bottom as an indicator of where the trailer needs to end up.

If it is a two-lane ramp, don't back down the centre, use one lane and stick to it. Some people consistently back down the middle and, as often as not, it is because they don't have the confidence to reverse down a single lane. What they should do is practice.

When you have backed your boat into the water, don't dally, unhitch the boat and move it away quickly. There is no excuse for having a conversation on the ramp while your boat is sitting in the water on the trailer, especially if there are other people waiting to launch their craft. Many ramps have pontoons or small jetties and these are designed for people to moor their boats while either getting or parking their vehicles. Use them.

Steve's
FAVOURITE FIVE DESTINATIONS FOR BOAT FISHING

Bermagui, NSW (p. 107)
Main fish species: *marlin*, *tuna*

Breaksea Spit, Hervey Bay, Queensland (p. 328)
Main fish species: *GTs*, *mackerel*, *marlin*, *snapper*

Cairns, Queensland (p. 351)
Main fish species: *mackerel*, *wahoo*, *marlin*

Darwin, NT (p. 290)
Main fish species: *black jew*, *golden snapper*

Marion Bay, SA (p. 247)
Main fish species: *tailor, Samson fish*, *snapper*, *King George whiting*

If you have a drive-on drive-off trailer, you should make use of it. Not only is it easier to drive a boat on or off, it makes the operation fast. When driving a boat on, it is common for boat owners to leave their engines running and in gear to hold the boat against the hitch. Limit the time for this. Leaving your motor running in the prop wash isn't necessarily good for it.

If you have a GPS unit, take the time to mark the entrance to the boat ramp as a waypoint. If you are ever out at night and fog rolls in, the few seconds it took to mark the waypoint will save you a lot of worry.

ANCHORING

Keeping a boat in position and limiting movement in the form of swing is a critical element in fishing. Swinging boats cause lines to cross, tangles and can sometimes even cost the angler a good fish.

When fishing in bays you should always carry at least two types of anchor, one for mud or sand and one for reef. The secret of effective anchoring lies in the use of a long length of heavy chain. The boat moving up and down on the anchor rope is then only lifting the chain instead of levering the anchor up and down and bending the prongs. To improve on this, a rubber ring tied off the bow and attached to the anchor rope is a solid investment. As the boat rises and falls the ring stretches but there is no lifting action on the anchor.

Reef anchors are a necessity when fishing heavy ground. The advantage of a reef anchor is the soft prongs that will bend if the anchor becomes lodged. On heavy-duty multi-pronged anchors the failure of the anchor to bend often results in a lost anchor. In shallow ground, such as estuaries, a couple of long poles pushed into the bottom will do, and tied off to the boat, work as well as any anchor. In shallow areas where the bottom is thick mud, a solid lump of steel or lead also does the job well. In this case, you are relying on the weight to bury in the mud and hold in the soft ground, whereas anchors with forks or blades are unable to get any purchase.

Hooked up off Bermagui, NSW

In an estuary or bay where there is a strong current, a boat will normally hold reasonably well with the current. On days when wind and wave action are the major influences on boat movement, swing is a problem. There will always be times when the water is too rough to do anything except allow the boat to swing, but on most days you can reduce the amount of swing and drift.

There are a couple of ways to reduce boat movement. One is to employ a second anchor on the stern, or alternatively bridle rig the boat. Stern anchors can be a problem as there is a need to tether the anchor short to the boat. If you have too much anchor rope trailing astern, there is always the risk of a good fish getting tangled on the line.

Bridle rigging is often better. When the anchor is out, a loop is put in the anchor rope and another rope is attached through the loop. This is tied off on the stern cleat of the boat. By lengthening or shortening this rope, you change the angle of the boat and reduce movement.

You can also bridle rig with two anchors set out at about 45 degrees from the centre-line of the boat; a short rope looped about each anchor line and tied at the transom will mean only the stern can swing and it will be a minimal amount of movement, generally less than a couple of metres.

If fishing offshore, a sea anchor comes in handy to slow down the rate of drift. Many bay anglers fishing in a current employ sea anchors in the form of large buckets to hold the stern of their boats steady.

If raising the anchor presents problems, and you don't have an anchor winch, the way around this is to use a large polystyrene ball or heavy plastic float. When it comes time to raise the anchor, the float is placed on the anchor rope via a shackle. The boat is motored forward; this forces the float down the anchor rope to lift the anchor off the bottom.

ESTUARY FISHING

An estuary is the doorway to the sea; the tidal mouth of a river. The demarcation between estuary and river is where the upstream extremity of salt water, meets fresh water. For experienced anglers, tidal movement is the telling factor, and tide height and direction dictate where fish will be. Tidal streams enable big predators such as mulloway to move over shallow sandbars to hunt fish, prawns and crabs, and it is tidal streams that push feed across drop offs and weed lines to ambush predators like flathead. Browsers such as bream and whiting move with the rising waters too, as these give access to nippers, crabs and worms on mud and sand banks that may have been exposed, or are too shallow on low tide. Even small bait fish move upstream with the tide. However, high tides put more water between the fish, which can make fishing less productive.

An outgoing tide often brings with it a flurry of nervous water caused by bait fish that leave their departure until the last minute. On low tide, fish tend to congregate in the deeper holes or choke points. These are easier to discern as an estuary empties, which is why prime time, whatever the location, is the last couple of hours of ebb, and the first hour or so, of flood tide. By the time the small fish get going, predators have already taken up station. Flathead will be lying undercover on the edges of drop offs, mulloway, salmon and tailor will be patrolling the deeper holes, and barramundi will be waiting at the mouths of small creeks and drains. When fishing around, or on bridges and jetties where a current is running, always fish into the current as this is where fish will be waiting to ambush their food.

Whether you're sweating profusely or rugged up in woollies and wearing a beanie, estuaries in different climates have a lot in common. The key to their fishing tempo is tides, those comings and goings of the sea. Tides take some fish to their feed and alternately bring feed to fish. In the tropical north, estuary anglers are always in anticipation of a silver eruption, or perhaps the feel of a hard-pulling mangrove jack tearing off with the lure into a gnarled snag. As you move south, estuary species seem tamer by comparison. A big barra erupting from the water is an awesome sight – but so too is the slash of the gill cutters on an estuary perch; or the unfolding drama of a big dusky flathead lifted on its pectoral fins, dorsal fin erect as it readies to strike your lure.

From southern Queensland to southern NSW, yellowfin bream, flathead and sand whiting are the mainstay. Further south, from the south coast of NSW, through Victoria, Tasmania, SA and southern WA, dominant estuary species include black bream and flathead and, depending on location, there could be estuary perch, luderick, silver trevally, mullet or salmon. And these are just a few – there are many more including varieties of garfish, trevally, cod, mullet, shark and mulloway.

Regardless of water temperature or location, the methodology of estuary fishing is the same: predators such as barramundi, flathead and mulloway are caught on lures and live bait; and browsers such as bream and whiting on lures and dead bait. Most changes are made in tackle. Take spinning for example – down south, light lines and small lures dominate, whereas up north, lures are bigger and the outfits stronger.

The major attraction of an estuary for all fish is food. These waterways, many of them lined with mangrove trees, act as nurseries that give shelter and sustenance to small fish. It is a critical role in the marine cycle. It is in these tidal waters that fish eggs hatch and those hatchlings that aren't eaten grow into juvenile fish, feeding on zooplankton and learning survival skills. This food source, the plankton and juvenile fish, attracts other fish, which is why estuaries offer some of the best available fishing.

Estuary hot spots almost invariably involve a structure of some sort. Weed lines are great food sources for species that nibble on crustaceans or vegetation: decaying vegetation and softer sand attracts many burrowing creatures, which provide

Mangrove jack is a popular estuary sport fish

meals for browsers like whiting and bream, while luderick may feed on the weed, or the tiny shrimp and worms. Sand and mud banks attract fish too, especially those banks exposed at low tide. As water levels rise, fish will move onto the banks to suck nippers and sandworms. In some estuaries you can see where bream have been by the small craters they leave. A favourite area for estuary anglers is around oyster racks in those estuaries where oyster farming is undertaken. Bream are the most likely species but many other fish hang around these racks including flathead and garfish.

Anglers casting lures soon learn about the propensity of sought-after species to inhabit difficult areas. Easy snags are often the most heavily fished and consequently rarely produce the goods. If you want to catch fish it often comes down to risking a lure – the fish population seems to decrease in inverse proportion to the degree of difficulty associated with lure presentation.

Anglers who achieve consistent success fishing estuaries often have an acute sense of awareness in what to look for. The key ingredients to success (just as important as offering up the right bait or lure) is the ability to read the water and spot the telltale signposts of snags or weedbeds, perhaps the odd wink of a fish, and then understanding what is happening. Another sign is found on the snags where the fish have nibbled the barnacles, leaving lighter coloured scars on the dead timber. Flathead follow the bream upstream, but they often sunbake on the shallow sand flats waiting for a tasty morsel. On bright days in clear water you sometimes see flathead. One way of finding where they have been is to walk the flats at low tide and look for elongated teardrop shapes in the sand, indicating where a flathead has been laying.

A good pair of polaroid sunglasses is a must for fishing skinny waters for the likes of whiting. Anglers who seek this fish look for holes in the sand or weed where whiting will congregate. Over sand bottoms, whiting holes are simply identified as darker in colour than the surrounding water. These holes can range from a metre, up to several metres in length and on the right part of the tide can be real whiting hot spots.

Anglers should always be ready to make adjustments for weather events. On a visit to Mallacoota Inlet that was marred by persistent downpours, we stopped lure casting for bream and flathead and picked up a shovel and went looking for scrubworms. Rainfall runoff flushes worms into the estuary and the bream school near-drains in anticipation of feasting on red wrigglers – soft, succulent meat with a wriggle in the tail. Bream are a good example of a species with a reputation for being contrary. One day they will be easy, the following day it's like fishing for a different species. Bream will more likely be shy and finicky on bright sunny days, and easier to catch when there is cloud to dull the sun. Like most estuary species, bream often feed better around the change of tide. In areas where they feel relatively safe, such as in a large snag, they may feed at any time of the day or night.

Berley can be used to attract a host of species. It works from a boat or shore and because estuaries have a definable current, it is particularly effective. A key factor in shallow water berley operations is the terrain. The first thing to do is to find an area where there is both current and a slight drop off. Current is essential to disperse berley and dead flat ground is not as productive as uneven areas. A slight drop off, even if it's only 10cm or 15cm, can make all the difference.

LURES

In tropical estuaries, baitcaster outfits are preferred for large lure presentations, although many anglers prefer to use threadline outfits when flicking soft plastic lures, particularly with smaller or unweighted lures. The reels are spooled with 15kg breaking strain braid and 24kg leader material is attached. Popular lures include 10–12cm bibbed minnows such as Barra Classics, Laser Pros and B-52s. All brands of soft plastic produce results; however, there are so many toothy fish you soon discover that using them can be an expensive exercise. Cherubin (shrimp) and mullet are used as live bait for barramundi, and prawns are used for most species.

In temperate estuaries, threadline outfits are the standard and depending on how you want to fish, these can range in line classes from 2–8kg. Even though there is a large movement of anglers now working light tackle and small lures, bait fishers are still the largest contingent.

BAIT

Baits like prawn, pipi, shrimp, and sandworm are standard fare for most estuarine browsers like bream, mullet and whiting. Fish like salmon and tailor will take most baits as well as small lures. Estuary perch like live prawns and bass yabbies, while flathead are often fished for with live mullet, although a pilchard or prawn fished on the bottom also works. Mulloway require a different approach altogether – bait size goes up a notch and live baits such as mullet, tailor and salmon are good, as are squid and fish fillets.

RIGS

Fishing rigs vary to suit the species. Midwater to surface fish like garfish, mullet and luderick should be fished for under a float. When it comes to bottom feeders like bream, many anglers rig up a running sinker rig; however, unweighted bait allowed to sink naturally is often a better option, especially in and around snags. In southern estuaries lures, particularly small bibbed minnows and soft plastics, are good value on the likes of bream, perch, salmon, tailor and flathead.

Clint Logan caught this estuary perch in Mallacoota Inlet, East Gippsland, Victoria

Steve's FAVOURITE FIVE DESTINATIONS FOR ESTUARY FISHING

Goose Creek, Melville Island, NT (p. 313)
Main fish species: *saratoga*

Mallacoota Inlet, Victoria (p. 142)
Main fish species: *bream*, *estuary perch*, *flathead*

Trinity Inlet, Queensland (p. 355)
Main fish species: *barramundi*, *mangrove jack*

Waterpark Creek, Queensland (p. 343)
Main fish species: *barramundi*, *threadfin salmon*, *mulloway*, *giant trevally*

Lake Wonboyn, NSW (p. 114)
Main fish species: *bream*, *flathead*, *estuary perch*

An increasing number of anglers are fly-fishing in estuaries and accounting for most of the species mentioned. In temperate waters, the standard fly outfit is about an eight weight, with an intermediate or sinktip line and level line leader of 3–6kg breaking strain. Three of the best flies in temperate waters are the Clouser Minnow, Crazy Charlie and the Skinner's Shrimp in about 1/0–3/0 sizes. In the tropics, 10 weight outfits with intermediate or fast sink lines and heavy leaders in the 20kg class are common. Flies to use include Bendback Deceivers, Clousers and Pink Things (Whistlers) about 4/0–5/0.

Lake Eildon, Victoria, during the drought years of the mid-2000s; the structure of drowned trees is clearly visible and this is where native fish and redfin are to be found

LAKE FISHING

Australia's lakes are cyclical in that they offer boom or bust fishing. The fish are not natural, having been stocked, and how well a lake will fish is often determined by external factors – such as the weather.

In the spring of 2010, Australia was a sodden place as rains of Biblical proportions caused widespread flooding from Queensland to Victoria. In Queensland, dams stocked with millions of barramundi overflowed and, in some instances such as Lake Awoonga, thousands of barramundi were washed over the dam wall. In Victoria, the rains broke the decade-long drought. Dustbowls filled and became lakes again and Fisheries Victoria rushed to take advantage, buying trout to put into the new lakes. In July 2011, I was catching brown and rainbow trout in Lake Tooliorook that weighed more than 1kg – trout that nine months previous had been yearlings of 200–300g, in a lake that didn't exist at all a year earlier. This is the way of lake fishing: take what is available while it is on offer.

Lakes and impoundments are stocked with a variety of species ranging from European imports like trout, redfin and carp to native species like yellowbelly, Murray cod and sooty grunter. Lakes have also been used to stock other native species – such as barramundi and Australian bass – outside their normal habitat.

In the days when trout ruled in southern Australia, fisheries used to talk about cold water (trout) and warm water (cod) species. It was a simplistic division, and it was wrong. Native fish such as Murray cod will tolerate low water temperatures, but survive better than trout when water temperatures are high. Not all European imports suffer in warm water – redfin and carp thrive when temperatures rise. Carp are very temperature tolerant, but the range of redfin is limited by the thermal barrier effect of latitudes of the upper Murray Darling – i.e. they don't like high altitude. Most lakes are stocked, so it is easy to divide fishing methods by species.

Native fish on lures require specialised techniques. You have to know where the fish are likely to be lurking and then offer a lure with all the right attributes: colour, action and depth are the keys to success.

Philip Stathis with a 67cm brown trout caught in Lake Purrumbete, Victoria

TROUT

Lake fishing tactics vary for different species of trout. Trout can be caught on bait, lures or flies, but lake trout differ from trout living in streams in the way that they move around and hunt (rather than taking up residence behind a rock or log to wait for the current to bring food). In the case of brown trout, you often find them close to shore, swimming along the margins as they forage for food around weed beds. Rainbow trout often like to stay out a little wider, so boat anglers work the calm strips of water known as wind lanes where there is sometimes a concentration of insects.

Tackle for spinning, trolling or bait fishing trout is about a 3kg threadline outfit. Trout love a fresh worm, scrubworm or the garden variety, mudeye, gudgeon or minnow. Many anglers achieve success using a dough mix or Powerbait, an artificial bait that comes in a range of colours. There are several methods – the most common is a bait set below a bubble float. A small cork between the float and hook regulates bait depth, which for casting purposes should be no more than the length of the rod.

Hooks used depend on the bait. Mudeye require a small No. 14 to No. 10 hook that is passed gently through the wing casing. For glassies and worms, a No. 6 to No. 4 in a baitholder pattern will suffice. Minnow and gudgeon are popular live baits and when they are used, a No. 8 or No. 10 hook is employed. If you prefer to fish with artificial bait, then use a paternoster rig with No. 6 hooks.

If lures are preferred then you can troll or spin. Trolling has a big following among lake anglers. In deep lakes during the warm months, anglers employ downriggers to keep their lures deep where the water is cooler. Flatline trolling is preferred in all lakes during the cold months. When trolling, try to work areas where fish are likely to hang out. As well as weed beds and snags, this also includes rocky points and drop offs. The most popular trolling lures for trout are winged lures like Tassie Devils and Loftys, or bibbed minnows. A favourite in some lakes is to rig up an attractor and trail a mudeye or lure.

Anglers who spin from shore work areas where trout are likely to be feeding, such as close to weed beds. Lures for trout are wide and varied, ranging from small, bibbed lures and soft plastics to bladed lures like Celtas. Many anglers spin with Tassie Devil–style lures, but these are difficult in shallow water. Anglers, concerned over the welfare of the fish they catch and preferring to release them, replace trebles with single hooks with the barbs flattened so that fish can be released in good health.

Fly-fishers work similar terrain to lure fishers. Use a five- to six-weight outfit with intermediate sink-tip lines for wet flies when there is no surface activity or the trout are hunting smelt. Successful wet fly patterns include gold beadhead nymphs, Tom Jones, Micks Scruffy, Chaser, Red Tag and Bullen Merri Special. When trout are feeding on top, dry flies will produce results. In this scenario, a floating line is used in conjunction with flies that match the hatch. Dry flies include Royal Wulff, Coachman, Red Tag, Red Spinner, Adams, Elk Hair Caddis, Snowflake Caddis and grasshopper patterns.

CARP

The European carp may be bad for the environment but perhaps we need to accept and understand that they are here to stay. Carp breed and grow so quickly that it's unlikely their numbers will diminish. Female carp produce up to 146,000 eggs per kilogram of body weight, and the ability of female carp to produce eggs does not decline with age. Many carp have been found up to 25 years of age.

The negative aspects of carp are well documented, but the benefits are understated and rarely promoted. This fish is underrated as a sport fish here and, because they are prolific, it is a species worth using to teach young anglers how to hook, fight and land a fish. A big carp is a credible opponent on light tackle and there are many closet carp anglers among the older generation.

Another important carp benefit is its role as a 'cod lolly'. Carp are a major food source for Murray cod, and I recall one senior Victorian Fisheries officer telling me that, 'cod pop carp down like aspirin.' Consider the benefits this has had for the more popular species like yellowbelly and silver perch. A big cod has a big engine and it takes a lot to feed, and judging by the partially digested fish bones that cod sometimes regurgitate when caught, carp are high on the menu. Remember, it is a fine thing to rejuvenate Murray cod into the Murray–Darling system through breeding and stocking, but they have to be fed.

Carp are not difficult to catch, put up a solid fight on the rod and there are no bag or size limits. A 3kg spin outfit is about right. You will also need a pea-size ball sinker, swivel and a long shank No. 6 hook. Use a running sinker rig, with a leader of about 1m from the swivel to the hook.

The first thing to do when you go carp fishing is to take a can of sweet corn. This is top bait for carp, as are cheese and maggots. A few corn kernels spread about the water where you fish will act as a berley. Thread on four or five pieces of corn and cast your bait close to weed beds. Corn can be improved as bait by adding scent – soaking the corn kernels in fish oil and dyeing the kernels with red food dye. It is important to keep a tight line – carp are somehow able to suck corn kernels off a hook without you knowing. When a good carp takes your bait, expect a vigorous strike, so be alert and ready to grab your rod when the action begins.

REDFIN

Redfin is a ferocious predator that will take baits, lure and flies. The easiest way to catch redfin is to thread a scrubworm onto a hook and drop it down among stands of dead timber. You will also hook them using a worm under a pencil float or on live minnow or gudgeon using a 3kg threadline outfit. The key to using a pencil float is that enough split shot is placed on the line below the float to keep it low in the water and upright. Set the depth to suit the area. In deep

Dane Geran caught these redfin in Victoria's Mallee

water go a full rod length; in shallow water, it is important the bait is kept off the bottom.

Redfin are aggressive and will attack the same lures used for trout. When you spin for redfin, work your lure past areas of cover, which can be logs, dead trees or weedbeds. Sometimes you will have to retrieve your lure past the same area a few times to induce a strike. While the same lures and flies will account for redfin, another favourite is the Baltic Bobber and Ice Jig. These lures are designed to be fished straight up and down and produce good results in timber or on the drift where the lure is allowed to jig up and down near the bottom. The best time to work lures for redfin seems to be about an hour or so before sunset, and it is my experience that the hotter the day the better the fishing.

A very productive way to keep a school on the boil is to release a fish after it has been attached to a line and float. The school will follow their trussed up comrade wherever it swims. Simply direct casts at the float.

NATIVES

Native fish like Murray cod, golden (yellowbelly) and silver perch will all take bait including bardi grubs, yabbies, shrimp and scrubworms. Most anglers who baitfish for native species prefer to have their baits on or near the bottom. The simplest rig for bait fishing is to use a pea-size ball sinker and allow it to run to the hook. Some anglers prefer to use running sinker rigs with a leader for the cod, and paternoster style rigs for the yellowbelly. Hook size for baits can range from a 6/0 Suicide for a large yabbie down to a No. 2 or No. 4 long shank for shrimp and bardi grubs respectively. Bobbing with lures and bait is popular in heavily timbered areas for yellowbelly. This is a method whereby the bait is dropped to the bottom, lifted a metre or so and then lifted and dropped.

Australian bass caught by Rod Harrison in Lake Wivenhoe, Queensland

Trolling or spinning for native fish requires specialised techniques. First, you have to know where the fish are likely to be lurking and then offer a lure with all the right attributes: colour, action and depth are the keys to success. If you prefer trolling then big, wide action, lures do best. Some popular lures are the Oargee, Stumpjumper, Poltergeist and Boomerang. You have to fish so close to snags and other structure that if you aren't fouled every now and again you are not close enough. Gelspun lines come into their own for trolling as you can feel when your lure is bouncing over submerged logs.

When it comes to spinning, many anglers use spinnerbaits or smaller versions of the bibbed lures like the Stumpjumper. Native fish can be caught on lures at night – surface lures like the Halco Night Walker work well after sunset, as do flies like the Dahlberg Diver and Deceiver patterns tied for neutral buoyancy.

AUSTRALIAN BASS

Australian bass are stocked in lakes and impoundments in northern NSW and southern Queensland – as far north as Lake Monduran, well out of its natural range. The milder, briefer winters mean a longer grow out period, which occurs through the warm months. This means the bass grow faster and bigger in these impoundments than they do in their natural environments further south. In Victoria, this feisty fish has been released into Blue Rock Dam and Lake Glenmaggie in Gippsland.

Tackle is a 3–5kg baitcaster or threadline outfit with a 5kg breaking strain fluorocarbon leader. Bass are caught mainly on lures, but will take flies and bait. Deep diving lures, bibless crankbaits, shallow running bibbed minnows and surface lures all account for bass. Use the divers in deeper water – when spinning or trolling edges and rocky points, crankbaits and shallow diving minnow lures are productive. Spinnerbaits and soft plastic lures do well and, for night fishing, the Halco Night Walker has proven deadly.

An eight-weight outfit is about ideal for fly-fishing. Use a floating or slow-sink intermediate line and a leader of about 2m minimum with a level line (rather than tapered leader) of about 3–4kg breaking strain. Fly-fishers find frog patterns and the Dahlberg Diver good for top-water fishing and the Clouser Deep Minnow better for deeper water. In areas of lily pads, cast the fly or soft plastic onto the plants; as it comes off the leaf and onto the water the chances are a bass will be waiting.

Bait fishers tend to use live shrimp, which are lowered into likely bass holding areas and held at different depths.

Steve's

FAVOURITE FIVE DESTINATIONS FOR LAKE FISHING

Lake Awoonga, Queensland (p. 337)
Main fish species: *barramundi*

Lake Burley Griffin, ACT (p. 138)
Main fish species: *Murray cod, yellowbelly*

Lake Mulwala, NSW (p. 126)
Main fish species: *Murray cod, yellowbelly*

Lake Purrumbete, Victoria (p. 219)
Main fish species: *trout* and *salmon*

Lake Wivenhoe, Queensland (p. 324)
Main fish species: *Australian bass*

BARRAMUNDI

Hundreds of thousands of barramundi have been stocked in Queensland lakes and dams and even in Manton Dam in the NT. Late afternoon and evening fishing is popular as this species will feed through the dark hours.

Trolling and casting lures is popular and anglers working lures prefer baitcaster outfits spooled with 15kg breaking strain braid and a metre or so of 20–35kg leader. Most anglers prefer to work lures up to 15cm, mainly floating/diving minnow types. When spinning, the best lure presentation is an ultra slow, jerky retrieve featuring long pauses and slight twitches. This is particularly effective near snags, weed banks and, in some dams, lily pads, as the barramundi often wait in ambush in these areas. Soft plastic prawn and baitfish imitations, 50–75mm, produce good results. Soft plastics can be worked on the surface or deeper. When sinking lures are used, barramundi often taken on the drop – if this is unsuccessful, the lure should be worked slowly along the bottom in a slow, lift and drop action.

Bait fishers use prawn, live garfish, bony bream and spangled perch. Prawn baits are simply hooked with a 4/0 hook through the tail and a running sinker that runs down the line to the eye of the hook. Live baits are hooked through the jaw or in front of the first dorsal fin. Catfish are a major problem when bait fishing, which is why many anglers concentrate on lures.

Bill Neilsen caught this magnificent saratoga in Borumba Dam, Queensland

SOOTY GRUNTER

Looking like a black yellowbelly, the sooty grunter or chimney sweep as it is sometimes called, is stocked in many north Queensland dams. Sooties are an aggressive fish. Although similar in shape to yellowbelly, the sooty grunter has a heavier build and more pulling power. In dams, this fish can grow to about 8kg.

Tackle is a 3–5kg baitcaster or threadline outfit with a 5kg breaking strain fluorocarbon leader. Many sooties are caught by anglers trolling lures for barramundi. Anglers also catch these fish casting bibbed minnows, spinnerbaits or surface poppers. Bait fishers use lightly weighted prawn baits to achieve good results. Sooties are best sought among snags and under lily pads. Pound for pound their strike and deep flurries are the strongest of our freshwater fish.

SARATOGA

Saratoga take up territorial lines, patrolling their area to keep out intruders. Anglers cast lures and flies and therefore invade the fish's space – it reacts by taking the offering. What anglers most enjoy about saratoga is the take. It is sight-fishing much of the time and the angler has the opportunity to annoy a saratoga into making a strike, and watching the entire episode. Saratoga, once hooked, are not a difficult catch. It is just a matter of taking it easy and slowly working them to the net for careful release.

The basic outfit is a small baitcaster or threadline spooled with 6–10kg braid line. The Halco Night Walker surface lure is a favourite, although unweighted soft plastics retrieved in a jerky, hesitant action on or just below the surface will attract a bite. Fly-fishers use six- to eight-weight outfits with floating lines, and employ surface flies like the Dahlberg Diver, suspending flies like the 3D patterns and Lefty Deceivers.

PIER AND BRIDGE FISHING

Pier fishing appeals to anglers of all ages, and it's been that way for as long as I can remember. In my teen years there were days when my friends and I would wag school to go fishing down the local piers and jetties. There was more social interaction than fish, but we were serious about our fishing. Later, I caught sharks, tuna and yellowtail kingfish from piers, along with snapper, salmon and bream.

There are good reasons why these fabricated structures are popular: most offer stable platforms sometimes even car parking and shelter, and most importantly, they produce fish.

These days there are fewer accessible piers compared to what was available 20 years ago. I guess it is inevitable that there will always be problems where anglers and officialdom cross.

Sometimes the fishing bans are introduced with good reason: vandalism is a problem, as are ever increasing costs of public liability insurance. I know of some piers where port authorities had to clamp down on anglers going underneath them to fish. In one case the snapper would bottle up under the pier, and where the snapper lurk anglers are sure to follow. The problem was that this particular pier – and others are in the same boat – had a lot of electrical wiring running about. The fear was that at some stage an angler might hook up and potentially cause serious injury.

The good news is that there are still enough piers to attract responsible anglers willing to obey the rules, and take their rubbish with them when they leave. And there are still many anglers who would rather fish from a pier, than from a boat or beach – that's how it is with piers.

Pier fishing is the home of the tackle trolley. I have seen anglers with tackle trolleys on piers near Cairns and Hervey Bay in Queensland, in NSW, Victoria and as far west as Arno Bay in SA. A wheeled trolley is an easier way to carry all the requirements for a long fishing session. Young anglers have been known to make towing hitches and attach a trolley to their bikes. As well as rods, reels and terminal tackle, anglers who use trolleys often carry all the home comforts like coolers, chairs, crab nets, stoves and cooking utensils.

The most telling feature of a productive pier is age. Like a good port, a pier needs time to mature and the older a pier is, the more heavily encrusted the pilings become with marine life. After a few seasons immersed in the water, pilings become barnacle encrusted and develop into vertical reefs. A cycle sees small fish move in, and larger fish subsequently follow. For anglers, those old pilings offer a fresh bait source for tasties like mussels, cunjevoi and crabs. The act of bait gathering, scraping mussels off with a rake for example, results in a neat little berley trail that enhances the piscatorial quality of the neighbourhood. Oddly enough, I've seen anglers scrape a piling for bait then move 20m along the pier before wetting a line. And, think of the naturally occurring berley trail created by anglers who throw their leftover bait in the water.

The most common species caught from a pier depends on where the pier is located. The waterfront at Mallacoota, Lakes Entrance and Hollands Landing are ever popular for the likes of silver trevally, bream, luderick, and mullet. Bay piers tend to produce mainly mullet, silver trevally, leatherjackets, trevalla (warehou), garfish, bream, snapper and squid. However, if you fish the pier at Lorne in Victoria you would also expect to catch salmon and barracouta. Merimbula and Tathra piers in southern NSW often produce bigger fare, including yellowtail kingfish and tuna. The pier at Hervey Bay in Queensland has a reputation for mackerel, trevally and tuna – it is a similar story with piers in WA and the NT where even barramundi are sometimes caught along with black jewfish.

Despite the food and shelter piers offer, the psyche of many pier anglers is to throw their baits far away from the structure they are standing on. But if you clamber about underneath a pier you will

Steve's

FAVOURITE FIVE DESTINATIONS FOR PIER AND BRIDGE FISHING

Broome, WA (p. 282)
Main fish species: *mackerel*, *trevally*

Lake Lonsdale, Victoria (p. 218)
Main fish species: *sharks*, *salmon*, *snapper*

St Leonards, Victoria (p. 187)
Main fish species: *snapper*

Tathra, NSW (p. 107)
Main fish species: *tuna*, *kingfish*, *sharks*

Urangan, Hervey Bay, Queensland (p. 327)
Main fish species: *mackerel*, *trevally*

be amazed at the amount of fish lingering around the pilings – so far back from the edge that they are in shadow. Experienced boat anglers, seeking species including silver trevally, trevalla (warehou), leatherjackets, snapper and mullet, know where the fish are located. Rather than fish away from the pier, these people often elect to tie up to the structure and fish between the pilings. This is a strange situation. You stand in a boat and see some anglers on the pier casting as far away from the structure as possible (and wishing they had a boat). And there you are in the boat trying to cast below the pier that the angler is standing on.

Piers are a favourite with anglers wanting to catch squid. During the day, squid will sometimes hang about piers, often staying in the shade underneath and jetting out to catch unsuspecting prey. By far the best time though is at night. Squid are attracted to lights and work the demarcation between the edge of the light beam and the dark water beyond. Anglers looking to fish a pier should always have a squid jig and a handline in their kit, just in case. This applies as much to southern anglers fishing places like Arno Bay in SA, as it does to anglers in southern Queensland or WA. Most anglers prefer to work prawn imitation jigs. These are cast, allowed to sink, and retrieved slowly in a stop-start motion. My preference is for baited jigs. These should be rigged up with the tail of the bait at the prongs if the jig is to be cast and retrieved. If you intend to simply leave the jig in the water suspended under a float, then reverse the way you put the bait on so that the head of the bait is at the prongs.

Outfits for pier fishing are basic. For smaller fish such as garfish, herring, trevally and mullet a light rod of about 2.5m with a threadline reel suited to lines of about 3–4kg breaking strain is required. And a variety of small sinkers, swivels, and a couple of quill floats as well as a selection of hooks from No. 8 through to about 2/0. For larger fish such as jewfish and snapper, go for a 3m surf rod and reel suited to lines of 7–9kg breaking strain. Sinkers should be ball or bean for running rigs, and start or pyramid for paternoster or fixed sinker rigs. I prefer 2/0–4/0 Suicide or Octopus pattern hooks, preferably chemically sharpened for snapper. For fish such as Australian salmon, you might find it preferable to come down to about 2/0, and if tailor or mackerel are preferred use ganged hooks and piano wire trace.

Some piers are popular with anglers chasing game fish like sharks, tuna and even marlin. Gamefishing was once the sole domain of the rich. That was until the advent of affordable sport fishing boats back in the 1970s. Even then, many people couldn't afford these craft, so they started to try for game fish from the shore. One of the favourite places was a pier fronting the ocean.

South Australian anglers have turned shark fishing from piers into an art form and in Victoria,

The pier at Marion Bay in SA is popular with local anglers

Point Lonsdale pier has a well-earned reputation for producing sharks. In southern NSW, Tathra pier earned a big reputation for sharks that included tiger and hammerhead varieties – along with the pier at Merimbula, this platform has been known to produce game fish such as longtail and yellowfin tuna, and yellowtail kingfish. Tropical piers such as Broome in WA and Hervey Bay in Queensland produce an amazing range of game fish.

Tackle requirements for shark fishing from a pier are much the same as for blue-water gamefishing. I recommend a 15kg gamefishing outfit for most sharks. The reel used should be capable of holding at least 800m of 15kg line, and by preference should be a lever drag model. As for the rod, a standard straight game rod is fine. These rods have a gimbal fitting at the base so you will need a gimbal belt to strap around your waist. Some anglers use a shoulder harness as this will help spread the load and relieve pressure on the angler's back and arms. In a long fight, you will be grateful for the investment.

The critical element in shark fishing is the trace. Wire trace should preferably be multi-strand and most anglers work a minimum 100kg breaking strain wire. When looping wire to crimp, many anglers use a Flemish eye, this acts as a shock absorber and can reduce wear on the wire caused by rubbing on the hook eye or swivel ring. The length of trace depends on the height of the pier off the water. You need to allow at least one metre extra when you bring a shark in. Be careful to wear gloves when handling wire. Swivels on the trace should be ball-bearing models suited to the breaking strain of the wire.

Hooks should be extra strong and sharp. Size 10/0 will handle most sharks. Mustad 7699 Sea masters COR are popular although some anglers have taken to Tuna Circles, size 16/0, which is relative to about 12/0 in conventional hook sizes. The key to the Tuna Circles is not to embed the hooks in the bait, but to have them rigged free. Always hone hooks before use, even if they have just come out of the packet. I prefer to have two hooks on the wire, the second one sliding.

Even though sharks are attracted by berley, I don't recommend this from piers – people using the local swimming beaches will not appreciate it. Fresh bait is the best. Fish fillets or whole squid do well. The basic rig to send bait out is a 20g balloon tied to the trace at the depth you want your bait to sit in the water column. About 3m is a good option for this depth. Providing you have a tail wind, the bait should head out to sea as far as you want it to go.

Live baiting is popular off many piers and this method accounts for most game fish. You can employ your 15kg game tackle for this. Slimy mackerel, yellowtail scad, salmon, silver trevally and pike are some fish that do well as live bait. These are rigged up on a 3m, 50kg breaking strain trace. Hook should be a Suicide pattern, 7/0–9/0. In this case a party balloon blown up to about 15cm is attached to the swivel at the top of the trace where it joins the main line. Use binding thread or 1kg monofilament to attach the balloon. When a fish hits the live bait the line attaching the balloon should break away.

Gamefishing is just one method. Many anglers spin for fish like salmon, tuna, trevally, mackerel, kingfish and bonito. For most fishing, anglers use a threadline outfit, usually in the 5–7kg line class.

Finally, there are bridges. Have you ever heard the saying, 'build a bridge and get over it?'

Port Campbell pier in Victoria's south-west offers up a range of species at different times of the year, from pinkies and salmon to barracouta and squid

A variation on that theme applies to mulloway, Australia's most enigmatic species – if you are going in search of mulloway and want somewhere to start, a bridge is about as good a place as anywhere.

Mulloway is among our most sought after and least caught species. What intrigues me about this species is the fetish it displays for bridges and bright lights. For a species with a seemingly shy, finicky nature, mulloway seem to revel in the bright lights and noise of big cities. This applies from Queensland to WA.

In southern Queensland, anglers fish for mulloway, or jews as they are more commonly called there, near bridges at places like Bribie Island, Brisbane and the Gold Coast canals. In the late afternoon when the soft plastic–bream brigade is coming off the water on the Nerang River on the Gold Coast, a second shift of boats is being launched by anglers going in search of mulloway.

Bridges are in favour in NSW in places like the Hawkesbury River. I fished this water with friend and Shimano Tackle boss, Colin Tannahill, who said one of the top mulloway spots was rail and road bridges running parallel to each other as they cross the river on the Sydney–Newcastle Fwy.

There are regular reports of mulloway being caught in the Yarra River in the heart of the Melbourne CBD in Victoria, where there are several bridges. Other areas of the Yarra to produce mulloway include the busy Docklands, the Bolte and Westgate bridges. These fish are often caught in another Melbourne River, the Maribyrnong, and are regularly seen swimming in the light beams that reflect onto the Barwon River from the bridge linking Barwon Heads with Ocean Grove.

Bridges also attract mulloway in SA where Adelaide's Port River is popular. In WA head west to Perth and the Swan River produces mulloway most of the year. Favourite mulloway haunts include the Canning, Narrows and Causeway bridges.

The reason mulloway are found around bridges is that as the water flows under the bridges the

Fishing for barramundi from a bridge spanning the flooded Mary River, NT

pylons create eddies that attract smaller fish; this in turn brings larger predators like mulloway to the area. Small fish are also attracted to light, and mulloway swim on the fringe of the light as they hunt unwary fish.

Anglers who chase mulloway reflect the fish, in that they are reclusive about what they are doing. A couple of fishing friends rang me to say they had done well on the mulloway in the Yarra River, catching fish up to 15kg. That was great news; except the fish had been caught a few weeks earlier and the mulloway had been off the bite for the month before I was told! It appears there are no friends in love, war or mulloway fishing.

RIVER FISHING

The uneven distribution of our rivers is characterised by the Australia climate – that never-ending cycle of drought and flood. We have plenty of rivers in places where they are taken for granted and none where they are most needed. But freshwater fish are wonderfully adaptive and have found an eco-niche despite the extremes.

Australia's river systems hold an assortment of native and imported fish species. In southern Australia, rainbow and brown trout, redfin and European carp were imported and have subsequently spread throughout many waterways. Intensive stocking regimes are helping the resurgence of native fish and Murray cod, golden perch (yellowbelly) and silver perch, and Australian bass are common captures in many areas.

In the mountainous regions, streams and rivers flow clear, their waters home to trout. In the lowlands, and pasturelands, rivers are often soiled. In northern climes in warmer waters, there is a gradual changeover from yellowbelly and Australian bass to sooty grunter, jungle perch and saratoga. Across the Top End, barramundi dominate.

River and stream fishing is more difficult than still waters because of currents and the nature of the terrain, such as levy banks and snags. When you fish in a river, where and how you fish is dictated by the species you are after. Knowing where the fish you seek are likely to be, and understanding why, is the surest way to achieving success.

Most fish like to shelter behind objects to stay out of the main force of a current. Native fish like Murray cod and yellowbelly have a predisposition for submerged timber, using logs and fallen trees both for shelter and places to launch an ambush. Both species are caught in most of the river systems from southern Queensland, through NSW and Victoria, and into SA. In many of the same waters silver perch, which are protected in some states, are plentiful.

Fly-fishing for trout in Nariel Creek, northern Victoria

Tasmania has no recreational native fish, the state's rivers being dominated by trout. The breaking of the decade-long drought in Victoria and NSW in 2010 brought a resurgence in trout fishing. Trout hunt differently to native fish in that they will shelter behind or in front of rocks or logs, which break the main force of the current, and will feed from the bottom to the surface depending on the insect activity on the day. The best trout waters are cool and well-oxygenated, usually in gravel-bottomed streams with a moderate to swift flow. Trout often use the cover of overhanging foliage along lowland riverbanks where they are likely to be found sipping shrimp.

Many anglers regard redfin as a fine table fish and for this reason it's one of the most sought after freshwater species. One of the easiest fish to catch, yet well thought of as a sport fish, redfin will take lures, fly and bait. Redfin can often be found schooling around dead trees, rocky points or beneath the grass verge overhanging a riverbank. Small redfin can run in plague proportions in some areas and are little more than nuisance value at best. Good quality redfin are another matter. In NSW, redfin are regarded as a noxious fish like European carp. Even though these fish wear noxious classifications in various states, this does not mean they are illegal to catch, nor does it detract from their sporting merits. However, there are laws in different states regarding what must happen to the fish after capture.

Carp have a larger following than many people are willing to admit. Classed as a noxious species, a big carp on light tackle will give anglers a run for their money. Most are caught on kitchen baits like corn kernels and cheese, fished on the bottom or under a float.

Australian bass is the toughest fish in southern rivers, in terms of difficulty and fighting ability for size. This species ranges from southern Queensland to East Gippsland in Victoria. Unless you are prepared to seek out remote areas and do it tough, trophy bass may prove elusive as these fish take station in pools, often surrounded by thick vegetation. As you might expect, the best pools holding the biggest fish are often remote and difficult to access, which is why bass suit the more adventurous anglers.

Sooty grunter is a fine tropical sport fish that can be caught on bait, lure and fly. In some rivers, sooties will school up under the cover of cluster fig trees and devour the orange fruit that falls off. In most waters, sooties are best sought among snags and under lily pads. Sometimes a school will be found hanging on an isolated fence post.

Saratoga can be seen along the water edge, patrolling a beat or pool often sheltered by overhanging vegetation. A solitary fish, saratoga is territorial and great to catch on surface flies and small poppers. Some anglers fish with soft plastic lures, but these lures work beneath the surface and when you fish this way, you lose the sight-fishing magic on the surface that makes saratoga fishing special. Saratoga females take their fertilised eggs into their mouths and keep them there until the first two or three days after hatching.

Barramundi are spawned in the salt and then move upstream onto the floodplains, living in fresh water until the following Wet season. All barramundi start out as males, and change sex when they are between 65cm and 75cm. In the freshwater environment, barra have a strong bronze colouring but change to silver as they move into salt water. You'll often find this species in holes on the floodplains of places like the Mary River System in the NT – and wherever there is a good snag the chances are barra will be schooled up, especially if there is a nearby drain or run-off.

Methods for beach, lake and river fishing

Fly-fishing

Fly-fishing is often perceived as being both difficult and expensive. This is a perception often promoted by the tweed and claret set. If you put in time and effort, and maybe take a few casting lessons, you will soon learn to cast well enough to present a fly in a small stream. As for the expense, it's a bit like buying clothes where labels, not quality, often dictate price.

You can buy a basic fly-fishing outfit for trout, consisting of rod, reel, backing, fly line, tapered leader and tippet, for less than a decent snapper or surf fishing outfit. The most popular outfit consists of a six-weight fly rod and reel to suit. Fly rods are based on line weights, for example a six-weight line. The reel is little more than a centrepin, and this is filled with a Dacron or braid line backing. If you want to fly-fish for barramundi or saratoga, then you would upsize to an eight-weight or ten-weight outfit. In-between, bass and yellowbelly can be caught on six- to eight-weight outfits. A small number of anglers fly-fish for Murray cod. Due to the size of the fish, ten-weight outfits are more common.

Next comes the fly line, which is attached to the backing. The most common fly line is a weight forward–floating line, which means the line has a taper that runs forward with most of the weight at the front of the line, and the line is designed to float. A variation on this line is the sink tip, where a portion of the fly line sinks. Intermediate and fast sink lines work best when presenting wet flies or large flies like Clouser Minnows and Lefty Deceivers.

Hooked up on a barramundi in Tommycut Creek, NT

Fly-fishers offering up small flies use a tapered leader that is attached to the fly line with either a nail knot or loop-to-loop connection. A tapered leader is what it says, line that tapers in diameter and strength, and most leaders are about 3m. They are designed to continue the taper in the fly line and help the fly 'turn over' during the cast. The thick end is attached to the fly line. A tippet is joined to the thin end of the tapered leader. This is a fine line, usually about 1–2.5kg breaking strain and a metre or so long. This leader in turn has the fly tied to the end. When large flies are on offer – say Dahlberg Divers for saratoga or Clousers for bass or barramundi – a level line is preferred to a tapered leader as there is no value in using a tapered leader on large flies.

Ancillary items for fly-fishing include a fly box, vest and waders. When the time comes to learn how to cast, seek professional advice from a specialist fly-fishing shop or pay for some basic casting instruction. Better to start out right than develop a casting technique that is limited by faults.

Extracting a lure needs to be done carefully

There are thousands of flies in use, but two basic types for trout are wet flies that work beneath the surface and dry flies that are designed to stay on top of the water. Here are some examples:

WETS: Gold bead head nymphs; Tom Jones; Woolly Bugger; Bagfly; Chaser, Matuka and mudeye patterns.

DRIES: Black Beetle (fished wet or dry); Coch-y-Bonddu; Rusty Dun and Orange Spinner; Adams; Royal Wulff and Red Tag.

Anglers chasing other species like saratoga, barramundi, sooty grunter, jungle perch, Murray cod and Australian bass will find four flies cover most scenarios successfully. Dahlberg Divers and various popping bugs are used for surface work, during daylight and at night. Underwater flies incorporate the various Whistler patterns, including the famous Pink Thing, Lefty Deceiver and Clouser Minnow.

Wading

If you fish rivers and streams consistently then eventually you will end up wading, whether fly-fishing or spinning. The combination of current and an uneven bottom peppered with smooth rocks can make movement difficult, until you get used to it. As you wade it is a case of one step at a time. Before taking each step, you should have already placed your front foot firmly and securely. One way to maintain balance is to use a wading stick. It doesn't have to be anything fancy, just so long as it is strong enough to take your weight.

Until you get used to wading, avoid stretches of fast water whenever possible, particularly if it is going to be above your knees. In slow water you can easily wade up to your waist and maintain your balance, but add a couple of knots to the water flow and life can become unsteady. Some anglers wear wading boots with felt soles believing, rightly, that these offer better grip.

Lures

These days, one of the joys of my summer is a stroll along Victoria's Barwon River – casting lures ranging from the Jensen Insect to tiny bibbed lures from Rebel and Rapala, as well as old bladed favourites like the Celtas – for about an hour or so before sunset. It has been my experience that the hotter the day has been, the better the fishing. When you spin with lures, you soon learn that a serious take will more likely be at your feet than in the middle of the river because that's where the redfin lie in wait. Sometimes you will have to retrieve your lure past the same area a few times to induce a strike.

Many freshwater anglers enjoy working lures on ultra-light tackle. A short flick stick weighing 2–3kg is one of the most versatile outfits available. The outfit won't suit big fish, but with a rod and reel combination in this line class, you can comfortably cast small lures in streams for trout or yellowbelly, or work surface minnows for saratoga and bass, or pluck a feisty small barramundi out of a billabong.

Rod choice is more important if you intend flicking small lures rather than fishing bait. The rod should be 1.9–2.1m in length, with a fine tip and sharp recovery action to suit lightweight casting. The rod determines the choice of reel. Choose a size 2000 threadline reel and check it is not too heavy for the rod – otherwise the combination will be ungainly to use. Always check that the reel has a bail arm roller and a smooth drag.

To get optimum performance, spool the reel with braid – you can use up to 6kg breaking strain braid, as this is still thinner than 3kg monofilament. However, when you do this, calibrate your drag setting to suit the rod: if your rod is suited to 3kg breaking strain your maximum drag setting should be about a quarter of this. For general fishing, monofilament works well enough and inexperienced anglers will have less trouble tying knots than they will using braid which requires specific knots for leader joins.

Steve's

FAVOURITE FIVE DESTINATIONS FOR RIVER FISHING

Daly River, NT (p. 292)
Main fish species: *barramundi*

Genoa River, Gipsy Point, Victoria (p. 142)
Main fish species: *flathead*, *bream*

Hawkesbury River, NSW (p. 92)
Main fish species: *bream*, *tailor*, *flathead*, *mulloway*

Murray River, Fort Courage, NSW (p. 136)
Main fish species: *Murray cod*, *yellowbelly*

Nariel Creek, Corryong, NSW (p. 124)
Main fish species: *trout*

Anglers who want to work lures will find the market is flooded with lures of different shapes, sizes and colours. Some are cheap copies of more expensive brands, but most seem to work – even if they need a little fine-tuning to make them swim straight. If you are trying lures for the first time, the best advice is to find out the lures that work best for the species and area. When in doubt, go with proven models – lures that have withstood time and change are a good starting point.

Small bladed Celta lures have been attracting trout in streams for as long as I can remember and Tassie Devils and bibbed minnows have a similar reputation in bigger rivers. Anglers are also using soft plastic lures with success. Anglers chasing yellowbelly in the Murray River have taken to working

Flathead love well presented lures

bibless minnows or 'crankbaits,' but of course you can also hook this fish on small, bibbed minnows like Stumpjumpers and spinnerbaits. Bass, sooties and saratoga will take poppers and surface minnows while barramundi will attack spinnerbaits, soft plastics and bibbed minnows. The key to success is speed and realism – the slower you can retrieve your lure while imparting some erratic action, the more likely you are to get a hook-up.

The problem with all lures is choice, and this is more so with soft plastics. Most plastics come with either a shad (flat) tail or a fine curl tail, and most have some special fish-attracting ingredient impregnated into the rubber body. The other thing that all soft plastics seem to have in common is that they work – unweighted on the surface, on the drop or dribbled prawn-like along the riverbed.

A few points are critical when luring. First, your lure needs to be where the fish are, and sometimes this can mean casting into a tangled mess of timber. Spinnerbaits are the best lures to use when casting into snags as you can often ease them through the timber. Secondly, presentation is critical. A lure should represent an easy feed for a predator and the lure needs to be worked, albeit slowly for most fish. Use the rod tip to impart a faltering movement into the lure and, for a few seconds, stop retrieving it.

Trolling is different from spinning. If anything, it is more difficult to master successfully in a river environment where current has to be allowed for constantly. Some anglers have taken to trolling from canoes and kayaks, which is fine down south; however, there is a point when you head north where a small watercraft becomes a crocodile lure. Unless you intend being the bait when you head to the tropics, leave your kayak at home.

The single most important thing I have learned about trolling is that an electric motor is better than any outboard, two-stroke or four-stroke. The latter may sound quiet, but they still have an underwater exhaust outlet.

Trout can be caught by trolling in rivers, and places like the Derwent in Tasmania are noted for the large brown trout caught on Tassie Devils. Bass are favourite trolling targets in southern Queensland impoundments where anglers troll deep divers. Redfin take most trolled lures including spinnerbaits, which also work on native fish.

Anglers who target Murray cod and barramundi essentially use the same tackle and techniques. The difference is in the lures being trolled: Murray cod lures are deep swimming with a wider swim action. Barramundi lures have a much tighter shimmy, but still swim deep for trolling. Most anglers who fish with lures prefer baitcaster outfits. The popular rod is rated for about 6kg breaking strain line but the reel is spooled with 15kg line, preferably braid. The reasons for this are twofold: braid is preferred over monofilament because it is thinner in diameter for breaking strain than monofilament, so heavier (thicker) braid is needed to counter wear and tear in timber. Thinner line means the lure swims deeper

Plastics are popular (and cheaper) for anglers chasing barra

and, because braid lacks stretch, the angler is able to feel what the lure is doing. If the lure hits mud, it will be a slower, almost dull vibration in the line; timber or rock sends sharp vibrations. When you attach your lure, use a loop knot as clips or snaps have a nasty habit of opening up at inopportune times – like when you are hooked-up.

Successful bibbed lures for Murray cod and yellowbelly include StumpJumper, Predatek Boomerang, Codzilla, Oargee, and the Bassman Codman series spinnerbaits, while Mumblers have a proven track record. Barramundi will take B-52s, Laser Pros, Killalures and Rapala X-Raps. You will save yourself a lot of money if you invest in a tackle-back; these relatively inexpensive devices are used to retrieve lures that become snagged.

Bait

Bait fishers chasing trout will find a light threadline outfit spooled with 2–3kg line does well. No. 8 to No. 6 size hooks will suit powerbait or scrubworms, a No. 12 or No. 14 for mudeyes and a No. 8 to No. 10 for minnow. Many stream anglers prefer to attach split shot to their line and allow the current to carry the bait downstream close to bank overhangs.

Outfit and bait for redfin is much the same. In my early teens, I used to fish for redfin from a kayak on the Murrumbidgee River near Wagga Wagga in NSW. The system was to put in upstream and drift down, stopping to fish around snags or where trees were casting a large shadow on the water. My favourite ploy was to fish with a worm under float, cast upstream, and allow it to drift in towards the snag or shade. If there was a good redfin about there was an excellent chance of the bait being taken. Redfin will also take minnow, and you can fish for them on the bottom or higher up the water column.

I mentioned carp fishing earlier and I don't know of anyone who bait fishes for saratoga. Yellowbelly and Murray cod anglers generally prefer 6–8kg threadline outfits, using a running sinker to a No. 2 to No. 4 straight hook or a 6/0 Suicide pattern. Best baits include bardi grubs, shrimp, yabbies and scrubworms. Cheese baits also do well. When fishing for big cod, a leader of a minimum 15kg breaking strain should be used as these fish have hundreds of small, sharp, rasping teeth that can wear through lighter leader material.

Barramundi will take live mullet and cherabin (giant freshwater shrimp which can be up to 20cm long) on hooks from 4/0–6/0, depending on bait size. Live prawns or popeye mullet set under a float make excellent baits when allowed to drift back into a snag or over a rock bar. Barra will sometimes crush and kill bait without taking it in so it pays to be alert. If this is happening, it may be the fish felt the line pressure too early and should have been given longer to take the bait properly.

Land-based gamefishing from rock ledges can produce fish like this yellowfin tuna caught by the author at Green Cape, NSW

ROCK-FISHING

As a sport, rock-fishing is addictive to the point that many anglers make the rocks their speciality, chasing a variety of species from game fish such as tuna and marlin – caught from ocean platforms such as Steep Point, Green Cape and Jervis Bay – to bread and butter species such as snapper, tailor and luderick, taken in more sheltered waters and from breakwalls at places like Portland (Victoria), Stockton Beach (NSW) and Noosa (Queensland).

Make no mistake – there is more variety to be had from rock ledges than just about anywhere else in the ocean, which helps explain why so many anglers are attracted by them. Whether it is the constant wave action and the potential danger it brings, or just the excitement of fishing, there is an ongoing fascination. On any given day on the rocks, an angler may be confronted by unexpected danger, be well rewarded for effort and have a heap of fun.

There are several methods employed to fish the rocks: bottom fishing, float fishing, unweighted baits and spinning. Most anglers chase bread and butter species like salmon, mullet, luderick, rock blackfish, tailor, trevally, sweep, garfish, King George whiting, barracouta and snapper.

The standard bait fishing outfit is much the same as employed in the surf and consists of a rod about 3–3.5m long, capable of casting sinkers up to 100g. The reel is a matter of choice, but most anglers tend toward a threadline in the south, and sidecast north of Sydney. Lines should be 7kg and when fishing the bottom the set-up used by most anglers is the same as that employed in the surf, commonly known as the paternoster rig. This consists of a couple of leaders running off a main line above the sinker.

Hook size and shape varies to suit bait being used. If you are employing pilchard pieces you will use a hook of about 3/0–4/0 in a Suicide pattern, while for bait like pipi or bluebait the size of the hook is reduced to about a No. 2 or 1/0. You will have a better hook-up rate with a medium shank Baitholder pattern for baits like bluebait, and a wide gap hook for pipi. When fishing the bottom from the rocks try to avoid fishing on reef as this can result in being snagged on rocks and weed. A pair of polarising sunglasses will help you spot the sand holes, which are the most likely feeding lanes for fish. Not only will you catch more, you will have fewer problems doing so.

Float fishing covers a wide spectrum of species and can account for just about everything except perhaps whiting, which fossick on the bottom for food. What you are likely to catch depends on where you put your bait and the type of bait used. Mussel or pipi under a float and kept in close to the wash will attract sweep and garfish – abalone gut or lettuce weed will attract luderick. Fish fillets cast further out and set deep might attract snapper and a dead fish allowed to float well offshore is a likely shark or, in northern climes, mackerel bait. Live bait such as a slimy mackerel or yakka put out beneath a balloon are used to attract game fish like tuna or even marlin.

One of the most effective techniques I have used is free-floating baits drifted down a wash spiced with berley. This method has accounted for a range of fish including snapper, salmon, and trevally. It's a simple, effective way of fishing but the berley, usually made up of pilchard pieces mixed with chook pellets and tuna oil, has to be maintained. As long as there is a berley trail, and the fish have something to feed on, they will hang around. When the berley (and therefore the food) stops, so do the fish. For both float fishing and free-drifting baits, the rod needs to be lighter and suited to casting lighter weights than the outfit mentioned earlier. A medium action rod of about 2.3–3m in length is fine. And because the rigs are much lighter you can use lighter lines, down to about 4kg, or even less if that is your preference. As there is no weight being cast, the best reel is either a sidecast or threadline.

Spinning is a popular pursuit off ledges. The most common species caught depends on location. In warm waters, mackerel and tuna are always likely. Further south in temperate waters, yellowtail kingfish, salmon, tailor and bonito are common. Metal lures such as the Halco Twisty and Halco Slice and Laser lures are popular. There is no need for extra-long rods or highly geared reels in southern waters; unless you happen across a school of kingfish in which case a 6:1 gear ratio is better than the usual 4:7 or 5:1. The optimum lure weight is from 28–56g for most species, and the rod should be a fast taper suited to the weight. My preference is for a rod of about 3m, preferably graphite, as this gives enough recovery on the cast to get the lure out the extra yard.

DANGERS OF ROCK-FISHING

I spent more than 20 years of my fishing time chasing big fish off the rocks. Land-based gamefishing is an exciting sport but one fraught with danger. While I was after tuna, sharks and marlin, other anglers would fish the same ledges for salmon, luderick and drummer. The fish might be different, but the risks associated with fishing from rock ledges were the same.

Putting out a live bait off the rocks

During those years there were many accidents, some that were tragic. Sadly, some were avoidable. Many accidents occurred on days when experienced rock fishermen wouldn't go down and fish due to the dangers from the big seas that were running.

Of the many factors to consider when choosing a suitable platform, the most important is safety. To ignore this aspect, particularly if you are fishing from rocky headlands, is akin to playing Russian roulette.

Rock-fishing can be dangerous

Sooner or later, no matter how lucky you think you are, you'll get yourself into trouble.

Victorian anglers have lost their lives after being swept from rocks at places such as the notorious Nobbies at Phillip Island. Due to the popularity of rock-fishing in NSW there has been a great loss of life. Take Jervis Bay, the most popular land-based gamefishing location in Australia. Crocodile Heads on the Beecroft Peninsula here is one of a number of top areas that have become notorious for the tragic loss of life. In the same area, Devil's Gorge is reputed to have claimed more than 20 anglers and Eve's Ravine is not for the faint-hearted.

Tragedies in NSW are not restricted to Jervis Bay, nor is it confined to the eastern states. If you checked the coroner's statistics in the west you would find an equally gruesome tale of 'death by misadventure' from ledges in WA as far apart as Albany in the south to Quobba, Carnarvon and parts further north. The stretch of coast that takes in Quobba Station is reputed to have claimed more than 30 lives.

There are some basic rules for rock-fishing that everyone considering fishing from the rocks should follow.

First, get local information about safety, tides, where the locals fish and when, what safety gear they take. Some ledges are not a fishable proposition under any circumstances; others are dangerous only when big seas are running. An idea of the state of the tides is also worthy of comment as it often happens that at low tide the seas will not wash over the ledge but later on, as the tide rises, the situation can become somewhat different. The first thing any angler should do before venturing down to fish from a rock ledge is to spare 15 minutes or so to study the pattern of the waves.

Second, never fish alone and always carry some form of lifeline in case you or your fishing buddy go for an unscheduled swim. A safety rope makes a lot of sense, and doesn't take up much room. Don't make the mistake of using a nylon rope, as a swimmer will have difficulty hanging on. Any rope should have a weighted flotation device at one end to enable it to be thrown. A polystyrene ball with a hole through the middle is ideal, but a plastic milk container part-filled with water will also do the job. Some anglers even wear life jackets that inflate when they hit the water.

Third, attention should be paid to your clothing. Ask yourself whether or not you can swim in the clothes you are wearing? Shoes are also important. Rock ledges can become slippery when it is raining or when there is a lot of spray coming over. Wearing shoes with plenty of tread will lessen the chances of falling over, or in for that matter.

Fourth, avoid diving into the water after another angler when conditions are rough and dangerous. The end result of this sort of bravery can be a double fatality and anyway, if the seas are that bad, you probably shouldn't be fishing.

Fifth, a first-aid kit is a sensible investment. Apart from shock, the worst thing about going in off the rocks can be the cuts you receive from the limpets and rocks. It makes no sense taking a first-aid kit along unless you know how to use it, so at the very least you should read the instructions. And don't leave your mobile phone in your car or back at camp as you may need to make an emergency call one day.

Anglers on the rocks have to be ever alert and mindful of waves. This is most important when fishing a ledge low to the sea. Under these circumstances it can prove fatal to relax and stop being vigilant – you just never know when that bigger-than-average wave might happen to thunder in over the ledge.

Remember, if in doubt don't fish. The fish are not worth the risk, find somewhere else where the fishing is safe and not so dangerous.

GAME FISH

Land-based gamefishing (LBG) is not a discipline for the faint-hearted. It requires an almost fanatical dedication and a willingness to endure conditions that would send many anglers packing, which probably explains why the numbers of LBG anglers have never been big. If there is anything in angling more exhilarating than being clean spooled by a game fish hooked from a land-based situation, I've yet to experience it. Encountering the power and surge of a big game fish in full flight, watching a kilometre or so of line melt off the spool and knowing you are powerless is the ultimate adrenalin pump.

LBG options vary by location. In Victoria and SA, sharks and yellowtail kingfish are the main target species. Along the southern NSW coast, kingfish, yellowfin tuna, marlin and sharks are caught. North of Sydney to southern Queensland, anglers can hook longtail tuna, mackerel, cobia and marlin. In WA, places like Carnarvon and Exmouth have their share of LBG anglers who hook mainly mackerel but also tuna and sharks. When LBG first started in the 1960s it was about high speed spinning, nowadays most big game fish are caught on live baitfish.

There are some specific tackle requirements that apply. For serious fish 15–24kg gamefishing outfits, preferably with lever drag reels capable of holding about 1000m of line, are standard fare. A shoulder harness and gimbal belt are essential equipment. The harness should be comfortable and the straps detachable to allow it to be fitted without the need for the angler to take his hands off the rod or reel. In almost every LBG situation a gaff of some sort will be required. Ideally, the gaff should be a single-piece unit long enough to reach a fish at the bottom of a swell on low tide. Aluminium tubing, 25mm in diameter with a minimum 3mm wall thickness, is about right while the hook gape should be about 75mm minimum.

A good average leader for this style of fishing is about 3m with a minimum 60kg breaking strain. To connect the leader to the main line, which should have a double, use a ball bearing game swivel. In areas where sharks or mackerel are prevalent, piano wire is used to prevent bite offs. The most popular set-up is the balloon rig and it is easy to make up.

Steve's

FAVOURITE FIVE DESTINATIONS FOR ROCK-FISHING

Green Cape, NSW (p. 113)
Main fish species: *tuna, yellowtail kingfish, marlin*

Sussex Inlet, Jervis Bay, NSW (p. 104)
Main fish species: *yellowtail kingfish, yellowfin and striped tuna, bonito, black and striped marlin, hammerhead, whaler sharks*

Lee breakwater, Portland, Victoria (p. 224)
Main fish species: *snapper, salmon, kingfish*

Quobba, WA (p. 276)
Main fish species: *Spanish mackerel, whaler sharks, golden trevally, cobia, sailfish, tailor*

Tathra, NSW (p. 107)
Main fish species: *tuna, kingfish, sharks*

A partially inflated balloon, approximately 15cm in diameter, is attached to the leader by a single strand of cotton or A-size binding thread. Keep the length of cotton to the balloon as short as possible and always tie it to the swivel. When a game fish strikes the bait, it will feel little resistance because the cotton breaks easily.

Hook styles and sizes are the next consideration. For most bait, hooks between 6/0 and 9/0 will suffice. There is a wide range of patterns suited to live baiting. Choose a chemically sharpened hook in the Suicide or Octopus patterns. Unlike normal hooks, these retain their sharpness in the water for long periods.

Gamefishing boats operate well offshore in all sorts of conditions

The range of fish that can be used as live baits is big but slimy mackerel and yakkas are the best. These can be caught from most rock ledges provided you employ some berley to attract them. Keep the bait alive in rock pools that are indirectly washed or sprayed by waves or bring a small wading pool and run an aerator.

The best place to hook a baitfish is just forward of the first dorsal fin. Avoid setting the hook too deep and, if using a hook with an offset point such as a Suicide, ensure the point is leaning forward when the hook is in the vertical position. If you don't do this – when the baitfish is pulling line out – the hook shank will be in the horizontal plane and the point, because of the offset, is likely to be embedded in the back of the bait. To get a baitfish to swim out, cast the fish into a wash where the undertow will assist it to swim out and away from the ledge. One of the tricks of this method is to allow plenty of slack line into the wash as even if the bait is reluctant to go, the undertow pulling your slack line out will force the issue.

FLIES

DRY FLIES

Flies are purpose-built insect imitations designed to fool a trout, unless of course the flies are what is known as search or stimulator patterns. These flies are not imitations of any specific insect, but rather a compilation of insects. The Geehi Beetle is such a fly – there is no such bug.

When it comes to the practice of fly-fishing, opinions vary of whether dry or wet flies are best. And there are some freshwater fly-fishers who specialise in trout but refuse to acknowledge saltwater fly-fishing in any form. Several fly-fishing writers have commented over the years on the difference between dry and wet fly-fishers. If you have ever read American fly-fishing writer John Gierach's work *Trout Bum* you will know that 'a 12in trout caught on a dry fly is four inches longer than a 12in trout caught on a nymph or streamer'.

So, what is a dry fly? In simple language it is an insect imitation designed to float on the surface of the water. The main difference for anglers to note between fishing a dry or a wet fly is that you watch the fish take the dry, and then you set the hook. This is not always necessary when a wet fly is employed.

Chopper Hopper

Baetid Dun

Geehi Beetle

Daves Hopper

Royal Wulff

Joselands Hackle Hopper

Stimulator

Knobby Hopper

WET FLIES

Wet flies are submersible flies and as such are the closest thing to a lure in fly-fishing. A wet fly is a nymph or streamer and is fished under the surface. If you want to get more technical, there are emerger flies. These float in the surface film (meniscus) and are designed to imitate an insect such as a mayfly that is emerging from its mudeye state.

Wet flies imitate insects in the nymphal stage such as mudeyes, beetles or alternatively small fish like smelt. The key difference is in the name and presentation because a wet fly is just that, whereas a dry fly sits on the surface.

Names like Greenwell's Glory, Woolly Bugger, Tyhappy Tickler and Tupps Indispensable sound odd but have one thing in common: they are all trout flies. Most fly-tyers are more deeply involved in entomology than normal fly-fishers. They have to be as their craft requires perfection. The flies they tie must not only look the same as the bug they are designed to imitate, but have a similar action in the water. If the trout are feeding on size 20 Damsel nymphs, then that is what you must offer.

Most fly-fishers admit there are days when science goes out the window. Days when you offer up something totally irregular, a fly pattern that matches no known local bug, in a size that is much bigger than the local insect population, and you suddenly start catching trout. I mean, why do rainbow trout like their nymph flies to have gold-bead heads? I can't think of a single bug that has a gold coloured bead on its head but you cannot argue with something that works.

Black Water Beetle

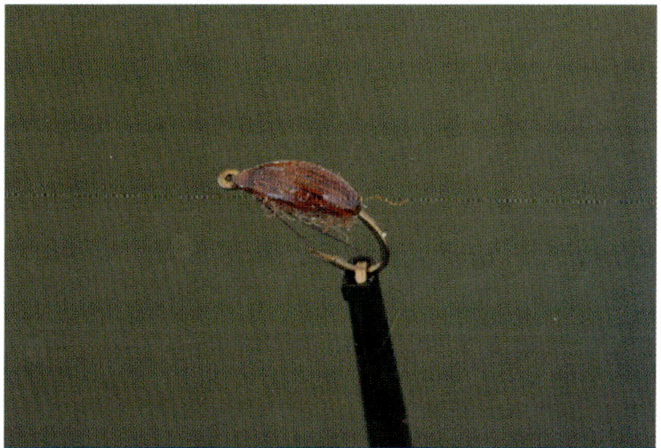

Brown Water Beetle

Beaded Woolly Bugger

Chartreuse Chaser

Big Eyed Woolly Bugger

Green Matuka

Olive Rabbit

Lazer Minnow

Gold Bead Head Nymph

Long Tailed Chaser

Micks Scruffy

Original Red Tag

Original Tom Jones

Sawyers Brown Nymph

SALTWATER FLIES

Delicate presentations to trout rising in mountain streams is the dream of many freshwater fly-fishers. The stream is running and the trout sipping. You cast a short arc, a tight loop and the way the line lays and the leader unfolds add up to a presentation that is, hopefully, as faint as a fairy kiss as your dry fly lands like a windflower on the crystal, effervescent water.

In some saltwater scenarios, you might undertake similar practices. Bream and estuary perch sipping ants off the surface in a south coast estuary. Or maybe a small patch of wary garfish schooling around pier pilings. You might even want to work similar flies, ant patterns, orange spinners or even an elk hair caddis.

It's a gentle, pleasant way to fish. It's also a lot of literary humbug – the sorts of 'once upon a time' stuff of dreams. There are those who like to portray an image of fly-fishing as a slow, delicate institution. But they're dreamers, not realists. A hot bite is a hot bite, regardless of where you are. The pace can be frenetic, and lobbing flies so they caress the water isn't always exactly what happens, even if we'd like it to be that way.

A hot bite in the salt can be even more chaotic. There will be situations when you might actually want to make the fly hit the water hard enough to splash. Some days it comes down to speed: how fast you can haul, cast and strip. Not much science in that. It all depends on the fish, the scenario and, of course, the fly-fisher's ability.

In practice, it is not as important in salt water to have the tournament caster's ability to place a fly within a small diameter ring. There is a wider margin for error, unless of course you happen to be working a set of snags. Most of us can put a fly about where we want it to be. Some days we are more accurate than others, and the more we try the better we are.

Many saltwater species tend to move around a fair bit, both because they are hunting and to avoid presenting an easy feed to a larger predator. That is the nature of the marine environment. While a trout might prefer to remain in its feeding lane, marine species are used to hunting and working for their supper.

This isn't to say that you can turn the water into froth and your fly into a missile and still catch fish – far from it. And, while swoffing is generally more forgiving of us less talented casters, when all the back casts are straightened, piscatorial results still come down to presentation. However, it isn't so much how you cast the fly to fish as the way you retrieve it past them.

Salmon Flies

Squid Fly

Garfly

A selection of Clouser Minnows used for flathead

Dusky flathead caught on a saltwater fly in the Wallagaraugh River near Mallacoota, Victoria

BAIT GATHERING

The ideal bait for any fish is one that occurs naturally in the environment being fished. Anglers fly-fishing overcome this problem by examining the local insects and making a fly pattern that ideally suits what they think the trout are feeding on – it's called matching the hatch. When it comes to bait gathering, the angler gets rewarded for effort.

FRESH WATER

BAITFISH: This category includes small fishes like gudgeon, minnow, galaxias and smelt. There are too many to list and the names vary with locality but most folk call the small fish minnows. In running waters, these fish school in backwaters and eddies, sometimes in little more than small pools surrounded by cumbungi or other grasses. In lakes, they will be found in the shallow – and sometimes under cover of – water grasses.

Rod Harrison caught this big Murray cod in the Murray River near Wentworth, NSW

There are two ways to catch them. One method is to sprinkle breadcrumbs to lure the fish and, when they are close, sweep them up in a handheld, fine-mesh net. A more successful method is to use a bait trap, which can be as simple as a clear plastic tube with an opening at one end. Enticements such as breadcrumbs are placed inside the tube, which is then put in shallow water. The bread lures the fish into the trap and, because it is clear, it is easy to tell when you have caught a few.

BARDI GRUBS: The bardi grub, which is top bait for Murray cod, is the larval stage of the ghost moth. These fat white grubs dig tunnels and mature in the ground after falling from the leaves where the adult moths lay their eggs. In these tunnels, they feed on the roots of adjacent gum trees until they mature, which happens in autumn at the first break.

Adult bardies are about 75–100mm long, and as thick as a man's finger. When they emerge, they leave their empty pupa cases sticking out of the ground. To catch bardi grubs you will need to purchase a bardi puller and take along a shovel. A bardi puller looks like a car speedometer cable. At one end it has a claw-like attachment consisting of four prongs with a noose of wire. At the other end of the puller is a knob or handle. When the cable is pushed in the tube the prongs open up, when the cable is pulled prongs and wire close.

The place to look is around the outer edge of the branch line of gum trees above the high water mark. According to the people I fish with along the Murray River, sugar-gum saplings are often the most productive trees. The shovel is used to scrape off about 25mm of topsoil. Work the bare ground and not grass. A good place to start will be where you find old casings on the ground, or exposed holes. Bardi holes are different to spider holes in that they have a sort of lining, but be aware that spiders sometimes take up residence in unused holes.

Once you have located a fresh bardi hole, the bardi puller is opened and inserted into the hole, ever so slowly, and gently manoeuvred over the head of the grub. The cable wire is then tightened so that the wire noose encircles the grub, which can then be retrieved from the hole. It pays to be careful as the grubs are soft and can be damaged easily. Always put the soil back after you have finished, and remember to leave some grubs in the ground so that they can continue the cycle.

To store bardi grubs, roll up a sheet of newspaper into a tube. Fold one end over and staple it, then place the grub in the open end, fold this over and staple it. Kept in a cool place (in the newspaper). A bardi grub will live for several weeks.

MUDEYES: The dragonfly nymph, mudeyes are found in dams and impoundments that have a good amount of vegetation under the water and around the edges. A mudeye net, which has a fine mesh, is dragged through the weed and mudeyes are trapped. It is usual to catch a few shrimp during this process and, if you are working the net near the bottom, sometimes yabbies are also trapped.

To keep mudeyes in good health, place them in a container with water from the dam where you caught them. If you need to store for a few days, then place a damp piece of cotton wool in the bottom of a margarine container, add a few small twigs or leaves and put the mudeyes in. Next, place the container in the fridge, the cold will send them into a form of hibernation and they will keep for many weeks. Be warned though, if you put too much water in the container the mudeyes are likely to drown while they are comatose.

WORMS: Everyone knows about worms and they have been top bait for most freshwater species for as long as people have been fishing. Worms like a dark, moist environment. In the garden you can keep the wrigglers on hand by establishing a permanent wet patch, which is then covered by a hessian bag, carpet or similar material. Scrubworms are just garden worms that, owing to their larger size, look as though they have been on steroids. To find them, the same formula applies – moist, dark areas are the best, and these are often close to water or under lush grass.

YABBIES: When the 10-year drought broke in south-eastern Australia in the spring of 2010, dry lakebeds filled quickly. A few weeks later anglers were catching loads of yabbies, not just from lakes but also from rivers like the Murray.

Yabbies are survivors. When a waterhole dries up, a yabbie burrows down to the moist soil in the water table below. This creature remains underground until water fills the catchment area, and it can do this for three years if necessary – a survival strategy that helps explain why yabbie numbers boomed after the floods. During hibernation, yabbies live off the meat in their claws and, to a lesser extent, the tail meat.

Anyone heading out to catch yabbies should first decide where to go and then read up on the regulations. There are differences in state laws governing yabbies. In SA and NSW, the daily take of yabbies by recreational fishers is limited to 200 regardless of size, and berried females must be returned. In Victoria, there is no requirement to return berried female yabbies, and the daily catch limit is based on a volume of 30l with no size restrictions.

Yabby Pots (Opera House nets) are banned in Victorian waters, but SA and NSW allow them with qualifications. If you are heading interstate and intend using an Opera House net, check the dimensions. Just because you bought a net at a tackle shop does not mean it is legal. SA anglers are permitted three nets but these must have a maximum funnel diameter of 7.5cm; in NSW, the maximum funnel diameter is 9cm and anglers are allowed five nets although their use is restricted to waters west of the Newell Highway and they cannot be deployed in trout waters or some listed waters where platypus are found. In both SA and NSW, the nets must be tagged with the name and address of the user.

Drop or hoop nets are allowed in SA, NSW and Victoria and these have size and number restrictions. In Victoria, anglers are allowed up to 10 hoop nets, and all states require nametags listing the anglers' details.

Yabbies are top bait for fish such as redfin and Murray cod, and even work well in estuaries for black bream. Meat is the standard yabbie bait but some anglers claim that rock melon is a better option when using a net. For those folk not in urgent need of a big juicy feed of fresh yabbies, the alternative way of catching them is on a handline. This is especially good fun with kids. All you need is a piece of string, a bit of meat and a net. First, find a dam or waterway where yabbies are likely to be. One way of spotting a likely dam is if you can see holes burrowed in around the banks. Next, tie your string around the meat, cast it out a few feet from the edge and allow it to settle on the bottom. When bringing your line up, do it slowly as the yabbie will continue to clutch the meat. When the bait and yabbie are near the surface, place the net under the yabbie before attempting to lift it out of the water.

SHRIMP: This is favourite bait for fish such as Murray cod, redfin, trout and yellowbelly. Shrimp come in all sizes, from monster 10cm beauties at Lake Mulwala to the smaller (five to a hook) varieties in southern rivers and estuaries. In northern Australia a giant freshwater shrimp called cherabin is popular bait for barramundi. There are a few methods of catching shrimp. One is to use a hoop net with a piece of chop or steak tied to the middle. This is lowered into the water and left there for an hour or so, depending on how many shrimp are about. When you think the time is right, it is a simple matter to raise the net and collect the shrimp.

Alternatively, use a long-handled shrimp net. Shrimp shelter under the vegetation along riverbanks and estuaries. The weed growth that gathers near boat ramps is often a productive area. Push the net through the water, into the weed, and lift it out. Another way is with a shrimp trap. These are cone shaped, with a join in the middle and a hole at each end to allow the shrimp to enter. Take a piece of meat, place it inside the trap and then set the trap alongside some reeds or submerged timber. The longer you leave the trap in the water, the more shrimp you are likely to catch. When camping it is a good system to leave the trap in the water most of the time, taking just enough shrimp out for bait as you require them.

SALT WATER

BAITFISH: Whether you fish with live bait, cube baits or fillets you still have to catch the fish. Bait availability and type depend on where you are but include garfish, salmon, mullet, silver trevally, yakka, slimy mackerel, tailor and hussar. It really does come down to location, as methods for catching them are similar. Baitfish jigs used in conjunction with a berley trail will catch yakkas and slimy mackerel. Sometimes the best method is to raise the fish to the surface in a berley trail – use small bait with no sinker.

CRABS: Experienced anglers looking for crabs for bait work their way along the rocks adjacent to the ocean poking long pieces of wire into likely crevices, looking under rocks and along mud flats at low tide, and sometimes in the tangle of seaweed along the shore.

CUNJEVOI: Found growing on rock ledges, it's best sought at the bottom of the tide. It is the dark red meat inside the hard outer skin of the cunje that is used as bait.

LETTUCE WEED: Favourite bait for luderick, lettuce weed is found growing on rock faces and in pools continually washed with water. The best lettuce weed is a bright green but southerners do well using brown weed.

MUSSELS: These molluscs will be found clinging to pier pilings or on reefs. It is advisable to wear gloves when trying to extract mussels from reef or rocks as they can have sharp edges that will cut flesh easily. Removal from pier pilings is banned in some areas. Mussels can often be found in water that can be reached with waders, or even shallower. In heavily populated areas mussels tend to suffer from exploitation and can be more difficult to find. On piles where it is allowed to take mussels, use a sturdy rake with a chicken wire bag or net hung below the rake to catch the shellfish as they fall off.

NIPPERS (BASS YABBIES): These crustaceans will account for fish ranging from bream through to mulloway. They live underground in mud and sand flats of estuaries and can also be found along some surf beaches under the wet sand. A clear indication of them being around are tell-tale holes left where they have burrowed. You can either dig them out with a spade or use a bait pump. Sometimes it will be necessary to use a couple of pumps to suck the yabbies in. The sand is then pushed out of the pump into a sieve, the sand filters through and the bait is left. This method will produce sandworms as well. The best flats to work will probably be about knee deep in water, with low tide the preferred time in most areas.

PIPIS: These are commonly found buried under the sand on beaches where the water washing over is just 10cm or 20cm deep (or exposed sand flats). To get them you can either dig a hole or twist with bare feet until you find a patch and then dig down with your hands. Pipis are usually found in colonies and once you find one, the rest are easy.

COCKLES: These molluscs live under sand and mud in estuary and bay weed-flats. The popular method of gathering them is to walk through the weed with bare feet, and because they live in colonies where you find one you will also find others.

SAND FLEAS: Anglers fishing for garfish in sheltered coves or from ocean fronting rocks often seek out sand fleas or hoppers, as they are also called, for bait. Sand fleas are found under rotting weed along ocean beaches – the best time to gather them is early morning when the air is cool and the hoppers are slow. To keep them fresh, put some damp sand in a bucket and bury them in it.

SANDWORMS: Apart from the bait pump a spade is an equally useful tool. Sandworms will be found over flats and damp areas when the tide is low; the best places are often under heavy banks of weed, which keep the sand moist. Some states have a ban on digging holes in the low-tide zone, so check your state regulations before starting to reshape the environment.

SQUID: One of the most versatile saltwater baits, squid can be easily caught using artificial or baited jigs. Most squid will be found lurking over grass beds but at night they are attracted to lights and hunt in the shadows on the edge of the beam.

Cherabin is another name for a large freshwater shrimp found in northern Australia

TRAVELLING

I spend an average of 20 weeks a year away somewhere. This is neither a boast nor a whinge; it's just plain matter of fact. In this job, you need fresh material, something you don't get sitting at home stoking the fires.

Do you travel light? Or are you one of those anglers who take everything, just in case? When you pack are you careful? Or do you toss everything into a bag or tube and hope it arrives safely at your destination?

A friend of mine often travelled on the good will of others in that it wasn't what he packed, but what he lacked. One time he drove more than 1000km to fish at Mallacoota Inlet in Victoria. On his way south from his home in southern Queensland he must have passed at least 100 supermarkets, yet when he arrived he had no food, save for some birdseed; he always carried birdseed for exactly that reason – to feed the birds. Then there were the dozen or so DVDs he brought along – several were unopened and were probably purchased on the drive down. The birds would be well fed and my mate would have music for his soul, if not food for his stomach. Not for the first time, he was banking on us sharing our tucker – and as he always carried enough tackle to fill a shop, I guess he gave as good as he got.

I used to pack gear on the assumption that you take everything because well ... you never know when something might crop up out of left field. I would head off for the rock ledges on the NSW south coast in search of game fish, somehow managing to pack some trout gear – just in case. Every angler's fishing trip nightmare unfolds in two parts: not catching fish, which includes finding that there are plenty of fish but you didn't bring along the right tackle; and being confronted with damaged equipment on arrival. It doesn't matter whether you are heading to exotic climes or going bush for a weekend, disaster awaits the unready, the unwary and even the conscientious packer.

First things first – how do you know if you have packed enough tackle? The best way is to think of every possible scenario, cover all options and then buy a few extras just in case. The golden rule for any fishing trip is to work out minimum tackle requirements, and add more. You can always wear the same shirt for a few days, rinsing it in the shower at the end of the week. However, if you don't have the right outfit you won't be able to fish properly, in which case you might as well stay at home. The key is to organise your tackle first, then think of clothing and anything else you might want to pack, and cut back from there.

Way back in the 1970s, during the height of the land-based gamefishing boom, I was travelling to Eden with long time rock-fishing buddy Ross Middleton in his station wagon. It was to be a three-week camping trip and the vehicle was packed so tight that I even had a car battery between my legs. Between Sale and Bairnsdale on the Princes Highway, opposite the Billabong Roadhouse, we came over a rise to find a Volkswagen Kombi van doing a u-turn in front of us. Ross swerved but we nicked the other car and it was enough to send us out of control and rolling (literally) down the highway. Tackle went everywhere and the bitumen was littered with the popular lures of the day – irons that went under names like Lyncher, Assassin and Coffin. The point being that if equipment is not packed properly, it will suffer in transit.

Fishing tackle is designed to undergo extremes in terms of handling and pressure. Fragile rods and reels don't last if they cannot take punishment on the water. The plain fact is that fishing tackle is less susceptible to damage on the water than it is while travelling, either on the road or in the air. The last thing you want, as you arrive where you hope the fish will be biting, is a bunch of broken fishing rods that are only good for garden stakes. This predicament is most often associated with air travel, and is usually blamed on rough baggage handling. Airport baggage handlers are not always to blame – broken tackle can also happen in cars and boats during a road trip. More often than not, the cause of the problem is a failure in the time and effort taken to pack equipment carefully.

Rods are the most fragile items, and the best way of ensuring they arrive at your destination in good condition is via a rod tube. It is not unknown for inexperienced travellers to invest in two-piece rods because they think aircraft cannot carry the longer, single-piece rods. It pays to check. I have regularly carried 3m long, one-piece rods in a tube. You might have a problem in a light plane, but most jets have room.

My standard rod tube for many years was made from 100mm PVC tube with screw-on caps. There are ready-made alternatives. These days I use a Plano rod tube. It is adjustable to a little over 3m and comes complete with latches designed to take locks. You will be amazed at how many rods you can pack into a tube, especially if you put tip to butt, and use an elastic band to hold them together. Rods should be packed tightly in a tube. If loose, a guide or tip may break. One way to pack them in tight is to use clothing. This has the advantage of leaving more room in the suitcase for tackle.

The best place to carry fishing reels is in the suitcase, firmly wrapped and protected by clothing. If you are using a threadline reel with fold-down handles, make sure the handle is folded before packing. Towels are great for wrapping reels in, and I always ensure there is clothing on all sides of the reels as this acts as a shock absorber if the suitcase is dropped. Oh, and be sure to service your reels

Many anglers make long road trips to find the fishing they want; this is the author's rig at Victoria River Roadhouse, NT

before packing – you'll love the smell of WD40 as you stand in the pre-dawn light.

I generally carry a backpack-style tackle box, one with small plastic trays that slide in and out. This will fold up and lay flat on the bottom of a suitcase – the plastic tray inserts can be spread around the suitcase. If you can't get enough gear in the trays, fill a few more and pack them loose in the suitcase.

Another worthwhile item is the zip-up folder bag that contains clip-seal plastic bags inside, which in turn are held in place by rings much like a school folder. These are handy for leaders, lures or flies. Importantly, these bags can be packed into small spaces where larger, solid items won't fit.

If towing a boat, put the suitcases in it, and the fragile items (tackle) in the vehicle. In aircraft, baggage load limits can be restrictive, but there are ways around them. For example, when travelling with your family or a group, you can usually bulk your entire luggage in together. The aggregate weight

Air boat launch in northern Australia

per family is sometimes better than the weight per individual. In the case of families, this works best when you are overseeing the packing arrangements. Be warned: do not let the family go on a mad spending spree while you're away. If you are like me, you are likely to come back with more tackle than you took on the trip.

The important thing about travelling is ensuring your fishing tackle arrives in good order. Work out the cost of replacing a few rods and reels compared with buying a few shirts and shorts and you will understand why it deserves priority.

SAFETY

Autumn is the season of travel for southern anglers wanting to head for northern Australia. The annual run-off that marks the end of the wet season is over, grasslands are drying and outback roads once more are turning to red dust. Whether towing a caravan, camper trailer, boat or bearing a car topper, big trips need careful planning. Take heed from the Latin proverb: 'haste manages all things badly'.

Hitching the car to the caravan, camper trailer or boat and turning the key to the engine is only part of the trip preparation. You need to know where you are going and research your destination. Many places across the Top End are similar to down south in terms of roads and access but you need to allow for difficulties specific to the tropics and unpopulated areas.

4WD VEHICLES

The 4WD is the main mode of transport for most anglers. Some 4WD vehicles are better than others in terms of handling ability and sturdiness. The make and model is your choice. A diesel engine is less affected by water and overall has more torque and, importantly, is infinitely more reliable than petrol motors. If going off-road, fit a snorkel to your vehicle in case you cross a river – in my northern travels shallow creek crossings are common in remote areas. Always seek local advice – you may be crossing a croc-infested stream.

Top End fishing guides I have dealt with prefer heavy-duty tyres, but not the extra wide ones seen on many vehicles down south. Wide tyres are regarded as too expensive and serve little purpose on the unmade roads. Speed can be a killer as control is easily lost on unmade roads, and towing a boat makes slower speed even more critical. Many unmade roads in the north have high, soft shoulders and it is easy to lose control as these, together with corrugations, seem worse on corners.

Boats and trailers need special attention. You might think you have a well-built boat on a rugged trailer, but after driving a few hundred kilometres across dirt roads, you start to find out otherwise. A boat continuously bouncing on a trailer can suffer cracks. It's not much fun to drive for a week only to find welds have cracked and your boat leaks. To eliminate this problem, tie old tyres on your trailer and put the boat on top of them. The tyres cushion the boat and reduce the likelihood of hull stress-fractures. When you arrive at your destination, remove the tyres and use the trailer normally. Remember to put the tyres back for your return trip.

Before going off-road seek local advice and spend time learning local rules and regulations. A permit is required to fish and travel independently through Aboriginal lands and in some areas, limits are put on the number of vehicles allowed through in a day. There are substantial fines for travellers without permits, and be aware of strict rules regarding alcohol.

PREPARATION

Most of my Top End fishing has been in company with experienced guides who take crocodiles more seriously than southern animal-rights activists. When fishing remote areas, or waters where crocodiles are plentiful, most guides bring a firearm and satellite phone. I am not suggesting you buy a firearm but a satellite phone is a sure-fire method of communication if the mobile phone runs out of coverage in remote regions.

Travelling anglers need to be cautious on outback dirt roads

Camping in remote areas is a cosmic experience, but it comes at a cost and you need to take account of basics like food and water, first aid and communication. Food is obvious, but water is equally necessary. Just because there is plenty of fresh water in billabongs doesn't mean it is accessible. Fetching water can be fraught with danger because of the crocodiles. If you haven't been up north and seen the number of crocodiles that are around, you are in for a surprise. When you set up camp, my advice is to avoid water and never clean your fish at camp, as this will attract the crocodiles.

CROCODILES

The crocodile is a symbol of fear: an overgrown lizard, it is the apex predator of its estuarine environment, a creature known to stalk prey and act out of opportunity. The crocodile will eat fish, birds, land animals, and humans – there is no discrimination; it is a diet of opportunity, not preference. Across the Top End, crocodiles are an unpleasant fact; their range extends up to 400km inland.

Crocodiles were hunted to the brink of extinction, and with numbers down to about 5000, were protected in 1971. The population is now estimated at more than 80,000, about 25,000 less than when the first Europeans arrived in Australia. There have been more than 20 fatal attacks in the NT since 1975.

Crocodiles can grow to 8m, and the biggest one ever shot was 8.4m in length; most are under 4.5m. The Mary River System in the NT has the world's largest crocodiles, over 4.3m, and the most concentrated population of saltwater crocodiles in the world.

Make no mistake: crocodiles are not your friends. People who are attacked by crocodiles rarely see, never mind hear them, beforehand.

Fishing from shore in crocodile-infested waters is a high-risk activity, but there is also danger when fishing from a boat. Anglers need to be aware of the risks, and need to realise that crocodiles as big as 5m can propel themselves out of the water by the force of their tail.

Crocodiles are a way of life across the Top End, and it pays to be cautious as these reptiles have been known to attack anglers in boats

I fished a river junction on the Liverpool River for a couple of hours with two other anglers, and we never saw a croc. At the end of the session, we decided to clean our barra before heading back to Maningrida. When the first barra frame went over the side, a crocodile appeared and ate it. You never know when crocodiles are around.

In June 2014, a 62-year-old man was taken by a 4.7m crocodile. The man was fishing from his boat at a remote waterhole on the South Alligator River System. NT police said the man was in a boat and washing or emptying a bucket at the time of the attack.

This wasn't the first time a crocodile attacked an angler in a boat. A report in the NT News in June 2014, said that in 2011, local angler Kevin Eccles was admitted to hospital after being savaged by a crocodile: 'A 2.5m (8.2ft) croc jumped out of the water and latched on to his shoulder while he was sitting in his 4.5m (14.7ft) boat. Mr Eccles had to poke the creature in the eye to force it to let go.'

The most famous example of a crocodile attacking boats concerned a saurian nicknamed Sweetheart. Sweetheart was the name given to a 5.1m saltwater crocodile responsible for a series of attacks on boats in Australia between 1974 and 1979. Sweetheart attacked outboard motors, dinghies, and fishing boats. In July 1979, Sweetheart was caught by a team from the Territory Parks and Wildlife Commission, but drowned while being transported. The crocodile's mounted body is now on permanent display at the Museum and Art Gallery of the Northern Territory.

Dick Eussen, now in his 70s and the elder statesman of Australian outdoors writers, has many a tale to tell of crocodile experiences. In the early days, Dick fished the billabongs and rivers of Kakadu in a 16ft Canadian canoe, and was bumped a couple of times by crocs, mainly females protecting their nests. His worst experience, and the last time he used a canoe in these waters, was on Leichardt Billabong on the Magela Wetlands.

'I was with Craig Miller; it was raining hard so we decided to leave the gun behind in the Land Rover,' Dick said.

'Craig was at the back of the canoe because he was heavier then me. We had only paddled about 100m from our launch site when this croc as long as our canoe appeared.

'The big croc came straight at the canoe, and we headed for shore. As the canoe hit the bank Craig ran out over the top of me, ran through a small overflow about 2ft deep to get to the car. As Craig was running through the overflow, the croc almost beached itself as it lunged at him.

'When he got to the car, Craig grabbed the gun and fired a couple of shots; the croc arched back and disappeared. It wasn't a heavy load so it wouldn't have done the croc any damage.

'Canoes were used a lot in those days as there was a belief that crocodiles did not attack boats, though my own experience told a different tale; I sold my canoe after three crocodile attacks,' Dick said.

Anyone who has been to Cahills Crossing on the East Alligator River will have seen anglers, sometimes knee-deep, fishing. Look upstream and downstream, and you will see crocodiles. It's a dangerous place, and one that proved fatal for an old fishing mate of Dick's, Kerry McLaughlin. On 17 May 1987, McLaughlin was taken by a croc as he waded across the crossing.

'Kerry was fishing on the Arnhemland side with three mates, and was wading back to get some beer when the croc took him, sweeping him off the crossing into deeper water,' Dick explained.

'Kerry tried to reach up for a branch, and still had his fishing rod in his hand, but the battle was already over. They found his body later on.'

Most people have enough sense not to fish in areas along the rivers where there is a potential for them to become the next meal for a crocodile. Moreover, in boats the concept of catch and release is all very well – but don't reach over the side and swim your barra. If you intend releasing the fish, spear it back into the water.

FIRST AID

First aid is commonsense, but buying a first-aid kit isn't much use if you don't know the proper procedures for applying bandages and the like. If going off road, a first-aid course is time well spent. You may never have to save a life, but you can take comfort in knowing you are prepared. An essential part of a first-aid kit is vinegar. In north Queensland there are signs warning of marine stingers, and in many places a bottle of vinegar is placed with a sign telling people to pour this on the wound, not to rub it, and to seek medical advice.

However, it now seems using vinegar as an antidote is wrong. In April 2014, researchers at James Cook University and Cairns hospital in far north Queensland cautioned against the use of vinegar on box jellyfish stings.

Pouring vinegar onto welts caused by the sting of the jellyfish has been the recommended first-aid treatment for decades; however, the researchers found vinegar promotes the discharge of box jellyfish venom.

In an ABC report, Associate Professor Jamie Seymour from the Australian Institute of Tropical Health and Medicine at the university said: 'You can increase the venom load in your victim by 50 per cent. That's a big amount, and is enough to make the difference, we think, between someone surviving and somebody dying.'

Finally, warning signs about stingers, crocodiles and poisonous trees are there for good reason. Read these signs carefully and you will enjoy the trip.

In Australia, the emergency number for ambulance, police and fire is 000.

GUIDE SCHOOL

In my job I need to be at the coalface and that means travelling a lot of the time to new destinations. In every case, the biggest help you can receive is local knowledge, sometimes it is courtesy of a guide at other times it is local anglers.

There is a growing trend among anglers to use charter boats or fishing guides to find out the whys and wherefores of fishing, according to Shaun Furtiere, skipper of the 7m Western Port charter boat *Think Big*.

Based on experience on this boat and others, I know that Shaun's comment makes sense, particularly for anglers new to an area or to boat fishing. Fishing guides and charter boat skippers can be a wealth of knowledge. Fishing off Cairns with Captain Bobby Jones, for example, I learned about smell. We were trolling baits for marlin along the outer edge of the Great Barrier Reef when Bob asked me if I could smell watermelon. It turns out that this distinctive odour is a sure sign of a fish kill in north Queensland waters. Mark Rushton at Queenscliff, Victoria, showed me the value of making a bait jig appear more natural for squid; and in the NT, Lindsay Mutimer taught me to wind lures slower to catch more barramundi.

There are endless lessons learned over many years from many guides and charter skippers – the real value of being on the boat is the hands-on approach. Shaun said many clients bought boats then spent long hours on the Internet or reading books, but didn't seem able to put what they read into practice. 'Most find it easier to come on a charter and I am happy to teach or show them anything they want to learn,' Shaun said, adding, 'it has got to a point where on many trips the charter is more about guiding and tuition than simply finding and hooking fish.'

The old time charter boat concept was like growing mushrooms – keep the clients in the dark and feed them 'you know what'. Fortunately, the industry has moved on. There is no mystique about fishing once you understand the basics, although these can change with species and region, which is why local knowledge is so important. Shaun said his clients are often after information like how to read a sounder or GPS unit, as well as fishing rigs and methods.

The cost of a charter may seem expensive, but when you weigh up the hands-on knowledge that can be gleaned from a cooperative skipper there is no better value for your dollar.

Not all guides are helpful: it was a long day and I was grumpy when I finally got off my plane in north Queensland. A young woman from the local tourism bureau met me at the airport and we sat down and went through my itinerary. It was then I realised that things looked like going from bad to worse. It seems the guide I was scheduled to fish with the following day had to be off the water before lunch; and on the second day, another guide wasn't sure whether or not he was going out. Being a guest, you have to take the good with the bad. I had a guide for the third day so I asked the woman to tell the guide who couldn't make up his mind that he wasn't required.

'I'm not sure I can do that,' she said.

'Then give me his phone details and I'll ring him and make up his mind for him,' I said.

Sounds a mite uppity but when I make a commitment, I try to stay true to my word. I don't tolerate ifs or maybes. When you make a commitment of time and money and someone breaks the deal for no good reason you have every right to be annoyed, especially after travelling for more than 12 hours.

Long-range charter vessel *Kanimbla*

It is a fact that in fishing magazines some writers fail to acknowledge the roles others played in their successes. I can produce a long list of fish that I probably would not have caught had it not been for the assistance given freely to me.

However, fishing guides can be a fickle lot. You get good ones and you get awful ones. I've fished with a few guides in my time, fine folk who treat you as equals and are ever ready to help clients who have shortfalls in their fishing abilities. Then there are those who are arrogant, supercilious people so wrapped in their own hubris that they develop a warped sense of importance.

One example of a problem guide that still sticks in my craw was when I was one of two anglers on a media familiarisation. The guide who was supposed to take us out had not arrived so the tour manager called in one of his off-duty guides. The guide in question had his girlfriend staying over and was none too pleased about the duty recall. That first day on the water, I thought we were in trouble when he brought his girlfriend along. Mind you, I didn't mind the girl – she was pleasant and well mannered.

I was troubled when our guide started handing out worn-out reels and lures with blunt hooks. It got worse when he brought out a range of new rods, reels and lures for the girlfriend and himself. When I told him the reel was no good he wanted to argue but then thought better and produced another slightly less decrepit reel. I didn't like that one either. Subsequently, he offered me one of his reels and then couldn't untangle the line! At that point, I knew it was going to be a long day.

That guide highlighted a point that too many people fail to take on board: get your money's worth. His mind wasn't on the job and substandard service deserved a substandard payment. Had I been a paying customer I would have demanded a refund.

At the opposite end of the scale is the pleasure you get when you go to a place and are treated to a delightful stay by an army of locals. Unpaid volunteers out to promote their region in true country fashion, which means hospitality with a capital H. This happened to me on the Dawson

River at Moura, a two-hour drive west of Gladstone in central Queensland. Better known for its prime cattle production and huge coalmines, the township and the nearby Dawson River is not exactly on most people's map of top fishing spots but the river holds barramundi, saratoga and yellowbelly.

I arrived at first light and was met by Craig Nowland, who introduced me to a few locals, and then put me into a boat with Ken Blyton. The action was slow paced but I was enjoying being on the water and we cracked the saratoga. Then at 10.15am Ken announced it was time to head for shore because, 'the ladies are bringing down morning tea'. Morning tea turned out to be fresh, hot scones, assorted cakes and coffee and tea. After that it was back on the water for a couple of hours before coming back to shore for lunch. This was an even bigger spread of fresh food than morning tea and it included some of the nicest steak and homemade sausages I have eaten. You cannot beat country hospitality.

Arnhem Land guide Lance Butler releases a barramundi

Hiring a guide is a good way to save time when trying to locate likely fishing spots. If the local guide doesn't know where the fish are, and what they are biting on, then either there are no fish or he's no good. However, a guide may cost you anywhere from $250–$600 a day depending on whether you are sharing the cost with other anglers. It might seem expensive but it's a matter of weighing up the options and the main ones are saving time and gaining a brief insight into years of knowledge.

When you pay for the services of a guide you have an expectation that it not only includes taking you to where the fish are, but also includes helping you catch fish. A guide with a professional outlook will carry a rod, but this is used as an instructive tool when needed to show the client what they are doing wrong. Sometimes words fail and it is necessary to demonstrate a cast, or even prove that there is a fish where the guide says. Most guides carry tackle for people who don't bring their own, supply a light lunch and produce results. At the end of the day, you are returned to your motel and pay the bill. No cleaning up of tackle or boat.

A competent guide is a big help. You learn new methods and it is an education to be on the water with some of these people. In deciding on a guide though, it pays to ask around. Guides from hell soon build reputations of notoriety that catch up with them. Make no mistake, if you fish with enough guides there will be days when you may want your money back. If I was to hire a guide and he started fishing without being invited to do so, I wouldn't pay. I might share the petrol costs, but that would be as far as I would go.

The bottom line is that if you intend going on a fishing trip with a guide or as part of a group, ask around. Word of mouth is the best gauge of who is worthwhile, and more to the point, who isn't.

In Cairns I had time on the water with a couple of guides who operate similarly, but in different ways. First there was Kieran Livingstone who runs one of those solid Cairns Custom Craft aluminiums. While most of the estuary systems had shut down, he decided to take a punt on Russell Heads, the junction and estuary system of the Russell and Mulgrave rivers. It was one of those windy, wet days when the sky was filled with dark clouds that hung low in the valleys to block out sunlight and turn the verdant mountains grey. Except for the warmth in the air, you could have been in Victoria in winter – at least there were no sandflies. As it turned out there was a bit of action. We had a hot bite of queenfish and were casting small poppers and flies at the marauding fish that were hunting along a sandbar. I couldn't see the sandbar – the combination of overcast sky and an alluvial river; however, Kieran assured me it existed.

Queenfish are a pretty fish with classic trevally lines but are skinny and don't weigh much. While there wasn't a fish under about a metre in length, those we caught ranged from about 7kg to perhaps 10kg. The action was fast and furious, lasting for more than three hours. A school of wolf herring had entered the estuary and were hunting with, and being hunted by, the queenfish. Wolf herring are one of the fiercest looking fish I've ever come across, and have a thick coating of slime. About 35–40cm long and shaped like a barracouta, the two front fangs on these herring come out of the top jaw parallel with the body.

Our outfits were 6kg with light spinning rods and threadline reels. Kieran said the key to working poppers was to keep them in the water and create an unbroken surface disturbance, as this is what attracts the fish. We employed a range of poppers, from the basic cigar-shaped, flat-nosed variety to ones that tapered at each end and had small propeller-like blades at the front and rear. Some of the lures were old favourites that had been carefully restored; others looked like they had just come out of the packet. Kieran will remember the trip as being the time he lost his favourite lure, the one with the propeller blades front and rear. I know that because he mentioned losing that lure several times in conversation. What irked him the most was that it was a one-off; he had never seen one quite like it in Australia.

No disrespect to the people who make poppers, but in my humble opinion the difference between a homemade popper and one with a famous brand name is about $30. I rate any colour, so long as it is white, to be good value on a popper. The truth about fishing with lures is the same truth that comes through with flies: confidence. If you believe in the counterfeit-offering then for some reason it will work better for you.

When a hook-up came, the queenfish would invariably leap out of the water several times, in between making long dashes for freedom. Sometimes the fish took a nose-down approach and all you could see was their tails churning up the surface, something Kieran said was common and known locally as 'the washing machine'.

Kieran's value as a guide was plain to see. There were other boats about the place with guides, but only one other managed to keep station with the fish. One guide on a boat labelled 'sportfishing' took his crew off bottom bouncing, another insisted on trolling through the middle of our casting range for minimal success. If I were on one of the other boats I'd have been asking for my money back.

On the same trip, I fished with another guide, Ross Finlayson, and in this case it was a bit of both worlds. Born and bred in Victoria, Ross skippered the game boat *Sea Baby IV* in those days and operated an estuary guiding business inshore, for which he used a Hewes flats boat.

Like Kieran, Ross is the consummate professional and we did all the right things with the Hewes. We fished the flats and mangroves at Port Douglas, flicking flies and lures among the barnacle-ridden roots in search of predator action. With limited success at Port Douglas we moved to the Mossman River to flick more lures and flies at steep, undercut banks and snags or, to be politically correct,

Cairns gameboat skippers Laurie Woodbridge (left) and Ross Finlayson (right) on the lookout for marlin

structure. Mind you, I find the word 'structure' incongruous. When I went to school 'structure' related to a building. In fishing terms, fallen trees, reef, rocks and even sunken vessels are referred to as structure. We caught an assortment of fish ranging from barramundi, tarpon and mangrove jacks to cod. It was fun fishing, except for the sandflies.

The real essence of Ross came through during an offshore bottom bouncing session. With other anglers on the boat choosing to use light game outfits to fish the bottom, or alternatively cube for mackerel, Ross brought out the handline.

'Let me show you guys how to catch coral trout,' said Ross. One bite, one coral trout; two bites, two coral trout, and so on until he had caught six of the delectable, seemingly impossible to catch, reef fish. There were those among our small group who were fishing on the bottom, on the same reef and using the same bait. We caught small mouth nannygai and mangrove jack. A few mackerel ate our baits, and in turn sharks ate the mackerel while the unfortunate fish were still on our lines. Not one of us, though, caught a coral trout.

Pulling in yet another trout of about 3kg, Ross couldn't help himself: 'There's a knack to this you know – you've just got to know what you're doing when you're dealing with these fish.'

Whether it be guiding along an overgrown mangrove estuary or trolling for mackerel or marlin, Ross was the guiding professional. But when the handline came out and the line went over the side he changed. The serious gameboat-skipper-come-estuary-fishing-guide adopted a new persona, one I would suggest that is commonplace among the kids fishing with handlines along the banks of the Broken River near his hometown of Shepparton.

Perhaps it's true what they say – you can take the man out of the bush, but you can't take the bush out of the man, and few of us ever let go of an old handline.

REGULATION PITFALLS

There are so many differences in fisheries rules and regulations between the states that it pays for visitors to research the relevant regulations for themselves (*see* following page).

Fishing regulations can be confusing. Take Murray cod season. In Victoria and NSW the season runs from 1 December–31 August. In SA the season usually opens on 1 January, however, there is no guarantee. In 2011, SA closed the Murray cod season a month earlier than Victoria and NSW, and this followed on from a two-year moratorium on fishing for Murray cod.

I am not about to debate the rationale of regulation changes, rather to show readers there are ongoing changes.

In 2011 there was a boom in the yabbie population across southern NSW, Victoria and SA. Most people enjoy a feed of yabbies, and catching them is a fun exercise that the family can enjoy; however, there are differences in the state laws governing yabbies. (*See* page 51 for information regarding different state regulations and yabbie fishing.)

In Tasmania you do not need a recreational fishing licence for saltwater or marine fishing but an Inland Fisheries Licence is required in inland waters, which includes some river mouths and estuaries. SA anglers do not require a fishing licence but Victorian and NSW anglers must buy a licence. In Queensland you do not need a recreational fishing licence; however, in 33 dams you are required to purchase a Stocked Impoundment Permit. The list of dams is available on www.dpi.qld.gov.au.

In case you haven't got the internet, here are the dams: Bill Gunn (Lake Dyer), Bjelke Petersen, Boondooma, Borumba, Burdekin Falls, Callide, Cania, Lake Clarendon, Connolly, Cooby, Coolmunda, Cressbrook, Eungella, Fairbairn, Glenlyon, Gordonbrook, Lake Gregory, Kinchant, Lenthalls, Leslie, Maroon, Moogerah, Lake MacDonald, Lake Monduran (Fred Haigh), North Pine, Peter Faust, Somerset, Storm King, Teemburra, Theresa Creek, Tinaroo Falls, Wivenhoe and Wuruma.

There are also different rules regarding fish sizes and the quantity you are allowed. You never know when a government department is going to spring something new too, which happened in SA with Murray cod, as already explained, but also in Queensland with snapper in 2011.

In Queensland the minimum size for snapper is 35cm and the bag limit is four. In 2011, the Queensland Department of Primary Industries instituted a six-week closed snapper season that began on 15 February and finished 31 March. The department said snapper were overfished and that the closed season was aimed at helping protect the sustainability of snapper stock. To effectively reduce fishing pressure, the closure also applied to the other main co-caught species of pearl perch and teraglin.

In SA the minimum length is 38cm but bag limits vary. In Gulf St Vincent, anglers are allowed five small snapper, 38–60cm, with a boat limit of 15. In all other SA waters anglers may catch ten small snapper (38–60cm) with a boat limit of 30. Large snapper, over 60cm, are limited to two per angler with a boat limit of six in all SA waters. SA has a closed snapper season and it is unlawful to take snapper from midday on 1 November to midday on 30 November.

There is no closed season for snapper in NSW or Victoria, but there are size and bag limit differences. In NSW, the minimum size for snapper is 30cm and the maximum number of fish that anglers are allowed to take is ten.

In Victoria, the minimum snapper size is 28cm and anglers are allowed up to ten snapper but, and this is the tricky bit, no more than three of those ten snapper may be equal to or bigger than 40cm.

In WA the fishing rules are mind-boggling. You are required to purchase a fishing licence if fishing from a boat; or for lobster, marron and abalone; or for net fishing; or freshwater fishing. Then comes the snapper, called pink snapper in the west. There are snapper tags, a snapper lottery and closed seasons that vary depending where you are.

In the south coast region, which takes in Albany and Esperance, snapper minimum size is 41cm and the daily bag limit is four. On the west coast, which takes in Augusta in the south and Kalbarri in the north, snapper minimum length is also 41cm; however, it changes to 50cm south of 31 degrees latitude, just north of Lancelin.

Colin Tannahill shows off a fine dusky flathead caught near the entrance to the Hawkesbury River, NSW

There is a closed snapper season in Cockburn and Warnbro Sounds from 1 October–31 January. There is sound reason for the closure as Cockburn Sound is the site of the largest known aggregations of snapper in the West Coast bio-region and is thought to be critical to the maintenance of adequate breeding stocks.

Snapper caught outside of the Sounds may be transported through, and landed within, Cockburn and Warnbro Sound during the closed season.

Confused? Well, there's more: on the Gascoyne coast, which starts at 27 degrees south between Kalbarri and Denham and goes north as far as Onslow, the bag limit for snapper is four fish with a 41cm minimum size. But, on the inner gulfs of Sharks Bay, the minimum size is 50cm and there is a maximum size of 70cm and the bag limit is one snapper.

And still, there are more rules and these relate to snapper fishing in Shark Bay. The Eastern Gulf has a closed season from 1 May–31 July. Denham Sound is open each year until the 15 tonne Total Allowable Catch (TAC) is reached.

Freycinet Estuary has a closed season from 15 August–30 September. Anglers must have a snapper tag to take snapper in the Freycinet Estuary – a limited number of tags are issued each year. When you arrive in the Kimberley, the bag limit for snapper is four and the minimum size is back to 41cm with no maximum size.

Mostly in WA a bag limit of two barramundi per angler applies, and in some places such as the Lower Ord and Broome areas, only one.

To run all the various rules and regulations, bag and size limit for species, and variations, would take more pages than in this book. However, as you can see, there is a need for travelling anglers to make themselves aware of different fisheries rules. Ignorance is rarely a reasonable defence in law.

Before you fish, check out each state and territory's regulations (*see* opposite page).

NSW
www.dpi.nsw.gov.au/fisheries/recreational/regulations

ACT
ACT regulations come under NSW

Victoria
www.dpi.vic.gov.au/fisheries/recreational-fishing/recreational-fishing-guide

SA
www.pir.sa.gov.au/fisheries/recreational_fishing/fishing_limits

WA
www.fish.wa.gov.au/fishing-and-aquaculture/recreational-fishing/recreational-fishing-rules/Pages/default.aspx

NT
www.nt.gov.au/d/Fisheries/recreational/index.shtml

Queensland
www.daff.qld.gov.au/fisheries/recreational/rules-regulations

Tasmania
Freshwater
www.ifs.tas.gov.au/fishery-management/recreational-fishery/angling-regulations/general-rules
Saltwater
www.dpipwe.tas.gov.au/sea-fishing-aquaculture/recreational-fishing/recreational-sea-fishing-licences

TOURNAMENTS AND COMPETITIONS

Ever wondered how many competitions or tournaments are held around Australia every year? Well, the simple answer is: far too many to keep track of them all. Here is a sample of the big ones.

Many competitions are run by local tourism authorities as a way of attracting visitors to a region so, if you know where you want to go and what you want to catch, go on the internet and do your research.

VICTORIA AND NSW

Some of the big competitions open to the public include the Yamaha Cod Classic at Lake Mulwala on the NSW–Victoria border that began in 1998. Organised from the beginning by Tony Bennett, the Cod Classic has grown to enormous proportions with more than 2500 anglers competing for seven boat-packages, among other prizes. As well as anglers, many families attend the event so the populations of Mulwala and Yarrawonga are boosted by more than 5000. The event is held on the first weekend of the Murray cod season, which starts on 1 December in NSW and Victoria. More information is available at: **www.codclassic.com.au**.

In Port Phillip, Victoria, the annual Tea Tree Snapper Competition hosted by the Snapper Point Angling Club is held every November on Melbourne Cup weekend, and has been popular since 1983. It averages about 2000 entrants who fish Port Phillip and Western Port for snapper. In 2011 the prizes on offer were valued at more than $100,000 and included three boats, along with plenty of other goodies like tackle. More information is available at: **www.teatreesnapper.org.au**.

Daly River Barra Nationals fishing competition at dawn, NT

SA

In SA, Whyalla's Australian Snapper Championship, held annually at Easter, has been going since 1991. The competition attracts hundreds of anglers from SA, Victoria, NSW and even the NT. To win this competition anglers need to land a snapper over 10kg. The smallest snapper to win was 9.9kg in 1992, however, most years sees the winner weighing in snapper between 13kg and 15kg. The biggest snapper weighed was a whopping 15.98kg – caught in 2003 by Whyalla local, Daniel Fell. More information is available at: **www.australiansnapper.com.au**.

Boats getting ready for the start of the Barra Nationals, NT

QUEENSLAND

Toyota was involved in the Fraser Island Fishing Expo for more than 20 years but the event seems to have gone into history. Still, there are many more competitions around the place, such as the Rocky Barra Bounty in Rockhampton.

NT

In the NT, two of the biggest events on the fishing calendar are the Barra Classic and Barra Nationals held on the Daly River.

The Barra Nationals is organised and run by the Palmerston Game Fishing Club and held in April or May. More information is available at: www.palmerstongamefishing.com.au. This event is followed by the Barra Classic, organised by the Darwin Game Fishing Club. Both are team events and have been going for more than 25 years. More information is available at: www.darwingamefishingclub.com.au.

The Australian Game Fishing Association has more than 60 'sanctioned tournaments' running in different ports around Australia. For example, in May you might want to join the blue-water action at Bermagui with the Canberra Game Fishing Club's annual yellowfin tuna tournament; the same month you could head south to chase southern bluefin tuna off Port MacDonnell in SA. September is a billfish tournament at Innisfail in Queensland and on it goes. The association's game fish tournament calendar covers the coastline and tournaments are based on best times. More information is available at: www.gfaa.asn.au.

Events held by the Australian National Sportfishing Association (ANSA) are organised at state level. More information is available at: www.ansa.com.au.

State-based ANSA clubs are at:

www.ansansw.com.au
www.ansavic.com.au
www.ansa-sa.org
www.ansaqld.com.au

The Australian Anglers Association holds annual fishing championships where state teams battle it out. State and member clubs also run separate events. More information on state affiliates is available at:

www.aaawa.iinet.net.au
www.aaavic.org
www.nswfca.com.au
www.fishpo.com.au

CATCH AND RELEASE

Angling has evolved a long way since the 1960s. I credit some significant events as catalysts for change during the past half 50 years.

First and foremost was the formation of the Australian National Sportfishing Association (ANSA) see **www.anas.com.au**. The organisation was formed in February 1967 in Cairns, and the first president was that doyen of outdoor writers, Vic McCristal. The founding editor of *Australian Angler,* Ron Calcutt, took every opportunity to promote ANSA and sportfishing.

In those days, McCristal and Calcutt were fishing gurus. Young anglers, myself included, joined up to be part of an organisation that promoted the new sportfishing ethos. Being young, we were impressionable and wanted more out of our fishing than killing. Sportfishing was seen as the ultimate challenge: angler against fish with the odds favouring the finned battlers. Mostly we steered an altruistic course – the bloodfest of competitions where success was measured in fish carcasses was not for us. We were sportfishers, and didn't have a blood lust. Well, almost. Some days we went feral and slipped back into old ways, killing more fish than we could use.

In 1974 McCristal stunned the fishing world with his book *Rivers and the Sea*. The book was thought-provoking, forthright and environmentally insightful. *Rivers and the Sea* was a timely release that fitted snugly in the mood of the moment and changed the way many anglers looked at our fishing environment.

The next major impact came from the Bearded Burbler, old Yibbidy Yibbidah himself: Rex Hunt. From the moment Rex kissed and released his first fish on television, the fishing scene changed forever. Overnight, catch and release fishing became the cool scene on all waters. In the ensuing years to about 2002 the changes slowed, but catch and release has become such a dominant part of fishing that many anglers no longer go fishing for a feed.

The industry introduced major tackle innovations, including Yo-Zuri squid jigs, Shimano Baitrunner reels, and Shakespeare Ugly Stik (solid tip) rods. Technology progressed and black-and-white paper sounders gave way to electronic units that were in colour and came with GPS, and other gadgetry that included tide charts and water temperature gauges.

Regarding fish handling, the Environet and lip-gripping tools came to the fore for those who wanted to catch fish and keep them in good health to return to the water. The biggest change was a soft plastic lure revolution driven by Shimano through noted anglers Steve Starling and Kaj Busch. Plastics weren't new, but they became an overnight sensation and one that attracted hordes of young anglers, most adopting catch and release. Plastics back then were lures with additives, today many plastics are moulded foodstuffs with additives – in other words they are bait.

A couple of years back a fishing columnist suggested that some of the new-age soft plastic lure brigade probably couldn't bait a hook or fillet a fish. If you use lures ad nauseam, and practise catch and release, then baiting and fish cleaning skills are redundant.

The strong emphasis on catch and release doesn't suit everyone. Many anglers quite rightly fish for a feed. This is as it should be. There is nothing wrong with taking a fish for the table – isn't that how fishing started?

Hidden away under every Columbia shirt or Gortex jacket is a primitive hunter-gatherer willing the angler to take a fish. For those who don't know how to fillet fish for the table, here's how it is done without going through the task of scaling.

FILLETING FISH

You will require a sharp filleting knife, a flat board and a pair of gloves. Mesh gloves will protect you from cutting yourself while cotton gloves, while offering no protection from the knife edge, help you to hold the fish.

First, hold the fish flat on the board, pierce the skin behind the front dorsal fin and cut diagonally across and through to the backbone. Then, keeping the knife flat against the backbone, run the blade towards the tail, and when you get to the tail push the point right through the side of the fillet. Now cut through to the tail.

When the fillets are removed, it is time to skin the fish. Hold the tough skin in one hand and using the flat-bladed knife, slice a small portion of the flesh away from the skin. This is where cotton gloves are handy as they allow you to get a better grip on the skin.

Next step is to remove the skin. To do so, make a slight incision through the flesh at the tail of the fillet and take hold of the skin. Now, keeping the knife blade at about 20 degrees off the horizontal, pull the skin towards you and the knife should slide easily to separate skin and flesh.

To rid yourself of bones on the rib cage, work your knife with small slices, feeling the blade around the bones.

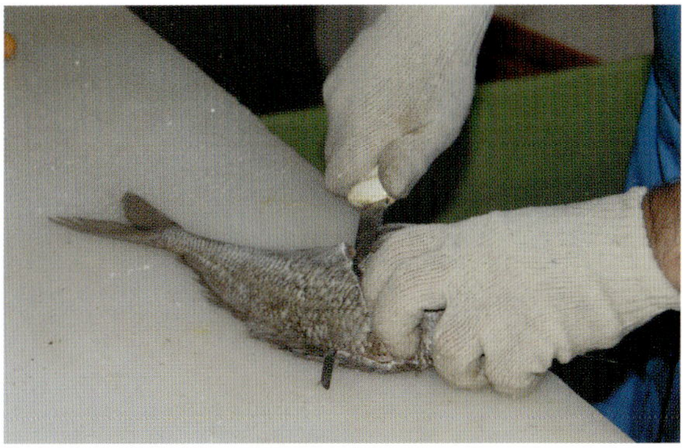

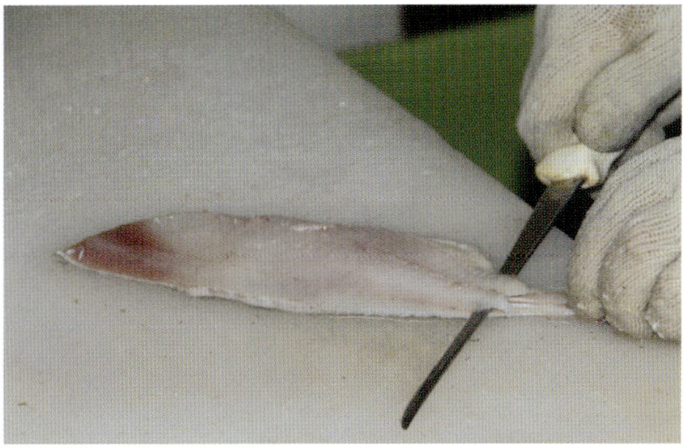

Friendly kookaburra at Maningrida Arnhem Land, NT

COOKING SEAFOOD

If you camp and fish for long enough you will eventually come across anglers who make cooking their catch something of a speciality. When I fished the rock ledges of southern NSW I met up with a couple of anglers who always made an effort to bake a big fish on the coals of a fire. Their preference was yellowtail kingfish or bonito. The method was simple: clean the fish, fill the gut cavity with foods like onion, mushroom, capsicum and the like, then seal the cavity with bacon before wrapping the package in foil.

Timing was everything. Big fish in the 12kg range could take up to 40 minutes, and they were checked constantly to ensure the flesh wasn't destroyed by leaving it in the coals for too long. When the baked fish was removed and the foil opened, the flesh flaked away and it was a free-for-all. The tucker was excellent. Some folks even ate the lips – something I could never come at.

Another method on the surf was to catch salmon, wrap them in wet newspaper, and put them in the coals. When the newspaper started to burn, the salmon was cooked. The ink didn't spoil the meal.

In Spencer Gulf, SA, catching blue swimmer crabs for the table is a popular pursuit. It's not a difficult task. You simply gather a hoop net, tie some fish onto the centre of the net and lower it to the bottom. In less than an hour, you lift the net and, if the crabs are co-operative, you will have several. I did this with Lawrie Birdseye and at the end of the day we cooked the crabs by boiling them. Unlike some crustaceans, blue swimmers do not require additives. They are sweet enough to eat straight out of the water.

In the tropical north, crabbing is a little different to the SA method, although the principle is the same. In this case the crabs are the much larger mud crabs, and crab pots made from heavy gauge wire mesh are used. The crab pots are a rectangular cage with narrow openings at either side, and bait is wired inside the cage to attract the crabs.

I went crabbing with Lindsay Mutimer when he was at the Arnhemland Barramundi Nature Lodge at Maningrida. It was a matter of setting the crab pots out along the edges of the mangrove estuaries, then going fishing for barramundi for the rest of the day. There were two critical elements to this system: first, the crab pot had to land on the bottom and lay flat; the second factor was to place the polystyrene marker buoy above the water in the mangroves. This was done not to hide the buoy, rather to keep it out of reach of the local crocodile population.

Tony Rigby was the Lodge chef and he gave me some of his seafood recipes:

Ginger beer batter

Ingredients

½ cup self-raising flour
½ cup cornflour
1 teaspoon garlic, chopped
½ teaspoon lemon pepper
½ stubby ginger beer

Method

To make the batter, place all dry ingredients in a bowl. While mixing, add ginger beer until consistency resembles thickened cream. Roll fish in flour, place in batter and deep fry at 180°C for three minutes.

Chilli mud crab

Ingredients

2 whole mud crabs
1 onion, chopped
4 shallots, chopped
1 tablespoon coriander, chopped
1 fresh chilli, sliced
1 tablespoon garlic, crushed
1 tablespoon ginger, crushed
2 cups sweet chilli sauce
3 cups tomato sauce
crispy fresh bread

Method

Shell and cut the crab into quarters – crack the claws by hitting them with the back of a large knife. In a large saucepan fry onion, shallots, coriander, chilli, garlic and ginger. Add sweet chilli and tomato sauce and bring to the boil. Add crabs and cover with lid. When the sauce comes back to the boil toss the crabs every minute for five minutes. Serve with crispy fresh bread.

Chilli squid

Ingredients

500g baby squid, cleaned
2 cups plain flour
½ cup cornflour
1 cup chilli flakes

Method

Cut the squid into bite-size pieces, leaving the heads whole. In a large bowl mix the plain flour, cornflour and chilli flakes. Separate the squid into approximately 150g batches and deep-fry at 200°C for 45 seconds. Place on plate and serve drizzled with a sauce of your choice.

SQUID

As sad as this may sound, my squid-eating friends have changed tactics. It used to be that they wanted to keep the biggest squid, which was fine – I prefer the small ones for bait. However, since discovering that small squid were sweeter, I find that I am now being left with the big specimens. The worst culprit in this is my food-writing buddy Bob Hart, who has the following to say about cooking calamari squid and pinkies on a barbecue:

> There are a few questions you should ask yourself when you decide to make a meal of freshly caught calamari:
>
> - Should I eat the big one, or a couple of the smaller ones?
> - Should I take the easy option, fire up the deep-fryer and cook salt-and-pepper squid?
> - Or should I behave like a serious fisherman and try the Vietnamese approach?

Frankly, if the squid is fresh enough, there are no wrong answers. Calamari, big or small, are delicious when they are fresh. And salt-and-pepper squid made with either big or small squid compares favourably with the more exotic Vietnamese approach. But as few Australian fishermen haven't the faintest idea how to approach the latter, let's give it a shot, because the final result is very, very special.

Extreme freshness is essential: Vietnamese fishermen often carry a charcoal brazier on their boats to cook this dish minutes after the cephalapod has been hauled aboard. This, even for me, is a step

Squid come out clean after a short session in a scaling bag

too far. But I am fascinated by the cooking method they use, and by the revelation that the skin of a calamari, which we go to so much trouble to remove, is similar to a thin pork crackling after the squid has been seared over hot charcoal. Try this:

Ingredients

calamari
3 small, fresh red chillies
3 tablespoons of coarse sea salt
lime

Method

Pull the tentacles, and everything attached to them, from the tube of the fresh calamari and put them aside for bait. Without skinning the tube or removing the flaps, split it lengthwise and open it out flat. Remove the cartilage. And that's it!

Make a paste by pounding together the chillies and sea salt using apestle and mortar. Spread both sides of the squid tube with this paste and place it into a flimsy, racquet-like, hinged grill – I bought mine in an Asian market for around $6. Clamp the grill shut.

Place the hinged grill over high, direct heat, ideally from a bed of charcoal, and cook 3–4 minutes a side. If you are able to cover it, as I do when I cook it in a Weber kettle, cook a large calamari for 4 minutes on the one side and 3 minutes on the other side; or cook a small calamari for 3, then 2 minutes.

Remove the calamari from the grill, cut it into strips and serve with a squeeze of lime. And that's it. Except, maybe, for a cold beer or three.

PINKIES

Now let's assume, just for a moment, that you are somebody who likes to catch their own pinkies. Or whatever it is you call infant snapper in your part of the world.

Should you be lucky enough catch them, you should also be prepared to cook them soon after – while they are still as stiff as boards – and remember, less is more.

So, when I harvest the occasional pinkie from the waters off Half Moon Bay, I cook them simply. Try my method for yourself.

Cleaning yellowbelly on the Murray River near Wentworth, NSW

Ingredients

pinkies, usually around 40cm and weighing about 800g
extra-virgin olive oil
salt
freshly ground black pepper
lemon slices
fennel slices

Method

First, scale and clean the fish, remembering to remove the gills, ideally in the water from which you caught them.

Oil each fish with extra-virgin olive oil and season well with salt and freshly ground black pepper. Now, slip alternating slices of lemon and fennel into the body cavities, and cut a couple of slices through to the backbone, across both sides of each fish.

Cook the fish on a covered gas barbecue (on a grill, not on a hotplate), or you can seal the fish in a frying pan before popping it into a hot oven (200°C) until it is cooked through. The fish is done when the flesh can be lifted away from the backbone, but remember: remove the fish from the heat before it reaches this point and rest it, loosely tented in foil, to finish cooking. Cooking time will depend on the heat source, but around 20 minutes, including a few minutes resting time, will wrap things up.

And one more tip: once you have placed the fish on your grill (which you have cleaned with a wire brush and then oiled, of course), leave it alone to give it time to begin to cook, and for the skin to release from the grill. You may not get a perfect result every time – much depends on your grill. But if you are careful the reuslt will be delicious.

I serve fresh pinkies cooked in this way with very little else: perhaps some melted butter, into which I squeeze a little lemon juice; or with a dollop of silky mash and a lightly dressed green salad on the side. And a glass or five of my favourite riesling.

Thanks to chefs Tony Rigby and Bob Hart for supplying content (including recipes from Bob's book Heat & Smoke*) for this section of the book.*

ONE-POT FISH MEAL

Thank you to Sandra Brunner for this recipe.

For people in a hurry, a one-pot meal may be the answer. Sandra uses ready-to-serve soups in her recipe, and says a 500g can does two meals. Avoid the varieties with meat, except chicken. Pumpkin, chicken and corn are favourites.

Ingredients

500g can pumpkin, chicken or corn soup
½ packet two-minute noodles
fish fillets cut into chunks
⅔ cup water

Method

In a saucepan or microwave-safe dish, stir together the soup with half a packet of crushed two-minute noodles (don't use the seasoning in the noodles packet), and the water. Heat until it's hot, then lay the fish fillets on the top and keep heating until the soup steams/simmers.

Flip the fish when it looks half-cooked, and give the soup a bit of a stir. Prod the fillet occasionally to see if it's cooked; it is cooked when it starts to break up.

CLIMATE CHANGE AFFECTING FISH MOVEMENTS

Climate change is the hot topic for many commentators. Scientists say our planet is undergoing change: the ice caps are melting, droughts are more common, storms are stronger, and sea levels are rising.

Naysayers, most of them extreme newspaper columnists or radio shock jocks, will have none of this.

I believe in science. Scientists tell us change is happening, and the change is having an impact on the marine environment.

In December 2008, Fisheries Victoria released a report titled *Victorian Climate Change Strategy for Fisheries and Aquaculture 2008–2018*. The report states that the world's climate is changing, and there are significant challenges ahead.

It says: 'Various climate change models predict higher temperatures, less rainfall, more extreme weather events and a warming of the oceans around Australia. The eastern and south-eastern Australian marine waters are considered the most vulnerable to the impacts of climate change in Australia.

'South-east Australian waters are warming most rapidly – a strengthening of the East Australia Current has resulted in a warming of the Tasman Sea at a rate that is greater than anywhere else in the Southern Hemisphere.'

Furthermore, the report points out that Victoria's marine waters were susceptible due to several features of its coastal region, including the influence of the East Australian Current, which has strengthened by 20 per cent in the past 50 years. This has led to eastern Bass Strait water temperatures rising faster than elsewhere in Australia and, according to some model projections, the rest of the world.

While temperatures of eastern Victorian waters are predicted to rise due to the strengthening East Australian Current, the report states that the cooler Flinders Current, upwelling events and a weakening of the warmer Leeuwin Current since the 1970s provides uncertainty for future conditions off western Victoria. The report predicts increasing levels of salinity in Victoria's bays and inlets due to increased evaporation.

The consequences of climate change, according to the report, include the decline in populations of some fish species, while others may increase and change their geographic distributions: 'In the ocean, warmer waters are expected to result in species moving southwards. These changes may lead to opportunities to target different species.'

Fast-forward to 2012, and a report by Dr Alistair Hobday, principal research scientist with the CSIRO Marine and Atmospheric Research division. Dr Hobday's report states that general ocean warming around Australia, in particular on the east coast, in combination with predicted strengthening of the East Australian Current, will see the distribution of a range of pelagic species extend southwards.

Recent years have seen a number of reports of fish detected south of their typical range limits on the east coast. On the west coast, changes in the strength of the Leeuwin Current are likely to have major implications for the distribution and abundance of some species, including Western Australian salmon and Australian herring in waters off SA.

Recent extreme events on the west coast have also seen pelagic species reported far to the south of their normal distribution. Changes in productivity, for example due to increased coastal upwelling, may lead to increases in abundance of some species, particularly of small coastal pelagic fishes, such as sardines and anchovy, in the upwelling system between Cape Otway and the central Great Australian Bight.

In southern Australia, scientists, divers and anglers are reporting new species. This movement of fish, as they follow warming waters aided by strengthening ocean currents, is an observable change caused by climate change.

Many of the changes are being tracked through Redmap, a citizen science program hosted by the Institute for Marine and Antarctic Studies at the University of Tasmania. Redmap stands for Range Extension Database and Mapping project. Redmap collects data to identify changes in marine life distribution. See **www.redmap.org.au**.

In 2014, the 2012 Marine Report Card was released, and it showed climate change is having an impact. Ninety-eight of Australia's leading marine scientists contributed to the 2012 Report Card.

The Report Card, which can be read at **www.oceanclimatechange.org.au**, says there is strong evidence of extensive southward movements of tropical fish and plankton species in south-east Australia, declines in abundance of temperate species, and the first signs of damage to shellfish due to ocean acidification.

The Report Card warns that Australia's reef systems are under threat from climate change. Off the east coast of Australia, the southward flowing East Australia Current is warming, and pushing further south, taking large open ocean fish like tuna and billfish with it. This region is a global warming hotspot, one of about 20 such ocean regions where the rate of warming is faster than the global average.

This is good news for southern anglers who are seeing species such as striped marlin, yellowfin

Being caught offshore in a storm is a mite scary at times

tuna and dolphin fish in their region. Closer to shore, yellowtail kingfish and cobia are being captured further south. The abundance of smaller coastal species such as sardines may increase in future – stronger upwelling of cool nutrient rich water in a range of coastal locations is expected to enhance their food supply.

While not a direct link to climate change, a marine heat wave along WA early in 2011 saw manta rays and whale sharks, found much further north, reported as far south as Albany. Marine algae were killed as waters warmed, and the northern abalone fishery was closed after stocks suffered mass mortality.

Many anglers believe a major change has occurred in our marine environment, at least off south-west Victoria. Since 2006, the offshore waters from Port Fairy to Port MacDonnell have been giving up southern bluefin tuna weighing more than 100kg. The event is significant given that no-one caught tuna that big before in Victorian waters.

In the 1980s, a dolphinfish was washed ashore at Eastern View along the Great Ocean Road, and in 2005, a dolphinfish was caught in Port Phillip. Small numbers are caught every year now offshore between Portland and Port MacDonnell in SA.

Weather is becoming less predictable as our climate continues to change

In 2008, half a dozen giant squid, cephalopods more than five metres long, were found floating by anglers fishing off Portland. Striped tuna have been caught off Lawrence Rock and broadbill swordfish, caught by trawlers, have been washed ashore along the southwest coastline.

Another example of perception versus reality occurred in Lonsdale Bay near the entrance to Port Phillip. In early June 2009, anglers were catching calamari squid to 2.5kg. This seemed early to me. Along the eastern seaboard, and off Indented Head and St Leonards on the Bellarine Peninsula, it is usual to hook squid weighing a kilogram or more in winter. Squid anglers say the serious squid run – the big spawners in Lonsdale Bay – doesn't start until late August, or thereabouts. If you thought you couldn't catch big squid in the bay in winter, then like me you were wrong. Former commercial fisherman, Mark Rushton, said it was usual to hook the big squid at this time, but they would not be in large numbers.

The story was similar with snapper in Port Phillip. Fifty years ago anglers and fisheries scientists widely believed that all snapper left Port Phillip in late autumn and that you couldn't catch them in winter. In reality, most snapper are gone from the bay by winter, but you can catch them right through the colder months. Corio Bay is famous for its winter snapper, and good winter catches are made off Williamstown, Hobsons Bay and Mornington in Port Phillip.

There was a time when most King George whiting anglers believed the peak time was in summer. Nowadays most serious whiting anglers chasing the bigger fish do best from late autumn through winter. Moreover, whiting is no longer a daylight fishery; many anglers fish well into the night, or start before sunrise and do better. Even traditional baits have changed; fresh squid and pilchard fillets have displaced pipi, sandworm and fresh mussel.

Forty years ago, there was a large-scale commercial fishing industry in Bass Strait based around the humble barracouta. Commercial fishermen in clinker boats with single cylinder putt-putt engines would troll Smiths jigs, or 15cm long lengths of coloured dowel, with an 8/0 hook attached. As a by-catch, fishermen used to bring small southern bluefin tuna back to port, and complain of the difficulty they had getting past the tuna to catch barracouta.

In the 1990s, a big tuna made its way into Queenscliff Harbour, and in December 1958, southern bluefin made it as far into Port Phillip as Corio Bay inner harbour. In 2010, flying fish were seen off Cape Schanck in Bass Strait, and there were football-field size schools of striped tuna running through the Strait. A few years ago, a school of longtail tuna swam up Wagonga Inlet at Narooma, and stayed for the winter.

Change never stops. It has been going on for longer than the debate over climate change, but not as significantly or for as long as what we are now experiencing. No one has a crystal ball to tell what the future holds. In the short term, southern anglers will encounter more warm water species, and few will complain. There are no indications of a decline in northern fish numbers, but in research and climate terms, it is still early days.

Where TO GO FISHING

NEW SOUTH WALES AND ACT

Steve's FAVOURITE DESTINATIONS FOR NSW AND ACT

There is so much world-class fishing on Sydney's doorstep that you wouldn't be blamed for not leaving the local waters. But when you do get out of town, the fishing, as good as it is, improves.

From the Queensland border to the Victorian border, there are hundreds of magnificent beaches offering up the likes of mulloway, tailor and salmon. The NSW estuary systems are highly productive for the likes of bream, dusky flathead and sand whiting, while upstream many of the rivers produce Australian bass. The clear, fast-running streams of the Snowy Mountains are a favourite destination for fly-fishers chasing trout with teeny flies on gossamer thin leaders, while the lowland rivers in the southern and northern areas of the state produce yellowbelly, silver perch and Murray cod. Offshore anglers chase marlin, yellowfin tuna, broadbill swordfish and yellowtail kingfish.

ACCOMMODATION

New South Wales' accommodation options cater to all types of holiday-makers, from high-end historic homesteads, to secluded mountain cottages or country pubs.

For more information visit www.visitnsw.com

Anglers fishing for yellowbelly and Murray cod among the dead red gums on Lake Mulwala

A high proportion of the biggest Murray cod can be found here
Hot fishing all year round
World-famous gamefishing
Murwillumbah
LAKE CLARRIE HALL
1
Moree
Bourke
Inverell
LAKE COPETON
Grafton
Lake Keepit
Armidale
Coffs Harbour
Cobar
Broken Hill
Tamworth
South West Rocks
2
Port Macquarie
Lake Glenbawn
Lake Burrendong
Mudgee
Rylstone
Kandos
Parkes
Port Stephens
Newcastle
WENTWORTH
Lithgow
HAWKESBURY RIVER
Windsor
Euston
Balranald
Griffith
Young
Lake Wyangala
3
SYDNEY
Port Hacking
Wollongong
Wemen (Vic.)
5
Wagga Wagga
Goulburn
Swan Hill (Vic.)
Barmah (Vic.)
Lake Burrinjuck
8
Nowra
CANBERRA
7
Mulwala
Albury
Yaouk Valley
4
Batemans Bay
Echuca (Vic.)
Khancoban
6
Narooma
Tom Groggin
Jindabyne
BERMAGUI
Tathra
Merimbula
Green Cape

1 NEW SOUTH WALES STATE PARKS

The successful push by state Fisheries departments to boost native fish species is highlighted by the quality of the fishing for the likes of Murray cod and yellowbelly now being realised in NSW state parks. **For more information visit www.stateparks.nsw.gov.au**

LAKE CLARRIE HALL

The most scenic water I have seen. To get to Clarrie Hall, drive to Murwillumbah, and then turn west through Uki and south on to the Doon Doon Rd. This is well stocked Australian-bass water.

ACCOMMODATION: For information on accommodation close to Lake Clarrie Hall visit www.sweetwaterfishing.com.au/AccommodationNSW.htm or www.bigvolcano.com.au/places/kunghur.htm

Angling is a buzz when you are into a hot bite. It is also a buzz when discovering new territory or out hooking with other anglers, observing their methods and techniques on their home waters. So it was when I fished Lake Clarrie Hall, west of Murwillumbah, with Gary Keillor.

At 800m above sea level, Clarrie Hall isn't as much a dam as a mountain lake. It looks like it belongs in the tropics. Built on Doon Doon Creek, it features hundreds of hectares of green lily pads that put a carpet of colour across the waterway when they flower, while the dark, craggy outline of Mount Warning looms on the skyline.

The main restriction on Clarrie Hall is that outboards are not allowed, so you need to bring either an electric motor or a canoe.

This was a fly-fishing trip and we were using eight-weight outfits, alternating a floating line with a slow sinker. We worked along the edges of the lily pads, casting to slight indentations and cutbacks, working the fly into channels or past suspected ambush points near islands of lily pads. Gary had some specially tied variations of the Dahlberg Diver flies with looped weed guards. Imitating frogs, the flies were cast to land gently on top of the lily pads, then bounced on to the water along the edge and made to pop and bloop.

For deeper retrieves, Deep Clouser Minnow flies were employed on slow sink lines. These were cast to the edges of the lilies, or around timber and allowed to sink to varying depths by using

Above: Dawn on magnificent Lake Clarrie Hall, northern NSW
Below: Gary Fitzgerald shows off an Australian bass he caught in Lake Clarrie Hall

a countdown method. It was a bit tricky to avoid hanging up on submerged timber or the forest of lily pad stalks that shoot up near the bottom.

It was also frustrating. We had **bass** slap, bang, roll over and do everything except stick their heads out and squirt water at us before we managed to keep one on a hook. That first fish probably weighed less than half a kilogram but was worth the effort. It nailed a yellow and orange Clouser retrieved in short, sharp bursts about a metre and a half below the surface along the fringe of the growth.

We caught many other bass that day, and missed a few big-shouldered fish that would have severely tested us.

Methods for Lake Clarrie Hall

TACKLE Lure fishing is the most popular method and light spin or baitcast outfits spooled with braid lines of about 5kg are preferred. This isn't so much because of the size of the bass, but their pulling power. A big bass in Clarrie Hall is about 40cm, but most of the fish are 37cm or less. For fly-fishing, an eight-weight outfit is about ideal. Use a floating or slow-sink intermediate line and a leader of at least 2m. Avoid a tapered leader, instead use a level line of about 3–4kg breaking strain, as the flies are not aerodynamic.

LURES AND FLIES When the bass are in deeper water, top lures include Halco Poltergeist. For working the edges, shallow-diving minnow lures, like Rapala CD3 and CD5s, are productive. For night fishing, the Halco Night Walker has proven deadly. Spinnerbaits and soft plastic lures can do well. Fly-fishers find the Dahlberg Diver good for top-water fishing, and the Clouser Deep Minnow better when working deeper.

LAKE COPETON

Lake Copeton is an excellent catchment dam, fed by the Gwydir River and run-off from the New England Tablelands. The lake is in northern NSW, about 46km west of Inverell on the Gwydir Hwy. The dam was constructed primarily as an irrigation, holding water to serve the cotton farms further west. At full capacity, the volume of water in Lake Copeton is about three times that of Sydney Harbour.

ACCOMMODATION: Copeton Waters State Park has cabins (bring your own linen), powered and unpowered campsites. The park is the first turn left after crossing the dam wall.
For more information visit
www.copeton.com.au

The lake is popular for angling and well stocked with **Murray cod**, **yellowbelly** and **silver perch** and has good numbers of **catfish** along with **redfin** and the noxious **carp**. If the lake has a problem, it is the size and the enormous amount of fishing opportunities. The Gwydir River end offers more in the way of scenic opportunity, and the small bays strewn with fallen timber are more protected.

I first fished this water in the mid 1990s with native fish specialist Rod Harrison. We stayed at Copeton Waters State Park and launched our boat from shore at Diamond Bay to make the 30km to our destination where the Gwydir River flowed into the lake.

We used baitcaster reels spooled with braid and cast diving lures to the edge of rocks and alongside the skeletal remains of treetops. Our *modus operandi* was to work rocky points, snags and drop-offs. The slightest irregularities in the shoreline or bottom are likely places, as are choke points where the water narrows and the current increases. It was in a choke point when the action went from hot to hotter.

A **yellowbelly** of about 2.5kg was putting up a valiant struggle after taking a lure and Rod was coaxing it along through the current. We were drifting through a stretch of fast water in a small canyon and, even though the fish was making life difficult by using its deep flank to hold in the current, it was almost a

Lake Copeton ranks among the top half dozen lakes for big Murray cod and yellowbelly

regulation battle. We had been on the lake trolling and spinning for a great fish since sunrise, more than eight hours ago. Then it happened as a huge flash of white emerged through the tannin coloured water as a big Murray cod rose from its lair to take a swipe at the struggling yellowbelly.

'Did you see the size of that bloody cod?' Rod asked, and we both felt a rush of adrenalin. Murray cod proved scarce and after two and a half days, we only managed two of the 'green fish' as Harro called them. Mostly we caught and released yellowbelly, good-sized fish that ranged in weight from 1–3.5kg. Mixed in with these were redfin and silver perch.

Even when the fishing was slow, there was still plenty of action. Water dragons provided plenty of fun. When one of these lizards spotted a lure in the water, it would clamber along the rocky shoreline, dive in and chase the lure. We made sure no lizard got close enough to hook up, but the sight of a reptilian head poking periscope-like out of the water pursuing a piece of coloured, vibrating plastic was good for a few laughs.

Back in the early 1990s, a Murray cod of 10kg was regarded as a good fish. These days the cod are up to 40kg. The yellowbelly average 2–3kg so you won't be on the water hooking tiddlers. The redfin are not huge, but they act more as a food source for other fish than an angling resource.

LAKE KEEPIT

Located about 54km west of Tamworth or 38km east of Gunnedah, Keepit is a shallow dam (as dams go) and owes its presence to an enormous natural depression at the lower end of the Namoi Valley. Compared to other lakes, Keepit has limited cover for native fish.

ACCOMMODATION: Lake Keepit, as it is also known, offers a range of accommodation styles including cabins, powered and unpowered sites and bush camping. All mod-cons are available, including an amenities block, kiosk, laundry, camp kitchen and barbecues. Visitors can buy food, fuel, fishing tackle and bait.
For more information visit
www.lakekeepit.com.au

The fish population consists of **Murray cod**, **yellowbelly** and **silver perch** and receives regular stockings. The waterway also holds **carp**, which are easy to catch around the shore, and provide entertainment for young anglers and fly-fishers who enjoy the fighting capabilities of this maligned species.

LAKE GLENBAWN

Lake Glenbawn is 160km north-west of Newcastle, just off the New England Hwy, and can be reached via Aberdeen or Scone, about 40km away.

The lake is noted for producing trophy-size native fish.

ACCOMMODATION: Lake Glenbawn has a range of accommodation options from cabins to powered and bush camping sites. A kiosk has basic food items.
For more information visit
www.lakeglenbawn.com.au

Yellowbelly to 15kg have been caught here, and **silver perch** to 7.5kg, which is 16lb on the imperial scale. A noted **Australian bass** lake, anglers can expect to hook this feisty species to 2kg and over. The lake was traditionally stocked with yellowbelly, **silver perch** and bass. However, **rainbow trout** were released to boost the fish population, and anglers who bottom-fish catch good bags of **eel-tailed catfish**.

Glenbawn offers a range of fish habitat, including snaggy runs and rocky banks, with weedbeds where lake margins permit. The skeletal tops of submerged trees offer cover for bass. Anglers in the know fish these areas with spinnerbaits and lipless crankbaits.

LAKE BURRENDONG

Lake Burrendong is built across the junction of the Macquarie and Cudgegong rivers, and is about an hour's drive from Dubbo or Orange.

ACCOMMODATION: Lake Burrendong has cabins, powered and unpowered sites. The camp area has an amenities block and laundry. Visitors can buy food, fuel, tackle and bait.
For more information visit
www.lakeburrendong.com.au

Constructed in the early 1960s, the lake produced outstanding catches of **Murray cod**, however, pollution from run-off caused fish kills and subsequently the waterway became best known as a **redfin** fishery through to the '90s, and then there was a **carp** invasion.

In recent years, NSW Fisheries increased native fish stocking, and fishing for **Murray cod** and **yellowbelly** has improved. **Catfish** and **yabbies** are also caught. Spring and summer are the best seasons for **yabbies**.

LAKE WYANGALA

Wyangala is a 30-minute drive south-east from Cowra or about two hours north of Canberra. The lake is huge, with a surface area two and a half times that of Sydney Harbour. The lake is situated below the confluence of the Lachlan and Abercrombie rivers and is a popular angling holiday destination.

ACCOMMODATION: Options include cabins, powered and bush camping sites. There are barbecues and an amenities block. Visitors can buy food, fuel, tackle and bait.
For more information visit
www.wyangalawaters.com.au

Anglers come here in search of **silver perch**, **yellowbelly**, **catfish**, **Murray cod** and **brown** and **rainbow trout**.

LAKE BURRINJUCK

Located about 60km south-west of Yass, Burrunjuck is New South Wales' oldest man-made lake. Burrunjuck was constructed in 1928 downstream of the junction of the Murrumbidgee and Goodradigbee rivers.

Yellowbelly are a favourite catch for anglers fishing NSW state parks

ACCOMMODATION: Visitors can choose from cabins and cottages, powered sites and bush camping.
For more information visit
www.stateparks.nsw.gov.au/burrinjuck_waters

The lake has abundant snag and rocky bank habitat and a solid fish population. Anglers who come here catch **Murray cod** and **yellowbelly**. Other species caught include **trout**, **redfin** and **carp**.

Methods for New South Wales state parks

Lure anglers prefer baitcaster outfits, 4–6kg and spool their reels with 15kg breaking strain braid. Trolling or casting lures will produce Murray cod, yellowbelly, silver perch and redfin. If fishing cod, use a minimum 15kg monofilament leader. Bait anglers tend to employ 4–6kg threadline outfits.

RIGS The simplest rig for bait fishing is to use a pea-size ball sinker and allow it to run to the hook. Some anglers prefer to use running sinker rigs with a leader for the cod, and paternoster style rigs for the yellowbelly. Hook size for baits are generally No.2 to No.4 long shank. Bobbing with lures and bait is popular in heavily timbered areas for redfin and yellowbelly. This is a method whereby the bait is dropped to the bottom, lifted a metre or so and then lifted and dropped.

BAIT Shrimp and yabbies are the two most popular baits, but scrubworms and woodgrubs will also produce solid results.

LURES Large bibbed, deep running lures are best for trolling. A few with a record of accomplishment include Stumpjumpers, Predatek Boomerangs, Halco Poltergeists and Bassman Spinnerbaits. Spinning with Minnow lures or working Spinnerbaits in the heavy timber and rocky gorges is productive.

2 NORTH COAST

COFFS HARBOUR

Coffs Harbour is located on the Pacific Hwy, six-and-a-half hours or 540km north of Sydney, or about five hours or 400km south of Brisbane.

Marlin, tuna and mackerel dominate the offshore gamefishing, while bottom bouncers do well on snapper and pearl perch. Land-based anglers can have a great time chasing mulloway or tailor in the surf, of fishing from the breakwall or ledges on Mutton Bird Island for mackerel, tuna, tailor and snapper.

ACCOMMODATION: As you would expect with a major destination, Coffs Harbour has a vast range of accommodation styles from campsites to hotels.
For more information visit
www.visitcoffsharbour.com

My introduction to fishing north of Sydney was at Coffs Harbour, an area with a diverse range of options. The first time I fished here I was into land-based gamefishing and spent most of my time on the ledges of Mutton Bird Island chasing **bonito**, **Spanish mackerel** and **longtail tuna**. Other anglers were after **drummer**, **bream** and **tailor**.

Offshore fishing is exceptional at times. Mackerel, **marlin**, **cobia**, tuna and **yellowtail kingfish** are just some of the game fish available. Bottom bouncers also do well.

My first trip offshore was a spur-of-the-moment event with a German angler called Hans. He was a permanent resident in the caravan park in which I was staying. Hans wanted someone to go out with him in his boat; I just wanted to get on the water after spending several days fishing from the rocks.

It was early April and the catch that day was a revelation in terms of quantity. We didn't head for the Solitary Islands or those areas that are now marine parks, but instead went south-east.

Our rigs were rudimentary: fixed sinker paternoster, two baits and that was about it. The bottom wasn't heavy reef; more like sand with intermittent reef patches.

Our baits were barely down when the action started. The first **snapper** was about 1.5kg, and from then on there was a steady stream of snapper up to 3.6kg, along with **pearl perch** and yellowtail kingfish. A couple of days later the local fishing club held a big fishing competition, and the bulk of the fish that weighed in were snapper. The biggest was about 4.5kg, but there were plenty around 1–2kg.

A long jetty juts out into the harbour and this is popular with families who can catch yellowtail, **trevally**, **garfish** and bream. The seawall that runs out from Corambirra Point is worth fishing for bream, drummer, tailor and even **mulloway**. Anglers here sometimes also hook mackerel and tuna. Estuary anglers can fish Coffs and Moonee creeks for **mangrove jack**, bream, **flathead**, **luderick**, trevally and **whiting**. Beach anglers fish for tailor, bream and mulloway.

Above: Mick Fletorides with a Coffs Harbour snapper
Below: Dale Attwell shows off a spotted mackerel, a common species along this stretch of the NSW coast

Above: Trial Beach is popular for many table species
Below: Fish Rock is a favourite destination for anglers and divers

SOUTH WEST ROCKS

Situated at the mouth of the Macleay River, South West Rocks is about 460km north of Sydney. Turn off the Pacific Hwy at Kempsey and drive for about 39km.

Top class estuary action is available for the likes of bream and flathead, while offshore anglers chase cobia, dolphinfish, tuna and marlin.

ACCOMMODATION: All tastes are catered for, just be sure to book in early for holidays.
For more information visit www.visitnsw.com/destinations/north-coast/south-west-rocks-area

When it comes to popularity, there are two types of fishing destinations: those that are hot all the time and those that wax and wane depending on the season. South West Rocks is in the first category. For as long as I can remember the area has enjoyed enormous favour as a fishing destination. Moreover, the reason it is popular isn't just fishing consistency, it's also the variety of species. Anglers have multiple options of beach, estuary or blue-water to choose from, so even when the weather cuts up rough, you can still fish somewhere.

The Macleay River carves its way from the mountains of the New England Plateau to the sea. The original mouth of the river was at Grassy Head, but during a flood in 1893 a new entrance was formed at South West Rocks.

The river mouth can produce big **mulloway** after a flood, with anglers lining the rock walls at the entrance to fish with live baits and large lures. The river also produces **bream**, **luderick**, **flathead** and **whiting**. The freshwater reaches of the river are highly regarded for native **bass**.

Among blue-water anglers, the Macleay River is known for its notorious bar that can make going offshore tricky. However, there is an alternative exit at Back Creek, not connected to the Macleay. The only problem here is that at low tide the creek can be far too shallow to motor along.

Offshore anglers have plenty of options. Some prefer to head north to Grassy Head; others go east around Laggers Point and then south-east to Fish Rock, which is south-east of Smoky Cape. The latter is regarded as one of the best offshore spots along this coast. About 16km east of the Macleay River entrance, and in 100m of water, is a Fish Attracting Device (GPS: S30.50.534, E153.11.803).

Offshore species caught in these waters include **marlin**, **wahoo**, **yellowtail kingfish**, **cobia**, **dolphinfish**, **spotted** and **Spanish mackerel**, **longtail** and **yellowfin tuna**, and **tailor**. For those who prefer to fish the bottom, the most sought-after fish include **snapper** and mulloway.

There are boat ramps at Kempsey, Frederickton, Smithtown, Gladstone, Jerseyville, Stuarts Point, Fishermans Reach and at the New Entrance, near South West Rocks.

Beach anglers have plenty on offer because of the variety of beaches and the fact that they face different directions – Trial Bay Beach, for example, faces west, one of the few beaches on the east coast to do so! Other popular beaches include Horseshoe Bay, Back Beach, Main Beach, Little Bay, Gap Beach, North Smoky and Smoky Beach.

PORT STEPHENS

Located about 220km or three hours north of Sydney via the F3 Fwy. From Newcastle, it is 50km or a 45-minute drive.

Regarded as one of the state's premier gamefishing ports, it also offers excellent estuary opportunities for bream, flathead, luderick and mulloway.

ACCOMMODATION: A major tourism centre, Port Stephens has a range of accommodation to suit all tastes.
For more information visit
www.portstephens.org.au

Port Stephens offers a mixed bag of quality species. Beach anglers do well on **tailor**, **whiting** and **mulloway**. Tomaree Head on the southern headland is a famous land-based gamefishing location for a wide range of species including **cobia**, **longtail** and **mackerel tuna**.

In addition to this top-class inshore fishery, the Port Stephens area gets even better offshore, with world-class blue-water fishing for game fish such as **striped**, **black** and **blue marlin**, **cobia**, **wahoo** and **sharks**.

A favourite area off Port Stephens is 'The Car Park'. It is a 40km run and many anglers launch at Little Beach, close to Nelson Bay. This ramp can handle three boats at a time, but sand build-up can be a problem and a 4WD is sometimes necessary. The Car Park is situated along the 160m line about 1.5km inside the Continental Shelf (GPS: S33.02.688, E153.24.403), and runs along the inside edge of an underwater canyon where eddies concentrate bait schools. The bait schools attract mainly striped or black marlin, with a few blue marlin and **sailfish** thrown into the mix.

Victorian angler Warren Carter shows off a big dusky flathead caught on a lure at Port Stephens

The average striped marlin is 60–80kg with the occasional 100kg fish being hooked. Black marlin range from 20kg up to 300kg. January and February are the best months for marlin, but March and April bring the cobia into the islands, and there are other species like **longtail tuna**, **yellowtail kingfish**, wahoo, and the delectable and seriously pretty **dolphinfish**.

When the game fish are not cooperating anglers can always go after **snapper**.

Broughton Island has marine park restrictions although some areas on the eastern side are still accessible. Anglers should check with the Marine Parks Authority NSW. The reefs and gutters around this island are famous for their snapper, with fish to 9kg that take soft plastic lures as well as bait. Little Gibber, a small headland inside Broughton Island, is a favourite for **longtail tuna** during April.

Methods for Coffs Harbour to Port Stephens

TACKLE Offshore tackle for game fish should range from 15–24kg outfits. Use 14/0 circle hooks and bridle rig live baits for trolling. Use leader up to 200kg with a minimum size of about 60kg. If mackerel are in good numbers, then piano wire trace usually makes more sense.

For live baiting, use 6/0 Suicide pattern hooks; for trolling, take a selection of skirted lures and large bibbed minnows like the Halco Laser Pros. Anglers have done well jigging for snapper over the reef systems using large, soft-plastic lures with shad tails.

Beach fishing here is very different from down south. The Alvey sidecast reel become more prominent as you move further north of Sydney. The standard surf outfit is a 4m rod fitted with a reel suited to line of about 8–10kg breaking strain. When tailor are running, many anglers rig ganged hooks and cast whole, unweighted pilchards. Night fishing, using baits such as squid or fish fillets, is the best chance for mulloway from the sand. Other species caught include dart, sand whiting and yellowfin bream. Sandworms, prawns and pipis are alternative baits. During a flood, keep an eye on the rock walls at the river entrances.

In the estuaries, a 3kg outfit consisting of a size 20 threadline reel and light spin stick will cover most lure and bait options. If working lures, spool up with braid. Unweighted baits fished in the snags work well for bream, while flathead are caught in areas where there are no snags. Always use a small lead (and none if possible). For bream, use a Baitholder pattern No. 4 hook, but go bigger for flathead, from a No. 2 to a 3/0. Best baits include prawns, beachworms and nippers. Chicken gut also works. Small lures work well, both hard-bodied, vibes and soft plastic.

HAWKESBURY RIVER

Brooklyn, on the Hawkesbury River, is located 24km north of central Sydney on the Sydney–Newcastle Fwy. Drive time depends on traffic but the turn-off to Brooklyn is just before the rail bridge.

Renowned for its big mulloway, this waterway also produces flathead, tailor, hairtail and bream.

ACCOMMODATION: The Hawkesbury region has all manner of accommodation available including houseboats.
For more information visit www.sydney.com/destinations/sydney/sydney-north/hawkesbury

The Hawkesbury River is regarded as one of the most consistent waters for big **mulloway**, or **jewfish** as they are called. It was with mulloway in mind that I went to the river to fish with Colin Tannahill. The river flows through Sydney's western suburbs as the Nepean River before changing to the Hawkesbury River at Windsor; downstream from the Sydney–Newcastle Fwy, where the famous rail bridge crosses, it becomes a broadwater.

We launched Colin's 6m boat at the George St ramp at Brooklyn at about 8.30am. The ramp is four lanes wide and features all amenities including mooring pontoons and fish cleaning facilities – none of which costs the boater anything. When it comes to services and facilities, boaters on the Hawkesbury River are well catered for. You can take a shower, fuel up and enjoy counter meals or even take-away of a cup of hot fish and chips. All this in an all-weather waterway boasting some of the best fishing in NSW,

Hawkesbury River Bridge is famous for the big mulloway and other fish caught around the support pilings

about an hour's drive north of the business heart of Sydney.

Our first stop was the Pittwater near Barrenjoey Head where we fished for **squid** to use as bait. Rain was pelting down and coming north along the Pittwater in squalls. Our problem was that the wind was blowing the boat along too fast for the squid jigs to work properly. Finally, we gave it away and headed for Patonga in Brisk Bay where, Colin said we might be able to catch squid out of the wind. What he didn't say was that Patonga comprises a pub and a fish and chip shop, both welcome sights on a windswept and wet day on the water.

Surrounded by heavily forested hills and steep cliffs, the 140km long river offers anglers a rich and varied range of piscine offerings ranging from **sand whiting,** squid and **yellowfin bream** to big **dusky flathead** and the ever-elusive mulloway**.** Best of all, as Patonga shows, it is an all-weather venue and you can always find shelter in the many arms, bays or headlands.

We started fishing seriously off a place called Flint and Steel Point; our target species was mulloway, and Colin had caught them here to 11kg. After an hour or two of pickers including a **'golden' toadfish** and the aptly named **shovelnose rays**, we decided to move. The problem was that the tide was incoming but the heavy rains meant a lot of fresh water was heading out. Our baits on the bottom were being pushed by the tide, but the boat was yawing badly due to a combination of freshwater flow and wind. Consequently, we headed for the relative shelter of Juno Point. We dropped the anchor about 100m off the point and started to fish about 50m away from a couple of anglers in a smaller tinnie. These anglers explained they were putting up with the rain because they had caught a 10kg mulloway the day before.

Fresh bait, preferably live bait, was the order of the day. We put out a bait rod and then rigged the main rods with squid and a live bream caught earlier and kept fresh in the bait tank. The bait rod never seemed to stop dipping over as species including sand whiting, **pinkies**, **yakkas** and bream consistently bit the tiny squid bait. Our neighbours were enjoying similar diversity by adding an octopus to the species list, and then landing a yellowfin bream of about 2kg. Mulloway were proving elusive, but we persisted for several hours. A couple of baits were sharked but there was no sign of the mulloway.

Colin said the top spots on the river for big mulloway are the upstream sides of the rail and road bridges that run alongside each other as they cross the river. As the water flows under the bridges, the pylons create eddies that attract smaller fish; this in turn brings larger predators like mulloway to the area. Land-based anglers fish for mulloway at Pelican Point, which is at the base of the road bridge on the southern shore. Many prefer to fish with lures.

Methods for Hawkesbury River

TACKLE Live baiting is the popular method for mulloway, and it accounts for some big flathead. Tackle for mulloway consists of an 8–10kg outfit. The rig is a running paternoster. Attach sinker directly to an Ezi-Rig slider so there is no leader to cause tangles. The main leader to the hook is about 24kg breaking strain and use a single, 6/0 Suicide hook.

For bait fishing, the rig was the same, albeit much lighter. Outfits were 3kg rods balanced with a small threadline reel. Hook sizes ranged from No. 6 to No. 4, medium shank Baitholder patterns. When fishing the Hawkesbury you will need a range of sinkers to compensate for tidal flow. Bomb sinkers with the swivel moulded in are best.

LITHGOW TO MUDGEE

Dunns Swamp is a highlight of the area for those who enjoy roughing it. It is located on the western border of the Wollemi National Park, 25km east of Rylestone, which is about 280km from Sydney via Lithgow. The drive takes about three-and-a-half hours from Sydney on a sealed road all the way except for the final 10km, which is gravel.

The waters along this stretch produce a range of species from Murray cod, silver perch and yellowbelly to bass and trout.

ACCOMMODATION: Lake Windamere, Rylstone Dam, Dunns Swamp, Lakes Lyell and Wallace offer up plenty of accommodation. At Dunns Swamp is a well-maintained campground and picnic area by the water with barbecues and tables. There is no running water or power and generators are banned. Vehicle-based camping is allowed in designated areas.
For more information visit
www.environment.nsw.gov.au
www.lithgow-tourism.com

Early settlers following in the footsteps of Blaxland, Wentworth and Lawson took three weeks of hard trudging to cross the majestic Blue Mountains. These days the drive from Penrith plains in western Sydney takes less than three hours. The steep terrain, higher altitudes and running streams of the western foothills provides the lakes with water conditions conducive to **trout**, and Oberon dam is amongst Australia's oldest notable trout lakes.

Onwards along the Mid Western Hwy, past bollard-shaped cooling towers and milder slopes clad with pine plantations and vineyards, is Lithgow. The stretch between Lithgow and Mudgee offers some exciting fishing in a series of waters with established native fish populations. Cooling storages for coal-fed power stations in the Lithgow/Wallerawang district have more recently come on-line. The combination of proximity to Sydney and trophy trout sees the piscatorial patronage having a favourable impact on tourism in the region.

Lake Lyell is a 248ha body of water built across the Coxs River near Lithgow. Originally built to provide cooling waters for local power stations, Lake Lyell now also serves as important recreational water. It has been stocked with **brown** and **rainbow trout** and **bass**. Some of the trout have grown to trophy-size, peaking at about 45cm.

The steep terrain over which Lake Lyell now sits gives it a narrow, deep profile that lends itself to trolling and downrigger techniques. Shore-based spinning or bubble-float techniques are productive from autumn through spring, as are deep-fly presentations, especially in pronounced narrows where the Cox's River enters.

Farmers Creek also flows into the lake. Both feeders are subject to strict closures and enforcement during the trout-breeding season in the cooler months.

The lake has well-appointed picnic and boat-launching facilities. Being within daytrip range of Sydney, it has become a very popular impoundment that's patronised by anglers armed with the latest tackle and techniques. When a bite is on, it's usual to see float-tubing anglers and state-of-the-art sportfishing boats mooching along, downriggers cocked.

Lake Wallace, also called Lake Wallerawang, is 155ha of relatively shallow and weedy water. It is

Above: **Lake Wallace holds brown and rainbow trout up to 5kg**
Below: **Dunns Swamp has a well-maintained campground and picnic area**

regularly stocked with trout of both denominations, the mix heavily biased towards **rainbow trout**. In 1998, it received a single infusion of 30,000 **bass**. The rainbow trout have proved spectacularly successful, with fish to 5kg being taken each year between autumn and spring. Lakeside picnic and playground facilities have been erected and unpowered boating is permitted.

Moving north towards Mudgee, you come across the twin Cudgegong River catchment towns of Rylstone and Kandos, snuggled in against the sandstone ridges of the Great Dividing Range.

Lake Rylstone covers 20ha and is stocked with **Murray cod**, **yellowbelly** and **silver perch**. It has no facilities. Fishing from the bank or unpowered craft is permitted.

Dunns Swamp (also known as Kandos Weir) since being incorporated into the Wollemi National Park, is a picturesque 100ha sanctuary that fills a sandstone gorge flanked by ochre outcrops and the greenery that goes with healthy cumbungi margins.

This waterway was the site of Australia's first successful private attempt at breeding native fish. In 1961, utilising ponds at the local cement works, a dedicated band of local anglers were successful in raising silver perch fingerlings. Residents of this former trout cod water include western strain Murray cod, yellowbelly, silver perch, **eel-tail catfish** and **river blackfish**. A direct result of the clear, tannin-stained waters is richly coloured, highly active fish that are a delight to catch.

The lake has clean, well-maintained **camping** facilities, including showers and flush toilets. Boaters need to be aware of a 10-horsepower restriction.

Weighing in at 10sqkm, Lake Windamere was built on the Cudgegong River 30km south of Mudgee. Many anglers regard this water as Australia's premier yellowbelly fishery. The lake also offers good fishing for other native fish including Murray cod, silver perch and catfish, along with brown and rainbow trout, **redfin** and **carp**.

An area immediately adjacent to the Cudgegong–Rylstone Rd is very productive. Rather than trudge the uneven obstacle course that the banks present, it has become a popular practice to bring boats in close.

Facilities include a caravan park and kiosk under the control of the Rylstone Shire Council.

Methods for Lithgow to Mudgee

LURES Lake Windemere has a high percentage of bank cover that suits both trollers and anglers who prefer cast-and-retrieve techniques. Baitfish profile-lures up to 10cm trolled along the edges of the rich and abundant weed beds have proven successful. Rocky banks and steeper drop-offs are popular with lure-casters. Effective retrieves are those punctuated by pauses and subtle twitches, with the water clarity often allowing anglers to see the fish strike their lures.

3 SYDNEY

SYDNEY HARBOUR

The bays and offshore waters surrounding Sydney are rich with fishing opportunities. Fish ranging from yellowfin bream and whiting to flathead, kingfish and marlin are all within easy reach of anglers who live in this region.

ACCOMMODATION: Every form of accommodation available in Australia is to be found in Sydney. If you have a boat, go for somewhere near a boat ramp. However, parking may be difficult and you may find it best to stay in a cabin at a caravan park where at least you will (or should) have a parking option for a boat. **For more information visit www.visitnsw.com**

Australia's coastal capital cities offer great fishing opportunities and we have early European settlers to thank for that. They chose sheltered bays that offered deep, safe anchorages for supply ships. Of all our capital cities, Sydney has the most to offer. Anglers here can fish for **bream** and **mulloway** in the estuaries, **tailor** and **kingfish** in the harbour or go offshore chasing **marlin** and **tuna**. That is just a very short list of what is on offer.

My flight from Melbourne to Sydney was a harbinger for the weather to come. There was no meal service on the flight, due, our pilot said, to the conditions. The foul weather left behind in Melbourne was following me up the east coast.

The next morning at the Rose Bay ferry wharf, where Al McGlashan picked me up, the wind was a 20-knot nor'easter but, as Al rightly pointed out, it doesn't matter in Sydney Harbour because there is always somewhere to fish. There were two other crewmembers: British Labour Party's former angling spokesman, Martin Salter, who retired from the House of Commons and now lives in Sydney, and young gun angler Thomas Eisenhammer.

Sydney Harbour produces a range of species like this Australian salmon caught on a soft plastic lure by Thomas Eisenhammer

First stop was Double Bay around the first headland west of Rose Bay on the southern side of the harbour. Several boats were already drifting and casting lures and flies to schools of fish busting up on the surface. The action was easy to spot by the birds, mainly seagulls, dropping onto the water to pick up scraps of baitfish left by the predators.

The target species were not big. We were using light tackle, 3–5kg spin outfits, and our main lure was a 15cm clear soft plastic called a Sluggo, which was rigged on a worm hook. Worm hooks are a strange shape and most often used when fishing terrain where a lure is likely to get hung up on weed or rocks. When properly rigged the worm hook point lays flat along the back of the lure and the bend of the hook protrudes below the lure to act as a weed guard.

The schooling fish were feeding on tiny baitfish less than 5cm long. Al assured me that even though our offerings didn't match-the-hatch – so to speak – these hungry little predators would chew them up. And he was right. The fish churning the water to suds turned out to be bonito, albeit small bonito averaging about 30cm long. These fish are like gold when you are looking for trolling baits, and great fun to catch on light tackle any day.

The only rule on Al's boat that morning concerned the cricket. Martin was keen enough to talk about the English team and how well they played in Adelaide.

'Oh, was there a match on?' Al queried, and it was back to the fish.

Martin is no slouch with a rod. He had three bonito in the boat before anyone else hooked up. Half an hour or so of small fish action and Al decided we should go out to North Head at the entrance to the harbour to check out conditions outside.

And conditions looked uncomfortable, at best. The sea was up and running, and the water temperature fell from 20°C in the harbour to a chilly 14°C. You can see cold water in the ocean; it has an aquamarine colour, the same as you see around icebergs where they enter the sea.

Still, we gave North Head a few drifts, casting soft plastic and popper lures into the white water caused by the surging sea breaking against rock ledges.

If you ever get the chance to go to North Head, look out for the aluminium ladders set up by the rock anglers. There are three levels from the top ledge, and it looks like madness for anyone to clamber down these ladders.

After about ten minutes of rocking, Al fired up the outboard and pointed his boat back into the harbour. There were reports of bonito, yellowtail kingfish, and salmon and tailor schools busting up along the northern shore so we headed first for Taylors Bay.

The method was the same and this time a few salmon and tailor were caught. Then we moved to Chowder Bay, next to Taylors Bay, fishing along as far as Bradley Head. There is a naval facility in Chowder

Martin Salter with a yellowtail kingfish caught on a soft plastic lure in Sydney Harbour

Bay with a couple of large mooring buoys, about the size of small road tankers. It was from underneath one of these that Martin, who had changed his lure to one with a weighted jig head, somehow plucked out a yellowtail kingfish. Tough little fighters, they go even harder on light gear and Martin was into his fish for about five minutes before he managed to bring it close to the boat.

Most of the action though was close to Bradley Head and Al says the fish sit in an eddy just inside the headland and ambush baitfish schools as they swim past.

As the action tapered off along these bays we moved into the middle of the harbour, and here the schools of fish were running along wind lanes. It was more of the same as far as bonito, tailor and salmon were concerned, but at least the action was constant. Every now and then you would spot a bigger splash, it kept us going because on every cast there was an outside chance on a big kingfish. We didn't hook a big king, but we had plenty of fun given conditions on a day so windy that fishing would be out of the question on most bays.

Sydney Harbour is the most sheltered harbour in Australia, but the best thing about this water is that it has oodles of fish.

LONG REEF

Fishing around Sydney is diverse and places like Long Reef between North Head and Manly are legend for gamefishing for species such as yellowtail kingfish. The wonderful aspect of these Sydney reef systems is that many are reasonably close to shore and access is easy from smaller sportfishing boats.

As Al McGlashan drove his boat down the Parramatta River, he took time out to point out deep holes or shallow banks where he has caught **bream** and **mulloway**. On this trip our destination was an old wreck. Originally a coal boat, the *Centurion* is simply called the Wreck. It is popular with anglers wanting to catch **yakkas (yellowtail scad)** or **slimy mackerel** for bait.

We called in at Rose Bay to collect Rod Findlay before working our way across to the Wreck, pausing to cast surface poppers and soft plastic lures at channel markers likely to hold **yellowtail kingfish**. At the Wreck the anchor went down and we started to berley to bring the bait nearer the surface. Problem was the baitfish were not keen on rising too high in the water column due to a school of yellowtail kingfish that insisted on swimming through the berley trail within a metre of the surface.

Catching baits wasn't difficult. A small hand line with a piece of pilchard on a No. 6 long shank hook did the job. Larger baits were allowed to drift down the water column for the **kings**, but they were too subtle, sucking off the soft pilchard without the hook. Live baits fared no better.

When the live well was full, we dropped into Manly to pick up Jack Scrine and then motored offshore past North Head and along the coast to Long Reef. The ocean looked flat but there was a big swell rolling in from the Tasman.

Al described this area is one of the most consistent he has come across for yellowtail kingfish. The sounder was showing a temperature reading of 20°C, and the bottom contour was a series of gutters and walls. There were clouds of baitfish and large arches that Al said were our target species.

Live **yellowtail scad** were hooked up and put into the water to be slow trolled along the back of a shallow reef where the swells rose steeply into turquoise coloured waves before crashing on the rocks. We were well away from the danger zone, and so too were the kingfish.

After a slow troll was unsuccessful, lures were rigged for jigging. Jack Scrine soon landed a 60cm king and Rod landed another that could have been its twin. We slowly worked our way northwest along an undersea wall towards a reef system called White Rock.

As the kingfish action moved from midwater to the surface, Al decided it was time to break out the surface poppers. Kingfish are inquisitive and often swim around stationary surface lures, striking the instant the lure is moved. Surface poppers are retrieved in a pull and stop motion, or else brought in at a steady rate with the angler pulling on the rod to make the lure bloop and splash.

For a couple of hours, we caught kingfish on poppers, and then on soft plastics and knife jigs and live yakkas. The action was consistent but we could not nail one of the bigger kings that we saw following hooked fish to the boat.

In the bait well was a lone **squid** and Rod decided to rig this up to troll as live bait. The squid lasted less than five minutes before it was taken. Rod missed the hook up but as the bait was undamaged he put it back out. Just five minutes more and the squid was taken again.

Jack Scrine with a yellowtail kingfish caught trolling live baits over Long Reef

Rod let the kingfish run, giving it time to turn and swallow the squid before putting his reel into gear and set the hook. This time there was no mistake: the rod doubled over and line poured off the reel under a heavy drag as about a metre of yellowtail kingfish dived for the safety of the reef.

The fight was short and sharp and in less than five minutes Rod brought the spent fish alongside to be gaffed and brought inboard. The reality of hooking kingfish is that in prolonged fights anglers generally lose. If the angler cannot turn a king on its initial dive the chances are it will drag the line through reef and bust him off. Kingfish are not called hoodlums without reason.

This bonito was caught on a jigged lure on Colours Reef

COLOURS REEF

Sydney anglers are lucky to have such a quality fishery within sight of the suburbs. One of the most popular fishing techniques is jigging and live baiting the reef systems that hug the coastline to the north and south of the entrance to Sydney Harbour. The Colours Reef, about 600m off South Head, is one of the more popular spots. It is so close to the Sydney CBD the locals could almost pop down for a fish during their lunch break.

I fished here with Al McGlashan. The morning began catching bait off Manly on the *Centurion* wreck. Bait catching tackle comprises a handline, a No. 6 to No. 8 hook, pilchards to use for bait and berley. The wreck is found on the sounder and the anchor dropped alongside; if the anchor lands on top of the wreck chances are it will become hopelessly lodged and that can be an expensive exercise as anchors are not cheap.

Berley is mulched and fed into the water. It takes about 20 minutes for the baitfish to get the scent and rise in the water column, and when they appear hooking them is easy. Most times though, the bait can be hooked easily enough by allowing the bait to drift down in the berley trail. You don't so much feel for a bite as watch the bait and spot the fish taking it. This style of visual fishing can be a lot of fun. If the baitfish stay deep then you will need to put a small split shot on your line to get the bait down. On a good day you can catch your bait, put it on the hook and send it back down into the jaws of a **kingfish**. On this day the **kings** were wary and on the small side, although this didn't stop them ripping baitfish off our lines.

With the live well full of baitfish, we headed for the Colours. The reef rises out of sand from 33–20m. It's not a big reef system but has a big reputation as a fish attractor and used to be a favourite haunt of **mulloway** anglers. There was a slight swell running but the weather was settled; blue sky, blue water and sunshine, a weather trifecta that is a panacea for anything that ails old salts.

Inshore and around the corner about 300m from South Head is the infamous suicide leap known as The Gap. This notorious landmark was of particular interest this day as we watched a helicopter skimming along the foot of the cliffs, filming. It is also a great area to troll live baits for **yellowtail kingfish**. When the seas are flat, rock fishers sometimes fish for **drummer**, **blackfish** and **snapper** just inside South Head Point, and Lady Jane Beach a little further inside the harbour, is also popular.

On the Colours there are two methods employed. The first is to use 15–24kg outfits and either jig with heavy metal lures or drift over the reef with live baits set deep. We were doing both. The boat was positioned for a drift over the reef and then lures and baits dropped. When the lures hit the reef, they were lifted and retrieved erratically at varying speeds. The baitfish were allowed to swim down deep and sometimes slow trolled.

Al watched the sounder and told us when we were over schools of fish. Most of the arches showing on the sounder screen were small, but there were a few bigger ones. Al said these are yellowtail kingfish. The first fish inboard was a small **amberjack**, followed quickly by another and then **bonito** and even **squid**. Had the kingfish been busting up on baitfish at the surface we would have changed over to popper lures and cast to the action.

The Colours reef offers variety. Inshore about 300m out from the cliffs is a ledge where large schools of **salmon** often congregate and this adds another dimension to the fishing on offer. Anglers fishing the Colours usually launch at Little Manly Cove boat ramp, about 5km away. When seas are flat, kayak fishers launch their craft inside South Head and troll lures along the Colours and sometimes in close to the cliffs.

BOTANY BAY

This bay is south of Sydney, and part of the Sydney metropolitan area. It has several artificial reefs established by NSW Department of Primary Industries.

Botany Bay produces an abundance of species. The fishable territory ranges from mangroves and sandflats to channels and bridge pilings where large **mulloway** hang.

Irony and circumstance go hand in hand. There I was, fishing a hot water outlet alongside the Kurnell refinery pier in Botany Bay, a few hundred metres from a monument dedicated to Captain James Cook's landing in Australia in April 1770. A year before, I was fishing from rocks on shore of the Hawaiian Island of Kona, about the same distance from another monument erected for Captain Cook, albeit one marking the place Cook was killed in February 1779.

In Botany Bay I fished with Brett Wilson, manager of the popular Squidgy lure account at Shimano. Brett was driving a 5.79m Bass boat

Captain Cook memorial at Kurnell on Botany Bay

powered by a 150-horsepower outboard. These boats are low in the water and laid out as fishing platforms. Designed for tournament fishing, with the aim of getting you to your destination in a hurry, this boat zipped along effortlessly at 105km/hr.

Brett collected me at a ramp near Captain Cook Bridge and headed straight across the bay to the refinery pier. When we arrived, he pointed out the boil of water that denoted the hot water outlet from the refinery. I was given a small spin stick with a Squidgy Flick Bait attached and told to cast into the middle of the boil. Brett worked a surface lure, a Stiffy Top Dog. As I retrieved, the **tailor** rose, boiling over the lure until one became hooked. It was a constant cast and hook process, with the occasional small **yellowtail kingfish** thrown in for good measure.

Because Brett's lure was on the surface, we could see the tailor bumping into each other as they tried to bite the lure. Brett caught six before he lost his lure. Tailor this size are called choppers. Their jaws are lined with razor sharp teeth that can cut through commercial nets or disable smaller fish by biting their tails off with scissor-like precision. It is why tailor anglers use ganged hooks in whole pilchards, and always leave the tails on their baits. Soft plastic lures stand no chance.

After an hour of solid hooking, and several lures later, Brett decided to move in search of some **bream** or **trevally**. We went several hundred metres and worked our lures along the bottom. The silver trevally proved co-operative but the bream were not interested.

Later that morning we drifted along the edge of the channel in Woolaware Bay, east of Captain Cook Bridge. This was a favourite **dusky flathead** area for Brett and the flathead were keen to chew on his Devilfish Vibes.

PORT HACKING

Port Hacking is south of Botany Bay but still part of the Sydney metropolitan spread.

Chris Cleaver shows off the quality of the dusky flathead available in Port Hacking

In my youth, **bream** was a species that anglers sought to put food on the table. It was a 'kill it and fillet' favourite. Both **yellowfin** and **black bream** were considered good fun but not much more than that. Bream fought well, but the sedentary nature of bait fishing – sitting around waiting for a bite – was ho-hum in terms of excitement.

Times have changed. The humble bream has moved to the top of the estuary sportfishing chain. This elevation reflects changes that have overtaken angling. A combination of bream fishing tournaments, the soft plastic lure revolution and slick marketing campaigns helped push the bream cause. The result was a groundswell of anglers moving to lure fishing and a boom in catch and release.

Modern lure fishing techniques have turned bream fishing on its head. These days anglers even sightfish bream in shallow water, which is what Brett Wilson, Colin Tannahill and I were aiming to do. We launched Brett's boat at a small sheltered ramp at Lilli Pilli in Port Hacking. These boats are ideal for lakes, estuaries and the metre or less of water we fished in Dolans Bay, several kilometres south-west of the boat ramp. Port Hacking is a sheltered bay dominated all around by two-, three- and more-storey homes that seem to hang precariously from the sides of steep embankments. Typical features of many homes are the boat sheds with rail lines running to the water. Alternatively, some properties have mooring jetties, and some have both.

Brett steered us into an area of extensive shallow sandflats interspersed with weed beds. We were fishing with ultra-light gear: small threadline outfits, 2kg line and Stiffy Fat Boy minnow lures. Brett explained the method was to drift over the flats, working the lures down to the weed beds where the bream would be feeding. If you caught weed, you were swimming the lure too deep. Lures were retrieved slowly, with a lift and tug on the line. As you stopped pulling the line, the rod tip was lowered and the lure rose in the water column as you wound up the slack; this was a likely time for a strike.

Experience at this style of fishing showed early when Brett spotted bream working, cast his lure and hooked up. It was a yellowfin bream of about 1kg. The fish was brought to the boat, the hooks removed and then it was released to be caught another day. Not one to waste time, Brett recast his lure, started to retrieve and was rewarded with another bream. Soon after, Colin hooked up and his fish was slightly bigger. That's how the fishing went for the next couple of hours. There weren't many bream, but enough to hold our interest. Brett said that when these flats were firing the bream fishing was unbelievable and it was common to hook large numbers. The flats hold other species, like **dusky flathead** and **sand whiting**.

There is more than bream in Port Hacking. During the previous couple of days anglers had been trolling squid and hooking into **yellowtail kingfish** to 15kg. Brett had to leave early so Colin and I went and collected his boat, launched and headed across the bay to Bundeena, an area Colin said was consistent for **squid**. It was late in the day, I had a plane to catch but if we caught squid then we would give the kings a go. Sadly, things don't always work the way you want and we couldn't hook enough squid to go trolling.

GUNNAMATTA BAY

Living in the suburbs of a capital city doesn't mean there is no quality fishing at hand. Sometimes it is on your doorstep, like Gunnamatta Bay, a part of Port Hacking where the shoreline is dominated by magnificent houses.

ACCOMMODATION: For more information visit www.visitnsw.com

Port Hacking consists of many smaller bays. The northern shoreline is dominated by multi-storey houses that seem to hang precariously from steep embankments. Most of these bayside homes come with boat sheds, mooring jetties or both.

On this day I was in the company of Colin and another Shimano employee, Chris Cleaver. First stop was across the bay at Bundeena. Colin and Chris said it was a hot spot for squid but plans don't always work out. We caught no **squid** but I was assured that was due to soiled water caused by heavy rainfall.

After missing out on squid we motored back to Gunnamatta Bay, casting soft plastic lures along the edges of the channel flanked by weed beds that covered the seabed in a mat running about 30m to shore. When a squid rose to a lure, Colin promptly cast a jig over the weed and hooked up.

Chris meanwhile was chasing bigger fare. He is one of a small number of anglers I have met who possess a talent for working small lures on light tackle. I saw Chris in action on the Gold Coast where he went against the flow by consistently producing fish when other anglers were catching donuts.

On this day, between downpours and shifting winds, Chris was in fine form and cleaned up. He fished a 2kg outfit and started out with a small Squidgy soft plastic with a wriggle tail. On successive casts he managed to pull a 60cm dusky flathead, followed by several small snapper and then hit on a school of silver trevally. When his lure was chewed out of recognition, he changed to a metal vibe, and promptly hooked a bigger flathead of about 70cm. It was a tough day in the office.

There is a fishing adage that you never leave fish to find fish. We moved around a few different areas but Gunnamatta Bay, about 200m from the boat ramp, proved to be the hot spot. **Silver trevally** were in good numbers along the main channel edges and undersize pinkies were a nuisance. A couple of oddities came up on lures, including a **fanbelly leatherjacket** and a **grinner**, an orange coloured fish with fine blue stripes running longitudinally along its back.

There was an area almost directly out from the boat ramp where the water was deeper and edged along a shallower sand bank. Chris was certain it was a good spot to pull a **mulloway**, or jewie as they call them. This didn't happen but it proved the top spot for big flathead when Chris managed to land an 85cm specimen. A catch that was more meritorious given he was using 3kg breaking strain leader; his explanation for this was that finer lines bring results. It's hard to argue with a man holding the proof.

Methods for Sydney

TACKLE For the smaller **kingfish**, **tailor**, **salmon** and **bonito**, 3–5kg spin outfits, and 15cm clear, unweighted soft plastics called Sluggos, which were rigged on a worm hook, or poppers. Offshore jigging and trolling live baits for bigger kingfish, 15–24kg outfits and either jig with heavy metal lures or drift over the reef with live baits set deep.

For the lighter fishing, for bream and flathead, a 2–3kg threadline outfit is used. The reel is spooled with braid with fluorocarbon leader of similar breaking strain attached. Fluorocarbon leader is invisible in the water, and shallow water **bream** are easily spooked so anglers need every advantage they can get. The rod needs to have sharp recovery for spinning.

LURES Lures used were bibbed minnows, in this instance Stiffy Minnows and Fat Boy models. Lures for the bottom species like flathead were Squidgy soft plastics and metal vibes.

4 SOUTH COAST

SUSSEX INLET

Sussex Inlet is on the NSW south coast about three hours drive from Sydney CBD.

ACCOMMODATION: Sussex Inlet has plenty of accommodation from caravan parks with cabins to powered or unpowered sites; houses are also available for rent. There is also accommodation to the north at Sanctuary Point and there are plenty of quality boat ramps.
For more information visit www.visitnsw.com/destinations/south-coast/jervis-bay-and-shoalhaven/sussex-inlet

The township of Sussex Inlet borders on one of many NSW estuary systems that have experienced a popularity boom since ultra-light small lure fishing took off just over a decade ago.

Sussex Inlet is best known for the large lake called St Georges Basin where the main target species include **dusky flathead**, with many over the 5kg mark. In October and November each year there are reports of flathead being caught weighing in at more than 9kg. As well, anglers can also expect to hook **yellowfin bream**, with smaller numbers of **black bream** in the same water. Other species are **snapper**, **tailor**, **sand whiting**, **luderick** and, sometimes, **mulloway**.

For those who prefer beach and rock fishing, there is much on offer. Jervis Bay, not far away as

Above: **Declan Betts shows off a small sand whiting**
Below: **Bernard Kong holds a dusky flathead caught in Sussex Inlet**

the crow flies, is regarded as the Mecca of land-based gamefishing and fish ranging from **marlin** and **yellowfin tuna** to big **yellowtail kingfish** are caught. On the beaches, **salmon**, mulloway and tailor can be caught.

If your boat is big enough you can head offshore via a bar crossing at the front of Sussex Inlet, which gives access to the Jervis Bay Canyons, Ulladulla Canyons and the Continental Shelf. Be aware that the bar crossing, like most bars, is not always easy; the seas can be dangerous on a run-out tide running into south or north-east swell.

St Georges Basin was one of the first waters to have an artificial reef established. There are several reefs, funded by NSW Recreational Fishing Licence fees.

Lake fishing is the most popular and the type of structures that hold fish are varied. You can fish shallow weedy flats, slow tapering banks to weed lines, tree-lined snag riddled edges in the creeks to deep holes and large undulating flats in the 5–6m range.

Fishing is generally better from October–late June: the flats fish best for bream from late October–early May; big flathead are most prevalent from early October–late January. Most mulloway are caught during autumn, around Easter.

NAROOMA OFFSHORE

This popular seaport destination takes about five hours driving on the Princes Hwy, south of Sydney, or eight hours from Melbourne.

The estuary has a huge reputation for flathead, bream, whiting and tailor, while offshore it is yellowfin tuna, yellowtail kingfish and marlin that are keenly sought after by anglers.

ACCOMMODATION: Narooma offers everything from campsites to houses.
For more information visit
www.eurobodalla.com.au/narooma

Narooma is one of those pleasant destinations that offers piscatorial delights most of the year, ranging from gamefishing offshore to rock, beach and estuary. Situated on Wagonga Inlet, the port is best known for its close access to Montague Island.

Narooma is most popular during summer and autumn, when boating anglers head offshore to Montague Island for **yellowtail kingfish**. Some travel further afield to the Continental Shelf, where they seek **striped** and **black marlin**. **Bonito** and **striped tuna** also run along the coast. Some anglers prefer a feed to a fight and concentrate on fishing the reef systems for **flathead**, **morwong** and **snapper**. In some years, the **yellowfin tuna** are about in good numbers around December.

Yellowfin are one of the toughest and most sought-after fish in these parts. Spectacularly colourful in the water, they're a fast-action eating machine with enough grunt to give the strongest angler a double hernia. Sizzling line-burning runs, sometimes in the vertical plane, are a trademark, while the fight that ensues can be more like an all-in brawl with fish and angler trading blow for blow. A stand-up fight in a rocking boat is difficult and anglers earn every kilogram.

The best time for yellowfin is late autumn through early winter. Conditions couldn't have been better when my fishing partner Richard Carr and I were more than 20 nautical miles north-east of Narooma on a calm, purple-hued sea. The cloud cover was high and thin. An ageing temperature gauge gave a digital reading of 17.4°C. Around us small shearwaters and gannets were feeding.

A walkway with fishing platforms runs along the north side of Wagonga Inlet, Narooma

Slimy mackerel, caught a little over an hour earlier and sliced neatly into cubes, lay spread across the bait board. I pumped the berley as Richard started feeding the cubes into the water. Hardly a word was spoken. This, to quote Charles Dickens, was a time of Great Expectations.

Less than half an hour later we had visitors. Whoosh! Whoosh! You think you can hear yellowfin as they come tearing through the berley trail. All you see is back or gilded flank as they dive through the slick to inhale a cube. On the surface a figure-eight eddy appeared where a fin had taken a cube barely 2m astern. The torpedo-shaped bulk of a fin displaces and sucks water down to cause the vortex.

Richard took a cube off the bait board and threaded it on the sharpened 9/0 hook attached to his 24kg outfit. Another cube went out, followed by the one with the hook in it. Matching the drift and sink rate of the free cubes, Richard inched line out. It was an urgent take. Richard pushed the lever on his reel up to strike mode, the line pulled tight and the fish's momentum sent the point of the hook home. This blue-water battle had begun.

Boat-ramp facilities here are free and excellent with fish-cleaning benches, but offshore anglers need to be aware of the notorious Narooma Bar. It has claimed many boats and several anglers have drowned trying to cross it. Always check the bar before venturing to the entrance, and ask for local advice on how best to handle it.

Narooma has various estuary species, including **bream**, **sand whiting**, **tailor** and flathead. Some of the locals regularly catch **mulloway**, while **luderick** can be found along the rock walls that mark the entrance bar to the ocean. For land-based anglers, there is a walkway around the northern shore of the estuary from the boat ramp upstream towards the bridge. This walkway has fishing platforms and is worth a visit. The rock ledges and beaches produce tailor, **salmon**, bonito and sometimes yellowtail kingfish and **longtail tuna**.

Game fishers start early, catching live bait on the bait grounds, Bermagui

BERMAGUI

If you drive about 30 minutes south of Narooma, as you would expect, the fishing opportunities are the same.

ACCOMMODATION: Camping grounds, motels and flats.
For more information visit www.visitnsw.com/destinations/south-coast/merimbula-and-sapphire-coast/bermagui

Bermagui is a small fishing port but a world-famous gamefishing destination. It owes its fame to an American western writer, Zane Grey, who went there in 1936. Little has changed since then. 'Bermi', as most people call it, still oozes character and people come here to catch **marlin**, **tuna** and **sharks**.

The offshore action is concentrated from the 12-mile reef (GPS: S36.30.000, E150.15.000) out to the first and second drop along the Continental Shelf. The influx of game fish is caused by the East Australian Current, a system of warm, nutrient-rich water that starts in the Coral Sea and flows along the east coast from Cape York to Tasmania. It's full of microscopic marine life such as plankton, which attracts small fish, which in turn attract larger fish and so the cycle goes, right up to big **yellowfin tuna** and marlin.

When the gamefishing slows, the rocky headlands and surf beaches provide plenty of sport for **Australian salmon**, with fish commonly caught up to 3kg. There is also plenty of estuary action provided by **bream**, **dusky flathead** and **trevally**.

TATHRA

Tathra is located 446km south of Sydney or about a one-hour drive north of Merimbula on the Sapphire Coast.

Tathra is a great family destination with a mixed bag of fishing. Saltwater anglers can choose from

Above: Beach fishing is popular at Tathra
Below: Tathra pier caters for large numbers of anglers

estuary, surf, rock and blue-water, while freshwater offerings include streams and dams.

ACCOMMODATION: A tourist town, Tathra has plenty of accommodation.
For more information visit
www.visitnsw.com

The major fishing attraction at Tathra is the pier. When I first went there in the 1970s, the pier was a rickety old platform littered with holes that you could easily fall through. At the time, the pier was popular with a small group of anglers who concentrated their efforts on catching **sharks.** These days the shark fishermen have gone, and some heavy restoration work has transformed the pier into a relatively safe fishing venue popular with families. Species caught here include **Australian salmon**, **yellowtail kingfish**, **bonito**, **tailor** and **tuna**. Around the pilings, **slimy mackerel**, **squid**, **yakkas** and **luderick** are common. The same species are caught from the rock ledges that run from the pier, south around the headland to Kianinny Bay. These ledges are definitely for adults only, and anglers need to keep an eye on the seas.

A concrete boat ramp is situated in Kianinny Bay. It is suited to boats up to 7m and offers good parking and cleaning facilities. The ramp can be difficult on days with a north-east or east wind.

Anglers launching here have the option of chasing blue-water game fish like **black** and **striped marlin**, **yellowfin**, **striped** and **albacore tuna**, and yellowtail kingfish; or bottom bouncing over the inshore reefs for species like **snapper** and **morwong**. The Continental Shelf is about 14 miles due east, and the famous Tathra canyons a couple of miles further out (GPS: TC NORTH1: S36.44.50, E150.19.70; TC NORTH2: S36.44.80, E150.25.00; TC SOUTH: S36.54.25, E150.21.30).

Tathra Beach runs north from the pier to the Bega River. Although the beach produces most of the common surf fish such as salmon and tailor, it also has a big reputation for **sand whiting** caught on sandworms and nippers.

The Bega River is worth a visit for **bream**, **flathead**, luderick, whiting and **estuary perch**.

For freshwater anglers, Brogo Dam near Bega is stocked with **Australian bass**, while the Bemboka River near Brown Mountain and Tantawangalow Creek near Candelo are worth a visit for **brown trout.**

MERIMBULA

About midway between Melbourne and Sydney, Merimbula is a tourism town that at one time boasted a higher occupancy rate than the Gold Coast. With that in mind, it pays to book well in advance if you intend going during holiday periods, particularly December to March.

This region offers gamefishing offshore for tuna, marlin and sharks, while the estuaries produce bream, mulloway, tailor, salmon, flathead and whiting.

ACCOMMODATION: Enough to suit all tastes and prices.

For more information visit www.sapphirecoast.com.au

Most visitors on family trips arrive at Merimbula with at least one fishing rod on board. Some give priority to the boat and tackle, then try to fit the family in around them.

A good boat ramp is situated near the causeway at the south end of town. From here, you can motor upstream into the Top Lake, go out under the Causeway Bridge into the bottom lake, or navigate the bar and head offshore.

Offshore the fishing is much the same as that encountered at Bermagui. The Continental Shelf is about 25km out, but there is often no need to travel that far when the warm current is running closer inshore. As well as game fish, the reefs, such as those near Haycock Point, will produce reasonable bags of **snapper** and inshore there are productive grounds for **flathead**.

The pier on the north side of town is excellent for anglers, with **luderick**, **slimy mackerel**, **salmon**, **bonito**, **tailor** and sometimes **yellowtail kingfish**. Large schools of slimy mackerel are generally around the pier. There is an expanse of rock ledges from the pier up to Tura Beach including Long and Short points. The rocks produce similar species to the pier.

Popular fishing beaches are Main, Middle and Tura and these produce mainly salmon, tailor, **gummy sharks** and **yellowfin bream**.

Merimbula Lake, relatively safe and protected, can be fished from the entrance to Boggy Creek, in the north-west corner of the Back Lake. The lake appears broad and shallow, but it offers a smorgasbord of piscine opportunities, including **mulloway**, **dusky flathead**, **bream**, tailor and **trevally**. Not only does the lake offer serious action, its safe and easy-to-access location lends itself to family fishing. A boat is handy, but not essential, and land-based anglers have the choice of pier, beach or wading.

To fish at the entrance, follow Bar Beach Rd along the northern side, or walk along the beach from the southern end. Mitchies Jetty on the southern side and Spencer Park on the north give anglers access to the channel that runs up past the bridge. Casting lures at the entrance can produce salmon

Sing Ling shows off a big mulloway that was caught in Merimbula Lake

and tailor. Fish the deeper water for luderick, whiting, flathead and bream. Boat anglers anchor along the edge of the channel.

The flats out from Lake Beach are popular for anglers working lures and flies but be careful not to disturb the oyster leases.

Opposite the hotel and just below the bridge is a popular boat jetty, which is the place to go if you want to book a fishing charter and head offshore, or hire a small tinnie, particularly if you intend fishing the deeper water areas of the Back Lake.

The bridge spanning Merimbula Lake is popular with anglers. Fishing is not allowed on the bridge but there are good access points to deep water on either side. On the western side, there is car parking and access is easy and safe. This is a popular area at night during summer when the tailor run, and large schools of trevally are sometimes seen feeding here.

Upriver from the bridge, the channel runs alongside oyster leases on the southern side and sand flats on the opposite bank. Bream can be seen mooching around the leases, but they are in shallow water and easily spooked. This channel makes a dogleg before entering the Back Lake, and near the entrance to the lake is a top spot to hook mulloway, tailor, bream and big dusky flathead. The water just out from the channel entrance is up to 8.5m deep and can produce mulloway at night.

The southern shore of the Back Lake has a couple of bays that can produce tailor, flathead and mulloway. Follow the shoreline around and you will come across other bays and heavy weed areas. The breaks in the weed are top spots for flathead, as is the entrance to Boggy Creek in the northwest corner. Anglers who fish for tailor tend to troll or cast lures into the feeding action. The tailor feed on anchovy schools and are easy to spot because the birds track them as they feed. During winter, fish up to 3.5kg can be caught.

Bream can be seen feeding around the oyster leases and will take lures. However, bait fishers using prawn or nippers fished on the bottom probably catch more bream, especially when working a berley trail. You are also likely to hook into good flathead, trevally or a tailor or two.

PAMBULA LAKE

Pambula Lake also known as the Broadwater, is just south of Merimbula, a short 15-minute drive.

ACCOMMODATION: For more information visit www.sapphirecoast.com.au

It produces good catches of **bream**, **dusky flathead**, **tailor**, **whiting**, **salmon**, **gummy sharks** and **mulloway**. I fished this water with Bruce Libbis on one of his 'off work' days. Originally from Colac in the Western District of Victoria, Bruce moved to the NSW South Coast more than 25 years ago, where he skippers *Rathlin 2*, a 12.5m Fly Bridge Steber, based at Merimbula. When not running charters, Bruce goes fishing.

We launched at the Pambula Lake boat ramp in the early morning. Despite its popularity and closeness to major population centres, the lake foreshores remain relatively pristine, with eucalypts growing to the water. We motored a few kilometres upstream to where the Yowaka and Pambula rivers flow into the lake. The stretch of river from the ramp to the river junction produces catches of flathead. During winter, when the **bream** are on their spawning run, large schools sometimes congregate along here as they move upstream.

The Yowaka River is noted **Australian bass** water. I fished here a few years ago with local fishing guide Micah Adams. Above the Princes Hwy, the river is easy to access from shore as Nethercote Rd runs parallel with the river for about 3km. Bass up to 3kg have been caught here.

In the shallow areas where the river joins the lake system we started to cast soft plastic lures over the flats and along the edges of channels. The flathead were finicky. A couple of fish were hooked and lost before Bruce brought the first one to the boat.

We headed downstream past the boat ramp, following the channel markers into the Broadwater, before stopping near some oyster leases at Honeysuckle Point where we cast lures for bream. Bream can be seen feeding around these leases and along rocky points where oyster colonies have established. You are not allowed inside the leases, but it is possible to hang back and cast towards them.

Bruce said the deeper water areas in the main part of the lake can produce some serious **gummy sharks** and **mulloway** in excess of 20kg. Schools of **tailor** hunt schools of anchovies in the main lake and during the colder weather tailor run to 2.5kg. Anglers spin, troll or work baits, following the movements of the tailor schools by watching the birds.

Salmon can be caught on lures in Pambula Lake

Downstream from Honeysuckle Point the river takes a sharp right hand turn at what is known as the Shark Hole. This is the deepest water in the lake and a top mulloway spot. From the Shark Hole a long, relatively shallow section runs to the sea. Every year the salmon run in good numbers in this Strait, and it also produces flathead, whiting and bream. When the salmon are running anglers work lures or flies, moving along the channel until they spot a school and then cast ahead of the school. In some years, the salmon average about 2kg.

Black marlin can be caught from the rock ledges at Green Cape

EDEN

Eden is a 35-minute drive south of Merimbula, or seven hours from Melbourne.

Anyone looking for fishing variety should visit Eden. Anglers come here to catch yellowtail kingfish, yellowfin tuna and marlin in the bluewater, or bottom bounce for snapper and flathead. There are estuaries that produce bream and flathead and beach anglers sometimes catch mulloway.

ACCOMMODATION: Eden is not as well endowed with accommodation options as Merimbula, but has all the usual types available from caravan parks along Twofold Bay to flats and motels.
For more information visit
www.coastalstays.com/eden

Angling opportunities include offshore game, reef, beach, estuary and pier. Eden nestles snugly on the shoreline of Twofold Bay and, unlike Merimbula and Narooma further north, the sheltered, deep-water harbour offers safe access to the ocean and has an all-weather boat ramp at Quarantine Bay.

The offshore waters can produce **marlin**, mainly **striped** and **black**, **bonito**, **yellowtail kingfish** and a variety of **sharks** including **hammerheads**, **blues**, **bronze whalers** and the acrobatic **mako**.

The top months for gamefishing are December–May, and you don't have to run far to find the action. A favourite area with game fishers is the Magic Triangle. This incorporates an area from Red Point, below Ben Boyd Tower (GPS: S37.06.030, E149.56.960) at the southern extremity of Twofold Bay, south along the coast about 4 miles to Mowarry Point, and out to sea for about the same distance.

When the East Australian Current is running inshore, this area can fire up for marlin and **tuna** that hunt baitfish migrating down the coast with the current.

Other top spots include Twofold Bay Canyon (GPS: S37.09.400, E150.23.000) and Green Cape Canyon (S37.17.100, E150.23.300).

Inshore reef fishing is excellent and you can expect to catch **snapper**, **morwong**, **leatherjacket**, **nannygai**, **flathead** and **gummy sharks**. If your intentions are to run wide, there are plenty of deep reefs at 50–250 fathoms, and these produce **morwong**, leatherjackets, **blue-eyed trevalla** and **hapuka**. Mowarry Point is a favourite with anglers chasing yellowtail kingfish, which can be up to 20kg.

It's also worth dropping a line into Twofold Bay. The piers in the harbour produce plenty of small baitfish such as **slimy mackerel** and **yakkas** and the fishing waters around the woodchip pier can be productive, particularly for yellowtail kingfish. Bonito are often found inside the bay along with flathead and **whiting**.

Land-based anglers can fish rock, beach and estuary. The rocks at Worang Point have produced tuna, marlin, sharks, **salmon**, **tailor** and **luderick**. Aslings and Boydtown Beaches are easy to access and can produce **mulloway**, **yellowfin bream**, tailor, salmon and gummy sharks. Curalo Lagoon, next to Aslings Beach and the Nullica River is worth fishing for bream and flathead. The Towamba River in Kiah Inlet is sheltered and a favourite with families. Whale Beach, on the north side of Kiah Inlet, is regarded as the best of the beaches, but access is difficult and anglers bring their boats across the bay and fish just offshore.

GREEN CAPE

This place is part of the Ben Boyd National Park, about a 40-minute drive south of Eden. Turn left at the sign to the Edrom Woodchip Mill. Follow the road until you see a sign to the Green Cape Lighthouse. The road is rough and dusty but well signposted. Watch out for the lyre birds, wallabies and kangaroos.

Land-based fishing is a fixture from the rock ledges with tuna, kingfish and shark the most likely captures, but sometimes a marlin is caught.

ACCOMMODATION: There are two campgrounds, Saltwater Creek or Bittangabee. These have pit toilets, no power and you are advised to bring your own water. Alternative accommodation can be had at the Wonboyn Lake Resort, signposted on the lighthouse road.
For more campground information visit www.environment.nsw.gov.au/nationalparks; If you prefer to stay in a flat visit www.wonboynlakeresort.com.au

Anglers who fish the east coast often refer to the January–March period as the 'magic quarter', when the East Australian Current brings millions of baitfish that in turn attract large predators, like **marlin** and **tuna**. The current flows inshore along the coast, making game fish accessible to anglers fishing from rock ledges. The rock ledges on Green Cape, south of Eden, are among the best areas for this sport. The combination of big seas, slippery rocks and rampaging game fish that can empty your reel of a kilometre of line in seconds create an adrenaline-pumping trifecta.

An angler shows off a bonito caught spinning from the rocks at Green Cape

Green Cape often reflects the fishing further north at game-fish ports like Bermagui and Narooma. History indicates that when these ports fire, so too will the cape. And what a history Green Cape has: at least two **yellowfin tuna** landed over the 90kg mark and marlin to 100kg. Other species you may encounter off the rocks include **northern bluefin**, **yellowtail kingfish**, **mackerel tuna**, **striped tuna** and **bonito**.

Marlin show quirks, like one fish I hooked. The initial take was more in keeping with a trout sucking a worm off a hook; little ticks of the reel followed by a short run. Expecting a bonito, I held the rod and waited. A slow steady run followed so I set the hook. An explosion of speed and urgent power buckled the

Wonboyn Beach is popular for tailor and salmon

rod and sent the ratchet's staccato click up-tempo as a couple of hundred kilograms of black marlin took off. Half a kilometre of line later, there were a few head-and-shoulder appearances. Someone standing by my side muttered, 'you've turned him'. But I hadn't. That was the last anyone saw of that fish, and about a kilometre of line.

Twelve months earlier, Peter Bowden hooked a marlin from the same ledge. When Peter's bait went it was a dramatic take. One second he was playing ticky, tacky, touchwood, the next instant 3m of black marlin was flying above the calm sea where Peter's balloon had been. What ensued was the stuff of campfire legends. The marlin went supersonic, heading due east and vaulting over the low swells more than a dozen times in a scorching 700m dash for freedom. The marlin rose smack in the middle of a group of boats. Watching a small flotilla of boats trolling lures over what they thought was a free-jumping marlin was disconcerting. Fortunately, there was no disaster and Peter remained locked into the fish.

An immense struggle took place, in pumping that marlin back to the rocks. The struggle lasted almost an hour in 35°C heat. Unfortunately, somewhere in that time span the marlin died, sank and became wedged on a ledge. It was a sad end to a spectacular episode.

Be warned, rock-fishing is thrilling but dangerous.

LAKE WONBOYN

Lake Wonboyn is 30km south of Eden and is enveloped by mountains clothed in pristine forests, unspoilt beaches and abundant animal and birdlife. It is one of my all-time favourite spots. Located about halfway between Eden and the border with Victoria, this large estuary system suits serious anglers and families.

The lake is dotted with oyster leases and has a well earned reputation for its flathead, tailor, bream and estuary perch.

ACCOMMODATION: On the north or Green Cape side of the lake, accommodation is limited to the Wonboyn Lake Resort.

For more information visit
www.wonboynlakeresort.com.au

However, many visitors prefer to stay in the township of Wonboyn on the southern side of the lake where there is more alternative accommodation including caravans and cabins.

For more information visit www.sapphirecoast.com.au/regions/wonboyn.php

Some visitors to this estuary stay in the small township of Wonboyn, on the southern side. Others prefer the north side, staying at the Wonboyn Lake Resort. Either way you can fish the estuary or the surf.

Wonboyn Lake Resort is a selection of holiday cabins situated in the lee of the estuary where the Wonboyn River takes a sharp turn to the north. Features include boat-launching and mooring facilities, boat hire, a shop and part-time restaurant. The resort is located in a bush setting so there is plenty of wildlife around.

The inlet has a reputation for big **dusky flathead**, **bream**, **tailor**, **whiting**, **estuary perch** and the occasional **mulloway**. Among those who prefer the north side and stay at the Wonboyn Resort, there is generally a healthy contingent of rock-fishers. It's just 10 minutes away from some of Australia's best known rock-fishing platforms.

The surf-fishing can be excellent for **salmon** and tailor. One year an angler caught a 16kg **striped marlin** off the beach while fishing for tailor!

In the estuary, oyster racks and reefs, which produce mainly bream, are a favourite for many visitors. The flats and channels are best for flathead, while further upstream, the snags can fish well for both perch and bream. One of my favourite methods is to walk the extensive shallow sand flats near the mouth. This area can be reached from shore on the Green Cape side, so you don't need a boat.

Methods for South Coast

TACKLE

Gamefishing

Tackle for gamefishing doesn't come cheap. Most anglers work 15kg and 24kg gamefishing outfits. The cost of a quality outfit, that is rod and reel, can set you back more than $1500 but, barring accidents, the gear will last many years. Marlin fishing is about trolling. Most anglers troll live baits, such as slimy mackerel or striped tuna, at about 2km/hr. When the mackerel are schooling into bait balls, the marlin are often found below them and a live mackerel, rigged with a heavy sinker and dropped into the school and slowly towed out can produce a strike. Skirted lures and fish rigged up as 'skip baits' also work. These are trolled at higher speeds of 8–10km/hr. Teasers are used to attract fish. These include daisy chains of plastic squid, 'Birds' or large flashing reflectors such as the Witchdoctor or Reflector Bonito.

Surf-, pier- and rock-fishing

On the beaches, an 8–10kg surf outfit will cover most options, although if you are chasing whiting or spinning for salmon and tailor you can reduce your outfit size to about 4kg.

Land-based gamefishing from the rocks is popular on the South Coast and most anglers work 12–15kg gamefishing outfits for live baiting, and 10kg surf outfits for spinning.

Fishing for salmon and tailor is similar to elsewhere. For salmon, a paternoster rig with size 3/0–4/0 hooks and bait such as pilchard is commonplace. Tailor can be caught on whole

Wonboyn Lake Resort offers mooring facilities for visitors staying in a cabin

pilchards rigged with ganged hooks. Spinning using chrome lures works for both species.

Estuary fishing

In the estuaries, outfits in the 3kg range suit best. A 2–3kg threadline outfit will cover most fishing options. Choose a rod with a fast tip action that is light enough to cast small lures or lightly weighted baits. If you are after mulloway then use heavier outfits in the 6–8kg line class. Fly-fishers will find 6–8kg weight outfits suitable. An intermediate or slow sink fly line will cover most options. Work 5kg level line leaders straight to the fly.

When tailor are about, anglers will use ganged hooks and cast unweighted pilchards out.

A No. 6 to No. 4 Baitholder pattern will suit the whiting and trevally, a No. 4 for bream and a No. 4 to 3/0 for the flathead. For mullet and luderick, fish with your bait under a pencil float, and use a No. 6 hook and smaller baits.

A running sinker rig, with the sinker running down to the hook, is popular. For mulloway, use a leader of about 24kg breaking strain and 6/0 Suicide pattern hooks on a paternoster rig or else under a bobby cork.

Trolling and spinning has developed a strong following and anglers can do well using bibbed minnow or soft plastic lures. Fly-fishers will find small baitfish patterns such as the Lefty Deceiver and Deep Clouser Minnow effective, along with small Pink Things and Crazy Charlies.

In terms of popularity, lure and fly-fishing still rank well behind traditional bait methods and prawns, pipis, squid and nippers (bass yabbies) are commonplace baits for most species. For the big flathead or mulloway, the preference among the bait fishing specialists is live mullet.

5 MURRUMBIDGEE RIVER

YAOUK VALLEY

Situated about 100km south-west of Queanbeyan, the drive to Yaouk Valley takes a little over two and a half hours through ranges covered with snow gums, messmate, peppermint, stringybark and alpine ash.

The streams and rivers in the valley are pristine trout waters, ideal for fly fishing. Access to streams is often a matter of stepping into the water where a bridge crosses a road as some property owners do not appreciate trespassers.

ACCOMMODATION: Not available. Adaminaby, 23km away, is the best option.

It was late autumn 1997 when I arrived in Canberra to fish with the late Chris Hole, fly-fisherman, author and painter. Chris offered to take me to some of his favourite trout streams that snake across the Yaouk Valley and feed into the fast-flowing Murrumbidgee below Tantangara Dam.

The bowl-shaped Yaouk Valley is fine grazing country, 1100m above sea level, where Merino sheep and Hereford cattle vie for snowgrass with eastern grey kangaroos and common wombats.

Chris was fond of small, sweet-water (crystal clear) streams. Fly-fishers crave the challenge of stalking skittish trout in clear, shallow water. The streams of the Yaouk Valley, which alternate between shallow riffles, deeper pools and glides, fit the bill nicely. In most places, they are just over a metre wide and less than a metre deep and the **brown trout** that thrive here feed on a variety of insect life, including nymphs, mayflies, midges, caddis flies and grasshoppers.

Chris preferred to fish with dry flies that float on the surface, favouring patterns such as the Adams, Red Tag and Royal Wulff, rating Humpy's well during the autumn grasshopper season. Fly-fishing is about matching the conditions; when the trout feed in the

Above: **The Murrumbidgee River downstream from Balranald**
Below: **Darren Brant shows off a fine Murray cod he caught on a lure**

meniscus (surface film) they are taking insects such as mayflies emerging from the nymphal stage into winged adults, or duns. If the trout are feeding below the surface, then nymph patterns are used. Chris's favourite wet flies included brown nymph, brown emerger, and a Hare and Copper.

For our sojourn, Chris produced a five-weight fly outfit and tied on a brown nymph. Working upstream, he flicked his line high on the back cast to avoid the shoulder-high tussocks and grass. On his first cast, Chris set the nymph down in a small pool at the bottom of a riffle and almost immediately a small brown trout shot out from its hide and inhaled the fly. Chris set the barbless hook, the prick enough to send the trout ballistic as it tried to dislodge the counterfeit nymph. According to Chris, the action was typical of these waterways.

'During the early part of the season you can catch and release 40 or 50 trout in a day,' he said. 'And despite the small size of the stream, there are large trout, up to 2.5kg in the deeper pools.'

After lunch we concentrated on the Murrumbidgee River. The trout we caught weighed up to about 500g. Spring is a good time to catch them, but Chris said the best time was early autumn when the fish are fat and at their prime.

WAGGA WAGGA

The largest inland city in NSW, Wagga Wagga is thought to mean crow in the language of the original inhabitants, the Wiradjuri people. The city is about halfway between Melbourne and Sydney and is a major inland transport hub for agriculture.

Expect Murray cod, yellowbelly and redfin in the Murrumbidgee.

ACCOMMODATION: A city this size has the lot; it's just a matter of looking.
For more information visit www.waggawaggaaustralia.com.au

In my early teens I lived in Wagga Wagga for about three years and spent many hours fishing from a kayak on the Murrumbidgee and at Lake Albert. The river held excellent numbers of **redfin**, and they were of good size, so this species was the focus of my fishing.

Murrumbidgee is a Wiradjuri word meaning 'big water,' and my memories of the Murrumbidgee are exactly that: a big, fast-flowing river, flanked by eucalypts and flood plains. Sadly, 40 years on, a word for 'low water' would be more apt.

On a recent trip I fished with local lure maker, Jason Mullavey of Muldoon Lures, who had warned me there was little water in the river and that he might have difficulty launching his boat, a 4m Quintrex Hornet Trophy, from the usual boat ramps.

With this in mind we drove to nearby Wiradjuri Reserve in north Wagga Wagga. A shallow stretch of river with a firm sand and stone beach, it seemed an unlikely place to launch a boat. Jason was driving a fairly new 4WD and had no qualms about reversing car and trailer more than 20m into the river. Even then the water was so shallow that I wondered if he should back further.

Leaving the reserve, we motored upstream for a couple of kilometres to Hampden Bridge. The river has gouged a channel close to shore, and there are some heavy-duty snags and rock bars midstream. Overhanging willow trees add to the available cover for native fish such as **Murray cod** and **yellowbelly**.

Jason put the 30-horsepower outboard into a little bit better than idle and we trolled our lures along the strike zones of snags and drop-offs. In some areas, we drifted and cast to indentations along the riverbank, allowing the lures to sit for a couple of seconds before starting the slow retrieve. We worked the fringes with our lures for several hours to no avail. Other boats stopped to check that we weren't catching anything and offered similar tales of piscine woe. The river is low and dirty, and the drought on land has extended beneath the surface.

River fishing for native species can be like that. Sometimes all it takes to bring the fish on is an upstream rise in water levels, or a barometric shift. Jason assured me that Murray cod to about 10kg are caught along this stretch of river, and he knew of a 35kg cod being caught nearby. This stretch also produces yellowbelly to 2.8kg, **redfin** to 2kg, **silver perch**, **river blackfish** and **eel-tailed catfish** – albeit not on this day.

While most anglers fish the river from shallow-draught tinnies, I remembered the advantages of using a kayak in my youth. It allowed me to go under overhanging willow trees to fish dark, sheltered areas where boat anglers often could not go.

BALRANALD

Balranald is located where the Sturt Hwy crosses the Murrumbidgee River in southern NSW. Although it is part of NSW, Balranald receives Victorian television stations. The ill-fated Burke and Wills expedition crossed the Murrumbidgee River at Balranald on their journey to cross Australia from Melbourne to the Gulf of Carpentaria in September, 1860.

This is Murray cod and yellowbelly water.

ACCOMMODATION: The town has a large, well-cared for caravan and camping park with the usual range of cabins. There are several motels in town.
For more information visit www.balranald.nsw.gov.au

The drive from the Monaro to Wagga Wagga and on to Balranald gives some idea of the Murrumbidgee's length and also of how much a river can change over the course of its flow.

Near Balranald, the river has been slowed by irrigation infrastructure and the first obvious difference is the steep clay banks and the number of snags. Every fallen tree and log has fish-holding potential and for a relatively small river, there are some big **Murray cod** waiting to ambush your lures or suck in a big bardi grub.

I fished in a boat with three other anglers and our modus operandi was to motor along to a snag, then drift and cast spinnerbait lures into the timber in the hope of catching a big cod or **yellowbelly**. Tony Bennett cast first. As he slowly retrieved his lure, a cod followed, missing the lure but leaving a telltale swirl at the surface. Three other lures were immediately cast to the same spot, a system affectionately known as 'seagulling'. I was in luck and about 12kg of Murray cod was soon netted, photographed and released. We caught nine cod and a similar number of yellowbelly on a day the boys rated as slow.

About 30km upstream from Balranald as the crow flies, there is a weir at Redbank, and further up, another weir at Maud, which is a popular fishing spot. The problem with heading upstream from Balranald is that the river is shallow and snags make navigation difficult. There are plenty of snags downstream, but the wider and deeper river makes it easier to get around. Another weir on the downstream leg is about half an hour by boat.

Anglers who achieve success in this part of the river can thank the dedicated efforts of the local angling club, which has put more than 100,000 native fish into the river. This proactive approach helps maintain the fish populations until nature provides the vital floods needed to improve numbers naturally.

Methods for Murrumbidgee River

TACKLE When bait fishing, a 6kg outfit will cover yellowbelly, while for Murray cod it can pay to follow the trend among lure trollers and work heavier tackle, using braid lines of 15–24kg breaking strain, as they are much thinner than equivalent monofilament. Leader material is important if fishing for big cod, and this should also be about 15–24kg breaking strain. Hook sizes for baits are generally No. 2 to No. 4 long shank. A 10kg baitcaster outfit is recommended if you want to cast lures for cod and yellowbelly.

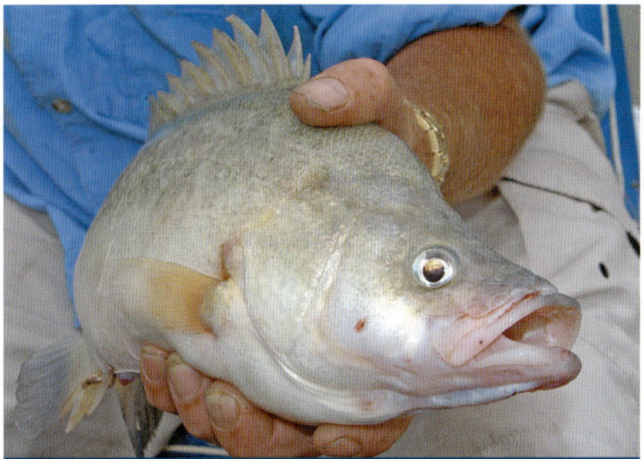

Yellowbelly or golden perch are prolific in the Murrumbidgee River

BAIT Bardi grub is the favoured cod bait followed by shrimp, yabbies, scrub worms and cheese. If you have trouble putting cheese on the hook, try putting some cheese on a Chux Superwipe cloth and melting it in a microwave oven. The cloth can then be cut into strips and presented on the hook.

RIGS When bait fishing, the simplest rig is a small ball sinker, allowing it to run down to the hook. Some anglers prefer to use running sinker rigs with a leader for cod and paternoster-style rigs for yellowbelly. The paternoster is sometimes a better option when fishing from shore as it helps to keep the bait off the bottom. In a boat, drop the bait to the bottom and then wind it up a metre or so. Drifting in the current and bobbing bait off the bottom can be effective for yellowbelly.

LURES The Murrumbidgee has a fairly consistent water depth of 4m with occasional 6m holes. If trolling for Murray cod, use a

The pondage is one of many fishing options available at Khancoban

selection of large bibbed minnows including Muldoon, AC Invader, RMG 80mm Poltergeist and No. 1 to No. 2 StumpJumpers. Step back a size for yellowbelly. Much depends on getting the lure down to the fish and if your lure is bouncing off the bottom then you know it is deep enough. When trolling upstream, work bigger lures than when downstream. Smaller lures can be used to cast to snags, and Spinnerbaits, which are less likely to hook up on timber, are popular for this style of fishing.

6 SNOWY MOUNTAINS

If you like the bush and clear mountain streams where you can fish for trout, then the Snowy Mountains offers excellent opportunities. Rivers up this way are part of our fishing folklore, particularly among fly-fishers. Several of my friends take off into the mountains, park their cars along isolated tracks and backpack through the bush to spend a few days fishing pristine waters. This is the extreme end of fishing, ideal when you are young and fit.

KHANCOBAN

The town was established to house workers involved in the Snowy Mountains Scheme, Australia's largest engineering project. The Snowy Mountains region provided the backdrop for the *Silver Brumby* collection of children's books by Australian author Elyne Mitchell.

Many trout fishers, particularly those adept with the fly, regard Khancoban as home base for trout fishing.

ACCOMMODATION: Includes units, houses and a caravan park.
For more information visit www.visitnsw.com/destinations/snowy-mountains/tumbarumba-area/khancoban

The biggest water in the area is Khancoban Pondage, fed by the Swampy Plain River and Khancoban Creek. The pondage is stocked with **rainbow** and **brown trout** and has a large **redfin** population, with fish to 2kg.

Redfin numbers have exploded in the pondage and most anglers aren't happy because the redfin eat the small, fingerling trout as they are liberated. To get around this, NSW Fisheries is releasing trout upstream in the feeder creeks, where hopefully they will survive until they are big enough to turn the tables and eat the redfin.

Being part of the Snowy Mountains Hydro Electric Scheme, the pondage has fluctuating water levels. During one particularly dry summer, water flows into the Swampy Plain River Anabranch were so diminished that the anabranch dried up and everything in it died.

The main restrictions for anglers here are in the streams that flow through private property. All methods – bait, lure and fly – are employed, but anglers who troll lures seem to achieve more consistent success.

GEEHI

Geehi is about 30km east of Khancoban on the Alpine Way. You can't miss it; when you see the bridge with the Swampy Plains River, simply turn off.

The Geehi River is an iconic waterway in the heart of the *Man From Snowy River* country. Trout are caught here, brown and rainbow, and the waterway has a sort of iconic status among fly fishers.

ACCOMMODATION: The Geehi Recreation area on the Swampy Plains River has campsites.
For more information visit www.environment.nsw.gov.au

Geehi Flat offers easy access and good fishing.

The camping area includes toilets and a stone hut that can be used for cooking. A paved brick path along the river from the car parking area to the toilets seems out of place in a national park, and in such a pristine environment. Camping is rudimentary but very pleasant, with cleared grass areas surrounded by dogwood and peppermint gums. Drive through the first area and follow the track, and you'll come across several stone huts, such as Old Geehi Hut and Keeble's Hut. These are used for shelter, but no one is allowed to take them over, so they are free to all comers.

Keeble's Hut is a must see. Arthur Keeble, an engineer on the Kiewa Hydro Electric Scheme, built the hut over six weeks in 1948 for Arthur and Flo Nankervis and friends. Its outstanding feature is the actual-size painting of an 8lb 14oz (4kg) brown trout on the door. The plaque alongside the painting says Mrs A. Nankervis caught the **trout** in February 1954 on a dry Jock Scott fly. Now, if that isn't enough to get you fishing the Swampy then nothing will!

I fished with Andy Zarro and Neil Bennetts, and they directed me to ford the river in a couple of places until we arrived at our destination, just above where Bogong Creek flows into the Swampy. For a backdrop we had the magnificent, super-steep Geehi Walls. Neil, who combines shearing and farming with being a fishing guide, is a fourth-generation mountain man. He told how his father and grandfather used to drive cattle over the Geehi Walls to feed on the mountain grasses.

The Swampy River was low and clear and there was concern that the trout would see us before we had a chance to put a fly over them. Neil rigged up a two-fly rig, using a dry Stimulator pattern to act as a strike indicator above a gold beadhead brown nymph. Andy preferred to work just the dry fly, a Geehi beetle. One angler walked the river casting his fly at riffles, runs and pools, and the rest of us stayed out of sight of the trout on the riverbank.

Walking through the scrub dodging wombat holes and always alert for snakes, the presence of deer was all-too obvious. Small trees had branches broken and debarked by deer scraping their antlers. In some heavily wooded areas, the deer had created clearings making access easier.

Trout were proving wary and the fishing was slow. Bright sun and shallow clear water are not ideal trout-fishing conditions. After a couple of hours we decided to try our luck in Bogong Creek, which had cover, so the trout would be less likely to see us.

Neil went first and soon managed to catch and release several small brown trout.

Fishing is as much about experiencing the outdoors as it is catching trophies. We didn't catch any monsters, but the great outdoors was breathtaking.

INDI RIVER

Taking the Alpine Way out of Khancoban and heading about 50km towards Thredbo, you come to Tom Groggin Station. Locals say the river flowing alongside the station is the Indi River – or the upper reaches of the Murray River, depending on which map you read.

This spot is great for rainbow and brown trout.

The Snowy Mountains abound with scenic rivers like the Indi, which is a great fishing spot

ACCOMMODATION: Drive a little further on from Tom Groggin Station and you will come to Tom Groggin Camping Area, the best opportunity for an overnight stay.

Tom Groggin is on the Victorian side of the river and it was here that A.B. 'Banjo' Paterson is thought to have met Jack Riley and been inspired to write one of our most famous bush poems, *The Man From Snowy River*. Drive a little further and you come to the Tom Groggin picnic area. By passing through here and following the 4WD track for a couple of kilometres, you reach the river again. Drive across it and you are on Davies Plains Track.

Neil Bennetts, Andy Zarro and I parked on Davies Plains Track, walked back across the river and started to work our way upstream. We couldn't get to the river from the Victorian side due to the blackberries. They're not as thick on the NSW side, although it was tricky working our way through flowering dogwoods and peppermint eucalypts with delicate fly rods in hand. Upstream of the ford, the river narrows, deepens and runs faster. It is gorge country with boulders lining the river edges between steep sloping sides, and trout hang in the pools along the edges of the current.

Neil said we had to hang back from the edge. The sun was out and the **trout** were easily frightened by shadows on the water. As Andy and I stayed back in the shadows under the bush, Neil crouched and worked his way to the edge of the boulder. Staying about a metre away from the edge, and out of sight of any fish below, he laid out several false casts and sent his Stimulator dry fly upstream to land in a pool on the far side of the river. The first cast was unsuccessful so he tried again. Each time the fly landed in a different pocket of water, and he watched it closely for any rises. A couple of small trout showed interest then turned away at the last moment. Neil had to watch his back cast due to the overhanging bushes, but he obviously had done this many times before, and kept working the fly around boulders and pools.

Well stocked with brown and rainbow trout, and Atlantic salmon, Lake Jindabyne is a fabulous fishery

The sun remained bright and the water clear, so trout proved wary and fishing was slow.

Perseverance finally paid off when, a few hundred metres upstream, Neil found a small **rainbow trout** of about 450g that wanted to eat his fly. Once he'd broken the drought, other trout followed.

A kilometre or so upstream from the ford we came across a series of shallow rapids and, above them, a large pool. Trout could be seen taking insects on the surface near some overhanging dogwood. Andy took off upriver, worked his way around the pool to cast across to the rising trout. He hooked up quickly, this time with a **brown trout** that took his Geehi beetle dry fly.

The fish weren't big, but Neil said he had caught brown trout to 1.8kg in this water.

LAKE JINDABYNE

The lake is half the size of Sydney Harbour, making it one of the largest bodies of fresh water in Australia. For Sydney people, the easiest way is to drive through Canberra down to Cooma. From Melbourne, I prefer to go via Cann River on the Monaro Hwy.

Lake Jindabyne sits on the eastern edge of Kosciuszko National Park and rates as one of southern Australia's best trout waters.

ACCOMMODATION: Plenty of it due to the lake's close proximity to the NSW snow fields.
For more information visit www.visitnsw.com/destinations/snowy-mountains/jindabyne-area

The lake is stocked with **rainbow** and **brown trout**, and **Atlantic salmon**. Some of the fish are in the trophy class. The trout average about 1kg but fish to 5kg are caught every year.

Several rivers flow in or out of the lake, including the Snowy, Thredbo and Eucumbene. There is a public boat ramp near the Snowline Caravan Park and, as with many lakes, the most consistent good catches have come from anglers trolling. During summer, downrigger trolling is common, but late in the day and at night the fish move inshore so that bait-, fly- and lure-fishers have good opportunities.

In autumn and winter, the trout move into the rivers to spawn upstream. Anglers will do well at this time if they walk along the shoreline with polarising sunglasses. Bait fishing is allowed in the lake, but not in the rivers.

NARIEL CREEK

Still in Victoria, the quick way from Melbourne is to drive up the Hume Hwy and turn off at Wodonga, following the shoreline of Lake Hume through to Tallangatta and then on to Corryong. It is about 120km from Wodonga. Jack Riley, a hermit stockman whose horseriding skills made him the inspiration for A. B. 'Banjo' Paterson's poem *The Man from Snowy River* was buried at Corryong.

ACCOMMODATION: A couple of caravan parks and three motels and a hotel are available.
Corryong Tourist Information Centre: (02) 6076 2277

A favourite dry fly among fly-fishers casting to rising **trout** in the Snowy Mountains and north-east Victoria is the Geehi beetle. This marvellous pattern is named after a non-existent beetle. It's a fly that trout could easily mistake for any number of bugs.

Andy Zarro tied a Geehi beetle to his tippet before we headed up Nariel Creek. Andy enjoys dry fly-fishing more than presenting wet flies like nymphs and streamers. Dries, however, need an insect hatch to bring the trout to the surface to feed.

On this day, the Nariel, like most creeks in the high country, was running low and clear – a little too low and clear for Andy's liking. Nevertheless, he persisted with the Geehi beetle. The first fish was a small brown trout of about 600g that was sitting in the shade of overhanging branches at the bottom of a run, waiting for dinner to be served up by the current.

Fly-fisher keeping low as he presents a fly to trout in Nariel Creek

Andy worked his way across the creek, staying low to avoid spooking the trout. He cast upstream and allowed the fly to drift into the trout's feeding lane. The take was instant, the hook-up lasting seconds and then the trout jumped free of the barbless hook.

The first time I fished this water was in the early 1990s with legendary fly-fishing guide and instructor, the late Mike Spry. Operating as Spry Fly at Khancoban, Mike's stomping grounds were the lush alpine river flats fed by the Snowy Mountains. That first day fishing with Mike was unforgettable, but not because of the trout. I met Mike on the creek downstream from the highway. As we were talking, one of his students came up from the creek, white-faced and breathless. He has been standing on a sandbank in the river when a red-bellied black snake swam across and curled up next to him.

'You must mean a snake like those,' said Mike, pointing at two snakes writhing and twisting around each other not 20m away. He motioned for me to follow and take photos, which I did from two steps behind Mike. Every time the camera shutter clicked, the two snakes turned and hissed.

That evening as the Kosciusko mayflies were doing their ritual vertical dance over the Nariel River Mike said: 'They're males searching for females. We'll work Royal Wulff (dry flies) and float them down to the pool where the trout should be.'

Mike left a lasting legacy: many of Australia's fly-fishers and guides credit him with teaching them the basic fly-fishing skills.

Andy was a friend of Mike, so it was appropriate that I fished the Nariel with him. As we worked upstream, he decided to change tactics. Dry flies weren't working, so he opted for a gold beadhead nymph below a strike indicator. At the next pool he was hit first cast, landing a neat **brown trout** of about 750g. He pulled three more from the same pool before we moved on. The Nariel has offered such good fishing for as long as anyone can remember, which is why it is rated among the top fly-fishing streams for trout.

Methods for Snowy Mountains

TACKLE Fly gear consisted of six-weight outfits with weight-forward floating lines. Leaders were 5m long with a 1m, 2kg tippet.

FLIES Flies were Geehi beetle and Stimulator dry flies, and gold beadhead nymphs fished below an indicator. Some fly-fishers use a dry fly as an indicator and attach the nymph to a tippet running from the hook of the dry fly.

CLOTHING This is snake country, so wear waders. As well as red-bellied blacks, there are healthy populations of browns, copperheads and tigers, all of them showing a liking for riverbanks. Polarising glasses are essential to protect your eyes and take the glare off the water so you can see the trout. Wear a wide-brimmed hat to cover your ears in summer, and always use sunscreen after you have rigged your line.

Trout have small ears and can't hear you talk, but if you thump along the riverbanks or splash the water, there is every chance you will spook them. The golden rule when you hunt trout is to stay out of sight and move softly.

PARK PASSES Nowadays the user has to pay for the privilege of experiencing the environment. Driving across the Alpine Way through the Snowy Mountains from Jindabyne and heading towards Khancoban, I came across a Kosciuszko National Park tollbooth near Thredbo. The park rules are simple: if passing through, you are handed a day pass at no cost. If you intend spending time in the park, the cost of a day pass is about $27 from June–October, and $16 for the rest of the year. Annual passes cost around $190 per vehicle. Information can be found at www.environment.nsw.gov.au/nationalparks/parkfees.

7 MURRAY RIVER

LAKE HUME

The lake is about a four hour drive from Melbourne on the Hume Hwy and, for angling licence purposes, is managed by Fisheries Victoria. Lake Hume is hard to miss, being about six times bigger than Sydney Harbour. It holds big numbers of that culinary favourite of rural Australia, the redfin, as well as good populations of yellowbelly, Murray cod and trout.

ACCOMMODATION: Every conceivable form of accommodation is available in the twin cities of Albury–Wodonga.
For more information visit
www.alburywodongaaustralia.com.au

The creation of Lake Hume was responsible for the biggest verified Murray cod kill in Australia. As the reservoir started to fill in the 1930s, the rotting vegetation from the flooded forest generated hydrogen sulphide. To counter the algae that ensued, the authorities released large amounts of copper sulphate into the river, which had the effect of wiping out the native fish population from Albury to Corowa.

Albury–Wodonga is ideal for anyone seeking a variety of freshwater fishing. The list of fish species on offer reads like a *Who's Who* of southern Australian freshwater fish. It includes **Murray cod**, **yellowbelly**, **redfin**, **carp** and both **brown** and **rainbow trout**.

The Murray River is right on the doorstep and Lake Hume is less than 20km away. An hour's drive south puts you within casting distance of some of

Rod Mackenzie caught this big Murray cod on a spinnerbait

Victoria's best trout spots, including the Mitta Mitta River, the Kiewa River and Lake Dartmouth. To the east, it's a similar distance to the famous Nariel Creek at Corryong, the Swampy River and the excellent Khancoban pondage.

Most anglers who come up this way fish Lake Hume. If you decide to do the same, buy a Victorian Recreational Fishing Licence: it might be NSW water, but the lake comes under Fisheries Victoria jurisdiction.

I fished the lake with Wodonga fishing identity Robert 'Bluey' Williams. We arranged to meet at Ludlows boat ramp on the southern side of Lake Hume; about a 15-minute drive east of Wodonga. The ramp is long enough to be called a road. Lake Hume was low, at about 25 per cent capacity.

Bluey, who runs a tackle shop in Wodonga, uses a 5m barra punt with a 30-horsepower outboard. It was spacious, fast and easily manoeuvred as we fished among the stands of dead trees for redfin. According to Bluey, the redfin average 350–500g, and there are plenty of them. Our bait consisted of small yabbies and scrub worms. We moved from one stand of trees to another consistently finding fish on the sounder, then tying off the boat and dropping our baits.

You could see the fish on the sounder, but they weren't playing the game. Bluey caught a few, hooking one of the smaller fish and putting it down, explaining it was the best bait for the bigger reddies. An angler I spoke to that evening caught more than 100 reddies in a session the day before. We didn't pull that many, but at least we had a taste.

Bluey said that one of the nice things about fishing broad water in a boat is that if the fish aren't biting, it's no big deal to run a few kilometres to another area. 'We could head towards Tallangatta and chase Murray cod, or the Bowna Arm for yellowbelly up to 10kg that often school near the entrance,' he explained. 'Bethanga Bay can be excellent for redfin to 2.5kg, and a lot of the trout guys troll lures near the Pines, which is close to Bethanga Bridge. The trout are up to 2.8kg but average about 950g.'

Bluey suggested the best time at the lake is August and September when there is an explosion of small baitfish (smelt) in the lake, which brings the trout on the bite. April and May can also be good months for trout. Native species such as cod and yellowbelly seem to prefer the warmer months.

Boat ramps on the lake are located at Ludlows, Bowna Arm, Pines (Bethanga Bridge) and the Lake Hume Resort, which is near the dam wall.

LAKE MULWALA

Lake Mulwala separates the Victorian and NSW towns of Yarrawonga and Mulwala. It is a little over three hours' drive from Melbourne. It is situated on the Murray River about 1992km from the river mouth and is regarded as the best impoundment Murray cod fishery in Australia. This is due to the exceptional growth rates cod in this water achieve compared to cod liberated in other waters. As well as cod, there are yellowbelly, redfin, carp and sometimes the occasional trout that has come down the Ovens River.

ACCOMMODATION: Loads of places to stay from waterfront caravan parks to motels.
For more information visit www.yarrawongamulwala.com.au

Above: Casting lures around sunken timber on Lake Mulwala at sunset can produce spectacular strikes from Murray cod
Below: A large Murray cod

The lake dates back to 1937, when the Murray River was dammed to create a large body of water for irrigation. However, the lake is more than irrigation storage; it is a major drawcard and largely responsible for the booming tourism industry – particularly anglers – in Yarrawonga–Mulwala. The Cod Classic is held here every December to mark the opening of Murray cod season, and it regularly attracts more than 2500 anglers and their families, making it by far the biggest freshwater fishing competition in Australia.

Lake Mulwala is about 12km long and 4km wide. The Murray and Ovens rivers join at the east end of the lake at Bundalong, and the Murray River bed passes through the southern shore, which at about 14m is the deepest part of the lake. Anglers fishing here require a NSW recreational fishing licence.

The lake is particularly attractive to anglers because the red gum forest wasn't completely cleared before the lake was created. In 1937, the River Murray Commission refused to undertake the tree-clearing program proposed by the citizens of Yarrawonga–Mulwala, so the following year some of the locals began felling the trees themselves. Only a few were cut down and those that were toppled were never removed. The result is a lake full of structure, with ideal habitat for species such as **cod** and **yellowbelly**.

The standing timber is also popular with nesting cockatoos. It seems cod have difficulty distinguishing between eggs cast out of their nests

These anglers are casting spinnerbait lures to snags along the Murray River

by cockatoos, and stray golf balls landing in the lake. Many cod have been found with golf balls in their stomachs.

The lake has long been highly regarded for the quantity and quality of the fish that can be caught. Many anglers and fisheries people rate the lake as the nation's most productive Murray cod water. While most cod are in the 2–3kg range, captures of 20kg and bigger are also possible. Yellowbelly are prolific, and **European carp** are everywhere.

You don't need a boat to catch fish in the lake, although it helps. Plenty of cod, yellowbelly, **redfin** and carp are caught from shore, and sometimes even **trout** that have strayed down the Ovens River.

SWAN HILL

Swan Hill is about 335km north-west of Melbourne on the banks of the Murray. The local tourism authority promotes the city as the Heart of the Murray, but when anglers see the giant Murray cod that overlooks the river, they know what Swan Hill is all about. Like Balranald, the city has a connection to the ill-fated Burke and Wills expedition with a Moreton Bay fig tree planted in 1860 to commemorate the expedition as it passed through.

ACCOMMODATION: Swan Hill has every type of accommodation from camping and caravan parks to first class motels. The Swan Hill Region Information Centre is located close to the River Precinct and Giant Cod. Staff at the centre have all accommodation details.
For more information visit www.swanhillonline.com

From Mulwala to Swan Hill there are excellent fishing opportunities. Some of the top spots along this stretch include Barmah, Echuca and the famous Torrumbarry Weir.

This is **cod** country. Local angling stories in this part of the world revolve around cod. One fish was evidently so big it had gravel rash on its belly and a sunburned back. Nobody knows how much the cod weighed, but three of its scales were used to roof a backyard dunny ... so the story goes.

If you are into catching cod, **yellowbelly** and **redfin**, then Swan Hill is a great place to start. As well as the Murray, the Neimur, Wakool, Edwards, Little Murray and Murrumbidgee rivers are all within about a 40-minute drive. For those who prefer lakes, close options include Lakes Boga, Charm and Kangaroo, all of which fish well during the warmer months.

The Murray River is no longer a river in the purest sense of the word. It is controlled water divided into a series of pools by weirs and dams. The best fishing is upstream of the main bridge. Water on the downstream side is shallow and needs to be navigated carefully.

About half a kilometre downstream of the bridge, on the Victorian side, is an all-weather ramp. Access is from Milloo St.

Popular spots include the willows near Murray Downs and, several kilometres further upstream, Pental Island. The latter has a solid reputation for producing big cod. Pental Island has a caravan park and boats can be launched from the bank. An all-weather ramp is also available there.

Three nearby lakes provide excellent angling, provided they are holding water. Drive out of Swan Hill towards Kerang, and you'll come across Lake Boga, about 10km out of town, then Lake Kangaroo (20km) and finally Lake Charm, about 30km away. All three are better known as part of the Kerang wetlands system and hold plentiful stocks of redfin to 2kg, bigger **carp** and, since 2004, Fisheries Victoria have stocked them with Murray cod and yellowbelly. The stocking commenced following the buy-back of inland commercial fishing licences.

The presence of Murray cod might be good news for native fish aficionados, but most anglers who fish here do so for redfin. It is the same right across the Wimmera and Mallee regions. Wherever you find large, relatively shallow lakes you also seem to find solid populations of redfin, even in some town-water supply dams.

Redfin is a European import, not quite as high on Victorian Fisheries pest scale as carp, but it's one of rural Victoria's most popular freshwater sport fish. It's something of a biological enigma among European imports – not only does it fight well and make excellent table fare, but it often bites better when the water warms up. When brown and rainbow trout are gasping for oxygen, the redfin is highly active and feeding.

Jim Credlin, the owner of the Swan Hill tackle store, is a big fan of these lakes. Lake Boga has 906ha of water, with a boat ramp, picnic area, caravan park and all facilities. Jim told me he was amazed that the redfin were still in this lake as it has been allowed to run dry, and yet when it refilled 'the redfin just reappeared'.

Lake Kangaroo is about 980ha and has boat ramps and caravan parks on the northern and western shores. This lake is not as popular with waterskiers. Good bank fishing is available and one of the best areas is close to the regulator at the Swan Hill end of the lake.

Lake Charm is about half the area of the other two lakes and features a caravan park and good boat ramp that can handle larger craft. It contains a big population of redfin as well as Murray cod, yellowbelly and carp.

For the land-based angler there are plenty of areas to wet a line. One of the best is on the foreshore of the Hiawatha Caravan Park. Jim said another popular area is the bank near the regulator that controls water flow between little Lake Charm and big Lake Charm.

Just keep your fingers crossed that the lakes hold water.

TOL TOL

The area is about 5km east of the soldier settlement town of Robinvale, via the Murray Valley Hwy and then on to the Tol Tol loop road. To get to this stretch of river, turn left on the Tol Tol Rd until you reach Invincible Bend Rd, which runs down to the river. Then go down any of the bush tracks that lead to the riverbank.

The biggest attraction here is the fish, yellowbelly and big Murray cod.

ACCOMMODATION: The banks of the Murray River are home to thousands of campers during holidays because campsites are free on long stretches of the riverbank, especially on the Victorian side. There is no accommodation at Tol Tol, but the riverbank is sparsely covered by trees and bush making it a popular area for campers.

I made my first serious **Murray cod** trip on the Murray River near Robinvale and for years was asked not to write about such a special stretch of river that produces a higher-than-average proportion of big cod. It wasn't my backyard so I did the proper thing. Then, when other fishing writers spilled the beans, the anglers who showed me the area, local cod gurus Rod Mackenzie and Gus Storer, decided it was okay for me to tell people about Tol Tol.

The Murray River is one of the most accessible campgrounds in Australia. Wherever you go along the river in a boat, you seem to come across small groups of campers in out-of-the-way locations. This was how it was at Tol Tol. A swag and billy trip – one of those experiences where a wash is a swim in the river, and a nature walk is taken with a shovel in one hand and a roll of toilet paper in the other.

There is no boat ramp so boats are launched over a low-lying section of riverbank using a 4WD. Head upstream for 3km and you arrive at Belsar Island, and halfway between the island and camp is a pumping station at Millers Bend. Both these areas are known for cod and **yellowbelly**. On my first trip, the four-day tally was eight Murray cod weighing more than 10kg each, with the best fish nudging the lie detector to 19kg. On subsequent trips to Tol Tol with Rod and Gus, we've caught cod to 33kg, plus a few bruising strikes that failed to hook up.

Gus Storer caught this 50kg Murray cod in the Murray River

ROBINVALE

From Melbourne, go to Ballarat then take the Sea Lake Hwy through St Arnaud, Sea Lake and Manangatang.

This is native fish water where Murray cod grow to 40kg plus and yellowbelly are plentiful.

ACCOMMODATION: If you are not into camping with a tent or swag along the Murray River, the best place to seek out accommodation is Robinvale. Everything from riverbank caravan parks to motels is available. For more information visit www.murrayriver.com.au/robinvale/accommodation

We trolled at little more than a fast walking pace, the electric motor giving off a light humming noise. Behind the boat, a couple of large bibbed lures were swimming deep, about a metre off the bottom, their action pulsing through the fine braid line like a heartbeat.

We were trolling in about 6.5m of water over a rock bar that rose about a metre from the riverbed. On each pass several large **cod** could be seen on the sounder screen. The cod showed up as oversized boomerangs with blood-red centres fading to blue and green on the edges. These were big fish, but they weren't cooperating.

Water clarity was okay; put your arm in the water up to your elbow and you could still see your hand. We changed lures, offered different colours and actions, but the cod had shut down, as they often do when the water level or barometer fall. A slight rise in the water can bring the cod on with a hot bite, but this didn't happen.

What might surprise is that we were fishing within sight of Robinvale, so close to town that waterski boats were coming past regularly. Cod in excess of 40kg have been caught here. The main feature that attracts the big fish to this stretch of the river is the deep, slow-moving pool and underwater structure including rock bars and fallen timber.

Robinvale has plenty of deep water, and the river near Robinvale Bridge has also produced many big cod. The river runs for about 6km downstream to Euston Lock and again features plenty of deep, pool water that attracts big fish.

Many anglers fish the major course of the Murray around Nine Mile Island. The island features shallow backwaters and heaps of birdlife, including eagles. It is separated from the Victorian bank by a cut that produces good numbers of smaller cod to about 10kg and **yellowbelly**. Although the cut is a part of the Murray River, it is Victorian water.

For boaters who don't mind launching off the bank, many of the roads behind the Robinvale racecourse lead to the river and there are plenty of low-lying areas. Alternatively, public boat ramps can be found next to the Riverside Caravan Park at Robinvale and just downstream of the bridge on the Victorian side of the river. Another ramp is located at Euston on the NSW side.

Carp caught on fly in the Murray River

EUSTON

The small river port of Euston, downstream from Robinvale is a major agricultural base for fruit orchards and grape production.

Fishing is the same as for Robinvale.

ACCOMMODATION: A hotel, motel and caravan park are available.
For more information visit www.murrayriver.com.au/euston/accommodation

Euston began as Boomiarcool Station in 1847, growing into a small township and subsequently a busy inland port, from which a fleet of paddlesteamers and barges transported the consignments of wool and wheat along the Murray to various NSW, Victorian and SA townships. These days the region is better known for its vineyards, market gardens, orchards and big **Murray cod**.

One of the vagaries of the Murray River is that small stretches of river produce consistently better results than other areas. It is about 4km from Robinvale Bridge to Lock 15, and Euston sits about halfway along on this stretch of river, on the NSW side. The water is predominantly deep with rock bars and old snags providing cover for a good number of large Murray cod.

Trolling for Murray cod from a boat on the Murray River

A large concrete ramp is situated behind the Euston club. The club itself has accommodation set on the banks of the river providing easy access to both the boat ramp and a selection of bank fishing.

Upstream of the club a caravan park also provides accommodation with river views and ample access to bank fishing.

As it is contained behind a lock, the river at Euston is virtually free of current, so ideal for those using electric motors.

If you are lure fishing, a selection of deep divers will be essential. The large dead river gums still standing along some sections of the river are prime locations to fish with bait or small hard-bodied lures for large **yellowbelly**. This is best done in periods of low light when the fish are less skittish. Below the lock, the river takes on a different appearance. Here the current picks up and the river is paved with rock bars and shallow snags. It is a great area to work spinnerbait lures or shallow-running, hard-bodied lures.

BOYANDA

The red ochre cliff near the Boyanda grape farm is a popular launch site for anglers fishing the Murray River midway between Robinvale and the small horticultural town of Wemen. A track follows the river from Happy Valley Shop at the southern end of Robinvale. Go to the end of this road, turn left at the crossroads, and then right to Boyanda, following a dirt track along the river to the boat ramp. The track runs all the way to Wemen along the Victorian side of the river and there are plenty of places to camp.

This is Murray cod country.

ACCOMMODATION: For more information visit www.murrayriver.com.au/robinvale/accommodation

The boat ramp is a rugged dry-weather 4WD launch site only on a rough clay incline. Situated downstream of the cliffs, it is a stark reminder that city folk have pleasures that the bushy never knows.

With plenty of rock bars both up- and downstream from the ramp, this is a surprisingly peaceful stretch of water devoid of high-speed powerboats. Upstream where the river bends, skirting the towering red cliffs, the water starts to show promise for large **Murray cod** as it takes on more depth. The bank is littered with large red rocks and similar rocks would also be strewn along the bottom of the river, providing perfect hiding places for a cod or two.

CURLWAA

Curlwaa is across the river from Mildura about 1km downstream of the Abbotsford drawbridge between Dareton and Wentworth. The golden rule of big fish is that they like structure, so don't stray too far from the bridge – it's the best structure there is in this stretch of river for Murray cod, while yellowbelly stay undercover in the snags along the riverbank.

ACCOMMODATION: As much as you want in Mildura, or downstream a few kilometres at Wentworth.
For more information visit
www.visitmildura.com.au/mildura-visitor-information-and-booking-centre

The boat ramp is nothing flash – a basic dirt facility suited to smaller boats. A kilometre or so upstream from the ramp is the old Abbotsford drawbridge, and the river on the NSW side is littered with fallen trees, deep holes and channels – ideal **cod** water.

On one of my visits, most anglers were fishing the opposite bank's lightly treed flood plains accessible by family wagon. A few boats were trolling lures along that bank, concentrating their efforts around the huge concrete piles supporting the bridge. Big fish like bridges, make no mistake about that, but on this day, the best fish were in the deep holes on the Curlwaa side. By bouncing slow-trolled lures off the rock on the bottom and feeling them through the fallen timber, I got solid results with **yellowbelly** to 1.5kg and Murray cod to 16kg. When I asked a couple of locals about this stretch of the river they said: 'Oh, yeah. It's good cod water isn't it? We prefer not to talk too much about it.'

MILDURA

Mildura is in north-west Victoria, but we've included it in this NSW section as the Murray River is a NSW water, so anglers who fish the river on the Mildura side require a NSW Recreational Fishing Licence.

Mildura is 90km from the SA border and is renowned for its fishing opportunities. Every season anglers trolling the deeper sections of pool water in the Murray River crack some thumping Murray cod, while yellowbelly to a couple of kilograms are a common catch on bait and lures. Redfin, carp and catfish can also be caught.

ACCOMMODATION: Mildura is a regional hub and has plenty of caravan parks and motels, and houseboat hire is available.
For more information visit
www.murrayriver.com.au/mildura/accommodation

The Mildura area offers some excellent fishing for both cod and yellowbelly and fishes best early in the season, tapering off a bit as the summer heat soars often to the mid 40-degree range. Early morning and evening into the night are your best times in summer. As the weather cools, the river traffic slows, and the fish once more begin to feed. This bite escalates as the water temperature falls in autumn; however, the bite slows down in winter. Nevertheless, anglers with the patience to target big cod can do well in winter, and through to the close of cod season on 31 August.

Construction of the Mildura Weir and Lock 11 was completed in 1927, and since then it has ensured a stable pool system for local irrigation. It also provided a deep-water refuge with ample structure and minimal flow for large **Murray cod**. The link between pool water and large cod is no great secret, and anglers have used this information to target big cod for many years. The combination of deep water, minimal flow and hidden snags in a large stretch of river is the Who's Who of big cod real estate, and the pool water above most of the locks along the Murray provide these conditions.

As you cross Mildura's Chaffey Bridge from NSW into Victoria, there is a concrete boat ramp just upstream to the left of the bridge. The stretch of river from here upstream to Gol Gol is deep water that is often productive for anglers trolling large lures.

Above: **Nick Wells with a nicely sized Murray cod caught on a spinnerbait lure in the Murray River**
Below: **Shrimp are easy to catch and make excellent bait for most fish in the river**

Any lure that can run at about seven metres puts you in with a chance. There is little visible bank-side structure, as most of the timber is hidden from view. If you are operating a sounder, you will notice the large amount of bottom structure: Old logs, rock formations, and the occasional car, especially near the bridge, will show on the screen.

What you will also notice is that much of the fish holding structure marks up wide of the bank. This is indicative of pool water fishing, and takes time to adjust to. Some anglers struggle to get their head around fishing so wide in the river, but most of the big cod are caught at least a third of the way across the river. From a fish's perspective, wide snags see little fishing related pressure and are prime locations for big fish to hold in relative peace.

From Gol Gol, the upstream bank-side structure is more visible, and this structure provides excellent casting opportunities for both cod and **yellowbelly**. On several of the bends, large dead trees still stand where they have succumbed to the rise in water level. These are great locations to cast hard body and spinnerbait lures. A proven technique is to stay wide of the vertical structure, and cast towards the base of the trees. Most of the standing timber has shed numerous limbs over the years, and these now lie on the riverbed between the tree and the boat. You can expect a strike from the first wind of the handle to the last as the lure reaches the rod tip. When using larger spinnerbaits with upsized Colorado blades, it can pay to pause your retrieve about halfway through to allow the lure to sink. The sudden change in lure direction can incite a cod shadowing the lure to strike. Other times, the strike may come deeper in the water column as the spinnerbait flutters back down towards the snags, and into the deep-water zone.

There are many good locations to troll or cast all the way upstream from Gol Gol to Redcliffs, and beyond. You could spend a lifetime fishing this single stretch of river and not even scratch the surface of possibilities that lay hidden in the depths. There is a concrete boat ramp behind the township of Redcliffs in a reserve close to the power station. Riverside **camping** is available in this reserve.

Head the other way, and go downstream from Mildura's Lock 11, and the water starts off a little

shallow but has ample structure for casting. Good numbers of **yellowbelly** are often caught below the lock on bait and lures. Many of the snags are old nature, and big cod skulk among the hollowed remains. There are a good number of deep holes along this section, and these produce large cod on trolled lures. As you continue downstream, there are several other locations with concrete boat ramps including Merbein and Coomealla.

Horseshoe Bend, also referred to as Merbein Common, was once the site of the original pump that serviced the Merbein irrigation area. Located 10km north-west of Mildura, on the Old Wentworth Rd, the Common has a concrete boat ramp and bank **camping** available. The pump hole has produced numerous big cod over the years. Just down from the Coomealla boat ramp, anglers fishing the clay bank are often rewarded with good catches of yellowbelly. This is also a good location to troll a lure for cod. There is 53km of pool water to fish between Mildura and Wentworth at Lock 10, and all of it a chance.

Near Wentworth, Cowra Station is a popular troll run marked with patches of rock and some deep timber snags. This stretch of water produces good fish every season. There are dozens of locations as you continue upstream to cast and troll before you come to the Abbottsford Bridge. There are concrete boat ramps just downstream of the bridge on both the Victorian and NSW banks. Watch how far you back down the Victorian ramp though as it is not positioned far enough out, and you could easily drop the wheels off the back end. **Camping** is permitted on the Victorian side downstream of the boat ramp for several kilometres.

WENTWORTH

From Mildura, take the Silver City Hwy towards Broken Hill. Follow the Murray River for much of the way and on the left, as you reach the Darling River just before entering Wentworth, is an excellent boat ramp facility.

The Murray River from Wentworth upstream to Curlwaa produces consistent captures of big Murray cod and yellowbelly.

ACCOMMODATION: Caravan parks, motels and houseboats are all available.
For more information visit www.visitwentworth.com.au

As you work your way down the Murray, you'll find locks near most of the major towns. The locks create deep, holding water, which is especially good news for anglers chasing **Murray cod**. There's one at Wentworth, just across the river from Mildura. The town of Wentworth marks the junction of the Murray and Darling rivers. On my visit the Murray was clear and green, the Darling, however, was its usual murky self.

My introduction to Wentworth was unusual. At sea you often see birds working in conjunction with pelagic predators. Small fish are rounded up and pushed to the surface, where birds and fish alike feast together. But I didn't expect to see a similar event on the Murray River. Shags were rounding up small bream, pushing them into balls towards the surface where pelicans, terns and even a kite were able to feast on the bounty.

There are two boat ramps at Wentworth: one is in the Darling River near the Highway Bridge and another on the Murray, on the left just before the bridge as you are entering town. We had two boats and we launched at Wentworth at about 8am. I was fishing with Gus Storer, and Rod Mackenzie was fishing with my son Michael. Gus and I only had an electric motor so Rod towed us a few kilometres upstream and then we cast off the rope and started trolling.

This was winter, a time few regard as prime for cod, but according to Rod, the cod have to eat sometime. 'One thing I can guarantee,' he said, 'is that if you hook a cod it will be a good fish.'

Three hours and a couple of fat **yellowbelly** later and Rod hooked up a cod. The fish was a beauty

Above: Australia's native freshwater fish take cover in timber and often come on the bite in the predawn light
Below: Big nets are required to land big Murray cod like this 30kg fish netted near Fort Courage for Rod Mackenzie by Michael Cooper

that weighed 26kg and was subsequently released to fight another day. (There are not enough big Murray cod left to be killing them.) We missed another cod and that was it for the day. Eight hours trolling for one fish.

For all that, I suspect winter is as good a time as any to fish here. After all, I returned the following year, in the depths of winter, and a group of eight anglers caught more than 15 Murray cod of 15–30kg in a four-day session.

FORT COURAGE

Sitting like a green oasis surrounded by red Mallee sand and saltbush, Fort Courage is my favourite destination on the Murray River. Little more than a caravan park with a boat ramp, Fort Courage is about 20km drive out of Wentworth on the road to Renmark.

If you want to fish the Murray and want to go somewhere unique and fishable, this is the place. Expect Murray cod, yellowbelly and the only registered fish cleaning bench on the Murray.

ACCOMMODATION: Bunk house, cabins, campsites.
Fort Courage Caravan Park: (03) 5027 3097

Fort Courage has great fishing for families or angling groups, and it is a fine example of what a committed group of anglers can achieve.

As you drive along the Renmark Rd, the only vegetation is saltbush and lignum. This is sunburnt country; dry and flat, with a few red sandhills. I remember coming along this road after a shower of rain and having to avoid running over lizards that were drinking from puddles on the bitumen. There are tracks leading off on both sides, but no homesteads to be seen. And although the road roughly follows the Murray River, the only water you come across is the Darling River Anabranch, renowned for its capacity to produce bucket loads of big **yabbies** after floods.

The sign to Fort Courage is clearly marked and you turn left and drive for about 1km over unsealed road. It's owned by Wentworth Services Angling Club, which purchased the land when the previous owners ran into financial difficulty. The park is a credit to the club members who volunteer their time to keep improving what is already an excellent venue. It consists of about 40ha of river frontage, with shade trees and green lawns, powered van sites, heaps of unpowered sites and air-conditioned cabins as well as a toilet and shower block.

The first time I stayed at Fort Courage, we caught **Murray cod** to about 17kg and heaps of smaller **yellowbelly**. What I remember most about that first trip was the day it was too hot to be on the water. The temperature topped 40°C so along with a few other campers we spent the afternoon in the shade of the communal cooking area. On return trips, I've often spent evenings around the large fireplace to keep warm.

The emphasis in the park is on communal gatherings. The cooking area is under cover and there are several sets of tables and chairs. The barbecue consists of a large hot plate, or there are two Weber barbecues for those who prefer a roast. Even the log fire is used for cooking, as campers bring over their camp ovens to sit them on hot coals.

The old boat ramp, with its narrow concrete strips lined on either side by gutters, was replaced and there are several mooring poles along the riverbank for anglers who prefer to leave their boats on the river at night. It also has what the members believe is the only registered fish-cleaning bench along the Murray in NSW.

The fishing here can be excellent. Upstream you can go as far as the lock at Wentworth, and downstream about 40km to Lock 9, below Moorna Station. It is an ideal base camp to fish Frenchmans and Deadmans creeks, the Rufus River and the anabranch. Cod and yellowbelly are the most sought-after species, but anglers also catch **redfin** and plenty of them target yabbies at the right time of year.

Methods for Murray River

TACKLE If you are after redfin or yellowbelly, take along a 3kg outfit. For Murray cod, use an 8kg threadline outfit when bait fishing and, for trolling or casting lures, a 10kg baitcaster outfit spooled with 15kg breaking strain.

RIGS Redfin and yellowbelly can be caught using running sinker rigs and No. 4 medium shank hooks. For Murray cod, you will need to increase the size of your outfit to about 10kg.

A running sinker rig is okay, but use a leader of about 15kg breaking strain. You will need to adjust hook sizes up to about 6/0 depending on the size of the bait. The paternoster rig is sometimes a better option when fishing from shore to keep the bait off the bottom.

BAIT Shrimp, scrub worms and yabbies will attract yellowbelly. Scrub worms and minnow work best on redfin. Murray cod will take bardi grubs, shrimp and scrub worms, and have shown a distinct liking for cheese.

LURES Anglers who troll lures will find Tassie Devils suited to redfin, with bigger, bibbed lures like Oargees, Stumpjumpers, Muldoons, Poltergeist and Predatek Boomerangs a better proposition on cod and yellowbelly. Spinnerbaits are ideal for casting into and around heavy timber such as you find at Lake Mulwala.

When trolling upstream, work bigger lures than when trolling downstream. Vibe lures are popular with anglers casting for yellowbelly.

8 AUSTRALIAN CAPITAL TERRITORY

LAKE BURLEY GRIFFIN

Lake Burley Griffin was constructed in 1963 after the Molonglo River was dammed, and was named after Canberra's designer. The lake is about 11km long, 1.2km at its widest point and has an average depth of 4m. It is a social lake on the water and around its 35km shoreline where skaters, walkers, runners and bike riders make full use of the bitumen pathway.

The most sought-after fish in Lake Burley Griffin, in order of preference, are the Murray cod and then yellowbelly. Most anglers I fished with talk about nothing else, especially the cod.

ACCOMMODATION: There is plenty of accommodation available in and around Canberra. Everything from hostels for backpackers to self-contained flats.

For more information visit www.visitcanberra.com.au

There is truth in the words of poet Robert Burns: 'The best-laid schemes o' mice an' men.' Anglers know that sometimes plans go awry with fish, as well.

So it was with a visit to Canberra. Local angler Shaun Anderson was all set to take me fishing for a couple of days. Plans were going great, until someone made Shaun an offer for his boat. The boat was on the market as Shaun had a new one on order. Two days before we were to go fishing, the offer came in – too good to refuse.

'Hope you don't mind being shore based?' Shaun asked. I thought about it for five seconds, realised there was a better story angle if we caught fish walking the lake, and said, 'Let's go'.

How often do you find yourself in a strange city without a boat and wanting to go fishing? I found Canberra is a place where a boat is handy, but not a necessity, especially if fishing in Lake Burley Griffin.

Shaun showed me several places around the lake where he expected we could catch **yellowbelly** and **redfin**. **Murray cod** were out of season so we kept our lure sizes down.

First stop was Scrivener Dam. Shaun works Jackal lures and these are essentially a sinking lure, a bibless minnow with inbuilt rattles. He cast, allowed the lure to sink to the bottom and then retrieved slow through a series of lifts and an ultra-slow retrieve. He has caught fish in close to the wall of the dam, but not on this day.

Our next stop was a small backwater near the local golf course and not too far from the Governor General's house. There were a couple of yellowbelly but the fishing was slow at first.

The day before, Shaun was hooking yellowbelly to 55cm but today they were not cooperating. It was about 4pm when the action started. Shaun hooked up and several other yellowbelly rose to the occasion, following the hooked fish about and attempting to get in on the action.

A few casts after that fish was landed, photographed and released, Shaun was on to another. It was just a matter of time, said Shaun, before the fish cooperated.

Since 1980, Lake Burley Griffin has been regularly stocked with native species indigenous to the Molonglo River. The stocking has established good populations of yellowbelly and Murray cod, fish

Shaun Anderson caught this yellowbelly on a lure in Lake Burley Griffin

that were lost to mining pollution of the river in the first half of the 20th century. One of the motives for raising the level of Murray cod and **golden perch** is to balance the ecosystem by having them act as native predators of other fish.

When we finished here it was late in the day so we waited until the morning to go to another spot, Lennox Gardens. There was a Tiger boat regatta going on, several skull crews were being coached, and the pathway was a moving mass of walkers and bike riders. Saturday morning in Lennox Gardens is not the sort of place I would normally be found fishing, but Shaun rates the area as a hot spot for lure casting for native fishes, and he is right.

The shoreline consists of a rock wall, and in the water there are more rocks before the water drops away sharply. A redfin took my Spinnerbait lure, and a few minutes later up came a yellowbelly. Only this fish wasn't on a lure, or following a lure in. Rather, it was mooching among the rocks for a feed of yabbies.

'A lot of the yellas we catch in the lake seem to gorge themselves on yabbies,' Shaun explained. The fish, 45–50cm long, had no sooner disappeared into the deeper water and Shaun was hooked up again. This fish measured at least 55cm. Well built with heavy shoulders and a large belly, its skin was a golden hue on the shoulders fading to an olive green down the flank.

Later we headed over to the Black Mountain side of the lake where lawns gave way to trees and scrub, albeit fringed by the bike track, and the fishing was equally impressive.

We wandered a few kilometres along the Black Mountain shoreline of the lake, casting lures where we could between trees. When a few boating anglers came by, working the same snags we were casting to, I was pleasantly surprised to learn we were catching more fish.

Shaun had said the yellowbelly in the lake were trophy quality, and he was right. But how often do you go to a major city, fish in the centre of town on foot and come away with a good result? Canberra's feature lake is an impressive fishery, and we didn't even try for Murray cod, which can top a metre in length.

VICTORIA

Steve's
FAVOURITE DESTINATIONS FOR VICTORIA

The Garden State might not be the biggest state, but it offers a diverse range of fishing with the advantage that it can all be reached within a day's travel. The Gippsland Lakes region is regarded as the black bream capital of Australia, while East Gippsland estuaries further north offer bream and dusky flathead that rival anything available in the northern states.

In the misery of a Victorian winter there are big trout to be caught in the lakes and salmon runs along the surf. Every spring, anglers experience an annual snapper migration into Western Port and Port Phillip, where they also catch big calamari squid and King George whiting. And if fresh water is your preference there are the clear alpine streams in the north-east. In the south-west anglers can hook 9kg snapper from the Lee Breakwater at Portland or 10kg mulloway in the Glenelg River at Nelson. And every autumn, there is a run of southern bluefin tuna with fish of more than 100kg being hooked from Cape Otway to the SA border.

ACCOMMODATION

Victoria offers a plentiful and eclectic range of accommodation options, including countryside spa villas, vineyard guesthouses and self-contained cottages.

For more information visit www.visitvictoria.com

Fishing in East Gippsland offers anglers heaps of variety with a scenic backdrop

One of the state's best trout lakes
Snowy River: best action along this Aussie icon is between Orbost & Marlo
Annual salmon run autumn–winter
Mildura
Ouyen
Swan Hill
Lake Charm
Kerang
Echuca
Dimboola
Horsham
Lake Toolondo
Bendigo
Shepparton
Nagambie
Myrtleford
Mount Beauty
Mitta Mitta
Falls Creek
Anglers Rest
Kyneton
Thornton
Eildon
Omeo
Casterton
MELBOURNE
Maramingo Creek
Nelson
PORTLAND
LAKE PURRUMBETE
Werribee
Corio
Geelong
Sandringham
Bairnsdale
Swan Reach
Orbost
MALLACOOTA INLET
QUEENSCLIFF
Hollands Landing
Lakes Entrance
Warrnambool
Anglesea
Lorne
Cowes
Peterborough
Apollo Bay
Inverloch
Port Welshpool
VENUS BAY
Port Albert
Sandy Point
Port Phillip
BASS STRAIT
1
2
3
4
5
6
7
8
9
10
11
12

1 EAST GIPPSLAND

MALLACOOTA INLET

To get to Mallacoota Inlet, turn right at the sleepy little hamlet of Genoa, just inside the Victoria–NSW border.

A quality sports fishery, and undoubtedly Victoria's best water for big, dusky flathead, the inlet also produces bream, estuary perch, mulloway and tailor among others. The fishing is so good at times that when you drive up the Princes Hwy from Melbourne, it can be hard to go past.

ACCOMMODATION: Everything from guesthouses and basic campsites to motels is available.
For more information visit
www.discovereastgippsland.com.au

Mallacoota Inlet is one of Victoria's largest estuaries. The Genoa and Wallagaraugh rivers and a host of smaller creeks and streams feed the inlet. The Wallagaraugh River joins the Genoa just above Gipsy Point, and this river in turn continues down to the sea at Mallacoota. There are smaller feeder rivers like the Betka and Maramingo, as well as bays, inlets and backwaters. Mountains and heavily forested shoreline offer shelter from the elements so that regardless of weather, there is always some protected water to fish.

This part of the world is popular with tourists and highly regarded by anglers both for the diversity and quality of fish. Anglers find plenty of joy here chasing **black** and **yellowfin bream**, **dusky flathead**, **luderick**, **mullet**, **trevally**, **sand whiting**, **estuary perch**, **garfish**, **Australian salmon**, **tailor** and **mulloway**, and **prawning** is popular with each new moon in summer and early autumn.

Like any waterway, it is a matter of looking around to find the right spot. The choice is wide, with many bays, inlets and backwaters. Finding good spots is much easier if you have a boat.

For those who want to stay close to camp, excellent whiting, mullet and trevally can be caught at Mallacoota. The wharf area is popular with holidaymakers who also take reasonable numbers of bream, **leatherjacket**, tailor and luderick. Some of the more common baits include prawns, bass yabbies and sandworms, with weed a favourite of luderick.

Black bream are the most sought-after species in the inlet. In most areas, it is a matter of finding likely looking snags and fishing around them.

The Narrows area, which is a neck of water joining the top and bottom lakes, is a hotspot for bream, flathead and the odd mulloway. The best fishing for mulloway is during summer nights. Baker Bight and Swimming Point are also well regarded for mulloway.

Live bait is best for dusky flathead, and Goodwin Sands east of Snapper Point at the southern end of The Narrows, is a noted flathead area during the warmer months. Many anglers access the area by boat and then wade and cast lures and flies for flathead.

A few better known areas for big flathead include Cape Horn and the inlets to Coleman and Muddy creeks.

GIPSY POINT

Gipsy Point is well signposted on the Mallacoota Rd from Genoa; it's a signposted left turn about half way between Mallacoota and Genoa.

If you are after dusky flathead and black bream, then Gipsy Point – which marks the junction of the Wallagaraugh and Genoa rivers – offers easy access to some of the best fishing in the inlet.

ACCOMMODATION: Accommodation is available but families are advised that Mallacoota is a better option.
For more information visit the website
www.discovereastgippsland.com.au

Above: **Gipsy Point has an excellent boat ramp and pier facilities**
Below: **Black bream are sought after for their fighting and eating qualities**

There are two boat ramps and mooring jetties at Gipsy Point. The main ramp is on the north side and this has a large jetty. A smaller ramp offers access to the Genoa River on the southern side of the point.

The area features shallow sand flats, channels, weed beds and fallen trees. **Bream** can be caught near the snags and close to the bank where there is overhanging vegetation, rock walls and deeper water.

When looking for areas holding bream there are a couple of indicators. The first are scars left on snags from barnacles that have been chewed off by bream. A second indicator is fresh diggings or craters on the sandbanks where these fish have been foraging for worms, crabs and yabbies.

You don't have to travel far to find fish. Two of the biggest bream I have seen came from the rocks directly across river from the main boat ramp, and upstream about a kilometre in a small, shallow inlet just before the junction. Both fish topped 1.83kg and were caught on the same day about one hour apart. One fish fell to a soft plastic lure, the other a fresh scrub worm.

Some of the biggest **dusky flathead** in southern Australia can be found in the same area. Fish to 8kg

The waterfront is a productive destination for anglers visiting Mallacoota Inlet

have been caught on baits, lures and flies. The biggest fish are in the deeper water, but lure- and fly-fishers often prefer to work the shallow grounds because they like to see their fish. A favourite area for me is across river from the main boat ramp. A shallow, weedy area with a submerged sandbar dividing it from the river, this water has consistently produced good flathead fishing.

WALLAGARAUGH RIVER

Part of Mallacoota Inlet, to get to the river launch at Gipsy Point, motor upstream, taking the left hand fork. Alternatively, follow the Princes Hwy for about 5km past Genoa and there is a dirt road off to the right with the sign Wallagaraugh River Retreat.

The upper reaches hold bass in pools.

ACCOMMODATION: An all-time favourite, Wallagaraugh River Retreat just south of the NSW border offers cabin, caravan and tent sites. Unlike most caravan parks, the property runs on generator power, evenings only.
Wallagaraugh River Retreat: (03) 5158 8211.

The Wallagaraugh River is in southern NSW and northern Victoria. It's a big river, wide and deep in parts. Upstream, near where the Princes Hwy crosses the river, it breaks out into pools.

For anglers who regularly fish at Mallacoota, the Wallagaraugh is well known. Some fishing reports from this part of the world refer to the Genoa River, when in fact the fish were caught in the Wallagaraugh, which flows into the Genoa upstream of Gipsy Point.

In the Wallagaraugh, just upstream from Gipsy Point, there is a long stretch of riverbank snags where **bream** and **estuary perch** of 1–2kg are a realistic expectation through winter and spring. The river is a patchwork of muddy backwaters, sandbars and snags. The depth varies from knee deep to about 3m. Some shallows carry ribbon weed, making them difficult to fish. No channels are marked and due to the depth variations, you need to be careful when boating, as the channel tends to swap sides along the river.

I fished here when Melbourne and the rest of southern Victoria were subject to havoc-wreaking gale-force winds, rain and hail. On the Wallagaraugh, the water was calm. Low-lying cumulus clouds were scuttling around the ranges, but there was no wind, the sun was out and the fish were on the bite. I was spinning for **dusky flathead** with Clint Logan. Clint and his wife Debbie, both keen anglers, used to own the Wallagaraugh River Retreat camping and caravan park.

A clearing mist around dawn on the Genoa River

Drifting over shallow flats, it was difficult to relate to climate conditions at home. Nor did I care. I don't think about home when I'm fishing, and I never, ever turn the phone on. When you're out on the water there are issues that are more serious: the action at hand.

On this day, the big flathead were hungry. Clint and I were fishing from his 4.2m flat-bottomed aluminium boat, which features a built-in floor that makes these small craft stable and ideal platforms for this style of fishing. A bow-mounted electric motor gave us the ability to sneak around without disturbing our quarry.

We were offering snacks of tiny Halco Scorpions, Legends and the like. Trying to induce a strike, we would flick our lures out and retrieve slowly. Twitch, pause and crank; an action we hoped was imitating a crippled baitfish. In America they call lures worked like this 'jerk baits'. To me this is spinning, and this day everything was working. The flathead, like the weather, were cooperating and we were enjoying tight lines and bowed rods on some reasonable fish.

Flatheads are predators and I enjoy fishing for them. When a big dusky strikes, the take is aggressive and hard. The large head shakes and sometimes the fish breaks the surface attempting to toss the lure. There are more than 30 species of flathead in our waters, but it is the inshore species, such as the dusky and the yank, that offer anglers an exceptional challenge. Flathead will take dead baits, live baits, lures and flies. You can work them up a berley trail, or simply sight-fish them on days when the water is clear.

To say Clint is a keen angler might be an understatement. 'Every day I try to put some time in on the water,' Clint said. 'Debbie really runs the business, I just work around the place and take off fishing when I can.' This can annoy Debbie, who also prefers being on the water. On one visit during late winter, Debbie had given Clint the week off to fish with me. Clint told me the **bream** were starting to run and the flathead were moving upriver after a minor flood; it was a promising time. A couple of bream topping 1.6kg are nothing to sneeze at, and this water regularly produces dusky flathead in excess of 5kg.

The week before I arrived, father and son anglers Ted and Cameron Whittam caught and released more than 100 flathead, several of them better than 4kg.

Ted and Cameron left and took the weather with them. The wind blew and the rain fell for a couple of days, but Clint and I simply edged close to shore and fished in the lee of the tea trees. Our first stop was some sand- and mudflats a few kilometres downstream from the retreat, about 10 minutes by boat. We were spinning with 3kg outfits and the first hook-up was a 3.63kg flathead that scoffed a small Halco Scorpion.

When the flathead fishing backed off we went in search of black bream. Bream in excess of 2kg had been caught in the weeks before my arrival and Debbie had been doing particularly well. These are big bream by anyone's measure. Our chosen method was to use unweighted prawns and fish the snags along the river. We were unable to top the 2kg mark, but you can't complain when the average bream was about 1kg.

Grant McFarlane shows off an 84cm dusky flathead caught in the Genoa River in Mallacoota Inlet

This wasn't good enough for Debbie. There is a little bit of piscatorial competition between her and Clint, and she was chomping at the bit to get on the water to show us how it was done. With Debbie fishing with local Genoa resident Gary McCorkell in another boat, we leapfrogged each other along the river. Clint managed a fish of about 1.58kg; Gary did the same. There were plenty of 1kg fish, and Debbie went closest to the 2kg mark with a fish of 1.75kg.

Clint uses bait, lure and fly. The choice of method comes down to conditions and the species. Likely looking snags are fished with unweighted prawns for bream or estuary perch. Areas where the river shallows and there are sand flats lined with weed beds are the domains of the big duskies. Here lures take preference over the prawns. A patch of grass on the bank in front of a sand bank is always worth a cast. Nevertheless, a prawn can still yield a bream as these fish often move into shallow water to forage on overcast days. Clint has caught dusky flathead to 6.4kg (14lb on the old scale, which is the proper weight for fish among old timers) and likes to tell of the monster he lost after a 40-minute battle. As we motored along the river from one fish-yielding snag to another, Clint pointed out recently fallen trees that 'have the potential to be good **perch**- or bream-holding areas in spring'.

This pristine part of the world gets better the further away from civilisation you head. Wattle and tea tree line most of the riverbank. As the banks rise to the ranges, a forest of Gippsland grey box and manna gums takes over. One stretch of the river boasts a rainforest, with tall trees and dense scrub covered in verdant green vines. If you weren't so far south, you'd swear you were in North Queensland fishing along the Daintree. Mind you, there are no crocodiles in the Wallagaraugh, although the goannas in this part of the world can grow to a fair size.

Upstream from the Wallagaraugh River Retreat, past Johnson Bridge, is the famous Bullring. Known for its bream, the Bullring is a bend in the river with a small island and plenty of rushes and trees. The area is often very productive.

If you motor upstream as far as you can go, you reach a wall of rocks. Secure the boat on the north side of the river, scramble through the scrub and you reach the first of the freshwater pools, known for their **Australian bass**. Bass are a freshwater species and sometimes tracking them down can mean a solid slog through the bush. The more isolated and rugged the terrain, the more likely you are to find this fish.

MARAMINGO CREEK

One of the most exciting, albeit also one of the most frustrating, days I experienced in an estuary took place in Maramingo Creek, an offshoot of the Genoa River. To get there, follow the Genoa River upstream from the junction with the Wallagaraugh until you come to a fork. Take the right-hand fork and you are in Maramingo Creek.

On this day, I was fishing with Clint Logan and we were after **estuary perch**. This fish closely resembles Australian bass, but bass is a freshwater fish, whereas estuary perch live in the saltwater estuaries.

An estuary perch in a snag is the toughest estuary fish in southern waters. I have always rated yellowtail kingfish one of the most uncompromising, hard-hitting fish I have come across. These green-backed bandits strike and then dive straight for the nearest reef in a sudden power surge. The fight is often measured in seconds between hook up and bust up. Estuary perch are in that class, albeit in a different aqua sphere. The biggest and best perch (they can grow to more than 5kg) live among the heavier fallen timber, where they school or lay in wait to ambush their prey under the cover of waterlogged branches. The heavier the snag, the more likely you are to find them in numbers.

Our first snag was a fallen tea tree, across the river from a sea-eagle nest. This cluster of large and small branches was a haven for estuary perch, and a prospective nightmare for anglers. The snag didn't look difficult to fish so much as impossible. Above the surface, the needle-like shrubbery made casting difficult. Lures had to be flicked under branches through tunnels of opportunity. Getting your lure into the snag was only half the battle. Once inside that shady overhang, the lure would sink through a criss-crossed maze of barnacle-encrusted branches and you needed total control and good eyesight to direct the lure away from disaster.

Clint is blessed with lightning-fast reflexes (honed over years of snake catching) and an uncanny, natural casting ability. When questioned about the snag, Clint gave a conspiratorial smile and replied with a classic drawl delivered (deliberately I suspect) at about the same speed as a constipated tortoise climbing a sand dune: 'don't worry about it mate, she'll be right.'

Clint was casting a small prawn-imitation lure. Nine times in ten casts, the lure landed in a hole bordered by a triangular cross of logs. It was a matter of being patient and persistent. 'I know the perch are here,' Clint assured me. 'Sometimes you just have to keep working the lure to get a result.'

I clung to the prickly branches to hold the boat on station while Clint flicked his lure into a hole on the dark side of the overhang. Letting the lure sink, he gave it a twitch, lift and drop. 'You have to watch your line all the time and strike as soon as the slack starts to be taken up,' he explained. There were several misses, but no cusses. Then the hook-up came and Clint, fishing with the drag almost locked up, hauled the perch away from the tea tree badlands into open water. From here, the fight was cleaner, the fish more controllable and eventually it was steered into an Environet where the hook could be removed and the fish released unharmed: a battle won in less time than it takes some anglers to tie a knot.

When Bemm River opens to the sea, anglers do well spinning for salmon and tailor in the channel

One way of bringing perch out from a lair is to cast a lure with a loud rattle at the snag. Take the hooks off so you will not snag or hook up. When the perch come out chasing the lure, toss another lure or a fly in behind them so that the fish, already steamed up and aggressive, will strike this offering on their way back – the take will be in clean water away from the snag.

At night, the perch often leave the snags and can be found mooching along weed beds. This is when they are at their most vulnerable. For anglers who want a fairer fight in more open waters, this is a good option.

The problem with perch is that the more you lose, the keener you become to hook another one. Forget the cost of tackle – it's addictive and for those anglers with a masochistic bent, Maramingo Creek has much to offer. You will also hook good numbers of **bream** in the snags and **dusky flathead** along the banks near gutters.

WINGAN INLET

Wingan Inlet is located about 30km south of Mallacoota on the Princes Hwy.

It's a great place if you enjoy isolation and good fishing for bream, poddy mullet, flathead, luderick and, upstream in the freshwater pools, Australian bass.

ACCOMMODATION: Camping is permitted but make sure the road is open as some access roads in East Gippsland are subject to seasonal closures.
For more information visit www.parkweb.vic.gov.au

Little known but well worth fishing for **bream** and **flathead**, the inlet is in Croajingolong National Park. The Wingan River snakes its way through the inlet, which is about 2km long and a few hundred metres wide. It is ideal for kayak fishing and upstream in the freshwater **Australian bass** can be caught. Beach fishing produces **salmon**, **tailor**, **yellowfin bream** and **gummy sharks**.

TAMBOON INLET

The turn-off to Tamboon Inlet is at Cann River on Princes Hwy. Take the Tamboon Inlet Rd, veering left onto Point Hicks Rd for about 5km before turning right on to Peach Tree Creek Track, which takes you to the boat launch area and jetty.

As with all East Gippsland estuaries, this one produces bream, flathead, luderick, tailor and salmon.

ACCOMMODATION: Some private-owned holiday flats and national park campsites. There are no

shops, power or water, so campers are advised to take everything they need. The camping area has toilets but that is about all.
For more information visit
www.discovereastgippsland.com.au

The hamlet of Tamboon comprises 12 or so houses and holiday flats. The estuary isn't always open to the sea but when it is, the fishing reaches its peak. In the estuary are **luderick**, **bream**, **mullet**, **trevally**, **salmon**, **tailor** and big **dusky flathead**. Because of its remoteness, the area doesn't suffer from overfishing.

BEMM RIVER

This place is located at Sydenham Inlet, about half way between Orbost and Cann River. Look out for wallabies on the roadside as you drive in and, if you have a boat, be sure to take enough fuel to last you.

Estuary perch are caught in the river, dusky flathead, bream and luderick in the lake and, when it is open, the inlet channel can be excellent for salmon and trevally.

ACCOMMODATION: Camping, hotel and flats.
For more information visit
www.bemmriver.org.au

In estuary terms, this waterway is a superstar, regarded by many as Victoria's best **bream** and **estuary perch** fishery. It may be remote, but those who prefer not to fish among crowds regard this as a bonus.

My first recollections of Bemm River were in reading the late Jack Dyer's football report in the *Truth* newspaper. During summer the column changed from Dyer 'ere to the Bemm River report. While Dyer and the *Truth* are no longer with us, Bemm River is fishing as well as ever.

Bemm River flows into Sydenham Inlet, which is better known as 'the lake' in fishing reports from the area. Most people also call the area Bemm River after the township, but the correct name of the settlement is simply 'Bemm'.

Bemm River built its reputation on bream but is popular with lure and fly-fishing specialists seeking estuary perch and **dusky flathead**. Other species include **luderick**, which can be over 2kg, **mullet**, **silver trevally**, **tailor** and **Australian salmon**. The beaches can fish well for salmon, tailor and **gummy sharks** but access to some beaches is difficult.

The estuary covers an area of about 10sqkm and is 4km from east to west and 3km from north to south at the widest points. There are two boat ramps, but the only one worth using is at the southern arm of Bobs Bay opposite Bemm River Hotel. The boat ramp has a floating pontoon-style jetty and in 2008, the carpark was elevated more than a metre with 1400 tonnes of rock so that it wouldn't flood when the entrance to the sea was blocked, as it often is.

Dave Sturgess, who operates Bemm River Holiday Lodge, says that as with Lake Tyers, further south, the opening of Bemm River to the sea is important, especially for anglers who reap the rewards. The lake is shallow, with an average depth of about 2m. Anglers are advised to take care when the entrance is open due to strong currents, and to be aware that on windy days the water can cut up rough. While this water is best known for its bream, luderick and estuary perch are also found in the lake, where they hunt small fish along the weed lines.

The entrance channel to the ocean at the south-east corner of the lake attracts many anglers. It has the deepest water in the system and is the place to go for tailor, salmon, yellowfin bream and silver trevally.

The river is always worth a solid session for bream and estuary perch, which can be found mooching among the snags in the river and near the river entrance. The challenge after a hook-up is extracting one of these bruisers from its place of residence.

Two things you should know if going to Bemm River: the road in has plenty of 'grasshoppers' (wallabies), and if you have a boat you'll need to bring your own fuel. If you don't want to tow your own boat to Bemm, hire boats are available from the Bemm River Holiday Lodge.

Surf fishers are well catered for and Pearl Point, Pyoot Bay, Gurnai, Ocean and Binn beaches will all produce good runs of tailor, salmon and gummy sharks.

MARLO

The turn-off is at Orbost on the Princess Hwy between Lakes Entrance and Cann River. As you come down the highway to Orbost, turn left onto Marlo Rd, this takes you back under the highway.

One of the state's most productive estuaries, the species caught here include Australian bass upstream in the rivers, estuary perch, luderick, mullet, bream, flathead, tailor and salmon.

ACCOMMODATION: Caravan and campsites, cabins and motels.
For more information visit www.discovereastgippsland.com.au

In the annals of Australian folklore, the Snowy River is one of the icons. Anglers know that most of the action is in the lower reaches downstream from Orbost to Marlo where the river flows to the sea.

Lynton McCormack caught this 44cm bream in Marlo

The road in closely follows the Snowy River for about half of its 14km, and there are several fishing platforms.

The estuary takes in the Brodribb River, which feeds into the Snowy River, and Cabbage Tree Creek that flows into the Brodribb below the shallow Lake Curlip. Sought-after species in this estuary include **bream**, **luderick**, **mullet**, **estuary perch**, **salmon**, **tailor**, **silver trevally** and **dusky flathead**. During summer and autumn, **prawns** run in Frenchs Narrows on the new moon. If you want to put in some serious fishing time in the estuary you will need a boat to get to most of the places, particularly up the Brodribb River and Cabbage Tree Creek. A concrete ramp is located near the Old Marlo Road on the Brodribb and another ramp is situated at Marlo near the jetty.

Lake Corringle, north-west of the Snowy and Brodribb junction is another shallow lake similar to Lake Curlip. Both these lakes are shallow, up to about 2m deep, and are best for luderick and mullet, but fish well for bream at night.

Anyone who has fished East Gippsland estuaries would expect dusky flathead to be a dominant species, however even though some are caught, they are not in great numbers and in my experience are best sought in Frenchs Narrows back to First Island.

In the fresh water, the Snowy River has a well-established reputation for **brown trout** and **Australian bass**. The Brodribb also carries some trout. Cabbage Tree Creek is reputed to hold Australian bass upstream where there is heavy growth but you may need a kayak to reach the best places. The Yeerung River to the east, accessed via Cape Conran Rd and then Yeerung River Rd, offers bream and estuary perch and is suited to kayak fishing.

My early memories of Marlo are of being on a newspaper assignment with photographer Mark Griffin and taking time off to wade the beaches, spinning for salmon and tailor with small chrome lures. It was a memorable introduction not because of the fishing, but because it was winter and I had no suitable clothing so I stripped down to underpants and proceeded to fish and freeze. Popular beaches are near the estuary entrance, and along the Cape Conran Road, which runs all the way to the Yeerung River. **Gummy**, **school** and **seven gill sharks**, **flathead**, **yellowfin bream**, salmon, tailor, silver trevally and mullet comprise the bulk of the fish caught.

Anglers who want to fish offshore can launch at West Cape, near Cape Conran, but the ramp is exposed to the vagaries of the ocean and it pays to seek local advice as to the likely weather conditions.

Methods for Mallacoota Inlet to Marlo

TACKLE In the estuaries, a small threadline and light spin stick will suffice for most bait and lure fishing. A size 20 threadline spooled with 3kg monofilament or 4kg braid is ideal. The rod needs to have sharp recovery so you can flick a lightweight lure or unweighted bait more accurately. It is important the rod isn't too soft when fishing snags, as you may need a bit of grunt to steer a bream, bass or estuary perch away from a snag.

If fly-fishing, a 6–8-weight outfit will suit most scenarios. Work an intermediate (slow sink) or floating line with a minimum leader length of 2m.

Most surf rods are about 3–3.5m long and capable of casting sinkers or lures up to 120g. How far you cast on a beach depends on where the channels or gutters are. Some days they will be almost at your feet. An 8–10kg threadline outfit is a good starting point.

RIGS Unweighted baits fished in the snags work well for bream and estuary perch, while flathead are caught in areas where there are no snags. A bit of deep water combined with mud is often best for flathead, but they also have a penchant for weed-bed edges and sand in knee-deep water. Sinkers are a liability you can do without whenever conditions allow. If fishing from shore, you sometimes can't avoid rigging up with a running sinker rig. Always use as small a lead as conditions allow. When

Fish cleaning facilities at the waterfront in Mallacoota

working bait, it can pay to drift your offering along the front of a snag or mangrove system. Remember fish generally face out of snags and when they are hungry, or annoyed enough, they will come out and take the bait.

Luderick and mullet are usually caught mid-water. Fish with your bait under a float, and use a No. 6 hook and smaller baits for both species. Estuary perch will take baits, lures and flies. Bait fishing is similar to lake trout in that a bubble float is preferred. Use a leader of about a metre of 6kg breaking strain leader and size No. 6 to No. 4 Baitholder or similar pattern hook. For bream, use a Baitholder pattern No. 4 hook, but go bigger for flathead from a No. 2 to a 3/0. Bass are found in freshwater, often in pools bordered by rocks or fallen timber and covered or at least shaded.

Australian salmon is the mainstay species for surf fishing and most anglers fish a simple two-dropper paternoster rig. The top dropper has a surf popper or saltwater fly instead of bait, the bottom dropper a 3/0–4/0 long shank or Suicide pattern hook. For tailor, gang three or four 3/0–4/0 long shank hooks and use a whole fish for bait.

Sinker type depends on conditions. In calm water with little side drift, a bomb sinker is suitable. However, in rough water with side drift most anglers use star or grapnel sinkers, which have wires jutting out that dig into the sand. The best way to attach any

Matty Campbell with a large dusky flathead, typical of what is available in East Gippsland estuaries

sinker is with a clip swivel as this allows quick and easy changing of sinker weights to suit conditions.

BAIT Top baits in estuaries include shrimp, peeled prawn, scrub worms, sandworms, bass yabbies and crickets.

In the surf, use fresh salmon fillets for gummy sharks, and pilchards or squid for salmon. Tailor will take a whole pilchard or small mullet or salmon that is cast and retrieved slowly in the surf.

In rough water, when the salmon are running, use salted baits, as these will take more punishment.

LURES Most small hard-bodied lures work in these estuaries. Soft plastic lures have a proven record and the Vibe-style lures – metal and plastic – are accounting for large numbers of fish. It is important to have alternatives as some days fish will take soft plastic lures, and on other days show a preference for small, bibbed minnow lures. Hard-bodied lures are presented with a pause and twitch technique to imitate a crippled baitfish. For soft plastics, the presentation procedure is a simple lift and drop. Regardless of lure type, the retrieve needs to be ultra-slow for all species – unless of course they inhale the lure on the first drop after it hits the water.

Fly-fishers will find shrimp imitation patterns such as Skinners Shrimp, Woolly Bugger, Crazy Charlie or a small Clouser Minnow do well on bream, flathead, estuary perch and mullet. Luderick can sometimes be enticed to take a weed-imitation fly that is fished in a berley.

In the surf, chrome or white metal slices work as well as any lures.

NINETY MILE BEACH

In autumn, large schools of **salmon**, along with **gummy sharks** and **mulloway**, hit Victoria's beaches. **Snapper** can still be caught, along with increasing numbers of **yelloweye mullet**.

One of the most popular beaches in this season is Ninety Mile Beach, which runs from Lakes Entrance south to McLoughlins Beach. It incorporates some of Victoria's best known surf fishing spots, including East Beach at Lakes Entrance, Ocean Grange, Loch Sport, Golden Beach, Seaspray, McGaurans, Woodside, Reeves and McLoughlins beaches.

Species caught include Australian salmon, **flathead**, gummy sharks, **whiting**, **silver trevally**, mullet, **tailor**, mulloway, snapper and **sharks** including **bronze whalers**, **school**, **thresher** and **hammerhead**.

The change of tide is a peak time to fish the surf. Big predators like mulloway are best sought at night or overcast days. Smaller fish, like salmon, mullet and whiting, will bite best around sunrise and sunset, particularly if a high tide coincides with changing light conditions. Some beaches fish better on low tide, others work the opposite way around. I prefer the low tide as this gives easier access to gutters and holes, although gutters and holes can change after a storm. One week you may have to wade out into chest-high water at low tide to reach a good gutter system, the next week it could be running close to the beach.

Storms also bring weed and side drift; however a strong blow can herald several days of top conditions for the likes of salmon. Anglers who spin will have little or no problem with side drift, but weed can annoy everyone. Weed is always worse on the rising tide than the falling. One ploy that works on some beaches is to start fishing about two hours after the tide has started running off. Sometimes the current will pull much of the troublesome weed back out to sea and make fishing better.

Anglers often launch small tinnies to fish over the close-in offshore reefs for big snapper. Popular beaches where this is done include Seaspray, Golden, Woodside and McLaughlins. The same beaches have a reputation for producing large sharks, mainly bronze whalers.

The only spot you can't fish on Ninety Mile Beach is a 28sqkm marine park south of Seaspray. It starts near Merriman Creek and runs along the beach for 5km, past the outlet drain from Lake Denison, and for 3 nautical miles seaward.

Methods for Ninety Mile Beach

TACKLE An 8kg threadline outfit is a good starting point. Most surf rods are about 3.5m long and capable of casting sinkers or lures up to 120g. Casting distance is governed by gutter locations. There are days, particularly after a storm, when the surf will have carved out channels very close to shore.

Australian salmon is the most sought-after fish; it's also the easiest to catch and most numerous. A simple two-dropper paternoster rig will suffice for salmon. The top dropper has a surf popper or soft plastic lure instead of bait, the bottom dropper a 3/0–4/0 hook.

For close-in species, like yelloweye mullet, employ a standard running sinker rig and use a No. 6 Baitholder pattern hook. If mulloway or gummy sharks are more in your line then a leader of about 30kg breaking strain is used on a running paternoster rig. Hook size should be at least 6/0 Suicide.

Sinker type depends on conditions. On days with minimal side drift, bomb or star sinkers may be adequate. If side drift is a problem, use a grapnel sinker. The best way to attach any sinker is with a clip swivel as this gives you a quick and easy way of changing sinker weights to suit conditions.

A rod holder is essential – make your own out of a metre-long piece of 50mm diameter PVC tube. As well as holding your rod tip high and above the waves, a rod holder is ideal for holding the rod when baiting up.

BAIT Common baits for salmon include whitebait, bluebait, pipi, pilchard and squid.

On rough days, salted baits last longer. The best place to have your bait is in the clean water behind the wave break. Yelloweye mullet are caught in close, sometimes in the whitewater, and pipi and sandworm are the best baits. Normal procedure for mullet is to encourage them in to the area with berley, which is thrown on to the beach where waves will come over and draw it back.

For the bigger fish like mulloway and gummy sharks, my advice is to fish into the night. Catch small fish like salmon, tailor and mullet, and either fillet them or use them as live bait for the larger predators that hunt along these beaches. Tailor and trevally fillets are especially effective on mulloway, as is fresh squid. If you come across tailor and bronze whaler sharks, then you can be reasonably sure that mulloway will be about to make up the trifecta, as these three species are often found together.

LURES When salmon run, spinning is a successful method. Metal lures in the 15–30g range will produce salmon and sometimes tailor. Productive lure colours include dark blue and green with mackerel pattern backs, and chrome. The key to successful spinning is to vary the sink rate of the lure and the retrieve rate. It's a matter of trial and error until you get the formula right for the day.

It's a large lake system, but Lake Tyers has enough facilities to cater for boat and shore-based anglers

2 GIPPSLAND LAKES

LAKE TYERS

About a 10-minute drive north-east of Lakes Entrance on the Princes Hwy, turn right on Lake Tyers Rd. Follow the road all the way down to the Waterwheel Tavern, and then decide where you want to go from there.

A water that holds big flathead and big bream, the lake also fishes well for tailor and trevally. Some years snapper have been trapped when the mouth has closed over. This is the black bream capital of Australia.

ACCOMMODATION: This region is one of the most popular holiday destinations for anglers. Accommodation options go from unpowered campsites to classy hotels and houseboats. There are guesthouses, flats and caravan parks. A great family destination with, if you need it, more than fishing on offer.
For more information visit www.discovereastgippsland.com.au

Lake Tyers is one of the most picturesque of the Gippsland Lakes, being surrounded by forest. Covering an area of about 16sqkm, Lake Tyers is the smallest lake and is not connected to any other lake or river. It is periodically closed to the sea, but offers some of the best fishing in the region, mostly **bream**, **luderick**, **flathead**, **garfish**, **salmon**, **tailor**, **silver trevally** and has been known to produce **snapper** to 50cm near the Glasshouse. The two main arms, Toorloo and Nowa Nowa, provide the most productive fishing spots. Small boats can be launched from Nowa Nowa and full boat-launching facilities are available at the Lake Tyers township.

On 26 June 2007, the lake opened to the sea naturally for the first time in nine years, and stayed open for six months. The previous natural opening of Lake Tyers occurred in June 1998, with the estuary closing again by January 1999. The entrance was artificially opened in 2002 when rising waters threatened nearby infrastructure and property, but closed naturally in January 2003. When the lake opened, Fisheries Victoria stated it was an important process that maintained the ecological health of the water. The system received a good flush, reducing organic loads and enabling adult fish to move in and out of the lake to spawn.

I fished Lake Tyers with local tackle shop proprietor and publican Ian Page. Ian and his brother Ken run the Waterwheel Tavern, which has a tackle store attached. What more could any angler want after a hot day on the water than a cold beer and easy access to bait and tackle? Our first stop was in the Toorloo Arm, which starts at Mill Point and is navigable several kilometres upstream as far as Burnt Bridge. In the Toorloo Arm, melaleucas grow right down to the water's edge, and behind them are stands of blackwood and then eucalypts. Next we headed into the Nowa Nowa Arm, past the Glasshouse and the Trident to Camerons Hole, which is about 13m deep, and then to Devils Hole, about 75 per cent of the way to Nowa Nowa from Lake Tyers. It is a whopping 20m deep.

Ian, who fishes mainly with soft plastics for bream and dusky flathead, says 'it is a lake with the lot'. While many anglers come to the lake for the bream up to 2kg, Ian loves the September run of dusky flathead because 'that's when the big flathead, up to 6kg sometimes, start to move in the lake'.

On my visit the fishing was slow, but the following week, Ian sent a report: 'Fished high up the lake near Devils Hole, bagged out on bream using prawn and pilchard fillets. Fishing a little slow, moved four times also picked up two flathead in deep water on pilchard. Only three–four weeks to wait for flatties to move to bottom lake, can't wait. Got the plastics ready. The surf is excellent with good catches of salmon on Scud Missiles on light gear and the bait guys are getting their share on bluebait.'

Lake Tyers has excellent boat-ramp facilities but newcomers should follow the channel markers and seek local advice on where the shallow sand banks are. When the lake isn't firing, or you are in need of a change, hit the surf. Salmon are the main catch at this time of year but you can also expect tailor and, if you fish at night, **gummy sharks**.

The Nowa Nowa Arm also fishes well, as does the main lake. And as well as bream to 1kg, this water produces some exceptional fishing for luderick, and holds some large dusky flathead to 40cm in the quiet bays and backwaters. **Pinkies** and tailor are caught in the main lake in the early morning and late afternoon. During summer, you can add garfish and silver trevally to the species list.

My first fishing experience of this area was in the 1990s with local angler Greg Jerkins. Greg organised a couple of canoes, some fresh shrimp and a trip up the Toorloo Arm, which he assured me was 'producing heaps of good bream'.

We launched the canoes at Cherry Tree Park and proceeded to paddle upstream for about 4km. Some of the arms off the Gippsland Lakes system are like overgrown ravines and trying to find your way on foot would require a good compass, a big axe and plenty of snake repellent.

Once I got the hang of the canoe and found some balance, the paddling was easy and well worth the effort. Only a few locals knew the bream were in the area so the fish were relatively untouched and not at all hook-shy. On this trip it was a matter of paddle the canoe to a likely looking snag, park the back end of the canoe against the shore and start fishing. You know that old line 'you should have been here yesterday', well, the fishing was so good I thought it was yesterday. Every snag produced fish, but not every fish was landed. The terrain took its

A fine pair of bream that were caught on hard-body lures in Lake Tyers

toll on tackle and bream – fish capable of sucking six carefully threaded shrimp off a hook in the twinkling of an eye are masters at snag tactics.

LAKES ENTRANCE

On the Princes Hwy, Lakes Entrance is the next major town after Bairnsdale. As you go through the hills before reaching the seaport there is a lookout on the right that gives a great view of the entrance way into Gippsland Lakes.

The many jetties give up consistent catches of luderick, silver trevally, salmon, tailor and bream.

ACCOMMODATION: Lakes Entrance has all types of accommodation, caravan parks and camping, B&Bs, hotels, motels and houses to rent.
For more information visit
www.discovereastgippsland.com.au/accommodation

Lakes Entrance is an ideal base for anglers wanting to fish the region. Facilities are excellent and it is within easy reach of places like the Tambo River and Lake Tyers. The township is situated along Cunninghame Arm.

The town jetties in the Cunninghame Arm, across the esplanade from the waterfront shops, are always popular. The fishing is consistent, helped no doubt by the shellfish and fish pieces falling over the side from the commercial fishing boats that berth here. The result is a wonderful berley trail that attracts a mixed bag of species including **silver trevally**, **Australian salmon**, **tailor**, **yelloweye mullet**, **bream** and **luderick**. Bream to 2kg and **dusky flathead** can be caught from the footbridge that gives access to Ninety Mile Beach. Surf anglers can expect to catch **Australian salmon**, **gummy shark**, **school shark**, yelloweye mullet and flathead.

As you enter Lakes Entrance from Melbourne, you cross over the main highway bridge spanning the North Arm. This is a popular fishing hole. While all of the aforementioned species can be caught, the prize is some big resident bream that always seem to be here frustrating anglers. The North Arm is a regular producer of **whiting**, yelloweye mullet, flathead and **garfish**.

Bullock Island is one of the most popular fishing spots, where bream, luderick, flathead and garfish can be caught. The rock wall and jetty on Bullock Island is another popular area. **Mulloway** are sometimes caught in the channel between Bullock and Rigby Islands, and in The Narrows between Rigby Island and the mainland.

The South Channel on the southern side of Flannagan Island offers open water for drift fishing. The Reeve Channel, on the northern side, is narrower but a better option, producing good catches of flathead, luderick, whiting and bream. Nearby, Nungurner features regularly in fishing reports from the area, particularly for whiting, flathead and mullet.

METUNG

Driving towards Lakes Entrance you will come across the Nicholson River and then the Tambo at Swan Reach. To go to Metung, turn right on to the Metung Rd and follow this down and it will bring you out to where the houseboats are moored.

As with most Gippsland Lakes waters, bream are the most sought after fish but you will also hook tailor, flathead, garfish and luderick.

Metung, on the western shore of Bancroft Bay, is a major centre for the cruise-boat industry. Whether you own one or want to hire a live-aboard boat for a few days, Metung is a prime spot. Surprisingly, for a town so reliant on boating, there is only one public ramp. This is located at Shaving Point and is a single lane ramp much in demand during holiday periods.

It is a short run east from Metung to Reeves Channel. Chinamans Creek to the north of Metung, and Box's Creek, a little further east in Bancroft Bay, are worth a fish. The latter is particularly good if you

need to get out of the weather or moor your boat for the night. If you leave Metung and go around Shaving Point heading west, you run into Lake King, a fabulous fishing water that has three of Victoria's top **bream** rivers flowing in: the Mitchell, Tambo and Nicholson.

Above: The entrance to the Gippsland Lakes at Lakes Entrance
Below: Damien Domagala with a big black bream caught in the Tambo River on a hard-body lure

TAMBO RIVER

Driving towards Lakes Entrance you will come across the Nicholson River and then the Tambo at Swan Reach.

The Tambo River is renowned for the quality of its **bream** fishing. From the mouth of the river at Lake King upstream past Johnsonville and Swan Reach, anglers can access long stretches of sheltered water above and below the Princes Hwy bridge. Access below the bridge is from the road to Metung. If you want to head upstream, follow the Upper Tambo Rd. Land-based access is also from McFarlanes Rd, downstream from Johnsonville boat ramp.

If you have a boat, there are vast areas of navigable water. Wide and reasonably deep in the lower reaches, the Tambo has large shallows upstream, but is navigable for about 20km. It becomes shallow soon after the cliffs.

There are plenty of local names for favourite bream fishing spots along the river, the better known including Whelans, the Lucerne Paddock, the Cliffs, the Rough Rd and the mouth. Drop in bait anywhere there is a snag and you will have a chance of catching a good fish.

NICHOLSON RIVER

Driving towards Lakes Entrance you will come across the Nicholson River.

The Nicholson is the shortest of the three waterways in the Bairnsdale area and is more affected by thawing snow than rainfall. The stretch near the railway bridge can be productive. A scenic waterway, it has limited land-based options and lacks the reputation of the Mitchell and Tambo rivers, but average size of **bream** is about the same and the river has less fishing pressure.

MITCHELL RIVER

Bairnsdale marks the start of the Gippsland Lakes region and is on the Mitchell River. To follow the course of this river, take the Bairnsdale–Paynesville Rd, it will take you past the Silt Jetties to Paynesville. **Estuary perch**, **bream** and **flathead** are the mainstay of the catch.

The estuary section of the Mitchell River begins at the rock barrier, about 5km upstream from Bairnsdale. Bream are caught all the way through to where the silt jetties enter Lake King. The jetties look like two long arms running parallel into the lake. The southern one runs for a couple of kilometres and has a graded track suitable for all vehicles. Access is via Rivermouth Rd out to Point Dawson, and as you drive out you'll come across several drive-off areas where you can park and fish. The main river is up to 4m deep along the silt jetties.

Upstream of the silt jetty, there is a fishing platform and boat ramp. The Cut, a shallow breakthrough to Jones Bay, is located at the start of the northern silt jetty across the river. This break often produces good fishing due to the number and variety of fish that continually move in and out of the river here.

Another top spot is Eagle Point Bluff, an escarpment upstream of the boat ramp on Masons Bend. It is a top bream spot, also noted for **luderick** and estuary perch. Access is via the Old Paynesville Rd. Two Bells below the boat ramp at Eagle Point is a popular area for anglers.

Above: Cam Whittam caught these bream in the Nicholson River on vibe lures
Below: A small black bream that took prawn bait

Departing Eagle Point, driving towards Bairnsdale, the river is on your right and there are many access points for land-based anglers. As you near the town you will come across one of the most famous fishing areas, the old butter factory, before reaching the main highway bridge. The other top area is the Backwater. To get there, cross the bridge to the east side of the river and turn left. The Mitchell River often produces bag-limit catches of bream at the cut near Shadoof Lodge, and the Backwater through to the Wy Yung Bridge.

LAKE VICTORIA

Within the area of Lake Victoria, Hollands Landing is a bit off the track. From Stratford on the Princes Hwy, before Bairnsdale, take the Stratford–Bengworden Rd to Perry Bridge, Meerlieu and then right onto Hollands Landing Rd. Highly regarded for its **bream**, the waters here also produce **flathead** and, sometimes, even **snapper**.

This lake joins Lake King at the popular boating and fishing town Paynesville, opposite Raymond Island. The piers on both sides of McMillan Strait here are popular with anglers, especially lure fishers who have found the combination of boat hulls and pier pilings an irresistible attraction for bream.

Hollands Landing, just inside the western entrance of Lake Victoria, offers a caravan park, shop, boat ramp and a jetty off the main drag from which it is worth wetting a line. Hollands Landing ramp gives direct access to McLennan Strait, a 9km long channel that bends and twists from Lake Victoria to Lake Wellington.

Places to fish in the Strait include the Woodpile, a cleared area about midway along the channel. Seacombe Landing, on the south side of the Strait also has a boat ramp, but is closer to Lake Wellington.

When fishing this water be aware the current can be strong and you may need to move several times before locating schools of bream.

Loch Sport seems a bit out of the way, but offers an alternative destination for anglers fishing this lake and has excellent boating facilities and causeway access to Ninety Mile Beach.

Methods for Gippsland Lakes

TACKLE A 2–3kg outfit consisting of a size 20 threadline reel and light spin stick will cover most lure- and bait-fishing options in the lakes. When working lures, your rod should have sharp tip recovery so you can flick a light lure accurately. Even with bait, you need to ensure your rod isn't too soft, as you may need some pulling power to steer a big bream away from a snag.

RIGS Unweighted baits fished in the snags work well for bream, while flathead are caught in areas where there are no snags. Sinkers are a liability you can do without when conditions allow. If fishing from shore, you sometimes can't avoid rigging up with a running sinker rig. Always use as small a lead as conditions allow. For bream, use a Baitholder pattern No. 4 hook, but go bigger for flathead, from a No. 2 to a 3/0. Luderick and mullet are best sought using a float rig with a size 6 long shank hook.

BAIT Baits include fresh prawn, shrimp and sandworm. Live mullet and pilchard strips can produce flathead, while luderick are best sought using lettuce weed or sandworm.

LURES Soft plastic lures do well on flathead and bream. Small curl tails do well on bream, stick baits and larger shad tails are better for flathead. Both species will take small hard-bodied lures and vibes.

3 SOUTH GIPPSLAND

PORT ALBERT

From Melbourne, go on the South Gippsland Hwy through Leongatha and Foster and finally onto the Port Albert Rd where the highway goes left to Yarram.

Renowned for its big **snapper** in the spring, this water also produces **King George whiting**, **flathead**, **trevally**, **mullet**, **garfish**, **gummy sharks** and **salmon** – to name a few species.

Port Albert has become increasingly popular with anglers looking for size and variety. The huge snapper remain a major attraction, but they are just one part of the piscatorial equation. Other fish include excellent King George whiting, salmon, **bream**, **snook**, **couta**, trevally, mullet, **cod** and garfish.

The list goes on, with **dusky flathead** being caught in excess of 4kg, particularly near the sand flats around places such as Manns Beach.

The Albert and Tarra rivers flow into the bay area on either side of Port Albert and both provide reasonable fishing for **brown trout** in the upper reaches as well as **estuary perch** nearer the entrance. As well as bait, the perch are susceptible to flies such as the Crazy Charlie. The Albert River is popular as an estuary fishing venue for flathead, trevally and salmon.

The Port Albert waterway is a conglomerate of islands surrounded by channels situated well inland at the western end of Ninety Mile Beach. At high tide most of it is navigable for small boats but when the tide falls, many boats find it necessary to stay in the main channels. Moreover, while the waterway can offer sheltered water, strong currents can sometimes make it extremely hazardous so local advice should be sought before venturing out.

A two-lane concrete ramp is located at Port Albert and boats to 8m in length can be launched as the ramp drops straight into deep water at high and low tide. Smaller boats to 5m can be launched at Robertsons Beach at high tide. Further east at Manns Beach, the locals and a few regulars have use of a tractor to launch their boats, while McLoughlins Beach has a concrete ramp, which is best at high tide for bigger boats.

Anglers heading offshore for snapper and **gummy sharks** sometimes prefer to head out through Shoal Inlet or McLoughlins Entrance. However, these are shallow exits and can be dangerous, particularly when the wind is blowing from the south.

Gummy sharks can reach serious proportions in this water, both inside the bay and offshore. Gummies in excess of 20kg have been caught, although most are 3–5kg. As the name implies, these sharks have no teeth; instead they have plates similar to rays and feed on much the same type of food as rays and snapper, which is why snapper anglers often catch gummies. Although not a difficult shark to land once hooked, gummy sharks try hard and a big one will run long and hard.

Fishing techniques are the same as for snapper, although gummy sharks are more partial to a solid berley trail and are found more often in shallower water than snapper. A running sinker rig with baits such as squid, pilchards, or fish strips works okay. There is no need for a wire trace but the leader should be about 10kg breaking strain to avoid wear on the hard skin of the sharks' backs.

Port Albert also has a reputation for better-than-average King George whiting, with many of the bigger fish taken in the deeper water and offshore. Because of the strong tidal influence, a paternoster rig with a single leader of up to 1m is sometimes the most effective method. A pyramid sinker is preferred in the deeper areas where the current is very strong. Instead of casting out and leaving the bait to sit on the seabed, anglers drop their bait to the bottom and then lift it and allow it to drop a little further behind the boat. This is done several times before the bait is retrieved and checked. When the strike comes, it will often be at the top of the lift, the whiting having followed the bait.

A quality boat ramp plus great fishing for snapper, King George whiting, salmon and gummy sharks make Port Welshpool a popular destination

Bass yabbies pumped from the flats are favourite bait in the deeper water while mussels also produce good catches but are best over the grass beds in the shallower water.

CORNER INLET (PORT WELSHPOOL)

The same directions as for Port Albert, except make a right turn onto Port Welshpool Road at Welshpool. Best known for its **King George whiting** and **flathead**.

The sheltered waters of Corner Inlet yield **snapper**, **salmon**, whiting and **trevally**, and the area is popular with game fishermen because it offers the safest ocean entrance between Westernport Bay and Eden in NSW. Port Welshpool is the major town and is situated at the entrance to Corner Inlet behind Little Snake Island. There is a hotel and boat hire.

Many fishable rivers, creeks and reservoirs are only a short distance inland – **brown trout** are fairly well distributed in the upper reaches of most of them, and **rainbow trout**, **blackfish**, **eels** and **perch** are also caught. The Agnes River can be productive for small brown trout and some blackfish.

The three-lane concrete ramp at Port Welshpool is well patronised by game fishermen heading into Bass Strait or down along Wilsons Promontory. Many boats head for Rabbit Island, Cliffy Island and the Seal Island group. The north-east point of the Promontory juts back into Corner Basin with places such as Freshwater Cove, Chinaman Beach and Tin Mine Cove.

Fishing the channels in Corner Basin, either from a boat or the shore is popular and anglers can expect catches of whiting, trevally and snapper.

A boat ramp suitable for boats up to 5m is situated between Duck Point and Townsend Point near Yanakie Beach. Another ramp is located at Toora but those in larger craft will need to watch the tide.

Above: Extended trailers are used to beach launch boats at Shallow Inlet
Below: King George whiting are among the sought-after species

SHALLOW INLET

Shallow Inlet is at Sandy Point. To get there, turn right off the South Gippsland Hwy soon after Meeniyan onto the Meeniyan–Promontory Rd; then right onto the Foster–Waratah Rd and left onto Waratah Rd and then continue on Sandy Point Rd. When you can drive no further you have reached Shallow Inlet. If reaching the inlet via Sandy Point or from the Wilsons Promontory side, turn from the Fish Creek–Yanakie Rd. The sand is so firm that boats are launched from the beach.

Salmon can school in large numbers but most of the fish caught are King George whiting, flathead, mullet and gummy sharks.

ACCOMMODATION: A range of accommodation is available within the township of Sandy Point, including a neat little caravan park, nestled in behind the sand dunes. Picnic facilities including barbecues, tables and toilets are provided on the foreshore neighbouring the Western Beach parking area. On the eastern shore of Shallow Inlet, visitors have the choice of accommodation at the caravan park and camping grounds off Lester Rd.
For more information visit www.turu.com.au/parks/vic/gippsland/sandy-point-holiday-park.aspx

Shallow Inlet is one of the few places in Victoria where you can launch your boat off the beach.

Coming in off the road, I was greeted by the sight of a Ford station wagon towing a 5.5m long tri-hull. The driver deftly drove across the wet sandy flats, turned his vehicle around and proceeded to extend the drawbar on his trailer. When all was ready, he reversed into the water, offloaded his boat and drove back to the dry sand area next to the sand dunes to park his vehicle. Another boat angler was already on the water, trolling for **salmon** a few hundred metres inside the entrance. On the beach next to the boat-launching area, there was just one other angler. It was a chilly day but he was well rugged up, at times standing waist-deep in water as he worked the channel edges for **yank flathead** with bait and lure.

The fishing might have been slow but you couldn't buy the view – the long stretches of sand, the rolling waves and the mountainous backdrop that is Wilsons Promontory.

As well as flathead, anglers who fish Shallow Inlet come to catch **King George whiting**, **garfish**, **yelloweye mullet**, **silver trevally**, **gummy sharks**, **snapper** and **Australian salmon**. As with all waters, time of year will dictate what you catch.

Anglers willing to venture offshore into Waratah Bay through the bar can do well. The bay is renowned for King George whiting and you can reliably expect to hook all Bass Strait species, including snapper, **sand flathead** and **barracouta**. The more daring may want to head to Glennie Islands chasing big **yellowtail kingfish**.

The first I heard of the big yellowtail schools at Glennie Islands was from a diver friend Rob Torelli. Rob, a six-times Australian Open Spearfishing Champion, is a free diver, meaning he doesn't use air tanks, and is one of a small band of skindivers who call themselves blue-water hunters. He gets in the water with a spear gun, starts up a berley trail, targets the species he wants, and then spears it. Some anglers probably look down their noses at this style of fishing, but Rob has always been selective.

Kings are both highly regarded and keenly sought because they are fish with a huge reputation for speed, tough fighting and excellent eating qualities – a true sportfish that experienced anglers know will test them out. On Australia Day 2008, Rob and his mate, Jozef Bednaret launched at Shallow Inlet and went to the Glennie Islands.

Rob reckons the schools of kingfish encountered over the 2009 Australia Day weekend were 'consistently bigger than any schools I have seen for 30 years'. Averaging about 15–20kg, they were feeding on large schools of cowanyoung and arrow squid.

Each diver landed a kingfish: Jozef's weighing 19.6kg and Rob's 17.35kg. Jozef's was the largest fish of any species ever taken by a spearfisher in Victoria and exceeded a 25-year-old record.

ANDERSON INLET

To reach Anderson Inlet follow the Bass Hwy past Western Port, through Wonthaggi to Inverloch. The inlet is a bit of a gem when you take in the Tarwin River as well. The inlet produces **salmon**, **King George whiting**, **silver trevally**, **pinkies** and **gummy sharks**.

Some would argue that Anderson Inlet isn't an estuary but a bay. It has three creeks, Screw, Pound and Cherry Tree, plus the Tarwin River flowing into it. The inlet is shallow and tidal. The entrance looks wide, but the actual channel is situated along the Inverloch shoreline.

Fisheries Victoria found 48 fish species in Anderson Inlet, including one of the healthiest populations of **estuary perch** in the state. Other species include pinkies, King George whiting, gummy sharks, **flathead**, salmon, silver trevally and sometimes **mulloway**.

During winter, salmon can run well in the inlet and anglers trolling metal lures do well on the Point Smythe side. Shore-based anglers often hook salmon after walking along the beach near the entrance and spinning.

From about October there is a run of **snapper** in Anderson Inlet that can reach up the main channel, sometimes extending past Maher's Landing to the lower reaches of the Tarwin River.

The bottom part of the inlet is generally the most productive. The shallow weed beds, interspersed with sand patches, sometimes offer good catches of snapper.

There is an exposed boat ramp at Mahers Landing and another at Inverloch. The Inverloch ramp is capable of handling two boats at a time and has a mooring jetty that is a popular fishing destination. If intending to go boating in the inlet, seek local advice as to the location of sandbars and mud banks.

TARWIN RIVER/VENUS BAY

Both of these places are located at the eastern end of Anderson Inlet, connected by a sealed road that follows the inlet shoreline around.

There are fishing platforms and a small boat ramp on the Tarwin River. It is the only Victorian estuarine water dominated by estuary perch rather than black bream. Venus Bay has five surf beaches, all numbered and signposted.

ACCOMMODATION: For more information visit www.promcountry.com.au

Estuary perch are the saltwater equivalent of Australian bass, and are highly regarded as sport fish. The Tarwin River is among the more exalted of Victoria's estuary systems with a solid reputation for producing estuary perch. It flows into Anderson Inlet.

Estuary perch, like this one caught by Martin Fellows, are the main target species in the Tarwin River

You would think it was a sure bet for black bream, but very few are caught compared to other estuaries where bream are the dominant species.

Estuary perch in this system can be unpredictable. Sometimes you will find them waiting in ambush in snags; on other days, they might be hunting along weed beds or on the channel edges. There are times when the perch work together in schools, stacking up like a pyramid, and other times when they hunt on their own. As a rule the bigger fish seem to travel in pairs.

During winter, the perch migrate to the estuary system of the Tarwin River to spawn. It is the opposite to the movement of black bream. During the warmer months, you will find the perch up the river, sometimes several kilometres above the main highway bridge.

On very high tides in the evening, look for newly covered grass flats at the mouth of the river. It is a good opportunity to work surface lures.

If you have success with estuary perch be aware of the razor-sharp cutters on the gill plates that can easily inflict painful cuts on the unwary angler.

Anglers fishing the river from shore will find easy bank access, as there are several purpose-built fishing platforms between the highway bridge and the boat ramp at Lower Tarwin. The boat ramp is narrow and can be very slippery at low tide.

The estuary has many shallow sandbars so if you are unfamiliar with the area take things nice and easy, particularly near the mouth of the river.

Victoria's annual run of **Australian salmon** hits the surf beaches in autumn and runs through the winter. South Gippsland beaches are traditionally among the hottest for salmon action. Winter sees beaches from Woolamai on Phillip Island through to Waratah Bay near Wilsons Promontory packed with anglers wearing waders and wielding long rods.

One of the most consistent areas is at Venus Bay where anglers can choose from five beaches, aptly named Beach Nos. 1–5.

I fished Beach No. 4 with local tackle shop proprietor David Walsh. When we arrived, there

There are five beaches numbered Nos. 1–5 at Venus Bay; this is beach No. 4 where the salmon are running

were already a couple of dozen anglers, spread across 300m or so of beach, most standing close to the access steps where there were several obvious gutters. The action of the surf carves out channels or gutters along the beaches, and these are easily distinguished by the darker appearance of the water. Waves rarely break over the deeper water – the roll comes in until it reaches the shallow edge of a gutter, then rises to break on shore.

Dave said the top time to fish the beaches was a couple of hours either side of high tide. First and last light was always good, but the fish seemed to move in and feed best around the top of the tide.

'One reason for this is the pipis,' Dave said. 'The water digs them out of their holes in the sand and they get washed out from shore creating a natural berley and that brings fish in to feed. Salmon do not have the dental equipment to open pipi shells but some would be damaged and opened, and this is what creates the berley.'

On this day, conditions were relatively calm and we didn't catch as many salmon as we would like. Experienced surf fishers will tell you they prefer a sea that is dumping waves and providing rough water as cover for salmon hunting small baitfish. Dave said July was, historically at least, the best month for salmon fishing on these beaches.

In winter, Venus Bay beaches produce salmon to 2.5kg, and during the night **gummy sharks** to 12kg are sometimes caught, usually with salmon fillet. Over the summer months, **sand flathead** to 50cm and **snapper** to 2kg can be caught.

Dave told the story of a whale being washed on to the beach during the warmer months: 'It was buried, but the waves dug it out again and the only way we could fish was with handkerchiefs over our mouths and noses to block the stench,' he said. 'Still, the fishing made the discomfort worthwhile. One angler managed to catch snapper to 5kg, and on either side of the whale carcass anglers were fishing for sharks.'

For anglers visiting Venus Bay, the most difficult beaches to access in terms of the walk-in are Beaches 3 and 5. The rest are an easy walk down some steps.

Methods for South Gippsland

TACKLE In the surf, the big question is whether you have the right gear. An 8–10kg threadline outfit is a good starting point. Most surf rods are about 3–3.5m long and capable of casting sinkers or lures up to 120g. Solid-tip rods dominate the market, but for my money are too soft on the tip and lack the recovery that assists with casting. Rod blank taper and construction determine distance, not the weight of the rod, which is why carbon fibre is popular. Not only is it considerably lighter, it has better recovery when casting, giving increased distance with lighter weights.

Australian salmon is the mainstay species and most anglers fish a simple two-dropper paternoster rig. The top dropper has a surf popper or saltwater fly instead of bait, the bottom dropper a 3/0–4/0 long shank or Suicide pattern hook. Sinker type depends on conditions. In calm water with little side drift, a bomb sinker is suitable. In rough water with side drift, most anglers use star or grapnel sinkers.

For estuary fishing, a 3kg outfit consisting of a size 20 threadline reel and light spin stick with a sharp action and plenty of recovery will cover most lure and bait fishing. It pays to avoid soft rods, as you will need some pulling power to steer the perch away from the snags.

Unweighted baits fished in the snags work well. Some anglers prefer to use bubble floats and drift them along the front of snags or weed beds. Use a Baitholder pattern No. 4 hook, but be prepared to downsize the hook to a No. 6 if using shrimp.

In the bays, a 3kg outfit consisting of a size 20 threadline reel and light spin stick with a sharp action and plenty of recovery will cover bait and lure fishing, including salmon. If gummy sharks or snapper are your target species, upsize your outfit to about 8kg.

A running paternoster rig will suffice for the gummy sharks. There is no need for a heavy leader, as they have no teeth. Use 4/0–6/0 Suicide pattern hooks.

Whiting and silver trevally can be caught fishing a running sinker rig with the bait on the bottom for whiting, and off the bottom for the trevally. If mullet or garfish are your target species, fish with a float and set your bait about a metre below the surface.

BAIT In the surf, preferred baits are fresh salmon fillets for gummy sharks and pilchards or squid for salmon. In rough water, when the salmon are running, use salted baits.

Salmon fillets and fresh squid are excellent baits for gummy sharks.

Bass yabbies are the best all-round bait and these can be sourced on the shallow mud flats with a bait pump. Other recommended baits to use include pipi, prawn, sandworm and mussel. Whitebait and pilchard strips will produce salmon, silver trevally and pinkies.

In the estuaries, baits like prawn, bass yabbies, crickets, scrub worms, grubs, shrimp and crickets will entice a strike.

LURES Small soft plastic and hard-bodied lures will attract perch to the hook. Estuary perch have a large mouth and will take 120mm long lures at times. Hard-bodied lures are presented with a pause and twitch technique to imitate a crippled baitfish; for soft plastics, a simple lift and drop procedure usually works. Regardless of lure type, the retrieve needs to be ultra slow. They will also attack flies such as Clouser Minnows and Bream Bunnies.

Most soft plastic lures will attract flathead. Fly-fishers tend to work flies like the Clouser Minnow, Crazy Charlie and Lefty Deceiver. Small hard-bodied lures also work on the flathead and salmon in the shallow areas. In deeper water, opt for metal jigs such as the Lazer, Halco Twisty or simple chrome slices. Lure weight should be chosen for casting to suit your outfit.

Cowes jetty is a popular fishing spot on Phillip Island in Western Port

4 WESTERN PORT

There are two highways out of Melbourne. Drive to Cranbourne and then onto the South Gippsland Hwy, which will take you down the east side past Corinella, San Remo and then to Cowes on Phillip Island. To go down the west side, to Hastings and Flinders, from Cranbourne take the Frankston Rd, then left onto Dandenong–Hastings Rd, then four roundabouts later take Flinders Rd.

Big King George whiting, big snapper, big gummy sharks and big squid. No bay in Victoria is so dominated by fish that are bigger than average.

ACCOMMODATION: For more information visit www.takeabreak.com.au/WesternPort/BaysandPeninsulas/accomodation

Western Port, about 60km south-east of Melbourne, is different in many ways from Port Phillip. It is about 40km long and almost 35km across at its widest, creating an area of water less than half that of Port Phillip. French Island in the centre and Philip Island at the entrance take up a large area.

Western Port is tricky water and inexperienced anglers should seek guidance when making a first foray here. The bay has a tidal flow that can push water through the eastern entrance at up to 7 knots, so even with 170–280g leads, you have no hope of hitting bottom in the shipping channel when the tide is moving. Mud banks can shift and unless you are familiar with the topography, stick to the marked channels. One way of spotting shallow banks is to look for the swans – they love shallow water. Drive around channel and bank markers, not over banks. It may be longer, but it's better for your boat and motor not to hit these banks.

Many piers and jetties are scattered around the bay, with Flinders on the Mornington Peninsula ever popular for anglers seeking **squid**. The pier at Corinella, on the eastern shore, has a reputation for **mulloway** and Cowes, on Phillip Island, is probably the most popular land-based destination. Piers can also be found at Balnarring, Tankerton, Stony Point, Hastings, Tooradin, Warneet, Newhaven and Rhyll, most of which will produce the likes of **King George whiting**, **snook**, **salmon**, **mullet**, **garfish**, **flathead** and **snapper**.

King George whiting come on in late spring and stay until autumn, which is the season for the **elephant fish** and big female **gummy sharks**. Snapper can be caught October–April, but November and December are the most consistent months for big snapper. Anglers also catch **thresher** and **seven gill sharks**, as well as the elusive **mulloway**.

MIDDLE SPIT

One of the most popular destinations for boating anglers is the Middle Spit, located along the western

Alex Greer caught this large calamari squid near Flinders in Western Port

shore of French Island. Regarded as a **whiting** hotspot, it's just a matter of knowing where to go and the tide to fish.

Hastings is a popular launching point for anglers wanting to work the spit, and the shallow banks and deeper channels of the western arm of the bay. The harbour is sheltered, and a deep-water ramp enables large trailer boats to be launched without difficulty.

Leaving the harbour is another matter. The channel snakes in from a long way out, the channel markers looking more like a forest than a navigational aid. One channel marker was knocked over on a recent trip, and I'm not surprised. The markers lack lights, relying on reflectors about as big as those on a child's pushbike.

If fishing these waters for the first time, try to have someone on board who knows the location of the fish and the shallow banks. I fished the Middle Spit with Colin Tannahill, who was taught how to fish Western Port by the legendary Bill Copeland.

Colin says he always tries to fish with wind and water in the same direction. The first rule of Western Port whiting fishing is to ensure your bait is on the bottom. Start with heavier sinkers, and then adjust when required weight is determined. When fishing deep-water marks, always pump fish up with the rod and wind, otherwise you will wear out the reel.

Finding fish may mean moving about. Some areas produce best at different times of tides, either flood or ebb. The window of opportunity for a hot whiting bite may be only 30 minutes, so it is good management to shell baits all the time, and to be about 30 baits ahead for when the fish come on. 'The last thing you want to be doing when the whiting come on is shelling baits,' Colin said. 'Try to work in with your fellow anglers to ensure a bait is always in the water at the strike zone – this can be critical on shallow marks.'

When looking for whiting, Colin suggests a good rule is to fish in 4–6m of water along the bank drop-offs. 'Try along a bank every 50–100m until you find fish. I often move 20 or 30 times in a session to either find fish or find fish of a size that I am after.'

Weed is a common problem. If you can find clean water, you will improve your chances. One trick is to use a brass ring to start the leader. The ring will catch most of the weed that works its way down the line and help keep your baits clean. Always remove any weed from terminal tackle and baits before putting baits back in the water. Berley is important, use shells at slack water so that they sink to the bottom and have less chance of being swept away when the tide flows. Ideally, put the berley in a weighted bucket on the seabed, and tie it off at the anchor spit so the berley comes back under the boat in fast water.

Tanna Shallow (GPS: S38.22.392, E145.15.376) is a shallow water mark of 3–6m, at the bottom of

Middle Spit, on the French Island side. You can fish right along this bank north towards the Cut and Middle Spit.

Tanna Special (GPS: S38.20.969, E145.16.094) is above the cut on the French Island side, with a depth range of 3–6m. Another shallow mark is Tortoise Head Bank (GPS: S38.25.060, E145.16.140) around the southern end of Tortoise Head, although you'll need to move towards Cowes or Rhyll until you locate the fish.

Stony Point (GPS: S38.22.352, E145.14.005) is a deep-water mark of 12–13m with a strong tidal flush. It is best fished in the last one to two hours of tide.

ELEPHANT TRIANGLE

Fishing for **elephant fish** in Western Port has become an institution. Anglers hang out for the first signs that the fish are starting to migrate into the bay. In general terms, the Elephant Triangle (GPS: S38.26.826, E145.19.165) is in the eastern side of Western Port, bordered by Rhyll, Tortoise Head and Corinella.

The first time I fished the Elephant Triangle was with Gordon Forrester. It was a move of last resort, having spent several days offshore for no reward. The season was early for elephants, but we pulled in a few on fresh **squid**. Despite the good weather, there weren't many boats on the water that day. On my next trip, the elephant bite was in full swing and the water was as busy as Bourke St Mall on Boxing Day.

Elephant fish are sharks that ripple their fins to swim, much the same as stingrays work their flaps. Strange-looking creatures with a proboscis like an elephant's trunk, they are long and silvery, have large teddy-bear eyes and a skin colour with a satin sheen. They fight well and are delicious into the bargain. They are found in the same terrain you would expect to catch gummy shark: mudflats, sand and rubble ground. A bonus for anglers fishing the triangle is that **pinkies** and sometimes **mulloway** are hooked.

Elephants in the triangle can be caught in water depths of 4–13m. Most anglers fishing lighter tackle prefer to hook them in the shallower water as they fight better when they haven't got depth on their side.

Wayne Snooks and Kye Anderson with a 27.5kg mulloway caught in Western Port

Elephant fish fight big for their size, often near the surface like an eagle ray. Most are in the 3–4kg range – a 6kg elephant is a good one. Despite their size, they can sometimes confuse you when you set the hook. The first run can be hard and fast, and you begin to wonder whether you have hooked a snapper or a ray.

COWES TO CAT BAY

Cowes to Cat Bay, along Phillip Island, is a popular area for anglers chasing **whiting**, **squid**, **snapper** and **gummy shark**.

Cowes jetty, a favourite with holidaymakers, is a productive platform that often produces **elephant fish** (in season), gummy sharks, **couta**, **pinkies**, squid, **Australian salmon**, **silver trevally** and **King George whiting**.

Further west, the Phillip Island ramp is shallow and can be difficult for drive-on trailers. The ramp is sheltered from east or southerly winds but exposed to winds from the north or west. It lacks mooring jetties and most locals use 2–3m extension arms on their trailers. Better boat ramps are at Rhyll, which is a 5km run by water to Cowes, or Stony Point on the mainland.

About a kilometre west of Cowes jetty is a yacht club. In front of the club a drop-off line goes from 5–10m, and is ideal for pulling in squid and King George whiting on the last of the ebb tide.

Further west, near Ventnor, are two lollipop markers about 200m apart on the beach. Fish between these for whiting and squid in shallow water on a rising tide, or on the 10m drop-off during the latter part of the ebb tide.

In the deeper drop-offs in Western Port, always put baits out at varying distances from the boat. Cast onto the bank and let the bait fall down it, or cast into the deep water and let the bait sink back to the bank to attract the whiting.

Just to the south-west of Ventnor is a rough set of eddies, part of McAffies Reef, but the turbulence lasts for only 500m.

Moving on towards Cat Bay, you can fish inshore of the 10m drop-off in about 5m of water and less. The area has plenty of weed patches harbouring whiting. Fish in closer to shore for squid, but give all the points a wide berth because of reefs. Cat Bay produces squid in good numbers and has a well-earned reputation for big King George whiting.

The most productive whiting water is about 400m off Cat Bay beach, in about 7m. There are many weed beds and it is easy to be hooked up in the weed when the boat swings, so use two anchors to keep the boat stationary. Unlike many areas of Western Port, Cat Bay doesn't have strong currents so you can spread rods around and get away with about an ounce (28g) of lead.

For anglers seeking bigger fish, the channel edge in about 15–20m of water from Buoys 11–1 produces snapper and big gummy sharks. Use a depth sounder and fish just off the hard bottom in the softer ground to avoid wrasse and other pickers. **School sharks** are often caught between Buoys 1–5, so many anglers employ clear, nylon-coated wire to avoid being bitten off, and also catch snapper on the wire. Swell against tide, particularly the last three hours of the ebb, can cause problems in the deeper water. The incoming or flood tide is normally the calmest, when the swell and tide are going in the same direction.

Be aware of tides. During spring tides, the run out can be very strong and you are likely to encounter rough conditions. The period from the first quarter to full moon and the last quarter to new moon are normally slower tides. A couple of days of south-west winds can cause a delay of up to one hour in the tide change, as the swell forges in from Bass Strait.

MOSQUITO CHANNEL

Corinella is about 115km south-east of Melbourne on the eastern side of Western Port. There is a jetty, slipway and a 24-hour all-tide boat ramp. Anglers who launch their boats here regard these waters as something special. After launching at Corinella you are within 5 minutes motoring of some of the most productive grounds in Western Port. The quality fish include **elephant fish**, **gummy shark**, **King George whiting**, **mulloway**, **sand flathead** and **snapper**.

It was about 5am and the ebb tide was flowing strongly when I ventured out with Brendan 'Winga' Wing in his 4.75m boat. We headed along the Mosquito Channel opposite Corinella along French Island. The water was calm with only a zephyr of a breeze. Our bait consisted of fresh squid that Winga caught the day before on the weed beds near Tortoise Head. It was quiet and we had five rods in the water, reels set in gear on a drag setting of about 1.5kg.

Winga knows these waters well. He has caught mulloway to 18kg off Corinella, and done it

Above: Steve Cooper with a gummy shark caught near the Western Entrance
Below: A mulloway taken off Corinella in Western Port

consistently; an enviable record. This success rate doesn't happen by accident. Winga said he believes in the 'one per centers' so everything that can be done to ensure success is done. On each outing, traces are re-tied, hooks checked for sharpness and knots tested at least twice.

However, the critical factor, according to Winga, is bait. 'Unless your bait is fresh, and by fresh I mean no more than one day old, you can forget about mulloway.'

The first strike came at about 5.30am. I took the rod, felt a couple of hard head knocks typical of mulloway and the hooks pulled out. We'd come out with bananas on board, something that is anathema to many boat skippers because they are said to bring bad luck. After dropping that first fish, doubts arose over the bananas, but we were on a myth-busting exercise. Then 20 minutes later, another strike buried the starboard side rod, this time the hooks held and a 7kg mulloway came to the net.

As we fished into late morning, elephant fish started to annoy us. There's nothing wrong with elephants, but we were after mulloway. It is due to the elephants, which glow with a satin sheen, and mulloway that Winga refers to this area as the 'Chrome Zone'. Part of our by-catch comprised fast-running **eagle rays** and three large **sharks** that couldn't be turned.

SNAPPER SPOTS

Many **snapper** anglers prefer to concentrate along the edges of the main shipping channels. The deep water running along the western shore of Phillip Island from the Nobbies to Cowes (Buoys 1–13) is a proven snapper area that fishes best on the last two hours of the floodtide. The deepwater drop-offs and reefs found out from Stony Point and Hanns Inlet are also choice snapper grounds.

Some excellent snapper captures have also been made in 5m or shallower, in areas like the easternmost tip of Pelican Island off Corinella and the southernmost tip of Elizabeth Island.

The stretch from Warneet to Tooradin will produce snapper. Boulton and Bouchier channels and Joe's Island are some of the most consistent producers.

Lysaughts (GPS: S38.17.372, E145.15.184) is on the bank and has a rough bottom of about 8m with plenty of cunje. It fishes best October–December, and the last 90 minutes of either tide can be productive. The Middle Channel (GPS: S38.19.216, E145.16.352) is similar to Lysaughts, in about 12m of water, on the edge of the channel off the Middle Spit. The bottom is well covered with weed and other habitat-forming growth.

Ventnor (S38.26.388, E145.12.650) is in 26m of water, and best fished on slack water, or when there are neap tides such as on the new moon. It can produce snapper October–March.

Behind the Hastings buoy (S38.19.188, E145.14.030) on the edge of the channel is 16m deep and a good spot to fish on the turn of the tide for 2–3kg snapper.

Methods for Western Port

TACKLE Snapper tackle in Western Port is generally heavier than that used in Port Phillip. Most anglers work 15kg outfits with solid tip rods. Using braid instead of monofilament line gives the angler the chance to reduce sinker weight. The same outfit is also suited to mulloway and gummy sharks.

The odd-looking elephant fish is a common capture during autumn in Western Port

Elephant fish, in the shallower water, can be caught on outfits down to about 3kg breaking strain. In deeper water, it is more practical to use a 6kg outfit. Soft tip or quiver-tip rods are popular for King George whiting, as they are light and sensitive for bite detection. The rod should be about 2.1–2.3m long, and needs some butt power to get the fish in. Balance the rod with a small spinning reel, and spool up with 3–4kg breaking strain lines. If you fancy working lighter sinkers, use a 5–10kg braid instead of monofilament line.

RIGS A running sinker, as light as the current will allow, and size 2/0–4/0 hooks, will suit elephant fish. When you hook an elephant fish, it will sometimes roll up in the line, causing the spine on its dorsal fin to cut the line, so employ a tough, monofilament trace of about 15kg breaking strain.

Fixed sinker or running paternoster rigs are used for whiting. A popular ploy when rigging up is to use red or lumo beads on the leader to the hook. Preferred hook sizes are No. 6 to No. 4, preferably in medium shank Baitholder patterns. You will need a range of sinkers to compensate for tidal flow. Bomb sinkers 14–50g will cover most situations.

Running paternoster is commonly employed for snapper, mulloway and gummy sharks. Use a 15–24kg monofilament leader about a metre long, and rig with two hooks size 4/0–6/0 Suicide pattern. Bait size dictates hook size. For big baits like squid heads, use either two 6/0 Suicide hooks or bridle-rig the bait using a Tuna Circle hook. For smaller baits like pilchards or silver whiting, two 4/0 Suicide hooks will prove effective.

BAIT Top baits include mussel, pipi and fresh squid for whiting and elephant fish. Gummy sharks can be caught on squid, fish fillets and eel. Snapper and mulloway will take fresh squid, pilchard and salmon fillets.

5 BASS STRAIT

A highly productive water that is also turbulent, Bass Strait runs from Wilsons Promontory in the east to Cape Otway in the west. Sometime dangerous, often unpredictable this waterway is the playground for the bulk of Victoria's offshore angling aficionados. Many have even moved to venturing offshore after dark, something restricted to a limited few before the advent of reasonably priced GPS systems.

The Strait is a bar on a grand scale. Some 40,000 square miles of ocean with an average depth of 70m. It sits between two oceans, the Southern Ocean to the west and the Tasman Sea along the eastern side, both of which drop off to 4200m. Consequently, the comparatively shallow water coupled with prevailing westerly winds funnelling through between Victoria and northern Tasmania can produce short, steep seas.

The fishing opportunities are diverse. Striped marlin and yellowfin tuna have been caught at the eastern end, off Flinders Island, while 150kg-plus southern bluefin tuna have been caught at the western extremity. In between, anglers chase all manner of fish from mako sharks to King George whiting. There are a host of opportunities.

ACCOMMODATION: The Strait is flanked by tourist-orientated towns and hamlets and there are plenty of rooms and campsites available.
For more information visit www.visitvictoria.com

Calm seas and blue water. A combination you are more likely to encounter off the east coast of Australia rather than Bass Strait. Nevertheless, these were the conditions that greeted us at Gunnamatta, about midway between Point Nepean and Flinders.

'Look at the colour of the water Steve, there's just gotta be sharks hanging around in this,' said Peter Smallwood, Queenscliff-based skipper of the 7m aluminium charter boat *Big Red*. Peter is one of an ever increasing number of charter boat skippers in this state. Twenty years ago charter boats were so rare they turned heads. Even ten years ago their numbers were limited. Times have changed so much that Peter says there is now stiff competition for the anglers' dollar.

This particular day I was on board as a guest. An extra decky to help out if required, take a few pics and fish. Most of the customers fish the bottom for whatever is biting. On the way out we'd trolled **plastic squid** around the Point Lonsdale reef area, catching **salmon** for live bait for **sharks**. The exercise hadn't taken long as the salmon had been running in big numbers in the area since late spring.

The run from Port Phillip Heads to Gunnamatta takes less than 20 minutes with 200-horsepower of Yamaha pushing you along. We stopped about 6km offshore in 26m of water. Upon arrival Peter's deckhand Ben Plumridge started working up a berley trail while the customers baited up the pre-rigged outfits and started fishing.

The drift brought forth a variety of reef fishes. **Red gurnard**, **flathead** and **blue throat wrasse** were prolific. **Snapper** were proving less cooperative. The inshore reefs of the Strait can produce good numbers of reds and many anglers have shunned Port Phillip's declining fortunes to seek snapper offshore. The keep-only-what-you-can-eat ethic is alive and well. Most fish were returned.

The first decent take of the day came but after several minutes he was bitten off. It was the catalyst for Peter to put the shark baits over. Not 10 minutes passed when the angler was again hard into a fish of unknown size. This time it ran him ragged from one side of the boat to the other. The fish stayed deep and ran hard but at least it didn't bite him off. When it was finally worked to the surface the reason why became obvious, a **gummy shark**. This was no ordinary gummy though. It was 1.6m long and weighed better than 22kg, or 50lb on the old scale. Fresh flake is popular table fare down

Brendan Wing shows off a 16kg yellowtail kingfish caught off Cape Schanck in Bass Strait

this way. The shark had no pups so it was quickly dispatched, cleaned to rid it of the ammonia in its gut cavity then tail wrapped and hung over the side to keep it fresh.

As the berley started to work **slimy mackerel** and **couta** followed the scent to the stern of the boat. I started working the feeding lane with the fly. A sinking line and weighted fly soon brought rewards. Sharks of the toothed variety though proved uncooperative.

Late in the day we observed frantic action off the Sorrento back beach. Hundreds of mutton birds were on the water that in turn was being turned to a froth by a feeding frenzy of salmon. As we motored over the sounder went red, a look over the side soon showed why: pilchards. The blue water was thick with a seemingly endless stream of **silver bullets**.

Once among the feeding mayhem spinning and fly-fishing became the order of the day. Mutton birds and terns followed the splashes of the hunting schools of salmon. Below the surface hundreds of tiny **pilchard** scales, glittering like diamonds in the afternoon sun, drifted like confetti in the current. There was no need to cast the flies. Cast and retrieve techniques were less effective than trailing the fly, allowing it to sink with a slow, jerky motion. The salmon simply inhaled and were hooked. Lures were also engulfed as they sank, although it was easier and less confusing to cast these away from the boat. These fish were averaging around the 1–1.5kg mark Except for bleeders, the salmon were returned to the water as fast as they could be caught. The action was steady, if not downright hectic.

But, this is the way fishing in Bass Strait can be sometimes. For most Victorians who have spent their time fishing inshore in bays, estuary or surf, a trip offshore into Bass Strait is guaranteed to surprise. You never know what you are going to catch from one day to the next. Many of the species are very different from their piscine cousins working the shallower waters inshore.

The attraction of Bass Strait varies with the anglers' tastes. For many anglers it is the abundance of sharks. Inshore reefs produce **bronze whalers**, **threshers** and **seven gill sharks**. Most shark fishers head for the 50m line where small and **XOS makos** and **blue sharks** can be abundant.

There are a host of other fishes. **Couta** can run in plague proportions during the summer, snapper are regular captures over reef systems and **tiger flathead** can be prolific over some of the sandy areas. As well you can expect other species such as **King George whiting**, salmon and **trevally** along with a wide range of reef dwellers including **gurnard**, blue throat wrasse and **sweep** to mention just three. **Arrow squid** also run in large numbers during the warmer months.

Steve Cooper shows off a thresher shark caught off Collendina; these sharks are common in waters between 20–45m deep along the coastline of Bass Strait

Pelagic species such as **southern bluefin** and **yellowtail kingfish** can also be had. However, these fish are seasonal. The bluefin have become irregular visitors while the kings are more numerous some years than others.

A typical day out for many would be heading offshore at first light and establishing a berley trail along the 50m line several kilometres offshore. The berley used generally consists of fish scraps mixed with bran and tuna oil. Carp, because of their oily texture, are a favourite additive for the berley pot.

The first fish to appear in the trail are usually couta and these can be more than one metre in length. When they are worked into a feeding frenzy, the action will become fast and furious. Sometimes the only sign the couta are about is consistent bite-offs fishing the bottom. When this happens heavy mono leaders or wire and heavy lures up to 170g are employed. The offshore current can be strong, hence the heavy lures.

Squid are a popular bait for sharks and aggressive arrow squid will also work into the berley. More aggressive than the popular southern calamari, experience has shown arrow squid can blast their ink stream the full length of a 4.7m boat! As for the sharks it is not uncommon to wait until the quarry is right up the trail and lurking at the stern of the boat before offering a bait. Sometimes it is a matter of choosing which shark. Be warned, every season anglers return with tales of XOS makos on the prowl and of outboard legs and berley buckets being attacked.

While squid, couta and salmon are all excellent baits, the Victorian obsession with pilchards and pipis

A fishy looking rock off Cape Schanck

remains undiminished and these are still by far the most popular bait types.

The wonderful thing about Bass Strait for most Victorians is its close proximity to major population centres, and the availability of a multitude of boat ramps to get there. The charter boats operating out of Port Phillip and Western Port have made access easier for those who either don't have a boat, or are concerned their craft may not be large enough. The majority of anglers working the Strait head from ramps from San Remo, at the eastern entrance to Westernport and Flinders on the western side. From Port Phillip the best ramp is at Queenscliff but there is also a facility at Sorrento.

Working west the Barwon River estuary has two ramps, the better one located on the Ocean Grove side of the river. Access to the Strait can sometimes be difficult and the river is shallow in places with rock that can damage motors. Just outside the mouth near the orange beacon, many boats drop anchor and fish for trevally and snapper. It is not unusual to hit the jackpot here with a large mulloway.

Torquay has an exposed ramp into the ocean at Fisherman's beach. Lorne also has a ramp fronting directly on to the ocean but many boat owners prefer to launch off a more protected stretch of beach alongside the reef on the western side of the pier. Apollo Bay is a sheltered harbour and the three lane ramp here is probably the best along the coast. It also offers access to excellent grounds off Cape Otway and Cape Patton.

The Strait offers anglers a diverse range of species. It is a year-round proposition although the late spring through to autumn are regarded by most as the more productive. While other pastures may look greener, the reality has always been of making the most of what you have. In this neck of the woods Bass Strait isn't a bad option.

CAPE SCHANCK

Cape Schanck is between the western entrance of Western Port and Point Nepean on the east side of Port Phillip.

Anglers fish off the rock ledges but better fishing is had from boats.

ACCOMMODATION: Visitors can stay at the lighthouse, RACV resort or a bed and breakfast. It won't suit boat owners who are best to stay further away at Flinders or Sorrento. There are plenty of options.
For more information visit
www.visitvictoria.com

Yellowtail kingfish have a reputation as one of Australia's toughest inshore game fish. Anglers relish the opportunity for a hook up; what follows is an adrenalin-pumping surge of power, with the king invariably diving for the shelter of the nearest reef.

In the 1970s and early 1980s, yellowtail kings were prolific in and around the notorious Rip, at the entrance to Port Phillip. These were big kings, up to 35kg and, at that size, wore the 'hoodlum' vernacular comfortably. There were some wonderful seasons, and anglers and commercial fisherman alike took large numbers. Then fish numbers started to drop, until one day, the big kings were gone.

Subsequent seasons saw mainly smaller kings, averaging about 4kg, but none of the monsters of those glory years. Consequently, Melbourne anglers who wanted to hook large kingfish in Victorian waters had two choices: travel to South Gippsland and fish near Wilsons Promontory or, alternatively, drive to Portland, about four hours away.

The good news is that large kingfish are back, closer to Melbourne albeit not in Port Phillip – as far as I know – but at least the fish are within an hour's drive of the city. Western Port anglers Brendan Wing and Gawaine Blake, of Think Big Charters and YouFishTV fame, were catching kings 7–15kg in Bass Strait. These are top fish by anyone's standards. The boys were alternating their grounds, working breaking reefs and headlands starting at Pyramid Rock on Phillip Island, Seal Rocks and west along the coast from West Head to Cape Schanck.

If you think a lot of water is covered, then you would be right. Our day started at the Stony Point boat ramp at 5.30am when we launched Brendan's 6.2m *Bar Crusher* and headed for a nearby pier to catch live bait in the form of **yakkas**. The anchor was put down, a berley trail started and the yakkas attacked our baitfish jigs. Not all were landed, a one-eyed seal had a good feed making the task of hooking and landing the bait that much longer.

With the live well full, Brendan pointed the boat south and motored towards West Head where we were to start the morning's fishing. The live baits were rigged and then lowered into the water. Trolling speed was barely walking pace and the boat was manoeuvred along the edges of white water zones, caused by the 2m swells that came in green before exploding into a white froth on the reefs and exposed rocks. It was a hairy business, not something beginners should try.

Brendan explains there is no single hot spot, 'one day you will find the kings schooling on a reef near West Head, the next time they could be a kilometre offshore or down near Pyramid Rock; we fish every likely area, using the sounder to locate reefs and baitfish, knowing that eventually we will locate the kings'.

We were half way between Cape Schanck and West Head, a good 40km from Stony Point, when the first positive signs showed. The sounder blanked out with huge balls of **baitfish** below, and about half a kilometre offshore we could see an angler hooked into a good fish. He said later that he was trolling a Halco Crazy Deep when the king hit. Sadly, the fight didn't last long and the king got away, as many do.

One of our live baits was knocked but there was no hook up. Then another king inhaled Gawaine's yakka and his rod doubled over and line poured off the spool. Brendan gunned the boat to set the hook and move us away from the reef. A few minutes of hard pumping and it was all sweat and cheers as Gawaine's 8kg king was netted. It was a beginning. Two more kings were landed later in the day and several others missed.

Methods for Bass Strait

TACKLE If you intend going after kingfish then you will need a 15kg outfit. My advice is to use a quality threadline outfit suited to jigging and gamefishing. This style of outfit will allow you to cast poppers and soft plastic lures, troll and bait fish. The only qualification other than strength is a smooth reel drag and a well-oiled bail arm roller.

Docklands in the Yarra River in Melbourne where anglers catch big mulloway, bream, snapper and other species

BAIT Kingfish can be caught on lures, live bait and squid strips. The choice of live bait is wide but yakkas, slimy mackerel, garfish and squid do well. Squid strips can be fished under a balloon and they can be trolled with good effect.

LURES Soft plastic lures, poppers and large minnow will produce results.

RIGS To avoid using a downrigger, due to the sharp undulating nature of the seabed, Brendan and Gawaine use the NSW alternative, which is a running paternoster rig. A heavy sinker on a light leader, tied to an easy rig that runs along the main line, holds the baitfish deep. A sinker stops the Ezi-rig, and 37kg breaking strain monofilament leader, about 2–3m long with an 8/0 hook attached, is tied to the swivel. Sinkers are cheaper than downrigger bombs and the system works well. The live baits we trolled were bridle rigged, although some anglers prefer a simpler method of hooking their baitfish through the nose.

6 MELBOURNE ESTUARIES

The age-old adage about the grass supposedly being greener somewhere else applies to fishing around Melbourne. Many anglers who head out of town do so because they don't believe any serious fishing is possible within sight and smell of the Big Smoke, but replacing a eucalyptus canopy with one of tiles doesn't automatically mean there are no fish to catch.

ACCOMMODATION: As fits any capital city, all types of accommodation are available in Melbourne from 5-star hotels to caravan parks.
For more information visit www.visitmelbourne.com

YARRA RIVER

Mulloway are one of the most sought and least caught Victorian species. Anglers often put in hundreds of hours in unsuccessful quests for a trophy of this enigmatic species. During autumn, reports tell of mulloway being caught from beaches and estuaries. Catches are often sporadic. But many anglers may be shocked to learn that the Yarra River is one of Victoria's most consistent mulloway waters.

A couple of fishing friends rang to tell me they were going to put in some serious time on the Yarra River chasing mulloway. They'd chased mulloway in other waters but had never been rewarded for their efforts. A month later one rang to report others were catching mulloway to 15kg. The following week he managed to catch one too, a fish of 8.5kg.

Experienced **bream** anglers know this species gravitates towards cover. You are as likely to find them snug-in against cumbungi grass as hovering among the rotting branches of a fallen tree. In industrial areas, such as Melbourne's Docklands, resident populations of bream school in shadowy areas beneath piers and feed on shellfish and crustaceans that live on the piles. Bream topping 1.5kg are regularly caught by anglers working lures around the rotting pilings of old piers around Victoria Docks.

The hot-water outlet for the Newport power station, better known as the 'Warmies', is a favourite for bream. The Warmies also produces **tailor**, **pinkies**, **mullet** and sometimes mulloway.

MARIBYRNONG RIVER

In the Maribyrnong River you can catch **bream** as far upstream as Canning St bridge in Avondale Heights. Look against the bluestone-lined banks, or under bridges and mooring jetties. On a visit to the Essendon Angling Club, several members told of their successes in the Maribyrnong River. The bulk of the fish were bream, but there was the occasional **mulloway**. Many of the members fished along the river adjacent to their clubrooms, a few hundred metres upstream from the Anglers Rest.

Suburban expansion has made the river an exciting place to fish, especially for black bream. The growth in mooring pontoons and bridge supports has replaced fallen trees in providing shelter for this shy, sometimes finicky fish, and the upsurge in popularity of lure fishing, particularly soft plastic and rubber lures, has turned the river into an exciting and productive area.

I fished the river in company with Cameron Whittam who loves working soft plastics – he had caught and released up to 30 bream in one session on the river. I was surprised to find the river in such a healthy looking state and with plenty of fish. We fished near the Canning St bridge. Bream were caught near the bridge and along the riverbank both upstream and down for about 100m. When we moved downstream, to The Boulevard in Maribyrnong – upstream from the Anglers Tavern – we found the fish beneath a long floating pontoon in front of the Essendon Angling Club house. The best bream for the session topped 32cm, although there were plenty that were a bit short of legal length.

PATTERSON RIVER

The Patterson River is well known for **bream**, and walking and bike tracks on both sides of the river offer ease of access for bank fishing. The most productive waters are in the marinas between the Mornington Peninsula Fwy and the Nepean Hwy bridges near the river mouth. Angling isn't allowed in Patterson Lakes Marina, which is the middle floodgate. In the marinas, the bream hang on the boat moorings, pier pilings and poles, so work as many places as you can until you find them. A word

Snapper like this can be caught in the Maribyrnong River within coo-ee of Flemington Racecourse

of caution though: unhook lures caught on ropes, otherwise more areas will be closed to fishing.

When the weather turns foul and the bay is too rough for boating, Melbourne anglers could do worse than fishing in the Patterson River at Carrum. This is one of the most consistent bream-producing waters in Victoria, and is only a few minutes' drive from the city. The main prize might be bream, but there are also **mullet** and occasionally **mulloway**. Never mind that the river seems built-in by suburbia, this very fishy stretch of water often produces good results when other areas are shut down.

While plenty of anglers fish the river from shore, many prefer to work the entire river by boat and there is an excellent boat ramp near the mouth. The landings along the boat ramps are popular, as is the bank above and below the ramps.

The maze that is Patterson Lakes, accessed via the first floodgate, is fishable and can be highly productive. Inner Harbour Marina, further upstream, is lesser known and not as heavily fished.

The Werribee River is a more traditional **bream** fishery and the river is well patronised by bream anglers. The best fishing is in late winter through to the end of October. Bream are caught from the mouth upstream as far as you can safely navigate. Top baits are sandworm and bass yabbies.

Methods for Melbourne estuaries

TACKLE When planning a trip, have enough tackle to cover more than one scenario. A 3kg threadline outfit is ideal for bream and pinkies. Bait fishers employ softer, longer rods than anglers who prefer lures. For bait fishing, the rod should be about 2.5m long; for casting lures, a 2m rod with a sharp recovery action is better suited. If you are chasing mulloway or bigger snapper in the Yarra, use an 8–10kg outfit. A medium taper rod of about 2.5m is okay, although you may prefer a longer rod from shore. The reel needs to have a smooth drag and a capacity of about 250m of line.

RIGS When bait fishing for bream or pinkies, use medium shank Baitholder hooks from No. 2 to No. 4. Take a selection of ball sinkers and use as light a lead as you can. The rig should be a standard running sinker.

For mulloway and bigger snapper, a running sinker rig with a leader of about 15–24kg breaking strain is employed. Hook size is controlled by bait size; a dual hook leader with 4/0 Suicide pattern hooks suits dead baits, and a single 6/0 Suicide hook for live bait. A running paternoster rig works well.

BAIT Bream baits include sandworm, pod worm, scrub worm, bass yabbies and freshwater yabbies. Pinkies will take all of these as well as squid strips and pilchard cubes. Mulloway will take fresh squid and live mullet and salmon. A few mulloway have been caught on raw chicken meat. If snapper are about, pilchard, fish fillets and squid will produce results.

LURES Soft plastic lures are popular for bream and pinkies, but small-bibbed minnows and metal vibes will also produce bream. Mulloway have been caught with large soft plastics, metal vibes and bibbed minnows.

7 PORT PHILLIP

Victorian Fisheries' surveys show that every year more than 330,000 anglers venture out to wet a line somewhere on Port Phillip's 1950sqkm expanse. That's a lot of people, but it's a big bay and the level of participation makes it one of Victoria's most popular recreational locations. To cater for the boating traffic more than 30 boat ramps are situated around the bay.

Snapper, King George whiting, gummy sharks, garfish, salmon, flathead and squid are the dominant fish.

ACCOMMODATION: Port Phillip has a range of accommodation to suit all budgets and tastes. For more information visit www.visitvictoria.com

WERRIBEE

The Werribee River is popular, both as an access point to the bay and the estuary itself. Excellent catches of **whiting** and **flathead** are made inshore near the weed beds. Further offshore, the deeper reefs have a big reputation for **snapper**. If you launch your boat in the river, stay in the marked channel and don't head out for deeper water until you have passed the large pile mark, as there is shallow ground to the right. Head left and you go to Campbells Cove, at the back of Point Cook airfield and the ageing RAAF jetty. This popular whiting ground also produces **pinkies**, **garfish** and flathead.

ALTONA TO WILLIAMSTOWN

The skyline stretching around the shore from Altona to Williamstown provides an unlikely backdrop for top fishing. Industry dominates, in particular refineries, with flames burning off gases.

However, anglers who fish here know these waters are among the bay's best for **snapper** and **King George whiting**. Some of the most consistent snapper fishing I have experienced in the bay has been on the inshore reefs that run from the breakwater pier at west Williamstown to the Altona boat ramp.

Anglers with a penchant for soft plastics or saltwater fly-fishing will find wading the grass beds along the shoreline and casting lures into the shallows can produce large **yank** and **sand flathead**.

The stretch offshore from the pier to the Altona ramp features intense reef systems that hold King George whiting, snapper, sometimes **elephant fish**, **gummy sharks** and the odd **ling**. **Snook** can be found in the shallow areas, while further offshore **pinkies** are dominant during the day, with larger snapper moving in at night. Inshore, grass beds offer good whiting fishing over summer and, sometimes, **Australian salmon** show in good numbers.

If you want big snapper, head for water 15m or deeper. You won't catch as many fish, but there the fishing is more about quality than quantity. If you just want a feed, start over the rubble and reef grounds closer inshore. The fishing can be frenetic when the snapper are in the area as they tend to school over small areas.

The second, more popular ramp is at Altona, but lack of car parking during the snapper season is a problem. The refinery lights make it difficult to find the ramp at night when returning, so mark the entrance in your GPS unit. Red sticks in front of the Altona ramp indicate dangerous reef. This ground

Michael Palatsides shows off a salmon caught off Altona on a metal lure

This scene at Mornington shows the popularity of boating and fishing on Port Phillip

produces good pinkies year round, yank flathead, whiting in patches along the reef edges, **pike** and salmon. The broken ground extends as far as the Altona pier.

At the Altona boat ramp a few years back, a chap drove up in his car, opened a car fridge and proceeded to remove several large snapper, 11–13kg. After placing the fish on the cleaning table, the gent returned to his car to collect a small shovel, which he used to scale the fish. As is usual when big fish appear on a cleaning table, a crowd gathered and questions were asked. An onlooker with a distinct southern Mediterranean accent spoke up:

'Hey mate, where you catch the snapper?'

'Point Cook', was the succinct response.

'Hey Joe,' the Maltese chap then called out, 'what did I tell you? I kill you Joe; I tell you we should'a been at Point Cook.'

After cleaning his catch of snapper, the lucky angler walked past a friend of mine and, with a wink and nod he grinned and said: 'don't worry about it mate, I just got back from Adelaide.'

West of the boat ramp, Altona pier on Pier St offers shallow-water fishing for King George whiting, **squid**, snook and, during a south-easterly blow, snapper can also be caught. About halfway between the pier and Altona ramp is Millers Rd, where you sometimes come across anglers with surf tackle fishing from the rocky shoreline for snapper. This early-season fishery produces good results.

The closest boat ramp to Williamstown is in the Yarra River at Newport. It is situated at the end of North Rd in the 'Warmies' channel that is the Newport power station cooling water. It is a dual-lane ramp with mooring jetties, a carpark, and wash down and cleaning table facilities. The breakwater pier at Williamstown is closed to fishing, but many land-based anglers fish from the carpark below the timeball tower. The bulk of their catch comprises King George whiting, **trevally**, salmon, snapper, and sometimes gummy sharks and flathead.

ST KILDA TO MORDIALLOC

St Kilda Marina in inner-city Melbourne gives boat anglers easy access to excellent **snapper** and **whiting** grounds. Inshore there is plenty of seagrass and sand areas for whiting while the deeper waters offer reef areas for snapper. The St Kilda Pier has produced snapper to 9kg at night. Also expect King George whiting, **garfish**, **salmon** and **leatherjackets**.

The Sandringham to Mordialloc area is excellent for King George whiting. The fish are found in the shallower areas where there is a mix of snags and weed. Some better known marks include the horse paddocks at Mordialloc and the clock tower at Sandringham. Black Rock is a hotspot for **pinkies** on soft plastics and these are found in water a little deeper than for whiting (3–5m on average) while big snapper are found in the deeper water (11–21m). **Flathead** abound in most areas but for larger flathead, aim for marks closer in, particularly in the early morning.

CARRUM TO MOUNT ELIZA

The Launching Way boat ramp facility at Carrum is the best in the bay but during snapper season anglers who haven't launched their boats and parked their cars by about 6am have to go elsewhere. Managed by Parks Victoria, Launching Way has four boat ramps and parking for about 275 cars with trailers. To maintain order, up to four staff direct traffic.

Carrum is popular because it is safe and close to the fish. Inshore grounds will produce **King George whiting**, **pinkies**, **squid**, **flathead** and **salmon**. Anglers also head to outer reefs and deeper water of 16–20m for big **snapper** and **gummy sharks**.

I fished out of here with charter skipper Mark Kassar, among others, and he taught me about moving baits and snapper. While many anglers work bow and stern anchors, or increase the size of their sinkers to hold baits in position, Mark allowed his boat to swing and used small sinkers so that the bait was on the move. He reckons small fish attacking a bait, even flathead, can attract larger fish.

Some of the best big baits include fish heads, such as whiting and couta, salmon and mullet, whole or cubed, and squid and cuttlefish heads and strips. Preferably use big baits in conjunction with berley, but use a berley pot that can be tripped open on the bottom rather than the pot attached to the stern of the boat. Snapper are on the bottom and a berley trail started at the surface thins too fast as it sinks.

The closest GPS marks popular with snapper anglers include Outer Artificial (S38.04.560, E145.02.340), Mile Bridge (S38.06.500, E145.05.400), Chelsea Reef (S38.03.534, E145.05.273) and the Hospital (S38.10.100, E145.02.500).

Frankston pier produces a variety of species but the main ones are **garfish**, salmon, squid and flathead. Canadian and Daveys bays at Mount Eliza are highly regarded for their whiting. Mornington Pier is highly regarded and regularly produces big snapper after a blow, as well as salmon, **mullet**, garfish and squid. Inshore reefs will produce whiting, pinkies, flathead and squid while the offshore waters are well known for their big snapper. The 19–21m line from Mornington to Mount Martha consistently produces snapper throughout the season, and often into winter.

Boat ramps are at Patterson River, North Rd Brighton, Ricketts Point (beach launch for small craft), Black Rock, Mordialloc Creek, Kananook Creek and Olivers Hill, Frankston, Mornington Pier, Fisherman's Beach Mornington, Dromana Safety Beach, McCrae, Rosebud, Rye, Tootgarook and Sorrento.

PORTSEA TO POINT NEPEAN

The annual **salmon** migration into the bay is part of a chain of fish migrations including **snapper** and **baitfish** species such as **sandy sprats** and **pilchards**, as well as **krill**. For the salmon, it isn't so much the need to breed, but the need to feed that brings them chasing the baitfish. As with all mass fish movements, the salmon run begins as a trickle. It peaks somewhere around late October into November.

A marine park has resulted in restricted access to large areas of the Lonsdale Bight so these days my favourite area for salmon is in and around reef and kelp beds near Point Nepean and Corsair Rock, and along the inside of Point Nepean down to Portsea.

Fishing in this region can test the mettle of your seamanship. The Rip is notorious for strong currents, contrary seas and pressure waves but when you bring the thrill of the hunt into the equation you have a challenging scenario. The quality and quantity of fish available, up to 4kg at times, can make a trip worthwhile. A salmon of this size is a good fish and a serious challenge for the light-tackle angler working lures or flies.

Boaters need to exercise caution in this area. Small boats are not a sensible option in the Rip, and usually the best time to be fishing is either on the floodtide or during slack water. On the outgoing or ebb tide, conditions can be dangerous, particularly when wind is pushing against the tide. If there is a swell, stay away from Corsair Rock.

Salmon schools move around. Some days they can be hunting krill in the middle of the Rip, on others they may be working along the fringes of the kelp just outside the reef at Point Nepean. The best place to find them is inside the bay at Point Nepean. Amid the bull kelp, there are channels where baitfish take cover and the salmon hunt along and through these channels, ganging up on the baitfish and herding them into clear water. Anglers who fish from the Point Lonsdale pier, or along Dog Rocks beach in the Lonsdale Bight sometimes encounter this sort of event in late December or January. On these days, often late in the afternoon and always about the top of the floodtide, a dense black cloud of pilchards is seen moving inshore. This is the prelude to a feeding frenzy. Sometimes the pilchards are so disorientated they beach themselves trying to get away.

Of course, this doesn't happen all the time. There are days when you catch salmon in good numbers and the only evidence that a feed is going on is the sight of diving birds hovering above the school. The birds are a giveaway for anglers, and when the salmon are schooled and hunting, obtaining a hook-up is easy.

Most anglers troll for salmon, using cheap skirted jigs with a small ball sinker in the head. White or pink colours do well, and the hook is a straight shank 3/0 or 4/0. When you are trolling, avoid driving over the top of the school as this will put them down and then they move. Inexperienced anglers who do this can incur the wrath of other anglers.

Trolling is successful but casting lures or flies is more fun. Inexpensive metal lures like chrome slices are ideal. If you decide to do this, replace the treble hooks with a single 3/0–4/0 straight shank hook as not only are these easier to remove, the salmon are less likely to throw them. Soft plastic lures also work well but don't bother with expensive minnows, as there is no need.

Saltwater fly-fishers will find 2/0–3/0 baitfish patterns, Clouser Minnows and Lefty Deceivers work as well as any. Colour is not critical but white, or combinations of blue and white or chartreuse and white, have worked well for me. Work a fast sink line on an eight-weight outfit and remember to give the fly time to sink before you start the retrieve. A fast strip often produces more strikes than a slow retrieve.

LONSDALE BIGHT

Lonsdale Bight is the more common name used for Lonsdale Bay. With lots of weed, waters affected by current and a high level of exposure when a southerly comes in, Lonsdale Bight is one the most productive all-round fishing areas in Port Phillip. The bight goes from Shortland Bluff to Point Lonsdale, but the southern half has been hived off for a marine park.

Point Lonsdale pier can produce **salmon**, **garfish**, **snapper** and **squid**. Snapper are best after a strong blow. Anglers catch snapper here as they migrate into the bay, and again in late March and April as the fish are on their way out. Salmon are always a chance, and a dedicated band of anglers still fish for sharks from the pier with **bronze whaler** and **seven-gill sharks** comprising the bulk of their catch.

During spring, Lonsdale Bight fires up for **calamari squid**, which move in over the kelp beds to deposit their jellybean-like eggs. **King George whiting** to 44cm are caught and the first appearance of spawning snapper is usually in September, depending on the weather. Solid rains forcing dirty water out of the Barwon River will turn the water turgid and give the reds cover to enter the bay. The best run of big snapper is in October and coincides with the best of the squid fishing, although the latter prefer clean water.

Bell Reef below the Queenscliff lighthouse at Shortland Bluff can only be fished on low water. **Silver trevally** run here during the spring until mid-summer and salmon schools often bottle up baitfish and work in close to the reef. Access to the reef is by wading from the beach below the carpark.

The beach below Cottage by the Sea will produce salmon, whiting and snapper. On very low tides, the beach is a hot spot for snapper fishing at night. Most snapper are in the 1.5–2kg range, but larger specimens to 5kg can be caught.

Most anglers fish in boats, and many anchor their craft on the reef that is an extension of Bell Reef, about 150m from shore and almost directly out from Cottage by the Sea. These grounds produce some good snapper at times, although the bulk of the catch is **pinkies** to about 2kg and above-average King George whiting.

The beaches that run back into Lonsdale Bight from the pier to Queenscliff can be productive, mainly for salmon. The peak period is a high tide coinciding with dawn or dusk.

Offshore in the bight, above-average King George whiting can be found over the sandy patches between the weeds. Best fishing is from late summer into early winter.

Above: **Point Lonsdale pier on the western side of Port Phillip Heads is a favourite with anglers chasing species from calamari squid and snapper to sharks**
Below: **King George whiting grow to large sizes in the Lonsdale Bight**

QUEENSCLIFF

Queenscliff harbour has a solid reputation for **mullet**, **silver trevally** and **salmon**. In some years, large runs of **couta** can be enjoyed in the harbour, and **garfish** are a common late-autumn visitor. On the debit side, the strong current makes fishing difficult, so the best times are at the top and bottom of the tides.

On Swan Island, there's a yacht club and a golf course, and a bridge connects the island to the mainland. Yachters and golfers seem to have more rights than anglers, as we are banned from stepping ashore on what is a military facility. But if you venture past the yacht club in a boat, you will find some flats worth fishing for **yank flathead**.

My plumber, Cam Whittam, is passionate about fishing. His speciality is small lures on the likes of **bream**, **flathead** and even **mulloway** in the Yarra River. After installing a washing machine at my place, we drove to Queenscliff to flick a few small lures for **trevally**, as you do.

Queenscliff pier is a popular destination for squid fishing

There was a steady run of silver trevally in the harbour, reasonable-sized fish to about 2kg. Anglers had been casting soft plastic lures to schools as they sheltered beneath boats in the marina. When the tide stops running, the trevally move out into the channel and bay area near the Swan Bay bridge.

The new marina was being built and when Cam and I arrived, the pier we wanted to fish was roped off with warning signs about asbestos removal. About the only place we could find to wet a line was from the mooring jetties about 50m west of the old scallop and abalone building.

It turned out that Andrew Malouf, a charter boat owner who I vaguely knew, had leased the building. We asked Andrew if we could gain access to the pier. Andrew has been running his charter business out of Queenscliff since the early 1990s and still loves to wet a line at any opportunity. 'Don't bother with the pier, I'll take you guys across the harbour in my boat and we'll tie up and fish,' Andrew said. He placed a 'Closed' sign on his office door and led the way to where his boat *Reel Thing* was moored.

It must be all of 30m across the harbour channel from Andrew's office to the old wooden structure opposite. Andrew's boat was 7.8m long with twin 135-horsepower, four-stroke outboards.

We tied up, Andrew put the berley over the side and said all we needed to do was work our lures and wait. Over the years, the harbour has proven a Godsend for more than one charter operator after a day outside when the fish were not cooperating.

On this day, the tide was flooding strongly, but we were on the spot and determined to fish. 'The trevally come in on the berley, and they hang in eddies along the current line,' Andrew said. Cam's line was in the water first and consequently brought the first trevally into the boat. Then Andrew hooked up. The fishing was easy and consistent; our best fish for the short session would have been about 1.5kg.

The best lures had been small plastic grubs with jig head weights down to 1lb 32oz. If you intend working soft plastics on these trevally, offer the lure up slowly. Several little tugs, let it sink, and then another couple of tugs is all the movement required. For the best fun, use a light outfit and make sure your leader is no more than about 3kg breaking strain, preferably fluorocarbon.

Fishing success is as much about detail as about time and effort. Top anglers set aside time to ensure everything is right, from fresh bait to sharp hooks. This came back to me while fishing on the Queenscliff grass beds with whiting specialist Roger Lewry. These grass beds, north of the harbour entrance, are one of the bay's top areas for **King George whiting**.

With anchor down and the boat sitting neatly in the current, Roger brought out a cuttlefish strip, placed it on the cutting board, and proceeded to soften it by pounding it with a meat tenderiser. The tenderising process not only softens the flesh, it forces the juices to the surface, making the bait more attractive. Most anglers fishing for whiting with squid or cuttlefish do the same. However, Roger makes one more small improvement: he cuts the tenderised strips of flesh off at an angle so the skin remains behind. 'I don't like the skin, I think it detracts from the soft, juicy bait,' he said.

Like most serious whiting anglers, Roger is good at it. He put five whiting in the boat before I landed a fish but, by way of appeasing me, said: 'Don't feel bad about it, I once landed 19 before the guy with me landed his first.'

I was on the water with Roger at 6am and back at the Queenscliff boat ramp inside two hours, with our legal limit of 20 whiting each. Taking a bag limit catch in such a short time happens to me rarely. However, people like Roger achieve this regularly. An old adage says 10 per cent of anglers catch 90 per cent of the fish. I'm not sure whether there is statistical evidence to support the claim, but by my estimation on this day, it is a fair assessment. It is about following the fish, putting in the time and effort, keeping records and, above all, paying attention to small details.

SWAN BAY

Swan Bay is a small offshoot of Port Phillip. The southern extremity is marked by the Queenscliff marina, the northern extremity by Edwards Point. A large portion of the bay is designated a marine park and off-limits to anglers, but enough fishing water remains to make it worthwhile. The marine park boundaries are easy to follow. Don't fish anywhere west of the Queenscliff boat ramp at the southern end of the bay. At the top end of Swan Bay, a series of orange poles on the west side of the channel, well inside the bay, delineate the park boundary.

The main area of Swan Bay is between Point Edwards and Swan Island. Relatively shallow, it has earned a reputation for **yank flathead** to about 4kg, **whiting**, **snook**, **garfish** and **salmon** in the warmer months. It is also a top **gummy shark** fishery.

The main navigation channel runs between Duck Island and Point Edwards, north-west of the Coles Channel Beacon. A short channel runs in close along the east face of Duck Island. Many anglers know of its existence, but few fish it as access means navigating a shallow sandbar. It is worth the effort because the channel has produced gummy sharks and flathead, as well as the occasional **mulloway** and **snapper**.

The main channel continues into the bay past Duck Island to the Swan Bay jetty, which is a popular fishing haunt for all of the species mentioned.

ST LEONARDS

One of the most vivid memories for me was the sight of Tilley lanterns glowing along the front of the old ramshackle pier at St Leonards during spring. During the 1970s, from October through November, this sight was common. The lights were created by anglers who swarmed on the pier when the **snapper** were running.

St Leonards is between Portarlington and Queenscliff, on the western shore of Port Phillip.

The pier and rockwall at St Leonards is famous for the big numbers of snapper caught here during October and November

Anglers still fish the pier for snapper, but most of the old structure has been pulled down, condemned as being too dangerous. It was a fair call given that most of the planks were missing. What is left of the pier limits the scope for land-based anglers, but snapper are still caught here every year in October and November, particularly when a good blow has discoloured the water. The pier can also be good for catching **squid** that move in under the lights at night.

Most of the fishing at St Leonards is offshore and a dual boat ramp with mooring jetty is situated about a kilometre south of the pier. This facility can be crowded at weekends and during holidays. Parking space is often inadequate, with anglers queuing to launch and retrieve their boats. If considering using the ramp, be aware that it is exposed to easterly winds.

The best thing about fishing at St Leonards is its consistency. Several years back, when the **whiting** were at a low ebb in the bay, St Leonards was about the only place to find them with any regularity. Moreover, you don't have to travel far. Most of the grass beds in front of the ramp out to the Coles Channel produce whiting. Some days you may need to move around, but that goes with the sport.

Another reason St Leonards is popular with boat anglers is that it is only a short run south to the entrance to Swan Bay, and Indented Head and Governor Reef aren't far to the north.

Snapper anglers launch here and fish the heavy ground in front of the low rock wall that extends from the pier. The more adventurous make the 40-minute run east across the bay to fish the deep water out from Mornington, often passing anglers who have come across the bay from the east.

INDENTED HEAD

Two of the top **King George whiting** spots are the Cabbage Patch (GPS: S38.06.285, E144.43.175) and Seven Hills (Black Shark) (S38.06.871, E144.44.627). The most consistent area for King George whiting, the Cabbage Patch is in about 10m of water. Seven Hills also known as Black Shark, is the widest reef on the Prince George Bank, and produces both **pinkies** and whiting at a depth of about 10m.

A major difference between Indented Head and most other areas of Port Phillip is that it has small inshore reefs mixed with grass beds. Boats dominate the fishing scene and a dual boat ramp with mooring jetty is sheltered from southerly sea breezes that blow in the afternoons. The ramp is relatively shallow and best suited to boats less than 6m. Weekends and holidays often see the ramp crowded and during peak times, queues are common and parking spaces at a premium.

One reason the area is popular is the Prince George Bank. Covering an area that runs 5km north and west, and 3km to the east of the ramp, the Prince George Bank is an extensive area of seagrass meadows interspersed with sand. Regarded as one of the bay's prime grounds for King George whiting, it regularly produces catches of other species including pinkies, **calamari squid**, **sand** and **yank flathead**, **snook**, **garfish** and **leatherjacket**.

At the northernmost point of the bank is the Prince George light, now marked simply as PG. At the light, the bank drops off on to reef. The edge of the reef can produce **snapper** while the heavy areas are good for big leatherjackets. There is a kelp bed hard in against the inshore side of the light and then Dead Mans Reef runs for half a kilometre west from the light towards Portarlington. This is popular with anglers trolling for snook.

Indented Head isn't just a small, table-fish port. Anglers who want bigger fare will find snapper and **gummy sharks** once they cross the bank and move over deeper water. Two kilometres past PG light and you are in 20m of prime gummy shark and snapper water.

Even when whiting are down in numbers around the bay, they are often encountered over the Prince George Bank. You don't have to travel far as most of the grass bed areas can produce whiting. A favourite early-season snapper spot is Grassy Point to Steeles Rocks, north-west of Indented Head. Between the mussel farms and the shore, about 600m out, a reef produces good numbers of snapper in October.

Anglers need to pay heed to the cardinal marks. In a line due east of the cardinal mark (two black balls) is shallow reef, so slow down and steer clear.

The breakwall that protects the harbour at Portarlington is a favourite place for land-based anglers chasing snapper, squid and salmon

Little Governor Reef, closest to the ramp at about 300m offshore, is dry at low tide. Between Little Governor and the ramp, there is about 4m of water. Governor Reef is a top spot for calamari squid.

PORTARLINGTON

Land-based anglers are well catered for at Portarlington. The main pier runs north–south, and at the end there is a breakwater that runs west–east. **Salmon** often run along here in good numbers. **Mullet**, **garfish** and **trevally** are caught in the harbour and **squid** are hooked at the end of the pier on the western side.

Seal Rocks is a few kilometres east of the harbour, and after a strong blow, this area can be a hotspot for snapper within a kilometre of shore. If you motor north-west across the channel, a large area of reef runs all the way to Point Wilson and takes in Arthur the Great. This is a top area for **snapper**, **sharks** and **whiting** when you are in less than 5m of water.

Point Richards is to the west of Portarlington. The main attraction for most anglers is the two-lane boat ramp and proximity to King George whiting and snapper grounds. The turn-off to the boat ramp is clearly signposted on the Geelong–Portarlington Rd. The 5m wide, dual ramp can be a problem when the wind is from north or west. Boaters should also be aware of the shallow sand banks immediately north of the ramp. Many anglers use Point Richards boat ramp as a starting place for longer trips into Port Phillip.

Mussel farms to the west of the boat ramp are popular with anglers chasing whiting and **pinkies**. Fishing within the farm boundaries is illegal, but you can fish close and berley works well.

Whiting are well spread and to find them, fish in less than 5m of water where seagrass is interspersed with sand holes. Seagrass beds can change from year to year, so each season usually warrants fishing in a different location.

Snapper run right along the channel edges so you never know where you are likely to find them in good numbers. Most snapper anglers fish within a couple of hundred metres of the channel. Some prefer to fish along the edges or alternatively in the old Steampacket Channel almost directly offshore. During spring and summer, most big snapper are caught on the north side of the channel. As autumn rolls in, snapper fishing is often better on the south side of the channel.

Cam Whittam shows off a good sized salmon caught spinning off Mount Martha

The deeper water produces **flathead**, **elephant fish** and **gummy sharks**.

On calm evenings, the glow of **flounder** lights along this stretch of coast is a common sight, with many sand areas attracting flounder in good numbers. Flounder spearing isn't exactly sportfishing, but flounder are tasty and there is always a good chance of spearing some flathead as well.

Methods for Port Phillip

TACKLE

Pier/beach

For smaller fish such as whiting, garfish, silver trevally and mullet, use a light rod of about 2.5m long with a threadline reel suited to lines of about 3–4kg breaking strain, and have on hand a variety of small sinkers, swivels, and a couple of quill floats as well as a selection of hooks from No. 8 through to about 2/0.

For larger fish, such as snapper, go for a 3m surf rod and reel suited to lines of 7–9kg breaking strain. Sinkers should be ball or bean for running rigs and start or pyramid for paternoster or fixed sinker rigs. I prefer 2/0–4/0 Suicide or Octopus pattern hooks, preferably chemically sharpened for snapper. For fish such as salmon or whiting, you might find it preferable to come down to about 2/0.

Boat

For small pan-size fish like whiting, flathead, mullet and salmon, there is rarely any need to use an outfit heavier than 3–4kg unless fishing strong tidal surges where heavier leads are required to hold bottom. A quiver-tip style rod coupled with a small threadline reel is my preferred outfit. Spool the reel with braid for better bite detection and employ monofilament on the leader to the hook. Use small swivels, hooks from No. 8 through to about 2/0 as well as a selection of small sinkers.

If you fish for whiting, remember the rig is not as important as ensuring the bait is below the sinker. For

Josh Hayden with a 4kg snapper that was caught in late autumn in Corio Bay

bigger fish like snapper, a 2m rod suited to 6–10kg lines is better. Hooks for snapper should be 4/0 for most situations with a running sinker rig.

8 CORIO BAY

An offshoot of Port Phillip and the main harbour for Geelong, to get here, take the Princess Hwy from Melbourne.

It was once the wool export centre of Australia but nowadays it is better known for its run of winter snapper but it consistently produces King George whiting, snook, salmon, garfish, squid, silver trevally and mullet.

ACCOMMODATION: For more information visit www.victoria.visitorsbureau.com.au

INNER HARBOUR

Following the inner harbour around from Bird Rock you pass Avalon Beach, which is little more than a collection of old huts. There is a boat ramp at the west end of Avalon Beach and the seagrass beds between the old channel and the shore are known for **King George whiting** and **flounder**. The old channel runs into the western end of the harbour, finishing in Corio Quay. The channel will produce **snapper**, particularly in spring.

At the northern end of the bay is Limeburners Bay, one of the most famous waters in Port Phillip. The Geelong Grammar School campus looks down on it and it is better known by most anglers as the 'Grammar School Lagoon'. It isn't big. Shaped like a figure eight, with two small bays divided in part by a spit of sand, the lagoon features a channel running from Corio Bay at the western entrance, and is separated from the main bay by another sand spit. At the back of the lagoon, Hovell Creek flows in past some mangroves.

Many anglers know the lagoon for its legendary winter snapper fishing. However, it offers a diverse year-round fishery with a mixed bag of species and is easily accessible for both boat- and shore-based angling. The wonderful aspect of this water is that you never know what you are likely to hook.

My most vivid memories of the lagoon are based around 4.20am, when the light in the school clock tower went off. That was the signal for regular anglers who fished the snapper here to change all baits in expectation of a fish at dawn.

Early morning snapper on Corio Bay

The channel edges can produce good catches of **yank flathead** to 2.5kg, and the same area is used by schools of **salmon** and **mullet**. Apart from the usual run of banjo sharks, stingrays and eagle rays, the lagoon can produce King George whiting, **gummy sharks** and even the occasional **mulloway**. Contrary to popular legend, snapper have been caught here in every month of the year, not just the colder months. Be prepared to move though. Most anglers employ depth sounders to mark fish before dropping anchor.

Hovell Creek is highly regarded for its bream fishing, but these fish are also taken from the sand spit on the southern shore and most likely school around the boat moorings of the Lagoon Boat Club.

Tide and current are major factors influencing the movement of fish in and out of this water. The best time to fish it is when the high tide coincides with sunrise. Fish such as snapper and mulloway move in on the floodtide to feed on the crabs, and leave on the ebb tide. If you catch a few fish when the tide is flooding, be sure to stay for a couple of hours of the run-off tide.

Flathead seem to be resident here most of the summer and autumn, and **bream** can be caught all year. The salmon and mullet are often best from about March through to October. In some years, schools of large salmon have taken up residence and anglers have done well trolling along the channel edges or casting from the beach using small silver wobblers.

WESTERN SHORE

Taking a southerly route around the bay from the lagoon you pass a large industrial and waterfront area. The next fishable water from shore is North Shore rocks, just outside the entrance to Corio Quay. During winter, **snapper** that have remained in the bay tend to congregate along the western shore and these rocks are popular for that reason. Land-based anglers don't have the mobility of boaters, but they still catch snapper.

Some other land-based spots worth fishing include St Helens boat harbour rock wall, Griffin gully jetty, Cunningham Pier and Limeburners Point breakwater on the southern shore. Cunningham Pier is particularly popular. It is privately owned and fishing hours are restricted, but you can drive your car on the pier and fish next to it.

In winter, boating anglers chasing snapper work along the western shore, from the entrance to Corio Quay, past St Helens, along Western Beach and between the Geelong Yacht Club marina and Cunningham Pier. Boat ramps are located at St Helens and Limeburners Point.

From spring to autumn, snapper can be caught along the channel edges and in the 'Paddock', on the east side of the shipping channel. Snapper sometimes need a trigger to start feeding: a strong blow from the east that stirs up the water, or full or new moon phases. The prime time to fish is generally an hour each side of a tide change.

STINGRAY BAY

Stingray Bay on the southern shore is properly called Stingaree Bay, but many anglers simply refer to it as Limeburners, due to the boat harbour at Limeburners Point. The boundary of the bay is roughly between the Limeburners Point boat ramp and the sand spit at Point Henry that abuts the main shipping channel.

This bay produces a consistent variety of quality species. Shore-based anglers can do well off the rock walls, catching **snapper**, **luderick**, **garfish**, **King George whiting** and **flathead**. For anglers with boats, King George whiting often run in good numbers, with the best results usually coming from the Spoil Ground, which is situated along the 5m line a couple of kilometres north-east of the ramp. First and last light is the optimum time for the better whiting, particularly when this coincides with a tide change. During the day, pinkies can be a problem. The Spoil Ground also turns up some good **flathead**, mainly yanks to 2kg.

Snapper are a serious prize in these waters and the biggest snapper are caught inside an imaginary line that runs from the boat ramp to the Point Henry weather station. In other words, work inside the bay in the shallower areas for the big snapper.

The best snapper fishing is from about mid-autumn through the winter months when the stingrays have moved on. Daylight snapper are mainly pinkies, and many of these will be undersize. After sunset though, bigger snapper in the 3–6kg bracket come and go. The run of fish isn't as consistent as some anglers like but it provides an opportunity to catch snapper through winter.

One of the quirks of this bay is the tidal flow. It doesn't seem to matter whether the tide is on the flood or the ebb; water movement is always east towards Point Henry.

The boat ramp consists of a double and a single ramp and will easily handle boats up to about 7m. There are pontoon jetties to tie your boat off, a well-lit carpark and a wash-down area. Unlike many Port Phillip ramps, there is no launching fee – yet – and the fish-cleaning facilities are a treat.

POINT HENRY

Point Henry is a sand spit point on the southern shore of Corio Bay and is the demarcation between the inner and outer harbours. It is distinctive in that there is a large aluminium smelter and a long pier used to unload raw alumina for the factory. The pier is officially unavailable to anglers although former employees of Alcoa, now closed, used to fish here when the aluminium smelter was in its heyday.

Anglers are able to launch small boats on the eastern side of the sand spit. Take care to check the shell grit is firm before you drive on it. Launching and retrieving boats is generally best at high tide. On low tide, anglers with small boats sometimes unhook their trailers and take them to their boats, pulling boat and trailer from the water with a towrope.

During summer, anglers trolling **garfish** alongside the pier sometimes hook **yellowtail kingfish** to about 6kg. Other species caught near the pier include **salmon**, **silver trevally**, **trevalla**, **flathead** and **snapper**. The grounds surrounding the pier are the most productive.

On the northern side, seagrass beds run out to the Wilson Spit Channel and these produce **King George whiting**, garfish, flathead and **snook**. Many anglers fish along the edges of both sides of the Wilson Spit Channel for snapper. On the northern side of this channel are some productive **whiting** areas in about 5m of water.

Anglers fishing for snapper on the southern side of the shipping channel often anchor near the ship-turning basin out from the end of the pier. Alternatively, on the south-east side of the structure towards the Curlewis Bank, there are seagrass beds and an old spoil ground. This is a favourite area for anglers working soft plastic lures for snapper, **rock flathead** and snook.

CURLEWIS BANK

Curlewis Bank is well regarded for **King George whiting** during late summer and autumn. However, this vast bank of sand, seagrass and spoil ground also produces **snapper**, **snook**, **squid** and **flathead**. It is popular with soft plastic lure fishers.

It was about 5.30am when I left Limeburners boat ramp and motored across Stingray Bay towards Point Henry on a 6m plate aluminium boat with Steve Stojanovski and Chris Vasilevski, who operate Firstcast Fishing Adventures. The boat was wide and purpose-built with a side console and casting platforms fore and aft.

Curlewis Bank runs from Point Henry to Portarlington on the southern side and is a mix of seagrass beds and rubble bottom where dredging spoil has been dumped. There are two spoil grounds, one out from the Sea Breeze Caravan Park, and the second closer to Clifton Springs off Hermsley Rd.

Our run from the ramp to the first fishing spot took about 10 minutes on the smooth water. It was still dark when the engine was switched off and we started to drift. In the background, I could hear the industrial hum of the aluminium smelter and the long, alumina-offloading pier.

Our rods were spin sticks with small threadline reels, spooled with fine 2–3kg braid line with about a rod-length of 3kg breaking strain fluorocarbon leader. At the business end were soft plastic lures, 10cm Berkley Minnow Gulps in Nuclear Chicken and Smelt (black and white) colours. These lures are more like bait. The maker promotes them as biodegradable because they dissolve in water. If you leave the packet unsealed for long enough, they do the same out of the water.

The weekend before my trip, a few locals enjoyed a good run on snapper. Reds to 5.2kg were caught on soft plastic lures and a few were lost as well. Steve and Chris are old hands at this game, and said the trick was not to retrieve the lure too fast, as this will attract flathead. Moreover, when a snapper inhales the lure, don't strike. Instead, set the hook by smoothly lifting the rod as the lure is taken. Steve said this technique evolved through experience. The boys fish ultra-light, and consequently a hard strike would most likely snap the line. He admitted to losing a few snapper using the cobweb-thin leader material, but said that most times the leader slipped between the snapper's teeth. To lose a fish you must first hook it, and the fine leader makes for better lure presentations.

The flathead here are mainly rock flathead, and this was the first time I had seen this essentially vegetarian species caught on line. It said something for the artificial flavouring of the lures.

Chris caught the first fish of the morning, a small snapper of about 800g, which was promptly brought on board. The lure was removed and the fish released unharmed. Next fish was a snapper of about

1.5kg, still only a pinkie, and small by the standards of the snapper that were being caught. Both men explained that many clients come on board with their GPS to get the marks of where they were, but that didn't make much sense given that we covered a wide area and were always drifting.

Over the next five hours we worked our way inshore along the bank, and out wide, fishing in water 5–7m deep. Seagrass with fine, fingernail-like shells attached dominates some areas of the bottom. In other areas, the seabed is hard and rubbly. At each spot, the outboard was turned off and the boat allowed to drift with wind or current. Lures were cast in the direction the boat was drifting. This meant that when you cast and the lure sank, your line was slack.

The method was to tighten the line, give a gentle lift to the lure and let it sink again, all the time slowly winding the reel to stay in touch and feel the lure.

It can be a slow business. There were pinkies and more pinkies, with a few flathead tossed in. The bigger snapper were proving elusive. It was the same with another crew working the same area. Nevertheless, as Steve said: 'It only takes one serious fish to make the trip worthwhile.'

CLIFTON SPRINGS

Clifton Springs is a sheltered harbour with a double boat ramp, mooring jetty and toilets. The facility is well signposted. To get there, take the Portarlington Rd out of Geelong and turn left at Jetty Rd just before Drysdale. Most anglers use this ramp to reach areas in Corio Bay outer harbour and western Port Phillip that are a bit far to reach from Corio Bay.

Snapper and **King George whiting** are the most sought-after species, but anglers also catch **flathead**, **garfish**, **snook**, **gummy shark**, **elephant fish** and **squid**.

The southern shore, from Clifton Springs through to Point Richards to the east, is home to extensive mussel farms. The hundreds of ropes hanging down with clusters of mussels growing on them are a big attraction to the fish. You are not allowed to fish in the farms, but you can fish near them.

Most snapper anglers fish along the channel edges. As you move away from the channel, the bottom is heavy reef that is hard on terminal tackle. To overcome this, most anglers anchor away from the channel and throw back towards it, as the banks along the top of the channel offer easier terrain. On a southerly, anglers fish the southern side of the channel; on a northerly they cross the channel and drop anchor to face the south.

One of the most popular areas is the bend that marks the junction of the Wilson Spit and Point

Andrew Dombrovskis with his catch of King George whiting caught off Clifton Springs

Richards Channels. Better known as the elbow, this area attracts a lot of boat traffic when the snapper are on the go. The mark is the former flashing channel marker – the current one has been moved about 150m along the channel towards Portarlington.

The north side of the channel, west of the Commonwealth Explosives Pier, is excellent ground for snapper, gummy shark and whiting. Whiting are found in areas where the weed bottom is interspersed with sand patches. These fish tend to move around so it may take a few drops to find a school.

If you motor west along the Wilson Spit Channel towards Geelong, you will come across the Wilson Spit Bank. Well regarded for its snapper fishing, the bank runs from the north shore of Corio Bay outer harbour to the southern shore near Clifton Springs where it meets Curlewis Bank. Buoy No. 5 on the north side and No. 6 on the south side of the channel mark the western edge of the bank; Buoys No. 3 and No. 4 mark the eastern edge. On the west side, the bank drops into about 8m of water, on the east side it is about 6m. On the south side of the channel, the bank averages about 5m, but drops to about 9m before Curlewis Bank, which runs out about 300m from the shore.

The average depth of Curlewis Bank is 2–3m, all the way back to Point Henry.

BIRD ROCK

An area that is on the north side of the outer harbour, opposite Point Henry, from Bird Rock east to an area known as the 'Quarries' (due to the large quarry on the shore), it produces **snapper** for most of the year. You'll also find that anglers fish here for **King George whiting**, **garfish**, **flathead**, **gummy shark** and **snook**. The best results have been from Bird Rock (Point Lillias) along the northern shore as far as the Quarries.

Be careful not to venture too close to Bird Rock because it is shallow for a fair way out. This rock used to be a popular land-based option, with anglers fishing the eastern face where it fronts a small bay, casting out about 50m into a channel that runs north–south along the eastern face.

POINT WILSON

Opposite Clifton Springs, the long Commonwealth Explosives Pier easily distinguishes Point Wilson. Boaters need to stay at least 300m away from the pier at all times. The waters surrounding the pier produce **snapper** and **King George whiting**.

Methods for inner harbour to Point Wilson

TACKLE A 3kg outfit is about right for whiting. Use a threadline reel balanced to suit a light rod of about 2.5m. Baitholder hooks from No. 4 to No. 6 will cover baits for whiting. Use a running sinker rig, and work a fine mist berley, preferably when there is some tide running.

Most anglers employ 8–10kg outfits for snapper, 4/0 Suicide pattern hooks, a selection of ball sinkers of different weights and some 15–24kg leader material. The standard snapper rig is a running sinker rig with a lead as light as conditions will allow.

BAIT King George whiting will take fresh squid, pipi, sandworm and mussel. For snapper, use salmon fillets, garfish, couta heads, fresh squid, sauries, silver whiting and pilchards.

BARWON RIVER

Sometimes going fishing in our southern rivers is about making the best of what is available, as is the case of the Barwon River, which flows through Geelong. Like the Yarra and Maribyrnong rivers, the coffee-coloured waters of the Barwon do not look inviting, but looks can deceive. Beneath its muddy exterior, there is a fishery worthy of a second look.

The headwaters of the Barwon River are in the Otway Ranges and the river flow is controlled by releases from the West Barwon Dam. From Pollocksford Bridge to Queens Park the river has pools, riffles, runs and rapids.

From Queens Park to Breakwater, wide deep stretches are the norm. At Breakwater, the runs are short and begin below a low-lying bridge. After Breakwater, the river meanders down to a second break, followed by several kilometres of salt water as it flows down to Lake Connewarre.

Geelong is Victoria's largest regional centre and for much of its course through the city the river is lined with industrial estates. Within casting distance of woollen mills, carpet and other factories, **redfin**, **blackfish**, **carp** and **eels** are caught. Victorian Fisheries stopped stocking **trout** in the river, saying the decision was taken to protect native fish, including **grayling** and **galaxids**. I thought it was a strange decision, given that trout were the main predator of redfin, carp and mosquito fish.

Redfin are one of the easiest fish to catch and are common at Queens Park, Shannon Park and Breakwater. Small redfin can run in plague proportions in some areas and are little more than nuisance value at best. The best quality redfin are caught an hour or so before sunset and the hotter the day, the better the fishing is.

The most sought after species in the river is carp. It may be a noxious species, but carp have been the saviours of fishing in many waters. They have been around so long that there is something of a subculture of carp anglers. Coarse fishers, who practise European river fishing methods, are common. Young anglers do most carp fishing, and it's a great way for them to hone their hooking and fish-fighting skills.

Methods for Barwon River

TACKLE For bait fishing or spinning, a light rod coupled with a small threadline reel and spooled with 2–3kg breaking strain lines will suffice. Bladed lures such as Celtas account for redfin, especially when cast along the riverbank and retrieved close to the overhanging grass.

RIGS The rig for smelt is simple. A No. 10 hook is tied to the end of the line; there are no swivels or sinkers. The hook is passed through both upper and lower jaws of the baitfish, as close to the lips as possible. If you need the fish to swim deeper then place a small piece of shot on the line about 45cm above the hook.

For carp, most anglers use a running sinker rig and Baitholder pattern hooks from No. 6 to No. 4.

BAIT Commonly used baits include worms, minnow and smelt for the redfin, crickets for river blackfish and corn for the ubiquitous carp. Berley helps to attract carp. The majority of bait fishing is in the slower, deeper waters from Buckley's Falls to the second break below Breakwater. Smelt and minnow are the major food sources for redfin.

BARWON RIVER ESTUARY

The Barwon River estuary enters Bass Strait about 10km west of Port Phillip Heads and it divides the holiday towns of Barwon Heads and Ocean Grove. This estuary is one of the most productive waterways in Victoria and can produce a wide range of species, including **silver trevally**, **King George whiting**, **mullet**, **salmon**, **flathead**, **luderick**, **elephant fish**, **pike** and **black bream**.

The estuary has a solid reputation as trophy fish water due to the number of big **mulloway**.

Reports of mulloway from the river seem to come just about every month, but the best fishing in terms of numbers is November–February and March–July for the bigger fish. Mulloway are caught from Lake Connewarre downstream to the mouth. A popular area is known as the Thunderbolt, about 500m downstream from the lake on the west bank. This is best fished from a boat. From the Thunderbolt downstream to the Sheepwash, at the

Above: Boat launching in the Barwon River at Ocean Grove
Below: Lachie and Bailey Cooper caught these salmon spinning with small metal lures near the Barwon Heads Bridge

end of Sheepwash Rd on the outskirts of Barwon Heads, the river has a deep channel that for the most part is close to the western bank. There are wide stretches of river between the Thunderbolt and the Sheepwash, and on the eastern bank several large drains feed water off the mangrove swamp. The entrances to these drains are natural feeding zones worth fishing as the tide is falling.

You can walk a long way upstream from the Sheepwash and find clear areas where the river channel hugs the bank. A boardwalk with landings for anglers to fish from has been installed several hundred metres upstream from Barwon Heads boat ramp. This will suit anglers with disabilities or people who simply prefer not to fish in mud or mangroves.

The boat ramp marks the end of land-based access to the river on the west side, as it becomes mangrove swamp, ideal for anglers with boats. The mangrove-lined inlets upstream of the Ocean Grove boat ramp hold reasonable bream and luderick. Sandworms combined with berley do well on the bream while weed or abalone gut is choice bait for luderick.

On the opposite side of the river is the Ocean Grove ramp, which is at the top of the broadwater that starts at the highway bridge. The floating boat-mooring jetty is popular with anglers, and some excellent hook-ups have been made from here.

Downstream of the ramp the river channel is clearly marked and when the mulloway are running it is common to see boats spread along the channel all the way to the mouth.

The 'Ozone' jetty on the Barwon Heads side above the highway bridge, and fishermen's pier below the bridge are worthwhile. The bridge has landings for anglers, and sometimes you can see mulloway on low tide at night, under the bridge lights. Anglers fishing from the beach on the eastern side of the river catch salmon, silver trevally, mullet and King George whiting and sometimes mulloway.

At times good schools of Australian salmon can be caught on small chrome lures. On slack water, and with the help of berley, mullet and salmon can be brought up the water column.

Methods for Barwon River estuary

TACKLE If you want big mulloway, start with a minimum 10kg outfit. Do not use wire; instead get some heavy monofilament of about 30kg minimum. Hook sizes vary to suit the size of the bait, but most anglers start at about 4/0, with 6/0 a standard among many specialists. Choice baits are squid, bass yabbies and live salmon, mullet or tailor, which are fished either under a float or off the bottom on a running paternoster sinker rig.

For whiting, bream and other smaller species, use a paternoster rig with No. 4 to No. 6 hooks.

9 GREAT OCEAN ROAD

From Melbourne, take the Princes Hwy to Geelong, follow the ring road to the other side then follow the signs to the Great Ocean Rd.

All forms of fishing are available somewhere along this magnificent roadway. Where else can you think of chasing sand fleas in the morning for garfish, and trolling skirted jigs offshore for 100kg tuna?

ACCOMMODATION: For more information visit www.greatoceanrd.org.au

Purpose-built fishing platforms were incorporated into the pier at Lorne when it was rebuilt

Victoria's Great Ocean Rd is a pandora's box of fishing adventure, ranging from rivers and estuary to surf and offshore. One of the state's most popular tourist destinations, this 300km stretch of bitumen runs from Torquay in the east to Warrnambool in the west. On the first leg, from Torquay to Apollo Bay, the road clings to the coast, separating steep verdant hills covered in eucalypts from pristine surf beaches and craggy rock ledges. Along the way, there are estuaries, townships and many neat fishing holes.

After Apollo Bay, the Great Ocean Rd heads inland, snaking its way through the lush Otway Ranges before returning to the coast near Princetown, and following the Southern Ocean to Warrnambool.

Anglers who come to the Great Ocean Rd seek everything from **brown trout** and **bream** to **snapper** and **sharks** and the good news is that, despite the route's popularity with tourists, fishing pressure has not been extreme. Every route has a starting point and a finishing point. In this case, the direction travelled at all times will be from east to west, that is from Torquay to Warrnambool

The offshore waters of western Bass Strait, from Torquay to Cape Otway, contain an abundance of similar species. These fish include **Australian salmon,** snapper**, barracouta, King George whiting, yellowtail kingfish, silver trevally, gummy sharks** and **arrow squid**. There are also reasonable numbers of larger sharks like **thresher, blue, mako, seven-gill** and **bronze whaler**. The best fishing is from late spring through to autumn, with late summer and early autumn my favourite due to the more settled weather.

Large migratory schools of **barracouta** follow pilchards and sandy sprats. Hungry and feisty, barracouta are a popular target for anglers who seek them for berley, bait, a feed or simply the sport they offer on light line. On some closer inshore reefs, particularly off Torquay, Anglesea, Lorne and Apollo Bay, you will find salmon and sometimes yellowtail kingfish. If you fish bait then work these inshore reefs and the sand patches between for silver trevally, snapper, **flathead** and King George whiting. Gummy sharks have become more abundant over these inshore reefs and every so often, you might hook into a thresher shark. Best baits include squid, pilchard pieces, and pipis. The annual run of arrow squid show in late summer and continue through the autumn. These are distinguished from the **southern calamari squid** by their distinctive, arrowhead tail. Arrow squid are more aggressive than calamari and can be caught on jigs as well as lures and even flies. Mako and blue sharks are keenly sought from the 50m line out.

Anglers find many rock ledges to fish from along the Great Ocean Rd

TORQUAY

Torquay is a coastal boomtown on the Great Ocean Rd, a place best known for surfing rather than fishing. During summer, Torquay beaches attract many visitors and the surfer cult is strong. But there is more to Torquay than riding a wave or getting a suntan. There are some serious fishing opportunities for beach and boat anglers.

An ocean front boat ramp is located at the western corner of Zeally Bay. It is a public ramp but the local fishing club has a tractor, which members use to launch and retrieve boats on the beach when the tide is too far out to use the ramp. Yellow Bluff and reefs running offshore from this bay and the front beach give the bay some protection from seas. There is a good case for building a breakwall and extending the ramp to give anglers better access to Bass Strait as the next closest boat ramp is in the river at Barwon Heads.

The species caught in the area include **King George whiting**, **salmon**, **barracouta**, **arrow squid**, **snapper**, **flathead**, **mulloway**, **yellowtail kingfish** as well as **sharks** including **blue**, **mako**, **bronze whaler**, **thresher** and **gummy**.

For boat anglers, the inshore and offshore fishing can be productive. Whiting to about 800g can be caught just a couple of hundred metres offshore, and many anglers head east towards Point Impossible to fish for whiting and snapper over the reefs. Offshore from Point Impossible there is a graveyard of shipwrecks that date back to World War II or earlier. Most of these are little

Rod Mackenzie shows off a salmon; this is the most popular surf species along the Great Ocean Rd

more than piles of rust on the bottom, but they have created reef that attracts all sorts of fish.

Water depth increases quickly out from the ramp and 30m of water is about 4km offshore. Large sand and rubble areas are excellent for mainly sand flathead, snapper and gummy sharks. In 40–60m of water, you will find good numbers of barracouta and arrow squid. The deeper water is popular for shark fishing and, when you go southwest towards Point Addis, deep water is closer to shore.

Beach fishing opportunities begin on Fishermans Beach, next to the ramp where mulloway and gummy sharks have been caught. Yellow Bluff, immediately west of the ramp, is fishable at low tide. The beaches that run from Yellow Bluff north-east to Point Impossible produce whiting, snapper (mainly **pinkies**), gummy sharks and mulloway. Favourite beaches along here include The Gap and Whites Beach. Driving along the back of the sand dunes you will notice a gap in the dunes, park your car here and walk on through. Whites Beach is past the Gap and is popular with nudists.

Jan Juc beach, west of Torquay, produces salmon and gummy sharks.

ANGLESEA AND AIREYS INLET

As you follow the Great Ocean Rd you come to the town of Anglesea – beach fishing opportunities are the same as Torquay, with the best fishing east of the Anglesea River, although you need to be aware of the Marine Park that extends west from Point Addis. Most anglers go here to fish the Anglesea River for **black bream** and **yelloweye mullet**, with the best fishing from the highway bridge upstream. A boat ramp is situated at Point Roadknight. Partially protected by the point, launching is difficult due to sand and swell, and the ramp is best suited to small boats.

Next stop is Aireys Inlet, just out of Anglesea, where the highway crosses Painkalac Creek. Small water, it is popular with bream anglers who fish mainly along the western bank, from the highway bridge downstream. Further along, beaches at Moggs Creek and Eastern View, alongside the Great Ocean Rd gateway sign, are popular destinations but are shallow and salmon is the mainstay of the catch.

LORNE

From Eastern View to Lorne there are many rock ledges and these produce big **King George whiting**, **mullet**, **silver trevally**, **snapper** and **salmon** at different times of the year. Winter is a top time for salmon but when they are not on the bite, **garfish** are a good alternative. Catching garfish from the rocks is a specialist technique. The Great Ocean Rd hosts a small number of specialist garfish anglers who have developed their techniques to a fine art. From late summer to the start of winter some of the biggest garfish you are likely to see are caught here. Fish in excess of 20in, and so thick that you cannot touch your thumb with your finger when you hold them.

The first time I came across this style of fishing for garfish was at Reedy Creek, a few kilometres east of Lorne. I was travelling with Andy Zarro and when we arrived at Reedy Creek a couple of local anglers, John Alsop and Keith Richmond, were already fishing. Both men were doing well on the gars, fishing from the sheltered cove, and we accepted an invitation to join in.

Anglers who fish the gars use light outfits. The rod is normally about 2.2m long and line should be about 3kg breaking strain. The rig consists of a float and a leader from 1.2–2m. Some anglers prefer to use berley floats instead of pencil floats as these are packed with berley that draws the garfish to the bait. Hooks range from No. 8 through to No. 14. Much depends on the gars when it comes to hooks. The smaller the garfish, the smaller the hook you may need to employ. In the deeper channels, a small amount of split shot on the leader helps to get the bait down deeper.

Bait is usually a small white bug known alternatively as a sand flea or sand hopper. Sand hoppers are found in the sand beneath rotting kelp. The best time to get them is on cold mornings when they barely move and you can pick them up easily. Once the day warms these little bugs start jumping about and catching them is difficult. To store the sand hoppers, put sand in a bucket and they will stay under the sand. When you want a couple for bait, simply move the sand aside and grab them. Another favourite bait is a maggot and during the warmer months these can be found among the rotting kelp weed on the rocks. If the weed is being washed by waves on the high tide it can be a top spot to fish as the waves pounding over the kelp will wash maggots into the ocean creating a natural food trail that will bring garfish in to feed.

On the way into Lorne is a ledge known as Jump Rock. This is a popular and consistent ledge that produces mainly salmon, silver trevally, barracouta, pinkies and mullet. As you drive into Lorne you come across Erskine River, a small estuary known to produce mullet, bream and **estuary perch**. Lorne is best known for pier fishing. Pier fishing has always been popular among Victorian anglers and Lorne pier is one of the standout destinations in terms of consistent results. Sometimes this pier suffers from being too popular and on weekends and during holiday periods it can be hopeless. If you want to fish the end of the pier, get down on Tuesday; hopefully by Saturday you might be where you want to be.

The good news for anglers who want to fish at Lorne is that a new purpose-built pier, with angling in mind, opened in 2007. The old wooden pier was a favourite destination for many anglers and their families. But it was built to accommodate the commercial fishing fleet and it was a case of standing room only on the pier when the salmon, silver trevally, garfish, squid, pinkies or barracouta were running.

The pier is a credit to everyone involved in the project. It sets a new standard as the best fishing

Recreational Licence Fund money was used to create a stairway down to the popular Artillery Rocks Ledge along the Great Ocean Rd

structure I have come across in Australia and is worth every cent that was spent. The pier is the same length (196m) and width as the old pier but flares out on each side at the end with stepped down fishing platforms complete with built in rod holders. This provides a selection of vantage points and levels and is readily accessible for pedestrians who no longer have to step over fishing rods (or get in the way) of anglers. Most importantly, there is more room for anglers.

The best time to fish the pier is after a strong blow from the east. When the seas are up and waves are pounding the reef, this pier can be exceptional for the salmon that hunt under the cover of white water. There is no boat ramp at Lorne but anglers launch their boats in a sandy strip in the Point Grey reef on the west side of the pier. It is suitable for small boats only.

APOLLO BAY

The drive to Apollo Bay from Melbourne is about two and a half hours.

Artillery Rocks, between Jamieson River and Wye River, is a popular ledge where anglers catch **salmon**, **barracouta**, **silver trevally**, **King George whiting** and **pinkies**. This is one of the safest ledges along this road and access is easy with the installation of a staircase. Further along, ledges at Boggaly Creek and Skenes Creek, just before Apollo Bay, offer good fishing for **garfish** and **mullet**.

Apollo Bay has a diversity of angling options including river, estuary, surf and offshore. And if

Barracouta are a common saltwater fish caught on lures from boats, piers and rock ledges along the Great Ocean Rd

none of these suit, you can fish the rocks or in the sheltered harbour. Anglers who come here seek everything from **brown trout** and bream to snapper and sharks. Despite the Great Ocean Rd's popularity with tourists, the fishing pressure at Apollo Bay has not been extreme.

The sheltered harbour has a boat ramp suited to large boats and is popular with anglers wanting to head offshore to fish the reefs for snapper, trevally, barracouta, squid and sharks, depending on the time of year. On good days, boats will head as far west as Cape Otway or east to Cape Patton where they fish for **morwong**, gummy sharks, snapper and sand flathead. Seek local advice before going to Cape Otway as there are extensive reef systems and the safest route is best determined on a navigation chart. Trolling for salmon along the back of the surf beaches is popular and an area off Skenes Creek known as the Waterfall produces good catches of King George whiting.

Australian salmon are the mainstay of the surf fishing. The main beaches are at Wild Dog Creek as you enter the outskirts of Apollo Bay, and Marengo a couple of kilometres on the west side of town. The best time to fish is from autumn through to spring. Wild Dog Creek is worth a try for brown trout but the best fishing is well upstream.

Apollo Bay offers pier and breakwater fishing. The harbour can produce barracouta, salmon, squid, mullet, silver trevally and **haddock (trevalla)** at times. **Shrimp**, top estuary bait, are often plentiful around the pilings. There are two breakwall arms and these will produce salmon and barracouta. The southern arm is more difficult to fish but often produces better results. Rock fishing is best near Marengo. As you walk west you will find plenty of options down as far as the Rifle Butts ledge, which is the third bay along. Expect to catch garfish, **sweep**, mullet, salmon, trevally, barracouta, pinkies and King George whiting.

Big Reef is 56km south-west of Apollo Bay and is about 10km long and 3–4km wide and rises from 80m to about 35m from the surface. The reef has many pinnacles and acts as a holding area for baitfish. **Yakkas** and **redbait** (sold to anglers for bait as Red Rockets), hang on the reef at about 20m deep for food and protection, which is why the tuna are there.

'There has been fish taken closer to shore as well,' Andrew Bounos wrote in an email to me. 'Rumour has it that one barrel is swimming around with a 50 Tiagra (game reel) in tow after a gimbal failed and the angler didn't have a good enough grip on his rod – wouldn't mind hooking that fish!'

On 17 April 2011 it was Apollo Bay's turn in the spotlight when a 153.5kg barrel was brought into the harbour to be weighed. It took three anglers four and a half hours to land the fish, which took a Rapala X Rap lure. By the second week of May, barrels to 144kg were still being caught; some of them taken on whole yakkas fished as dead bait in a cube trail.

The downside of the fantastic tuna action has been the numbers of boats that have been towed to port and, for the most part, because they ran out of fuel. Being so far offshore, it behoves the boat owner to keep an eye on fuel levels. For safety sake, boat skippers should notify someone of their destination and estimated time back at port and commonsense dictates that when you are two or three hours run from port, you should be fishing in company with at least one other boat.

The estuary fishing can be surprisingly good, even though the Barham River at Glen Aire, between Cape Otway and Johanna, doesn't look very appealing at first sight. **Bream**, **yelloweye mullet**, estuary perch and the occasional brown trout can be caught. Upstream, past the caravan park, the Barham River holds brown trout. The road to Paradise – yes, that's the name of the place – follows the river course and it changes from being a small deep stream in a deep cut to a wider, shallow stream with riffles, runs and pools. The further up you go, the smaller the trout become. Although this is the same with most of the Otway sweet water streams, shaded by dense stands of blackwoods, beech and fern that provide shady habitat for brown trout and a daunting challenge for fly-fishers.

AIRE RIVER

This area comprises estuary, surf and fresh water on the west side of Cape Otway. Aire River nestles in a valley along the foothills of the Otways. To get there, follow the Great Ocean Rd past the Cape Otway turn-off, and as you descend from the Otway Ranges turn left on Horden Vale Rd. This road starts as bitumen and turns to gravel. Follow this road until you see a track off to the right and a sign for the national park. If you cross a creek, you have gone too far. An alternative route is to continue on the Great Ocean Rd to Glenaire, where there is dry-weather access via Sand Rd.

The estuary comprises reeds in many areas. From spring through autumn, the green and brown hues of the river flats and mountains seem to light up. In the depths of winter, low-lying grey clouds can roll in, blanketing the estuary, and the valley acts as a funnel for icy, southerly winds that seem to come straight from Antarctica.

It is under such wintry conditions that the surf and estuary fishing can be exceptional. The estuary holds a solid population of **bream** to 46cm, **yelloweye mullet** and sometimes there are **brown trout**. Most bream are caught on shrimp, spider crabs or scrub worms. If you decide to net shrimp, then blanche them in hot water before using them, as they seem to attract fish better. When fishing with crabs as bait, leave your bail arm open and allow the bream to run. The fish will slow down or stop to swallow the crab and then take off again. This is the time to set the hook.

During winter, a major lure for anglers are the sea-run brown trout which are returning to the river to spawn and are often caught on lures around the old bridge pilings. On a visit here more than 20 years ago I witnessed an angler catch a 5kg trout on a chrome Wonder Wobbler. He was trolling the lure near the old bridge. Veteran Aire River angler Doug Lucas says the best method for the trout is to troll broken back minnow lures.

Beach fishing can be extraordinarily productive and the easiest and best way to get to the beach is to launch a small boat alongside the bridge. Walking to the beach across sand from where you park your car can be arduous. However, the hard slog is sometimes rewarded with fishing of a quality equal to anywhere in Victoria. I have seen **salmon** so thick they are like clouds in the water.

Gummy sharks are also caught at night and sometimes anglers manage a bonus in the form of a **mulloway** or **snapper**.

Best times to fish for salmon are sunrise and sunset, but for the bigger predators fish at night. The high tide can be productive, particularly if it coincides with dawn or dusk.

Look for gutters and channels. The best fish will be in the clean water away from the froth and sand being stirred by the wave action.

While the estuary and surf fishing can be excellent, this is an extreme stretch of water in terms of brown trout. The Aire begins life as a series of small trickles high in the Otways. As it grows, its crystal waters rush through verdant valleys dense with ferns, bushes and blackberries. Blackwood trees line much of its course and there are pine plantations. On the higher ridges, tall stands of mountain ash dominate an undulating skyline.

In the upper reaches, the trout are small, with 350g considered above average. However, in the lower reaches where the river is wider and deeper, some of the biggest trout you are likely to encounter in a river on mainland Australia lie waiting.

One of the prime fishing areas is the Aire crossing near Beech Forest. The area has picnic facilities and the river is easy to access. There is a weir at the crossing, below which the river turns into a series of riffles, runs and shallow pools.

The long stretches are narrow and shallow – broad, deep pools are as scarce as pan-size trout – but at least you can wander downstream a fair way without getting into too much trouble.

These weenie browns are colourful, nicely proportioned and most importantly, not always easy to hook. Size and quantity are irrelevant – the fly-fishing here is more about the challenge. Dry flies such as the Red Tag, Mayfly, Caddis imitations and Thorax patterns No. 16 to No. 22 can produce satisfying fishing. However, unless there is an obvious hatch underway, it's less about matching the hatch and more about pot-luck. The recipe for success still requires skill and application, but it comes with large dollops of frustration.

Oddly enough, size is less of a problem for spin fishers. The deeper stretches are best worked with thumbnail-sized minnow lures or else the ever-reliable Celta. Casting requires a refined, gentle touch. The dense foliage overhanging much of the water means that an underhand flick or a bow-and-arrow cast is more functional than the normal overhead style.

Lest you think the Aire is only about weenie browns, think again. The main course in this river, from the foothills to the ocean, holds a healthy population of sea-run browns equal in size to any found on the mainland of Australia. The lower reaches, where the Aire leaves the ranges and runs through verdant pastures to the Southern Ocean, are in stark contrast to the high country. After it leaves the hills, about 3–4km of river is dominated by a succession of deep logjam pools flanked by steep embankments. Where the Great Ocean Rd crosses, it changes again, with a lower riverbank and fewer logs. Further downstream the Aire forks, the eastern arm running into Lake Craven. The west fork joins with the Ford River, rejoining the main flow at the southern end of the lake.

The full potential of Lake Craven is unrealised. It has produced some estuary perch, and excellent trout caught mainly by anglers trolling in canoes and small craft. Most reports I have on the lake come from people who decided to have a bit of a troll in between bait sessions, the results often surprising them.

Big trout hunt all the way down to the sea. Most of those caught in the lower reaches are about 500g–3kg. These fish linger along the river edge, lying in wait under shelter of overhanging grass for shrimp, galaxias and insects. Shrimps are the most easily obtained bait; all you need is a long-handled fine mesh net and a coffee jar with moist sawdust to keep them alive. They are found living in the submerged watercress overhanging the riverbanks.

Local identity Stan Wright achieves top results by threading half a dozen of the little crustaceans onto a No. 4 Gamakatsu hook. The shrimp are too small to thread longitudinally, so the hook passes through the middle of the shrimp at right angles to its body. Stan describes the method as 'criss-crossing' and admitted it may be a bit unorthodox, but that it works for him.

He also believes in stealth, staying low, using the grass and cumbungi to mask his presence while slowly and quietly edging along the river. Stan's method was to cast an unweighted shrimp bait close to the edge. The bait was allowed to sink and then slowly brought to the surface. Every couple of paces the bait was checked and cast out again. The method is methodical, slow and very thorough. It is similar to a fly-fisher casting nymphs into every square metre of a creek, one step at a time.

The logjam pools upstream from the highway bridge are home to the biggest trout. Big, hook-jawed cannibals, merciless and mean, they offer up an irresistible challenge to an angler's skills. They feed as readily on other trout as they do big yabbies, elvers or small snakes weaving across the surface. Due to the terrain, these fish are not easy to catch. Successful anglers like Stan – who has caught them to 7kg – use live bait. His preference is for wood grubs, and he fishes at night.

Stan's method is basic. The grub is hooked through the collar, cast to the middle of a pool, and allowed to sink. As it runs down with the current, the grub is slowly retrieved; the critical strike time is just as the grub is nearing the surface. As big trout often take a tail-up vertical position in the water, the pull gives the impression of being snagged.

GELLIBRAND RIVER

A little further west from Aire River are Castle Cove and Johanna Beach; both produce fishing similar to the beach at Aire River. There is also good beach fishing at Princetown, at the mouth of the Gellibrand River.

Like the Aire, the Gellibrand River produces **bream** and sea-run **brown trout** in the lower reaches. It also has a solid population of **estuary perch**. Upstream, above the highway bridge anglers fish for **river blackfish** and trout equal to or even bigger than those in the Aire River. During winter, when the Aire and Gellibrand flood into the paddocks, the brown trout can be seen in the paddocks feeding on snails, worms and other insects caught by the rising water.

Sand flathead are much sought after by anglers because of their tasty meat

I first fished the Gellibrand with Colac angler Murray Kidman. Softly spoken and polite, Murray knew the Otway Ranges as well as a taxi driver knows suburban streets. Brown trout were Murray's specialty, the Gellibrand River his favourite water. Proof of Murray's ability was on show over the bar of the Gellibrand Hotel: a 4.6kg buck brown trout and a hen fish of 4.45kg.

The Gellibrand River begins its run to the east of Beech Forest at the West Gellibrand Dam. Flowing north then west in a huge arc, it turns south through dairy pastures and light forest before joining the Southern Ocean at Princetown.

It is not an easy river to fish. There are few areas where open water and gravel beds exist – for the most part, the Gellibrand is steep-sided and narrow. Long stretches are enclosed by temperate rainforest: blackwood, satin box and tree ferns in the upper reaches; blackberries and eucalypts lower down.

Boat ramp at Curdievale (Boggy Creek) on the Curdies River

As with the Aire River, the biggest fish are in the lower reaches, sea-run trout that lurk in deep, narrow runs or logjam pools. Murray said some of these sea-runners were 'at least 18lb (8kg)'. Murray worked tiny Rebel lures, 'Baby Brown Trout' and 'Baby Bass' models, no longer than the first joint on a man's thumb, and weighing less than 4g.

Murray would cast his lure upstream and down, working every square metre of holding water. It was a lesson in precision and control: wind, dense cover or fast running water, it made little difference. The lure flew to exactly the right place every time and always landed just a hand span from trouble. In spots where a cast would be a certain recipe for disaster, Murray made use of the current to run his lure those extra few centimetres into or around obstacles.

The estuary section produces bream, estuary perch, **yelloweye mullet** and sometimes **silver trevally**. The Gellibrand River has some of the state's largest estuary perch, with Fisheries Victoria research showing captures in excess of 3kg in the snags above the highway bridge.

Shrimp and minnow are the best baits, while the bream will also take slow-trolled lures.

Princetown Beach is well known for producing **salmon**, **gummy sharks** and, over summer, **snapper** to about 2kg.

Gibson Steps, a few kilometres west of Princetown, is a popular beach for anglers chasing salmon, **mullet** and gummy sharks. Port Campbell is a small commercial fishing pier in a cove, but enjoys good runs of **barracouta**, salmon, **squid**, **slimy mackerel**, mullet, silver trevally, **haddock** and **pinkie snapper** at times.

PETERBOROUGH

Peterborough has beach and estuary fishing. The estuary system is Curdies River, a noted **bream** river with fish to 1.5kg common. The best place to access the river is upstream at a place called Boggy Creek – a name well known locally, but not by cartographers. I have several different maps of Victoria and none of them shows this Boggy Creek. Mind you, when you see the bream firing in Curdies River, you can understand the general reluctance to tell the world about the place.

When you hear of someone heading down to Boggy Creek to fish the Curdies, they are actually going to Curdie Vale, a quiet out-of-the-way rural settlement about 10km north of Peterborough. Boggy Creek is the name of the local pub. As well as a pub, the settlement has a boat ramp that would put many big city ramps to shame.

The Curdies is not a big river. It starts out as small, unmarked outflow on the southern shore of Lake Purrumbete, near Camperdown. It's so small that unless you know what you are looking for, you will drive over it thinking it is just a drain. The river finishes at Peterborough as a lake-like shallow estuary that sometimes flows in to the sea.

There is a boat ramp above the main highway bridge at Peterborough. It is a basic concrete ramp with no facilities and is exposed to southerlies. The shallow water in the lower reaches makes boating on the estuary adventurous at best. Anyone contemplating doing so should seek local advice.

Most anglers fish in boats downstream from Boggy Creek. For much of its course, the river has more S-bends than a Grand Prix circuit, and is lined with cumbungi grass that makes bank fishing almost impossible. About halfway between the ramp and the estuary proper is a cleared area on the western shore locally called 'The Lodge'. Access is restricted through private property off Boggy Creek Rd.

On a recent visit, most anglers were fishing about a kilometre or so upstream from the estuary. The boats were pulled into the cumbungi, parallel with the river. Wind isn't a problem. Because of the cumbungi-lined banks and the constantly turning river, you can always find somewhere sheltered. Upstream of the Boggy Creek ramp, the river is more open but access is still through private land. As you head upstream, the river becomes shallower, snags are more common and, in places, the riverbank is overgrown with tea tree. The snags hold bream to more than 40cm and about 5km upstream is the Scout camp, an area that is known for its **estuary perch**.

The upstream waters have a small following of saltwater fly-fishers chasing bream and **estuary perch**. A few **mulloway** are caught in the river, up to 13.5kg. Much depends on whether the river mouth is open to the sea.

WARRNAMBOOL

Warrnambool is a big, tidy regional city. It's a great place to take the family for a holiday, particularly if you have fishing on your mind. All forms of angling are available, but the most popular water is the Hopkins River estuary. It is one of the state's best waters, with good numbers of **bream**, **estuary perch**, **mullet** and even **mulloway** when conditions are favourable. When the mouth is open to the sea, the Hopkins River is tidal for about 8km, almost to Allansford.

The Hopkins River estuary has two convenient boat ramps. The first is at the bottom of Jubilee Park Rd, and the other about a kilometre upstream from the main road bridge.

Land-based fishing in the water is also easy and accessible. The refurbished bridge near the mouth of the river is a popular destination, and lure and fly-fishers often wade around the Jubilee Park area for bream and perch.

The Merri River, to the west of town, can produce excellent **trout** fishing due to stocking by Fisheries Victoria. The river contains some of the largest riverine trout in Victoria, rivalling many better known south-west lakes in terms of size and quality. When released, most trout are yearlings weighing 50–150g. In productive water like the Merri River, these fish reach weights of over 1kg in their second year of life, and some of the longer lived trout grow to over 2kg and live for three or four years.

The pier at Port Campbell is a popular fishing spot, offering sheltered fishing conditions in an area noted for its big seas and strong winds

The Merri River is open all year to fishing up to the Bromfield Weir.

Levis Beach to the west of the city and Logans Beach Whale Sanctuary, adjacent to the Hopkins river mouth, can produce good catches of **salmon**, **yelloweye mullet** and sometimes mulloway.

Offshore at Warrnambool, beyond the 30m line, anglers catch **mako**, **blue**, **gummy**, **thresher** and **school sharks**. **Snapper** can be caught over the reefs, both inshore and offshore, while **nannygai** and **blue morwong** work along the 25m line. On the inshore reefs, salmon, **sweep**, **snook**, **couta** and **pike** are best fished with berley and unweighted bait. Salmon and **silver trevally** also haunt the close-in reef areas and **crayfish (southern rock lobster)** fishing is popular over the summer.

In Warrnambool Harbour, anglers fishing in among the boat moorings also do well for **King George whiting** and mullet. The breakwater is a popular venue where anglers catch mainly salmon, barracouta and **pinkies**, although snapper to 8kg have been caught.

Cam Whittam with a better than average black bream caught on a lure

Methods for Great Ocean Road

Estuaries

TACKLE A 3kg outfit is the most popular. This consists of a small threadline reel (about size 20) and a rod about 1.8m long with a soft tip for bait fishing. Longer rods with softer tips are preferred by some, as they are more forgiving of sticky drag systems. If you intend casting lures, then opt for a rod with a sharper tip action and recovery. Bream are a tough fish and many anglers keep their catch in a keeper net alongside the boat. This gives them the opportunity to keep on fishing when they have caught their bag limit, swapping fish when they hook a bigger one.

RIGS A running sinker rig, consisting of a pea-size ball sinker and a leader of about 1m works well. Sinkers should be as small as conditions allow. Unweighted baits are best if you intend fishing the upriver snags or casting into the undercut banks. The slower sink rate of an unweighted bait is often more attractive to bream and estuary perch.

Hook size is about a No. 4 medium shank such as a Baitholder pattern. Some anglers prefer to drop back to a No. 6 hook for shrimp and worm baits. Due to the barbs on the back of the shank, the Baitholder hook works best with soft baits.

BAIT Popular baits used here include podworms, scrub worms, shrimp, greyback minnow, brown shell, yabbies and crabs. The preferred bait, however, is fresh shrimp, which can be netted in the river. Buy a fine mesh net, find an area of riverbank not overgrown with cumbungi and drag the net through the under bank vegetation. Blanche the shrimp in boiling water, which will turn them white.

LURES Soft plastic lures are all the rage, but many anglers have reverted to small hard-bodied lures, bibbed minnows or adopted blade lures. These will catch bream and estuary perch.

Beach, pier and rocks

TACKLE An 8–10kg threadline outfit is a good starting point for these scenarios and a rod about 3–3.5m long, capable of casting sinkers or lures up to 120g. Solid-tip rods dominate the market, but for my money are too soft on the tip and lack the recovery that assists with casting. Rod taper and construction determine distance, not the weight of the rod, which is why carbon fibre is popular. Not only is it lighter, this material has better recovery when casting, giving increased distance with lighter weights.

How far you cast on a beach depends on where the channels or gutters are. Some days they will be almost at your feet.

RIGS If you are after big fish such as mulloway or gummy sharks, use big bait and 6/0 Suicide pattern hooks on a running paternoster rig. Australian salmon is the mainstay species and most anglers fish a simple two-dropper paternoster rig. The top dropper has a surf popper or saltwater fly instead of bait, the bottom dropper a 3/0–4/0 long shank or Suicide pattern hook. For fish such as whiting, you might find it preferable to come down to about 2/0.

Sinker type depends on conditions. In calm water with little side drift, a bomb sinker is suitable. However, in rough water with side drift, most anglers use star or grapnel sinkers, which have wires jutting out that dig into the sand. The best way to attach any sinker is with a clip swivel as this enables quick and easy changing of sinker weights to suit conditions.

On a beach, a rod holder is essential. You can make your own out of a metre-long piece of 50mm diameter PVC tube. As well as holding your rod tip high and above the waves, a rod holder is ideal for holding the rod when baiting up.

BAIT Use pilchards, squid, whitebait, bluebait, pipi, mussel and fish fillets. Salmon is especially good when the salmon are around and you are after larger fare.

Boat fishing

TACKLE There are two basic outfits to have on board. A 2m rod suited to 6–9kg lines will cover the bottom bouncing, trolling and spinning. Use small swivels, hooks from No. 6 through to about 4/0 as well as a selection of sinkers. In deep water, you will find braid line will allow you to fish deeper with lighter sinkers, and feel the bite better. If you want to catch sharks, a 15kg game rod and reel will suffice for most toothy denizens.

BAIT Same as for beach and pier.

Freshwater fishing

TACKLE In the mountains, light tackle is the go. For lure fishers, light 2–3kg outfits will suffice. This is great water for dry flies, but the trout can be skittish. Look at using four- or five-weight outfits and 1–2kg tippets in the small waters, and 3kg tippets in the lower reaches.

BAIT Top baits are shrimp, wood grubs and scrub worms. Shrimp are the most easily obtained bait; all you need is a long-handled fine mesh net and a coffee jar with moist sawdust to keep them alive. They are found living in submerged watercress overhanging the riverbanks. Thread half a dozen shrimp onto a No. 4 Baitholder hook. The shrimp are too small to thread longitudinally, so the hook passes through the middle of the shrimp at right angles to its body.

LURES Lure size, oddly enough, is less of a problem. The deeper stretches are best worked with thumbnail-size minnow lures or else the ever-reliable bladed lures. Casting takes a refined, gentle touch. The dense foliage overhanging much of the water often determines that an underhand flick or a bow-and-arrow cast is more functional than the normal overhead style.

FLIES In the upper reaches where the streams and fish are smaller, dry flies such as the Red Tag, Mayfly, Caddis imitations and Thorax patterns, from No. 16 through to about No. 22, can produce satisfying fishing. However, unless an obvious hatch is underway, it's less about matching the hatch and more about pot-luck. Success requires dedicated skill and application, as there can be large dollops of frustration.

In the lower reaches from the foothills to the sea, use wet flies such as Matuka, BMS, Clouser, Muddler Minnows or baitfish and shrimp patterns.

Offshore anglers seek out sharks like this mako that took a squid bait

10 SOUTH-WEST VICTORIA

LAKE WARTOOK

From Melbourne, take the Western Hwy to Ararat, then to Halls Gap and follow signs to the top of the Grampians.

The lake is mainly about trout and redfin.

ACCOMMODATION: The lake has no camping facilities, and camping is not allowed around the lake foreshore – so, if heading up this way, you will need to sleep elsewhere.
For more information visit www.grampiansvictoria.com.au

Drought and changes to irrigation methods during the so-called noughties, left many of Victoria's favourite fishing lakes dry. A drive through the Wimmera revealed once famous lakes including Toolondo, Lonsdale, Hindmarsh, Green, Pine and Dock Lake that in the latter stages of the ten-year drought, ranged from large billabongs to dustbowls.

Amid the cropping plains of the Wimmera, Lake Wartook stood as an oasis. Located less than an hour's drive from Horsham, it was usually full and surrounded by green, lush forest. It was hard to believe you were in the same country, never mind the same region.

Lake Wartook sits atop the Grampians National Park, 442m above sea level on the McKenzie River. The 1000ha lake, which is used for both domestic and irrigation storage, has a boat ramp. If taking a boat out, take care, as there are many submerged tree stumps. The deepest water is at the wall and between Bear Island and the western shore. There is no horsepower limit but a speed limit of five or eight knots (depending on which sign you read) applies, and boats with sleeping accommodation or toilets are banned.

The lake's reputation as a serious **brown trout** and **redfin** fishery is what really matters. Local angler, Bill Johnson, was a caretaker for the dam and being a keen angler, living in isolation beside the water was not exactly a hardship. '**Brown trout** in the lake are up to 3kg in size, with the average fish going between 1–2kg,' Bill said. 'The lake also holds **redfin** to about 2kg, **river blackfish** to 800g and **tench**.'

Importantly, you don't need a boat to catch fish. Bill said one of the most consistent spots on the lake, particularly from late autumn through the winter months, is along the dam wall.

LAKE FYANS

Like many Victorian waters, Lake Fyans suffered during the drought but the fish seemed to survive and recovered faster than most waters when the drought broke in October, 2010.

ACCOMMODATION: There is plenty of accommodation available at Stawell and Halls Gap but for those who like to be on the spot, you can stay at the lake.
For more information visit www.lakefyansholidaypark.com.au

Freshwater angling in Victoria was hard hit by the long drought that seems to have lasted for most of the Noughties. At the height of the dry, Fisheries Victoria struggled to find enough suitable waters to place all the 350,000 or so **trout** it releases annually.

In those dry years, as you drove through the Central, Wimmera and Mallee regions, grass could be seen in depressions that were once lakes. The hangover of the drought was that some lakes, created as they were by water authorities, have probably disappeared forever.

However, there is some good news. Lake Fyans, near Stawell on the edge of the Grampians, recovered quickly from the worst of the drought and is back in favour with anglers. The lake highlights how quickly recovery can come. In 2008, water levels in the 526ha lake were down to 13 per cent. The boat ramp near the caravan park was high and dry and revenue loss for the local community was tipped at $4 million.

With low water levels, no sign of rain and summer coming on, residents were concerned there would be a mass kill of trout and **redfin** that could leave thousands of fish putrefying around the lake shoreline. Fisheries Victoria initiated a program to salvage some dollars from the remaining trout by allowing a commercial netter to harvest the remaining fish.

During the previous six years, the lake had been stocked with an average 6000 rainbow trout and 6000 brown trout annually. At the time the harvesting program was announced, Fisheries estimated that up to 9000 rainbow trout and 12,000–15,000 brown trout over 1kg, and larger numbers of redfin, were in the lake.

The good news for anglers is that the lake is fishable once again and after a serious bout of stocking, is producing brown and rainbow trout to 2.8kg along with redfin to 1kg.

Carson Jacobs with a rainbow trout caught at Lake Toolondo

LAKE TOOLONDO

Lake Toolondo is located between Hamilton and Horsham; about four hours' drive from Melbourne. From Melbourne take the Western Hwy through Ballarat, Ararat to Horsham, then turn left onto Golf Course Rd and follow through to Horsham–Noradjuha Rd and then take the Natimuk–Hamilton Rd.

ACCOMMODATION: The Wash Tomorrow Caravan Park is situated at the southern end of the lake, and it has caravan and camping sites, and onsite vans. There is an earthen ramp, but this is far from the water when the lake levels are low. The campground is off John McPhees Rd, accessed from Telangatuk Rd.

To contact Trevor Holmes for Victorian Inland Charters, phone 0438 132 130.

For more information visit www.travelvictoria.com.au/horsham/accommodation

During the 1980s, Lake Toolondo was the hottest **trout** fishing still water in Victoria. So long as the lake had water, trout and **redfin** offered great fishing experiences around the tree-lined lakes. In August 2001, Lake Toolondo was at 10 per cent of its maximum level. As the drought persisted, Lake Toolondo reverted to the original Bartons Swamp. A Fisheries Victoria survey found **brown trout** to 3.5kg trapped in the receding waters.

The drought broke in October 2010, and in 2011 Bartons Swamp filled, and once more became Lake Toolondo. Fisheries acted and stocked brown and **rainbow trout**. By 2013, Toolondo was yielding trout better than 3kg.

The fishing became so good that fourth generation Wimmera angler, Trevor Holmes set up Victorian Inland Charters and concentrated on this lake. It seemed a good idea at the time as most anglers believed water in Lake Toolondo was guaranteed to be kept at a minimum level. A change in State Government changed that, and at the time of writing in 2014, the future of the lake is with Mother Nature.

In July 2013, the lake was at 34 per cent capacity. Twelve months later in July 2014, Trevor said the lake was at about 25 per cent capacity and 2.7m at its deepest point. As it declined, Toolondo reverted to three individual lakes, however, there was still plenty of good water.

The trout being caught in the lake are not even three years' old and yet many are in excess of 4kg. Trevor said the biggest trout he had seen was a rainbow trout that weighed about 5kg and was caught by a fly fisher casting from shore. Most rainbows weigh between 1.8–3.3kg. Brown trout to 4.35kg were also being caught in good numbers, along with redfin to 1.8kg.

There are boat ramps at both the north and southern ends of the lake. The northern ramp is concrete, and the southern ramp is dirt and located in the caravan park. Water levels dictate whether the ramps are usable.

The lake is heavily treed in most areas, and teeming with aquatic life including **mudeye**, **minnow**, **gudgeon** and **yabbies**. Algal blooms during periods of low water can close down the fishing opportunities.

Even when it is low, the Wimmera River has enough holes and structure to hold fish like yellowbelly and catfish

DIMBOOLA

From Melbourne take the Western Hwy through Ballarat, Ararat, Horsham and follow signs to Dimboola.

Freshwater catfish, yellowbelly, carp and redfin are some of the fish you are likely to encounter.

ACCOMMODATION: For more information visit www.travelvictoria.com.au/dimboola

At first sight the Wimmera River didn't look special. Barely flowing, it consisted of sandbars and fallen trees interspersed with shallows and a few deeper holes below the timber. I was fishing with local anglers, Bill Johnson and Laurie Liston. Soon after we crossed the river at Dimboola, we turned south into Little Desert National Park. Our destination was one of Bill's favourite catfish holes, but it wasn't marked on any map. To get there we turned on to one dusty, unmarked and unmade track after another, forever weaving and turning to dodge river gums and tea trees.

The Wimmera River marks the eastern boundary of Little Desert National Park. My first view of the stretch of water we were going to fish was uninspiring, but I held the faith. After all, Bill and Laurie assured me there would be catfish. The Wimmera River holds **carp**, **silver** and **golden perch (yellowbelly)**, **eel tailed catfish**, **redfin**, and some **Murray cod** up to about 28kg, as well as the usual small forage species. The river dries to a series of pools during summer but these retain permanent habitat.

Both anglers said the river was a magic place for anglers willing to paddle kayaks. 'You find there are holes all the way from Jeparit to Horsham and it's not difficult to work a kayak over the shallow sections,' Bill said.

My reason for being here this night was the **catfish**. It is the only place I know of in Victoria where catfish are the major part of the catch. The catfish, which weigh up to 2kg, were brought to the river from the Murray River by some local anglers, a process that spanned several generations.

'Catfish are an aggressive, predatory species, the flathead of the river,' Laurie said. The population of catfish boomed, their numbers such that this species dominates the angling scene and is credited with keeping **carp** numbers low.

The fishing was simple. Bill had brought along a bucket of worms, and using a running sinker rig with a No. 4 medium shank hook, he threaded two worms on the hook and cast his bait alongside the timber. Bill said peeled, raw yabbie tail was another excellent bait. Catfish are nocturnal feeders and bite best from dusk through to midnight.

'To achieve regular success you must place your bait in close to the timber,' he said.

We were fishing a small pool of water. An old tree lay partially across the water, its branches spread like tentacles and Bill put his bait hard in against the logs. Almost as soon as it got dark, the catfish came on the bite. They can be finicky feeders, sometimes the slightest line movement indicating that all that was left of the worm bait was probably a short piece of meat on the hook shank. At the slightest movement of line, we had to pick up our rod and be ready to set the hook and hang on because the bigger catfish would pull our line straight through the timber.

River blackfish are a sought-after species in the Wimmera River at Dimboola

A word of caution: Take care when handling catfish as they have three spines that will spike and inflict a stinging pain similar to a flathead. The spikes are located on the dorsal fin and on each pectoral fin.

LAKE TOOLIOROOK

From Melbourne take Princes Hwy to Geelong, then turn right on Hamilton Hwy through Inverleigh, Cressy and then Lismore. At Lismore turn left on Lismore–Skipton Rd for about 5km, the lake is on the left.

It's a well-stocked rainbow trout lake.

ACCOMMODATION: For more information visit www.lismore.vic.au/tourism/accommodation

Sometimes you hear stories of a hot bite and think to yourself, yeah another fairy story. Well here is the good oil on a drought breaker that began in the spring of 2010 and will continue through until the next major drought, which I hope is a long way off.

I had heard stories that Lake Tooliorook was fishing extremely well. A year before this trip the lake was dry, so off I went. In fact the **trout** bite was so hot I was worried the fish would come to the boat poached.

Better still, Lake Tooliorook isn't the only Victorian trout water with a hot bite, and it all came down to a seasonal change and, as unlikely as it sounds, some quick action by a government department. The extraordinary rainfall in 2010 caused devastation and heartache for many folks, but Victoria's trout anglers dined out on the results.

It was winter, closed season for trout in Victoria's rivers and, the same time the year before there were limited opportunities; the state was still in the grip of prolonged drought and many lakes were little more than swamps; some even dried up. The spring rains changed that. Empty lakes in the southwest and central parts of the state filled and, in some instances, overflowed.

It was an opportunity too good to miss for Fisheries Victoria and the department responded quickly to kick-start the lakes. Sourcing 187,500 brown and rainbow trout at short notice from its Snobs Creek Hatchery and private hatcheries, Fisheries began stocking the lakes with trout that went from 50g to yearlings. Six months later and some of those fish were weighing better than a kilogram. It was a phenomenal growth rate.

Fisheries would not normally stock fingerlings due to predator species like redfin. However, the redfin died as the lakes dried, so fingerling trout could be stocked without being eaten. In May 2011, anglers were catching these small trout as yearlings.

There has been much praise for Fisheries from caravan-park owners and small town shopkeepers to Victoria's peak angling lobby group, VRFish, whose chairman, Geoff Cramer, said the rapid stocking response had delivered the goods for freshwater anglers already with the yearling stockings paying off most of all.

'Anderson's Lagoon (better known as Hepburns Lagoon) near Ballarat was the standout performer. Big numbers of rainbow trout between 800g and 1kg were being caught just five months after release,' Mr Cramer said.

It is the same in many waters. Mr Cramer said: 'Rainbow trout to 700g were being caught at Newlyn Reservoir while Bostock Reservoir, near Ballan, yielded rainbows up to 500g. Greenhill Lake, near Ararat, was producing some rainbow trout up to 1kg while anglers have also enjoyed success at Tullaroop Reservoir, Lake Elingamite and Deep Lake further south.'

Lake Bolac in the Western District was also fishing well and Fisheries Victoria expects Lake Wendouree at Ballarat to be producing trout to 700g.

Fly-fishing writer Philip Weigall said he was surprised at how quickly the fisheries had turned around. He was concerned that trout food might have been a problem but all the bugs are back: midges, water beetles, mayflies and even baitfish.

'If you write anything,' Phil said, 'be sure to let your readers know that there is a bag limit of five trout a day.' Some anglers it seems have been taking advantage of the turnaround and going home with extra fish – perhaps trying to make up for the lost decade?

So, where should you fish? Well, waters stocked with rainbow trout only under the drought recovery program include:

Barkers Creek Reservoir, (4000), Lake Batyo Catyo (4000), Lake Beaufort (2000), Bostock Reservoir (5000), Lake Burrumbeet (5000), Deep Lake (2000), Hepburn Lagoon (20,000), Newlyn Reservoir (5000), Rocklands Reservoir (10,000), Lake Tooliorook (also called Lake Ettrick, 10,000), Lake Wendouree (90,000 fingerlings).

Some other waters were given a mix of trout. Cairn Curran Reservoir received 2500 browns and 7500 rainbows, Teddington Reservoir 1500 browns and 3000 rainbows; and Tullaroop Reservoir fish releases consisted of 5000 browns and the same number of rainbow trout. The odd water in all of this is Greenhill Lake, which was the only water to receive only brown trout, 1000.

To these numbers can be added another 500,000 trout stocked into Victoria's lakes before the spring rains. It leaves anglers with many options.

LAKE BOLAC

From Melbourne, take the Western Hwy to Ballarat, and then turn west on the Glenelg Hwy, driving through Skipton and then Lake Bolac.

In late 2011, Lake Bolac proved to be the hottest trout water in Victoria with anglers catching rainbow trout to 4kg. These were fish that 12 months earlier had been released as 50–70g yearlings. Redfin will come back and hopefully the trout will be sustained.

ACCOMMODATION: For more information visit www.travelvictoria.com.au/lakebolac

One of my favourite fishing activities after a hot summer day is to wander along the banks of the Barwon River in Geelong, casting lures for **redfin**. Redfin are a feisty, competitive fish that bites readily, and comes up well on the table. Many people underestimate the popularity of redfin, particularly in country areas. A Victorian poll of anglers to determine the most popular fish showed trout had the biggest following and redfin came in second, ahead of the iconic Murray cod and yellowbelly.

Victoria has plenty of redfin waters, and one of the best known is Lake Bolac, alongside the town of the same name in central Victoria. Surrounded by farms, the lake covers 1460ha and features foreshore camping and day-visitor facilities, picnic and beach areas, boat ramps, electric barbecues and hot showers. In short, this waterway is an ideal family holiday or day-visit destination.

Lake Bolac has a special standing among Victorian lakes. Few world records come from Victorian waters, let alone lakes. Sure, we claim world records for exceptional growth rates of trout in waters like Purrumbete and Bullen Merri, but you don't get International Game Fish Association recognition for growth rates.

Boat ramp at Lake Bolac

Well, Lake Bolac has a world record. On the Lake Bolac Angling Club bulletin board in the shelter next to the boat ramp is a framed newspaper clipping and a copy of an International Game Fish Association world record certificate. The certificate states that Bernard Murphy caught a 7.48kg (16lb 8oz) **short finned eel** on 17 November, 1998. The eel was an all tackle world record.

According to Victorian Fisheries, the lake is predominantly redfin water with fish to 875g and averaging about 500g. It also has short finned eels, **tench** and **carp**. There are some large **yellowbelly** from an earlier (1990) stocking, but anglers seldom take them, and some illegally stocked Murray cod. Not surprisingly, the lake is commercially fished for short-finned eels. Despite the world-record quality of the eels available, the anglers here were more interested in redfin. Since **trout** were stocked in 2010, these are the dominant species but rest assured, redfin will come back, they always do.

LAKE LONSDALE

Take the Western Hwy to Ballarat, Beaufort, Ararat, and then Stawell. Take the Grampians Rd towards Halls Gap, then turn right on Mt Dryden Rd.

Victoria's Wimmera region experienced a boom in recreational fishing in 2011: angling licence sales are up about 300 per cent and about half of those sales are directly attributable to the explosion in the yabbie population. It had been several years since anglers could consistently catch large numbers of yabbies. All that changed with the onset of the spring rains that broke the decade-long drought.

ACCOMMODATION: Lake Lonsdale is part of the Grampians Region where tourism plays a major role in the economy of many towns.

For more information visit www.visitvictoria.com/regions/grampians/accommodation.aspx

Redfin are a favourite among Wimmera anglers. Some years you will catch them to a couple of kilograms, but most times this fish is from 250g to about 1kg.

The bigger specimens tend to hang about structure such as logs, tree roots, shady overhangs and rockbars. A light line speciality, redfin hit a bait or lure well, and the fight is more dogged than most introduced species.

Redfin will take worm, gudgeon and minnow on the bottom, or fished under a quill float as well as most small lures.

Most waters affected by the rains were producing the best **yabbie** returns experienced for many years. Lake Lonsdale near Stawell has been a yabbie hotspot and Murray Burns, senior Fisheries Victoria officer at Horsham, said it was taking anglers about three hours to catch their 30L limit of yabbies. Lakes Hindmarsh and Natimuk and other west Wimmera Lakes also produce yabbies.

Yabbies are survivors. When a waterhole dries up, a yabbie burrows down to the moist soil at the water table below. This creature remains underground until water fills the catchment area, a survival strategy that helps explain why yabbie numbers boomed after the floods. During hibernation, yabbies live off the meat in their claws and, to a lesser extent, the tail meat.

For more on yabbies including state regulations, *see* page 51.

Lake Lonsdale has always been a favourite for anglers with a taste for redfin and yabbies; sometimes one is more dominant than the other

LAKES PURRUMBETE AND BULLEN MERRI

From Melbourne, take the Princess Hwy to Geelong, Winchelsea, Colac then Camperdown.

Arguably the deepest lakes in Victoria, the Western District Crater Lakes consistently produce the biggest brown and rainbow trout and, when stocked, can be counted on for Chinook and Atlantic salmon.

ACCOMMODATION: Caravan parks, cabins and motel accommodation are available.
For more information visit www.travelvictoria.com.au

When people talk about **trout** fishing in Victoria, the bulk of the serious action is in the Western District crater lakes. Of these Lake Purrumbete near Camperdown ranks in the top half a dozen trout lakes in the state in terms of quality, quantity and accessibility.

The 552ha lake is a freshwater legend, being a success story for as long as I can remember, due to heavy stocking rates of brown and **rainbow trout** and **Chinook salmon**. Some **Atlantic salmon** are also released. In addition, the lake has a good reputation for **redfin** that average about 1kg.

What attracts anglers more than quantity though is the fish quality. Trout and salmon achieve dramatic growth rates and, while most trout and salmon caught are 1–2kg, fish weighing 3kg and 4kg are not a rare capture. On trout opening day in September 2003, Altona angler Rodney Smith caught a 7.25kg monster **brown trout**, explaining it was one of several similar size trout he had seen that morning.

Lake Purrumbete is surrounded by private property and public access to the lake is restricted. There is a boat ramp and caravan park at the south-western corner and public shoreline access at Hoses Rocks, on the western shore, and through the quarry on the eastern side. After that it's shanks pony. Boats give easy access to all areas of the lake and shoreline. In 2009 a temporary boat launching facility was established near Hoses Rocks after the lake level fell so much that the usual boat ramp was left high and dry.

Lake Bullen Merri is a deep lake that produces spectacular results for trout, Chinook and Atlantic salmon

Big brown trout, like this 3.42kg specimen caught by Bruce Morrison, are part of the scene at Lake Purrumbete

Lake Bullen Merri at Camperdown is less than 20 minutes drive from Lake Purrumbete. A deep, volcanic lake with saline water, Bullen Merri is stocked with brown and rainbow trout, Atlantic and Chinook salmon, and **Australian bass**. Trout and salmon captures topping 4kg are not rare. The **bass** is slower growing than either trout or salmon and, unlike trout and salmon, it bites best when the weather is hot. Bass were put into the lake as a test to see if they would grow and hopefully offer anglers a summer fishing opportunity on the lake. Progress has been slow although bass to 1.3kg can be caught.

Access around the lake is easy. There are two boat ramps, one at the north-east corner near where the road ends at the fence, and the larger ramp at the southern end of the lake near the Bullen Merri Anglers Clubhouse.

For shore-based anglers, access is along the road that fronts the southern, western, and northern shores. Top spots include South Beach, near the boat ramp; Potters Point about halfway along the western shore, and the stretch from The Cave near the pine trees at the north end to the Coral at the eastern fence line. Fly-fishers do reasonably well near Potters Point and the South Beach.

A lot depends on where the fish are working on the day, the main problem with this lake is the wind because, regardless of the direction the wind is coming from, eventually it will swirl around and be in your face. Anglers trolling often tend to work their lures close to shore, with Potters and Wurrong points at the southern end well regarded.

KONONG WOOTONG RESERVOIR

Although just a ten-minute drive out of Coleraine, Konong Wootong isn't well signposted. To get there, take the Coleraine–Harrow Rd, turning off at Reservoir Rd. The water is surrounded by farmland and ringed by ancient pine trees that give some wind protection.

A small water with a big reputation for its trout fishing, and the Coleraine local chocolate factory will have you coming back for more.

ACCOMMODATION: For people who want to stay a few days, camping is permitted below the wall.
For more information visit www.southerngrampians.com.au/towns/coleraine.html

Coleraine in Victoria's Western District is in the heart of prime wool-growing country. The small town is also famous for its chocolate factory. Less well known among the general angling public is the **trout** fishery in the small impoundment just out of town, Konong Wootong Reservoir.

Konong Wootong Reservoir is a picturesque water constructed 80 years ago to supply the domestic water for Coleraine and Casterton. The 60ha impoundment is now solely a recreational fishery. Local angler Noel Vickery said it is one of the best trout fisheries in the state, and among the best public fly-fishing waters available. Noel has fished this water since 1947, and said it is a firm favourite with SA fly-fishers.

'The lake holds the world record growth for a **rainbow trout**,' he said. 'A two-year-old rainbow, stocked into the lake as fry, grew to 9lb 12oz.'

Noel said that fish went to the British Museum in London, but it was a long way short of the biggest trout to come out of this water. He can't remember the exact date but, in 1939, angler Dorothy Woolley caught a rainbow trout that weighed in at 14lb 10oz.

'She was fishing with mudeye and used a split cane rod and catgut line,' Noel said. 'The good quality of trout in this water attracted the Ballarat Fish Hatchery people who would come to the lake and strip the trout of their eggs for breeding purposes.'

According to Victorian Fisheries, this water holds **brown trout** that average about 1kg and

Structures like these weed beds around Konong Wootong Reservoir offer a haven for insect life and make a great food source for trout

are up to 2kg, rainbow trout and **redfin** to 1.6kg and the water is stocked regularly with brown and rainbow trout. Non-power boating is permitted. Many fly-fishers who come here fish from float tubes or canoes. For many, the early mayfly hatches in September and October are a major attraction. Despite many weed beds around the shoreline there are plenty of areas for shore-based anglers. A favourite area is the retaining wall at the Coleraine end, but look for snakes among the rocks.

Methods for Lake Wartook to Konong Wootong Reservoir

TACKLE Threadline outfits to about 3kg cover most options. Anglers bait fishing with bubble floats often prefer rods up to 3m long as these allow them to cast with longer leaders. Fly-fishers tend to work five–six-weight outfits and sinking lines.

BAIT Popular baits include mudeye, glassie, pilchard strips, worms, gudgeon and minnow. Manufactured bait like Powerbait also works well here at times.

RIGS Bait type dictates hook size. A mudeye, which is a dragonfly nymph, is a delicate creature and requires a small hook that is passed gently through the wing casing. A No. 14 to No. 10, 9287BZ-pattern hook is popular.

For most other baits, such as glassie, use a No. 6 to No. 4 Baitholder. A new hook on the market, the Mustad Demon, light gauge circle hook in size 2 is worth a look. The hook should be threaded through the bait from the tail and the point exposed in the region of the head. A half hitch is placed around the tail to keep the bait straight. Minnow and gudgeon require a No. 8 or No. 10 hook that is passed through the upper jaw of the fish, but not so deep as to harm it, again the light gauge, circle hook is ideal.

When fishing from shore, bubble floats are preferred over pencil floats by most anglers. A bubble float is not designed to keep bait suspended off the bottom at a set depth, rather it is designed to assist the angler to cast bait out. A bubble float has a tube that passes through the centre and this acts as a pump to fill the bubble with the required amount of water. The more water, the heavier the float, and the further the angler can cast. The line is passed through this tube and a small piece of cork is threaded on the line below the float but above the bait. This cork regulates bait depth. Ideally, this should be no more than the length of the rod to enable casting, hence the use of longer rods.

LURES Murray Wilson's Bullen Merri Special or BMS is a popular fly, as too is the Tom Jones, Black Matuka and Woolly Bugger patterns. Spinning, downrigging and flatline trolling techniques are all employed using bibbed minnow lures like Rapala CD5 and 7 and Halco Poltergeists, and winged lures such as Tassie Devils and Loftys.

PORT FAIRY

From Melbourne take the Princes Hwy through Geelong, Colac, Camperdown and Warrnambool to Port Fairy.

This town is a small, historic seaport with a big fish reputation – great white sharks and southern bluefin tuna top the list. Other fish caught include salmon, sweep and yellowtail kingfish in the ocean; bream, trevally and mulloway in the Moyne River.

ACCOMMODATION: For more information visit www.portfairyaccommodation.com

Port Fairy is an unimposing historic seaport situated about midway between Warrnambool and Portland. Moreover, while it might come across as a sleepy, seaside resort Port Fairy always seems to attract piscatorial headlines. During the 1960s and 70s, the headlines were about sharks – **great whites** to be precise.

The first time I heard of Port Fairy was in November 1964 when Melbourne skindiver Henri Bource joined the world's most exclusive club: those who have been attacked by a **great white shark** and survived. Henri lost a leg to a shark while diving in Dinghy Cove on the northern face of Lady Julia Percy Island, 16km away to the south-west. A decade later saw the release of the movie *Jaws*, which boosted the popularity of big gamefishing for Great Whites. Efforts were made to establish Port Fairy as a gamefishing port for Great Whites and for a short time it attracted people like film star Lee Marvin and country singer John Denver. Fishing for white sharks, which is now illegal, soon went out of vogue and this historic seaport faded from the fishing spotlight.

In the spring of 2005 the township was back in the news with **mulloway**, that enigma of the Victorian angler, being caught in the Moyne River in an area known as Belfast Lough. Apparently a few of the locals had managed to keep the mulloway quiet for some time.

On 19 March 2006 Port Fairy hit the piscatorial headlines again. This time it was a whopper: an 85kg **southern bluefin tuna**, at the time it was the biggest southern bluefin caught by an angler in Victorian waters. The tuna, which took Ken Hines and Cameron Ordner four hours to land, was caught in 550m of water 40km south-west of Port Fairy. As if to prove it wasn't a fluke, a few days later another bluefin of 60kg was caught.

The 2010 big run of tuna off Port Fairy started with a 144.6kg **bluefin** on 15 May when most anglers were fishing waters closer to Portland and Port MacDonnell. There were plenty of bluefin being caught off Portland so few anglers paid much attention to what was happening elsewhere. There were about 400 boats launching at Portland that weekend, and such was the chaos that trailer boats were lined up for more than a kilometre waiting to launch.

However, over that weekend of 16 and 17 May, more 100kg plus tuna were landed off Port Fairy and by Monday, many anglers were launching at Portland then motoring east for 50km to Port Fairy, or else launching in the Moyne River. Port Fairy became tuna central and it made the evening news on Friday 21 May, when a 154.6kg bluefin was caught. This fish is still the biggest caught in Victorian waters, but probably a long way short of the biggest tuna hooked.

Most anglers who fish at Port Fairy chase smaller fare. Offshore anglers can catch **mako**, **blue** and **thresher** sharks. The inshore reefs are home to the likes of **snapper**, **King George whiting**, **sweep** and **yellowtail kingfish**. The boat ramp is situated in the Moyne River and the entrance to the sea is safe.

East Beach can produce some excellent whiting fishing and, during winter, salmon to 4kg are often caught. For estuary anglers, the Moyne River is better known for its **bream**, **mullet** and **silver trevally** than it is for mulloway. The Garden St Bridge is a popular spot, while the breakwater at the entrance can produce **snapper**, **whiting** and **salmon**.

Even better news for anglers is that Port Fairy is near several other favourite fishing spots. To the east is Killarney Beach, where you can launch a small boat. A short drive west brings you to Yambuk Lake, a highly regarded **bream** water. Yambuk is well signposted. After taking the turn-off, follow the road through the caravan park to the boat ramp and picnic area. Bream are caught upstream and downstream. The lake, which is 500m upstream of the ramp, is shallow in many areas. Access to the river is difficult. Anglers fishing from boats 50–60m out, and casting back towards the shoreline, catch mostly bream.

Bob McPherson with a pair of southern bluefin tuna caught trolling skirted jigs off Cape Bridgewater

PORTLAND

The next city on from Port Fairy and a major rural industrial centre, Portland also offers easy access to some of the best saltwater fishing available in Victoria.

ACCOMMODATION: For more information visit www.travelvictoria.com.au/portland/accommodation

The **southern bluefin** run off Portland grew so quickly that the council installed another boat ramp to cope with the extra traffic. The area produces the most saltwater species caught in Victoria and this includes **snapper**, **calamari squid**, **yellowtail kingfish**, **salmon**, **barracouta** and **King George whiting**. 'I reckon Portland is Victoria's best kept angling secret,' local angler Bob McPherson told me. Bob made this statement in 2004; at the time, I believed he was right. Times change though and two years later Portland was no longer an angler's secret, becoming Victoria's major gamefishing destination following consistent captures of southern bluefin tuna and **albacore**. Portland had long held a solid reputation for a smaller run of bluefin tuna, fish to about 15kg. Nowadays anglers are on the water in search of 100kg plus tuna and the seaport has become Tuna Central. For all the **tuna** that have been landed, six or eight times as many have been hooked and lost due to tackle failures, inexperience or a combination of both.

Southern bluefin tuna are a serious game fish that will fully test experienced anglers with top shelf tackle. Anglers used to catching 100kg marlin off Bermagui have been on a steep learning curve,

Bluefin are running at Portland

finding these tuna much tougher opponents. Battles lasting more than three hours have been reported, with the anglers' tag teaming and still losing out.

There have been many reports of anglers being 'smoked' (clean spooled) on 24kg gear, and let's face it: any fish that can take 1000m of 24kg line in a single burst is a powerhouse. However, what more can you say about fish that have smoked anglers using heavier, 37kg tackle? Many experienced and reputable anglers have reported hooking fish twice as big as the 'average' 80kg tuna being caught.

No-one knew whether that first season was an aberration but the tuna have continued to show in subsequent years. One certainty though is that anglers now travel further offshore than ever before. On a trip off Portland with Albert Bruckner, Chris Hall, Bob McPherson and Dean Keilor, we travelled about 24 nautical miles south-west of Portland, and about the same distance offshore from Cape Bridgewater, to an area known as 'The Kink'. The water depth there is 180m, and it marks the start of the 'Horseshoe', a 14 nautical mile stretch of the Continental Shelf that runs in a south-east curve.

We saw a couple of tuna, small numbers of birds working along with dolphins. Unfortunately, like many other boats that day, we weren't where the fish were. One crew who were, and already had a 100kg plus tuna on board, came on the radio to report his crew were doing battle with another, bigger tuna. The fight lasted more than three hours before the fish, which had been brought near to the boat several times, finally won the day. That fish was estimated at being at least one-third bigger than the tuna they landed.

The durability of anglers never ceases to amaze. Conditions that day deteriorated steadily as a south-westerly picked up steam, pushing the seas on top of the swells into white caps and making the boat motion uncomfortable. How an angler could stand up in a small boat and battle a big tunny for hours under these conditions was a tribute to his determination.

More than 20 boats were offshore from Portland that day, and probably just as many came east from Port MacDonnell, just over the border. The only other Portland boat to have success managed to hook ten bluefin, losing four – an amazing effort. Unlike most boats, these anglers were not trolling all day. Instead, they opted to troll large bibbed minnows until they found the tuna, and then proceeded to cube them up with a berley trail as you do **yellowfin tuna** in NSW.

Simon Elliott caught this 11.1kg mulloway from the Lee Breakwater on bluebait

Many anglers are wondering what impact the tuna will have on Portland. Short term, the boat ramp will be crowded and accommodation in short supply. At times when the tuna are running hot more than 190 boats have launched at Portland. The capture of a single fish, the right fish, can be an amazing drawcard. In 1966, Richard Obach caught a 1064lb black marlin off Cairns in North Queensland. The catch broke the world record for 37kg line and was the catalyst that saw Cairns change from a sleepy sugar industry town into an international gamefishing city.

There is more to Portland than tuna, and whether you fish surf, rock or offshore, there is a variety of species. The former whaling settlement is the hub in the western Victorian saltwater angler's wheel, the fishing reads like a 'Who's Who' of southern Australian species. Expect to catch snapper, **Australian salmon**, King George whiting and even **mulloway**. There is **shark** fishing for species such as **threshers**, **makos** and **blues; snook** grow to over-size proportions and the harbour has solid runs of **haddock** (**trevalla**) and **silver trevally**.

The best thing about Portland is that even when the south-westers are whipping up the seas elsewhere, Portland Bay is relatively settled. In November and December, some of Portland's more innovative anglers catch **thresher sharks** on lures off the North Shore, out from Wally's Ramp at Allestree. A big hit over the summer and autumn in the same area is the annual run of yellowtail kingfish up to about 15kg.

Portland harbour has excellent boat launching facilities with fish cleaning benches and, unlike some ramps around the state, has running water and plenty of car parking. Many land-based anglers fish from the Lee breakwater, which is the eastern arm of the harbour. When the sea isn't kind, boats will often drop anchor to fish along the wall. The rock wall that runs east along Dutton Way to Snapper Point has produced mulloway, **whiting**, **gummy sharks** and snapper.

These privately owned, waterfront boat garages and decks along the Glenelg River at Nelson are an unusual sight on Victorian waters

Beach fishing is popular. There are many beaches to choose from. West of the city is Bridgewater Bay, with Shelly and Bridgewater beaches. Even further west is Discovery Bay, a vast beach that stretches from Cape Bridgewater to the Glenelg River estuary near the SA border. About 20km east of Portland is the famous Narrawong Beach.

Popular offshore areas include the Cod Splat, about 3km offshore from the Corkscrew (tower at the end of the southern Breakwall) and in line with Lady Julia Percy Island. King George whiting are fished heavily between Lawrence Rocks and Black Nose Point, while the North Shore of Portland Bay offers up just about everything.

NELSON

The longest navigable river in Victoria, Glenelg River crosses into SA a few kilometres upstream from Nelson, and then flows back into Victoria. The name Glenelg is also unique being a palindrome, that is the word reads the same backwards and forwards.

Black bream, mulloway and estuary perch are the most sought-after species.

ACCOMMODATION: Nelson Hotel offers some of the best steak available anywhere. It is difficult to go past the Nelson Hotel but there is other accommodation on offer.

For more information visit www.nelsonvictoria.com.au

The long river is one of the state's premier fisheries for **bream**, **estuary perch** and **mulloway**. Victoria has some excellent estuaries west of Melbourne, like the Barwon and Hopkins rivers, but none produce as many fish as consistently as the Glenelg.

The river runs beyond Victoria. At a place called Chapmans, a few kilometres upstream from Nelson, the river crosses into SA before snaking back into Victoria at Dry Creek. There are strict speed limits on the Glenelg and to launch at Nelson and motor upstream to some of the areas would take all day at 5 knots. Sapling Creek for example is 26km upstream from the river mouth, but you can get here in about 15 minutes from Nelson by road. Moreover, that's the beauty of this system – many boat ramps and landings are accessible by car. All you need is a map.

Parks Victoria has issued an excellent guide to the area called the Glenelg River Guide, Lower Glenelg National Park. It can be downloaded at: www.parkweb.vic.gov.au. The map covers the river from the river mouth upstream as far as Dartmoor, and it shows boat ramps, campsites and access roads. Anybody contemplating a trip down that way should get a copy of this map.

When the mulloway show, usually about October, the early action takes place at the lower end on the river at Taylors Straight and below Nelson near the mouth. As the season progresses you can expect to be hearing reports of mulloway and bream being caught further upstream at places like Sandy Waterholes, or further up at 'mulloway strait' near Sapling Creek.

Neil Shelton, who runs the Nelson Hotel, is a keen angler and he said: 'It usually follows that our mulloway move into the river after the run starts in SA.' In a good season, mulloway to about 20kg, bream to 1.8kg and estuary perch are caught. Many bream anglers hook mulloway as a by-catch.

Methods for Port Fairy to Nelson

TACKLE Surf fishers should look to their usual 3–4m rods spooled with 8–10kg lines. Boat anglers will find 8–10kg outfits suited to most inshore fishing and mulloway in the Glenelg, but should employ heavier outfits starting at about 15kg in the deeper water. If southern bluefin are your target species, look at serious game fishing tackle starting at 24kg.

For mulloway, use a 4/0 to 6/0 Suicide pattern hook and a minimum 15kg breaking strain leader. Mulloway can be caught on soft plastic lures, and the outfits used are the same as those employed on bream: a 2–3kg spin rod coupled with a size 20 threadline reel spooled with 125–200m of braid. The breaking strain of braid used depends on the angler, but 5kg through to 10kg is okay, just make sure you attach a 10kg monofilament leader. Most of the mulloway caught on soft plastic are hooked in the corner of the mouth so the leader is away from the teeth.

RIGS Estuary rigs can vary. For bream, a running sinker rig with a No. 4 Baitholder pattern hook is standard but be sure to keep the lead size small. If chasing mulloway then a running paternoster rig, with a 24kg leader and a 6/0 hook is a better option. Unweighted baits are preferable whenever you can use them. Trolling small bibbed lures close to the cliffs can produce good results, as can drifting and casting to the rocks and snags with either soft plastic or hard bodied lures.

In the surf, a fixed sinker rig with one or two leaders. For whiting, hooks should be about 2/0, for salmon upsize to size 3/0 or 4/0 hooks. If the salmon are on then put a surf popper rather than bait on the top leader. Anglers bottom fishing offshore generally use a fixed sinker rig and hooks from 3/0 to 6/0 depending on the fish sought.

Most of the tuna are caught on skirted jigs or bibless minnows. Trolling speed is from 8–12 knots, or until the lure is 'smoking' through the waves.

Wind on leaders of 100kg breaking strain should be used.

BAIT In the estuaries, use cut crab, pipis or sandworm for bream, For mulloway, live mullet are the preferred bait and these are either slow trolled or else fished under a float with the boat at anchor. Other baits include fresh squid, pilchards and fish fillets.

11 CENTRAL VICTORIA

Above: Eildon pondage is popular with fly-fishers
Below: Mick Hall shows off a quality rainbow trout caught in Eildon Pondage

LAKE EILDON

Lake Eildon is Victoria's most popular freshwater fishing spot. Part of its popularity is due to its proximity to metropolitan Melbourne. Lilydale is just a 90-minute drive away, either over the Black Spur or via Yea.

Lake Eildon is slowly being transformed into a major Murray cod and yellowbelly fishery. In 2010 a program to stock more than one million Murray cod into the lake was started by Fisheries Victoria. For anglers who prefer other fish there are redfin, carp and brown and rainbow trout to be caught.

ACCOMMODATION: For more information visit www.travelvictoria.com.au/eildon/accommodation

This is a big bit of water. At full capacity, the lake has about 515km of shoreline. Even at 20 per cent capacity, it still measures 35km from end to end.

The lake has been stocked with **rainbow** and **brown trout**, **yellowbelly** and **Murray cod** and has large numbers of **redfin** and **carp**. Summer and autumn are the seasons for redfin and native species; late autumn through winter into spring often producing the best trout fishing.

The Delatite River arm is popular for Murray cod and yellowbelly, although yellowbelly are more widespread. The best bite in the lake is often redfin and you can get good results in Jerusalem Creek, Fraser National Park and Taylor Bay.

For trout anglers, some of the most productive fishing occurs in arms serviced by rivers, such as the Big River and Goulburn River arms, and the main arm under the powerlines off Jerusalem Creek. In some years, brown and rainbow trout to 4kg are caught trolling using both downrigger and flat-line techniques. Concentrate in areas where trout are most likely to be hunting – that is, along drop-offs and weed beds where there is cover for small fish. The biggest trout are more often caught deep.

Other areas worth a look include Jerusalem Inlet, Coller Bay, Italian Bay, Taylor Bay, Bonnie Doon and Howqua Inlet.

Boat ramps are located at Peppin Point near Bonnie Doon, Coller Bay, Jerusalem Creek, Jamieson, Howqua, Macs Cove, Goughs Bay and the Lake Eildon boat harbour.

EILDON PONDAGE

Boating is not allowed on Eildon pondage, which is just below the dam wall at Eildon. Nevertheless, it is one of the most heavily fished waters in the state and is an ideal family spot, with barbecues and toilet facilities. This water is regularly stocked with **trout** from the nearby Snob's Creek Hatchery and has developed into one of the state's most consistent fisheries. As well as the usual run of yearlings, the hatchery also releases older brood fish. Some of these trout are 3–5kg. Many show the scars of hatchery existence in their well-worn tails.

Eildon pondage is divided into upper and lower sections. In the upper pondage, Cemetery Point, Fly Corner and Centre Bridge are angling favourites. In the lower pondage, Bourke St, Riverside Dr and Nursery Corner are well known. You can park your car right alongside where you intend to fish, and there are three designated disabled/wheelchair areas on Riverside Dr.

When word gets out that Fisheries Victoria has been stocking the pondage, anglers immediately assemble right around the pondage, lining up along Riverside Dr, Bourke St at the gates at the Goulburn River end, and near the bridge dividing the upper and lower pondages. The fishing includes **brown** and **rainbow trout** from about 1.2kg through to more than 4kg, and the fishing is about as easy as it gets.

When the fish are on, you don't have to wait for hours for a bite. The most difficult part is hooking the fish. They may be hatchery stock, but trout are wily wherever they come from.

Methods for Lake Eildon and Eildon pondage

TACKLE Most anglers work a 3kg outfit. This consists of a light rod about 2.1–2.3m long balanced with a small threadline reel. A net is an essential item if you are unsure of landing fish by hand. Trout don't have any spines, but native fish and redfin do.

RIGS Trolling with Ford Fender or Cowbell attractors in combination with lures such as rainbow pattern bibbed minnows or Tassie Devils is popular for trout. Downriggers can be used to get lures down to 30m if necessary, and this is often where the trophy trout are likely to be caught.

All of the lures work equally well for spinning, and you can add bladed lures like the Celtas to the list. The best results on lures come by varying depths and retrieve rates.

Native fish and redfin are more likely to be found in heavily wooded areas. Spinning among snags or trolling with small lures such as Stumpjumpers is popular.

Fly-fisher Mick Hall casts his line in the Rubicon River searching for trout

Yellowbelly can be caught on bait, lures and fly. Favourite baits include scrubworms and yabbies. For the most part, anglers after these species fish on the bottom with a running sinker rig or else lower their bait over the side of their boat, allow it to get to the bottom, then wind it up half a metre or so. Trolling can be productive working large bibbed minnow lures such as Halco Poltergeists and Stumpjumpers.

If fishing off the bottom in Eildon Pondage, as you do with mudeyes, use a bubble float. For maggots and mudeyes, you should be using about a No. 12 hook. For Powerbait or scrub worms a No. 8 to No. 6 medium shank Baitholder will do. When fishing shallow areas, a running sinker rig – that is, a leader to the hook below the sinker – is popular with anglers using Powerbait, as it floats off the bottom away from the yabbies. Some anglers attach a berley bin to their lines and allow it to act as a casting weight.

LURES AND FLIES Lure fishers will find small bladed lures do well. Plenty of trout have been caught here on silver wobblers and Tassie Devils. Fly-fishers tend to work five–six-weight outfits and intermediate- or slow-sink lines. Best flies are Long Tailed Chaser, Woolly Bugger and Matuka when working below the surface. If there is an insect hatch, choose a pattern to match the hatch, or opt for old faithfuls like the Adams, Red Tag or Elk Hair Caddis.

BAIT Best baits for trout are mudeyes and scrub worms. In Eildon Pondage, best of the local baits include scrub worms, maggots, mudeyes and Powerbait.

RUBICON RIVER

The Rubicon, one of Victoria's legendary **trout** waters, is popular with trout anglers who fish using all methods available. Rising in forested hills with a steep gradient in the headwaters, the river varies from shallow riffles and runs to deeper pools.

I first fished the Rubicon in the company of Eildon local Mick Hall. We fished several kilometres upstream, just below the power station at an area known as Kendalls. Instead of casting dry flies to rising trout we fished with gold beadhead nymphs below an indicator. It resulted in many brown trout to 1.2kg and smaller rainbow trout.

The turn-off to Kendalls is a few kilometres south of Thornton, and the road follows the Rubicon River to Rubicon township. This area is popular for bush campers, and fishes best early in the season when there is ample flow.

The most easily accessible area on the Rubicon is Tumbling Waters, located where the highway bridge crosses the river on the Thornton–Taggerty Rd, about 3km out of Thornton. This area features a toilet block, playground and barbecue facilities.

Downstream from Thornton is an area known as the 'Tennis Courts'. Access is restricted and depends on the property owners. The Goulburn Broken Catchment Management Authority in conjunction with Fisheries Victoria undertook to repair the riverbank as they removed willow trees. Boulders were added and undercut cover created along the banks. The latter idea was gleaned from the USA, where they call these undercuts 'Lunker Bunkers'. The system works well. Sadly, despite widespread willow removal along other waters, little has happened in the way of streamside rehabilitation.

As Mick and I walked the bank, scores of grasshoppers jumped out of our way. Seeking escape from our feet, some hoppers leapt too far, clearing the bank and landing on the water. The lucky ones ended up on rafts of gum leaves, the rest sat atop the water – a floating smorgasbord for hungry trout.

The Goulburn River is popular among fly-fishers, but flows vary and anglers need to be careful

The name Rubicon was made famous by Julius Caesar. When Caesar crossed the Rubicon's namesake in northern Italy with his 13th Legion more than 2000 years ago, it was an act of war against Rome. For Mick, the reluctance of the trout to sip his fly was an equal affront.

Mick is the most knowledgeable fly-fisher I know, a man with an international reputation for his exquisite fly-tying skills.

But Mick is more than a match for a wily opponent like Mr Speckles. He reduced his tippet size to about 1kg breaking strain and downsized his Chopper Hopper pattern fly two hook sizes to match the size of the grasshoppers. As soon as the fly kissed the water a trout rose to the bogus offering.

Rubicon trout are generally 250–650g, but much bigger trout can be caught. The Rubicon joins with the Goulburn River just below Thornton and the trout in the Goulburn use the Rubicon for spawning during winter. Late in the trout season, as the brown trout begin to move to their spawning areas, you hear of anglers catching trout to about 3kg. A few seasons back, at the start of the spawning run, a 7.93kg brown trout was found dying in the shallows above Tumbling Waters.

Methods for Rubicon River

TACKLE Bait and lure fishers will find small 2–3kg threadline outfits ideal. Bait should be presented unweighted, cast upstream and allowed to drift downstream along the banks to the fish. Use unweighted mudeyes, grasshoppers, worms and crickets on No. 8 to No. 14 hooks.

For lure fishers, small hard-bodied lures in rainbow trout or brown trout patterns are used. These are cast upstream and retrieved slowly past structure or along the banks.

Fly-fishers working dry flies often go down to four-weight outfits with a weight-forward floating line and a 2–3m long leader and 2kg tippet. When working nymphs a six-weight outfit is fine. Use an indicator about 45–60cm above the fly.

FLIES The best wet fly is the gold beadhead nymph. Popular dry flies include Royal Wulff, Grey or Rusty Duns, Chopper Hopper and Hackle Hopper, generally in sizes 14–16.

GOULBURN RIVER

The Goulburn River from Eildon Pondage to Alexandra is one of the most popular stretches of **trout** water in Victoria. Places like Thornton, 'Gilmore's Bridge' and the Breakaway, where the Acheron River joins with the Goulburn River, are legendary. Anglers who fish this river expect to catch **brown** and **rainbow trout**, **redfin** and **carp**. Trout are the primary target species.

Anyone contemplating a visit should note that river levels may rise and fall dramatically during summer when irrigation farming is underway. When this happens you need to look at where you can fish safely, even if that means sitting on the bank.

A lot of private property fronts the river, so access is limited. Access points between Eildon and Thornton along the Back Eildon Rd are at Point Hill Reserve, Blue Gums Caravan Park (convenient accommodation), Thoms La and the bridge at Thornton. On the Goulburn Valley Hwy, this stretch of river can be accessed at Walnuts River Reserve.

Between Thornton and Alexandra on the Goulburn Valley Hwy, you can get to the river at Gilmores Bridge about halfway between Thornton and Alexandra, McMartins Rd and the Twin Rivers Caravan Park at the Breakaway on Hobans Rd, which runs between the Goulburn Valley Hwy and the Maroondah Hwy. The Rubicon River joins with the Goulburn between McMartins La and the turf farm.

At Alexandra, the Goulburn River is accessible at the main road bridge and from Brooks Cutting. The Alexandra Bridge has a big reputation for producing redfin to about 1.3kg and some bigger trout on lures over summer.

Bait fishers do well along the stretch of river from Eildon to Thornton, due mainly to the consistently deeper water, while the river from Thornton to Alexandra is a favourite haunt of fly- and lure-fishers. The Breakaway, where the Acheron River joins with the Goulburn, is a favourite destination with many anglers choosing to stay beside the river in the conveniently situated caravan park.

From Seymour to Shepparton the river becomes a mixed species fishery with a stronger emphasis on native fish, with **Murray cod** and **yellowbelly** stocked near Nagambie. The river from Seymour to Nagambie is regarded as native fish water, even though there is still a lot of trout. Boating activity increases as you near Seymour, and wide action lures like Stumpjumpers are used while trolling near the logs and snags for cod and yellowbelly.

The Goulburn joins the Murray River near Echuca. On the way, it runs through Lake Nagambie and the Goulburn Weir, which hold good numbers of native fish and redfin. The Goulburn holds solid populations of native fish all the way to the Murray River.

NAGAMBIE

Nagambie is about a 90-minute drive north of Melbourne along the Hume Hwy. It's an easy drive, with or without a van in tow.

The Goulburn River feeds Lake Nagambie, and upstream and downstream of Nagambie, anglers fish for a variety of freshwater species.

ACCOMMODATION: There is caravan, camping and cabin accommodation available on the waterfront at Nagambie Lakes Leisure Park, Loddings Lane, Nagambie.
For more information visit
www.nagambielakespark.com.au

Nagambie is promoted to tourists as an area of wine, waterways, wetlands, wildlife, and thoroughbred horses. No matter what visitors come to the area for, most activities involve water, whether it is the Goulburn River or Lake Nagambie.

Local tourism information suggests Nagambie is a derivative of an Aboriginal word for lagoon. This is appropriate given that water is an intrinsic element of the town, and nowhere is this more evident than at Nagambie Lakes Leisure Park. Nagambie Lakes was created by the construction of Goulburn Weir in 1891. Built for irrigation, it was the first major diversion structure built in Australia. Close by is Kirwans Bridge, a rustic timber structure, and Chinamans Bridge, a 'strutted, stringer' style drawbridge.

The Goulburn River and Lake Nagambie are developing a reputation for **Murray cod** to about 20kg, **yellowbelly** to 2kg, **redfin** and **trout**. In recent years, Fisheries Victoria has put in a major effort to ensure these waters become a thriving native fish, fishery. Murray cod is the apex predator of our waterways, and as the cod grow, redfin and trout numbers will decrease as evidenced by the Murray River where anglers who seek Murray cod call trout 'speckled cod lollies'.

Methods for Goulburn River

TACKLE All methods of angling for trout are employed somewhere along the river. The river's trout reputation was built on fly-fishing, and the best fly-fishing is where the river shallows and gravel beds and runs are the main features.

A six-weight fly outfit with a weight-forward floating line and tippet section of about 2kg covers most options.

Bait and lure anglers will find a 2–3kg threadline outfit suitable.

Yellowbelly and Murray cod can be caught on bait and lures. A 3–4kg outfit will suffice for yellowbelly; use a heavier, 6–8kg rig for cod.

RIGS If fishing for trout, a long shank No. 6 hook is fine for worms, but if you are using mudeyes then you may want to drop down to a No. 12 or No. 14. Bubble floats are best for bait fishing in still waters, but in fast running water put some split shot on your line, cast upstream and allow the bait to bounce along near the river bed.

The popular bait rig for yellowbelly and cod is a running sinker, with the sinker allowed to run all the way to the hook. For yellowbelly, use as light a lead as you can and about a No. 2 medium shank hook, depending on the size of the bait.

For cod, generally use a No.2 to No. 4 long shank or up to a 6/0 Suicide pattern for large baits like bardi grubs. Use a minimum 15kg breaking strain leader for cod, on lures and bait.

FLIES Flies should suit what the trout are feeding on, but old standards like the Red Tag (wet or dry), Adams and ant and beetle patterns, Tom Jones, and gold beadhead nymphs should always be in your fly box.

LURES Small bladed lures like Celtas rarely fail for trout, or alternatively, small-bibbed minnows and even soft plastic worms do well.

Lure choice for cod and yellowbelly depends on where you fish. Lure suggestions include Bassman Spinnerbaits, Oargees, Stumpjumpers and Halco Poltergeists. In heavy timber use spinnerbaits; when trolling or casting into lightly wooded areas bibbed minnows do well, and they are best for trolling.

BAIT Best baits for trout are garden or scrub worms, mudeyes and crickets. Natural baits for yellowbelly and cod including bardi grubs, shrimp, scrub worms and yabbies. Cheese is also popular.

Brett Evans with a Murray cod caught in the Kerang Lakes

KERANG LAKES

The Kerang Lakes and associated channels have long been regarded as fishing hot spots. The best waters are Kow Swamp, Reedy Lakes, Lake Charm and Kangaroo Lake. All fish well for species that include **yellowbelly**, **redfin** and **Murray cod**.

The Reedy Lakes (there are three), Kangaroo and Lake Charm are just off the Murray Valley Hwy between Kerang and Swan Hill. Kow Swamp is further away, near Gunbower, southeast of Kerang on the Murray Valley Hwy. There are more lakes, but these ones seem to produce consistent results.

All the lakes hold **redfin, Murray cod** and **yellowbelly**. Some tall stories do the rounds when it comes to fish but here is one that is true. Fisheries scientist Theo Roughley wrote about a 24.5kg (54lb) **yellowbelly** caught in Kow Swamp in 1938 that was sold at the Melbourne market. Moreover, that fish was gutted!

Fisheries Victoria used Recreational Fishing Licence funds to buyback inland commercial fishing licences. Since 2004, Fisheries have been stocking these lakes with Murray cod and yellowbelly and the results are proof of reward for effort. While there is a natural native fish population, their numbers have been improved by reduced commercial fishing pressure and additional fish.

Redfin might be a European import, not quite as high on Victorian Fisheries pest scale as **carp**, but the species is one of rural Victoria's most popular freshwater sport fish. Plenty of anglers happily fish these lakes for redfin. This feisty English import has earned a reputation as a table delicacy and, when they grow to 2kg or more, is a worthy adversary.

Another aspect of the fishing in these lakes is that the interconnecting channels are also producing good catches. Lake Kangaroo is about 980ha and has boat ramps and caravan parks on the northern and western shores. Good bank fishing is available and one of the favourite areas is close to the regulator at the Swan Hill end of the lake. Unlike most waters, anglers do better here above the regulator rather than the more traditional fishing below.

Lake Charm is about half the area of Kangaroo Lake and features a caravan park and boat ramp. Charm holds a large population of redfin as well as Murray cod, yellowbelly and carp.

Above: Fly-fishing the Mitta Mitta River
Below: Geoff Lacey wades deep to cast a fly to rising trout in Mount Beauty Pondage

Kow Swamp is 2720ha and has **freshwater catfish**, which are protected and must be returned unharmed. Reedy Lakes are listed as First, Middle and Third. Reedy Lakes (First) is the smallest at 202ha but has a picnic area and a boat ramp. As these lakes are shallow, much of the fishing occurs in the interconnecting channels. Boating is banned in Middle Lake.

Methods for Kerang Lakes

TACKLE A 3kg outfit will suit most bait or lure fishing. Use a small threadline reel and a light, medium action rod with a sharp tip action to help detect bites or flick lures.

BAIT The most productive baits are small yabbies, shrimp, scrubworms and glassies, a small frozen baitfish more often associated with estuary and ocean fishing than freshwater. If you want to target cod, then use larger yabbies, bardi grubs or cheese. Hook size for bait fishing depends on the bait being used. The Baitholder patterns suit most applications and a No. 6 will suit shrimp, a No. 4 for the likes of scrubworms and yabbies but you may want to go up to a 3/0 for bardi grubs or big yabbies for the cod.

LURES Bladed lures and small-bibbed minnows that run a couple of feet below the surface suit redfin, while Murray cod and yellowbelly will take similar lures, as well as spinnerbaits.

Soft plastic lures have become popular and anglers have found these lures work well on redfin. Yellowbelly, which have tougher mouths, are more difficult to hook and while a few cod have been caught on soft plastics, this is still relatively new water in fishing terms. Soft plastic lures are cast and retrieved in a jigging action so that the presentation is essentially a lift and drop technique, which is the same as bobbing bait. An alternative method though is to rig the lure on a paternoster bait rig, instead of using bait, and drift.

12 ALPINE WATERS

So many rivers and streams are encompassed by the High Country that it is impossible to list them all. Most are clear, cool waters that offer ideal habitat for trout.

ACCOMMODATION: The ski fields are a winter playground so this area is well catered for with quality accommodation including caravan parks, motels and lodges.
For more information visit
www.alpinelink.com.au

KIEWA RIVER

High Country waterways are popular with fly-fishers looking for gin-clear water with good numbers of trout. In this regard, the Kiewa River near Mount Beauty rates as one of the state's best waters, although it fluctuates regularly with the demand for electricity.

One of the best stretches is from Dederang to the township of Mount Beauty, with **brown** and **rainbow trout** to 1.25kg, however most of the trout (mainly browns) will average 450–500g. Due to heat during summer, it pays to fish the fast water and shady areas during the day.

A long section of the upper Kiewa River, from Mount Beauty through Tawonga to Redbank is especially kind to anglers during the warmer months.

Local fishing guide Geoff Lacey says it is a 'blue-ribbon trout stream particularly suited to fly-fishers'. With plenty of clearance for a back cast, it is easy to see why fly-fishers enjoy walking this river, casting their flies to riffles, runs and pools.

The Kiewa River has two branches and both hold brown trout. The west branch is a typical mountain stream, with several kilometres of fishable water amid pristine surrounds with a self-sustaining population of brown trout. This water is lightly fished, with only a few access points. If wading up the stream, wear felt-soled wading boots to avoid heavy falls, as there is an extremely slippery basalt bottom in many parts of this stream. Always work upstream as the trout face this way and you are less likely to spook them. If nobody has been fishing for a few days fly-fishers can get a response to every second or third cast.

The east branch of the Kiewa River is rarely fished because most anglers consider it too dangerous due to regular and sudden rises in water level.

It is easily accessed at Bogong Village near the tennis courts and for several hundred metres upstream. It contains brown trout.

Rocky Valley Creek, another brown trout water, is lightly fished further upstream because of difficult access. Access to the creek is easy from Bogong Village and conditions are not difficult. Felt-soled wading boots are required. To access other areas, you'll need to make a long walk in from Bogong High Plains Rd.

LAKE GUY

Bogong Village is little more than workers' bunkhouses converted for outdoor adventure students and a few houses. The hamlet is set on a steep slope, and as you follow the road past the houses it snakes down the hill to picturesque Lake Guy.

The lake is not one of the better known **trout** fishing destinations, but Geoff Lacey says 'Lake Guy is the jewel in the crown of Bogong Village, a fantastic little fishery that holds good numbers of trout. It contains good-sized trout that are regularly caught by anglers trolling in small boats or canoes.'

Although the lake is deep, water levels fluctuate according to hydroelectric requirements and this means that shore-based anglers sometimes have access difficulties caused by thick mud along the edges.

North-east fly-fishing guide Scott McPherson shows off a brown trout caught on fly in the Mitta Mitta River

'This water provides good trolling conditions from spring through to about mid-December with trout to about 1.5kg regularly caught,' Geoff says.

Most of the trout are browns, but Lake Guy also has a reputation for producing rainbow trout.

FALLS CREEK

Rocky Valley reservoir at Falls Creek has been used as a venue for state and national fly-fishing championships. **Trout** to 3kg have been caught from the shore. Bait fishing using ultra-light rods and rigs is deadly during summer in the Rocky Valley and Pretty Valley reservoirs. However, choose your days carefully as the temperature in those high altitudes can be 15°C cooler than at Mount Beauty.

Pretty Valley Creek is fairly challenging to fish at the run-in to the reservoir, being wide in places and deep with a subtle flow and absolutely no streamside cover. In contrast, the run-out contains shallow runs with pools with lots of weeds and rocks and contains hundreds of small brown trout that beginner fly-fishers have no trouble in catching and releasing.

OMEO VALLEY

The Upper Mitta Mitta River at Angler's Rest appears to go the 'wrong' way, as it travels south to reach Dartmouth reservoir, which is far to the north. It flows out of the Bogong High Plains and down the Omeo Valley and contains wonderful pools, runs, glides and riffles; there is everything one could wish for in a quality trout stream. Self-sustaining populations of **brown** and **rainbow trout** can be seen rising in the tails of pools each summer evening just before dusk.

Murray crays are also a feature, although with minimum sizes in force, they are best left alone.

The Cobungra River is a typical mountain stream, much like the Bundara River. It is lightly fished and contains both rainbow and brown trout with lots of king brown snakes to contend with in summer.

Fly-fishers walking an alpine stream

Access is limited to the best stretches of the Cobungra River, and available mainly through local fishing guides. Tracks are rough and a 4WD with a winch is strongly recommended.

LAKE DARTMOUTH

Lake Dartmouth in northeast Victoria holds self-sustaining populations of **brown** and **rainbow trout**, **Macquarie perch**, **river blackfish**, **trout cod** and **carp**. The good news for anglers is that the lake and pondage (Lake Banimboola) are open to trout fishing year round.

The lake was formed in 1979 by damming the Mitta Mitta River. Trout and the threatened Macquarie perch thrived in the lake during the 1980s, and subsequently, Lake Dartmouth has developed a reputation as being one of Victoria's most consistent trout waters. It is one of just three Victorian fisheries where anglers are permitted to take Macquarie perch, one fish per day with a minimum legal length of 35cm. The closed season for perch is 1 October–31 December.

Main access to the lake is via Dartmouth village to the dam wall, or to Six-Mile Creek where there is a concrete boat ramp and full picnic facilities. There are several good campsites around the lake, most only accessible by boat: Eight Mile Creek, camping and toilets; Raymond Creek Dart Arm, no facilities; and Eustace Gap, no facilities and only accessible by boat or a track, and has been used for launching boats.

Lake Dartmouth is primarily used as a boat fishery as access around most of the shoreline is difficult for land-based anglers. The lake produces trout averaging about 750g–1kg, but trout in the 2–3kg classes can be expected.

Lake Banimboola, which is Dartmouth pondage, is popular water for land-based anglers using fly, bait and lure techniques. The lake, which is about 5km downstream from Lake Dartmouth, has limited access. The pondage is well stocked with brown and rainbow trout and there is good natural recruitment of wild-bred trout from inflowing streams and creeks. The average trout is about 1kg but trophies to 4kg are sometimes captured.

Anglers who prefer to fish running water will find much opportunity in the Lower Mitta Mitta River below the Pondage. Experienced anglers regard this river as one of Victoria's premier trout waters. As long as the water-flow from the Dartmouth is moving well, fly-fishing and spinning can be excellent. Another option is Snowy Creek, which flows out of the Bogong High Plains and into the Mitta Mitta River in the centre of the tiny township of Mitta Mitta. The creek contains mainly brown trout with some rainbow trout mixed in. Best fishing is often during summer, at dusk, when the bigger trout are rising.

LOWER MITTA MITTA

Wodonga-based fly-fishing guide Scott McPherson accompanied me on one trip on the lower Mitta Mitta. We were wading a stretch of river near Eskdale early in the morning. I recommend not only waders for this activity, but also a good set of thermal underwear – as refreshing and invigorating as the surrounds and fishing can be, cold is something you can do without.

The **trout**, mainly browns, were small and not cooperating, sipping tiny insects as they landed on the surface. These insects are so small that fly-fishers have been known to call them 'no-see-ums'. Every now and again a larger ring appeared, the signature of bigger trout. As we studied the water, we realised the bigger trout were working a beat, about 50m long. We could follow their movement by the rings.

We were working five-weight fly outfits, weight-forward floating fly lines and 4m long leaders that taper down to a fine tippet where the fly is attached. On the opposite bank, willow trees had been lopped and the wood was piled up in places ready for removal or burning. Scott tied on a Royal Humpy and began to work a shallow riffle. He was rewarded almost immediately with a hook-up, but the trout was small. That was the story of the day, albeit a nice day.

Snowy Creek flows out of the Bogong High Plains and into the Mitta Mitta River in the centre of the tiny township of Mitta Mitta. The creek contains mainly brown trout with some rainbow trout mixed in. Best fishing is often during summer, at dusk, when the bigger trout are rising.

LAKE BUFFALO

Two productive lakes in this region are Lake Buffalo, 20km south of Myrtleford, and Lake William Hovell, 60km south of Wangaratta. Both waters have boat-launching facilities, but fishing here can be difficult during summer because of the heat.

Redfin to 1.5kg can be caught in Lake Buffalo along with **Macquarie perch** to about 1kg, and **brown** and **rainbow trout**. The Buffalo River is a favourite fly-fishing water producing trout to 1.5kg. Redfin, **Murray cod**, Macquarie perch and **river blackfish** can also be caught. Yabbies, worms and crickets are among the best baits.

In Lake William Hovell, expect redfin to 2kg, brown trout to twice this size, river blackfish and Macquarie perch. The King River, below the lake, has trout, redfin, Macquarie perch and river blackfish.

Methods for alpine waters

TACKLE Brown trout are the dominant species, but there is a smattering of rainbow trout in some waters. Both species can be caught on bait using light threadline outfits, spooled with 2–3kg lines. Hook size varies with bait, a No. 6 is a big hook, and for mudeyes, you will find No. 12 a better size. The method is to either fish under a bubble float and drift the bait into deeper holes, or put a couple of pieces of split shot on the line to take the bait deeper, again casting upstream and allowing it to be washed into holes where larger fish are likely to wait.

Most anglers I came across were fly-fishing with five- and six-weight outfits, although a few were working outfits down to two-weight for finer presentations. Weight forward floating lines are the most popular, leader length ranges 3–4m, and tippet size is up to the individual, but can be gossamer-thin 1–2kg breaking strain for the small flies. As mentioned earlier, the slippery rocks in some areas make wading difficult, so wear felt-soled shoes if you intend to enter the water. Always work upstream as the trout face this way and you are less likely to spook them.

BAIT Popular baits include crickets, grasshoppers, maggots and scrubworms.

LURES Use small bladed lures like the No. 1 and No. 2 Celtas, or small bibbed minnows. Cast upstream and across, and be prepared to vary the retrieve rate. Soft plastic lures are proving successful in these streams.

FLIES Flies depend on the insects, and fly-fishers match the hatch. The Bogong Beauty is an excellent dry fly, along with size 14 Royal Wulffand Red Humpy. Other flies to use include Adams, Elk Hair Caddis, Stick Caddis and brown nymphs, including those tied with gold beadheads. Emerger and flying ant patterns can do well at times. Nymphs and Stick Caddis imitations can produce fish in the deeper water during the day. After dark, trout often rise in the back of large pools and a fly such as Craig's Nightime can be deadly.

SOUTH AUSTRALIA

Steve's

FAVOURITE DESTINATIONS FOR SOUTH AUSTRALIA

Fishing in SA is of a consistently high standard for species that seem to grow bigger than anywhere else in Australia. In Spencer Gulf, snapper up to 18kg have been caught; Investigator Strait has big samson fish and Coffin Bay produces even bigger yellowtail kingfish that sometimes give 50kg a nudge. The biggest King George whiting, some more than 2kg, come from these waters.

The state has hundreds of isolated surf beaches that can produce huge salmon and even bigger mulloway. Most ports have piers to fish from and you are allowed to drive your 4WD onto the beaches, which explains why they are so clean as anglers have somewhere to pack their rubbish and take it away. Just to cap the state off, the Murray River, from the NSW border, holds the biggest Murray cod in Australia, many of them weighing more than 40kg.

ACCOMMODATION

You're never far from somewhere to rest your head in SA.

For more information visit www.southaustralia.com

The pier in the sheltered harbour at Port MacDonnell is a popular and safe fishing venue for anglers

Site of the Australian Snapper Championships each Easter
Great white sharks (swimming is optional)!
A one-stop fishing destination with the lot
Marla
Oodnadatta
Innamincka
Coober Pedy
Marree
Roxby Downs
Leigh Creek
Parachilna
Woomera
Border Village
Yalata
5
Ceduna
Hawker
Quorn
Streaky Bay
WHYALLA
Point Lowly
ARNO BAY
Port Broughton
Wallaroo
4
Port Hughes
Moonta
COFFIN BAY
Ardrossan
2
ADELAIDE
MARION BAY
3
Goolwa
THE COORONG
1
Salt Creek
Kingston S.E.
Beachport
Port Macdonnell

1 THE COORONG

From Adelaide, follow the Princes Hwy to Murray Bridge, through to Tailem Bend and then onto Wellington and then Coorong. The magnificent beach is accessible to 4WD vehicles.

ACCOMMODATION: Most anglers sleep on the beach or in their vehicles. Bush camping is available at 42 Mile Crossing but life is a bit more civilised at Salt Creek where there is a roadhouse and caravan park. Kingston has a range of accommodation for anglers who prefer to stay in cabins or motel rooms. For more information visit
www.thecoorong.com
www.kingstondc.sa.gov.au

Above: Rod Mackenzie caught this gummy shark from the beach at 42 Mile Crossing
Below: sunset on the beach along the Coorong

The willing angler with a 4WD will find many opportunities on the stretch from the border with Victoria through to the Murray River mouth.

Many anglers will drive 6km across the border to Piccaninny Ponds in SA to access the beach and then come back towards the mouth of the Glenelg River, or go west towards Green Point. Others launch tinnies at Green Point to fish for big **snapper** and mulloway. The beach is firm enough to launch from, but watch for the big wash at the Victoria–SA border. It is a freshwater soak and you can drink the water, but it is large enough to suck in a car.

One of the best beach fishing places in the country is on Younghusband Peninsula, better known as The Coorong, between Kingston S.E. and the mouth of the Murray River at Goolwa, about 100km south of Adelaide. The Coorong has more than 100km of salt lake lagoons separated from the ocean by sand dunes, on the other side of which is a beach that you are allowed to drive on.

Species caught here include snapper, **mulloway**, **salmon**, **sharks**, **flathead** and any number of **stingrays** and other flatfish. Many fish caught here are big. **Gummy sharks** are up to 20kg, snapper 9kg and mulloway 35kg. Even the salmon come in XOS sizes up to 6kg, with 2–3kg being average.

Two of the easiest access points for those travelling from the east are 42 Mile Crossing and Tea Tree Crossing at Salt Creek, just off the Princes Hwy. You will need a 4WD with deflated tyres to negotiate the sand dunes. 42 Mile Crossing is the easier access point, as high water can close the crossing at Salt Creek.

Anglers who fish this beach often spend several days in makeshift camps. The roadhouse at Salt Creek has a good range of supplies, including bait and tackle. A permit is required to camp on the beach and these are available from Salt Creek or Policemans Point roadhouses, or Department of Environment and Heritage offices. There are also self-registration stations.

Loop tracks have been placed along the beach through the dunes to provide sheltered areas for camping. If you intend driving on the beach, stay well away from the water. It is safest to drive above the high-water mark. Avoid turning your wheels sharply, as you may become bogged.

The best time to fish here is when the wind is blowing from the north. It settles the sea and reduces side drift. Experienced surf fishers will appreciate the lack of kelp weed, much lighter ribbon weed taking its place. Provided you use long rods to keep the line out of the waves and sinkers with wire grapples, you can hold bottom most of the time.

KINGSTON S.E.

Kingston S.E. is a picturesque seaside town nestled on the waters of Lacepede Bay. It is part of the Limestone Coast and its rugged beauty is shared by its coastal neighbours like Cape Jaffa, Robe and Beachport.

The ocean's relative calm at Kingston S.E. offers a range of fishing opportunities, both in and offshore. **King George whiting**, **snapper** and **gummy sharks** are regular catches, as are the delectable **southern rock lobsters**, better known as **crayfish**.

There are two boat ramps, at Kingston S.E. and Cape Jaffa. The ramps are open year round.

For pier anglers, there is a jetty at Kingston S.E. maintained for recreational use, and a commercial jetty at Cape Jaffa used by the fishing fleet. Both jetties fish well in the evenings. Fish that are caught include **Australian herring (tommy ruff)**, **whiting**, **garfish**, **mullet**, **mulloway**, **flathead**, **snapper** and **trevally**.

To the north of Kingston S.E. is Long Beach, which runs from Kingston S.E. to the Murray Mouth. Long Beach finishes at the southern end of The Coorong and is regarded by many anglers as one of Australia's premier beach fishing destinations.

For more than 35 years, Kingston S.E. Lions Club has run an annual surf fishing competition in January at Long Beach. In 2014, more than 950 anglers entered. However, be wary of the sea when driving on the beach. In January 2007, many anglers fishing the competition were caught out by a king tide that buried their cars under tonnes of sand, and about 30 vehicles were stranded at camps dotted along the 50km stretch of beach between Kingston S.E. and Salt Creek further north.

The area is popular among anglers seeking crayfish among the inshore reefs. The open crayfish season runs from October through until the end of May. During this period, recreational anglers can obtain an amateur pot licence and try their hand at catching a feed of southern rock lobsters.

Strict bag and size limits are enforced on this fishery as are the means pertaining to the capture of these shell-encrusted delicacies. A southern rock lobster can grow to 10kg; however, the average size caught by anglers is less than half this size.

Cray pots are baited with fresh fish. Carp, which have an oily flesh, are one of the best baits. The bait is placed in small plastic holders that are wired into the pot. This in turn attracts the crayfish inside where they are unable to steal the bait or climb back out.

Setting the traps requires patience. Crayfish live under ledges and along drop-offs so anglers need

Jemma Storer holds up a fine crayfish (southern rock lobster) caught at Kingston S.E.

to use their sounders to read the seabed and find a suitable rough area. Once this is done, the pots are then thrown overboard on the end of a long rope that is attached to a couple of floats and your licence tag. Some anglers hold the rope and allow the net to drag across the bottom until it wedges up against a bit of reef. The crayfish hide under the ledges and this ensures the pot is directly outside their door. The nets are left in overnight as crayfish do most of their moving and feeding under the cover of darkness.

The middle tail fin on each crayfish must be cut in half in a straight line to distinguish it as an amateur catch that is not saleable.

Methods for the Coorong

TACKLE Surf-fishing tackle consists of a rod about 3.5m long suited to 10–12kg breaking strain line, and capable of casting sinkers up to 100g. Balance it with a large threadline or overhead reel that can hold at least 300m of line. If you decide to use braid line then you can go to 15kg breaking strain. Braid is thinner than monofilament so is less affected by drift, but it also tangles into impossible bird nests and doesn't have the same degree of abrasion resistance as the thicker monofilament lines. Distance isn't always important, but comes in handy on those days when the channels or gutters are well out from the beach.

RIGS Australian salmon is the mainstay species of the southern surf angler and they need no special leader. Most anglers fish a simple two-dropper paternoster rig. The top dropper has a surf popper or soft plastic lure instead of bait, the bottom dropper a 3/0–4/0 long shank, or Suicide pattern hook.

A running paternoster rig is the choice of most anglers chasing large fish such as mulloway, snapper or gummy sharks. For the big fish, a leader of about 25–30kg breaking strain is employed with size 6/0 Suicide pattern hooks and a grapnel sinker. Star sinkers are not as effective as those with the grapples on the bottom. The latter seem to dig into the ribbon weed and hang on much better. Use a clip swivel as this allows you a fast and easy way of changing sinker weights to suit conditions.

Rod holders are essential. No need to buy them though: make your own by purchasing about a metre of 50mm diameter PVC tubing, and cut a 45-degree angle on one end.

A small nylon bait board is one of the handiest items you can take, as it can be difficult filleting a fish or cutting a squid strip on sand.

BAIT Anglers wanting to catch bigger fish prefer to work big baits like squid heads or strips. Alternatively, fresh salmon fillets do well.

If you are chasing salmon then small squid strips, pilchard or whitebait will attract bites.

2 YORKE PENINSULA

ARDROSSAN

To get here from Adelaide take the Port Wakefield Rd then turn onto the Copper Coast Hwy to Ardrossan.

Located on the east side of the Yorke Peninsula, Ardrossan is bountiful water just 150km west of Adelaide, so is a popular weekend fishing destination.

ACCOMMODATION: The peninsula is a popular destination for anglers due to its closeness to Adelaide so there are plenty of rooms, cabins and even houses to rent.
For more information visit www.southaustralia.com/regions/yorke-peninsula.aspx

Two piers, only one of them accessible to anglers, dominate the grain town of Ardrossan but it is a well-patronised fishing platform long enough for locals to devise trolleys to carry all their fishing tackle. Looking out on the long pier at Ardrossan, it's striking how much equipment anglers take with them. Some have so much tackle that trolleys are needed to cart tackle boxes, rods, reels, bait and crab nets.

Everyone seems to have a crab drop net and a selection of squid jigs. It's no wonder – the pier has a big reputation for producing both **blue swimmer crabs** and **squid** in good numbers. It also produces school **mulloway** to about 90cm, **salmon**, **King George whiting**, **Australian herring (tommy ruff)** and **mullet**.

Blue swimmer crabs are tasty and any month containing an 'R' is regarded as a crabbing month, especially January–April. Not everyone works a drop net though. Another method used for crabbing is raking, where an angler will wade and rake sandy patches. As the rake goes over the top of a crab, it sticks its claws out and gives away its hiding place. On seeing this, the angler carefully scoops the crab out. The best crab-raking areas are to the north and south of town.

Boating anglers are well serviced with an excellent boat-launching facility adjacent to the bulk-loading jetty south of the fishing pier. During summer, anglers fishing near the pier have caught **yellowtail kingfish** to 20kg.

Offshore fishing is mainly about **snapper** and King George whiting. The best known snapper area is the Ardrossan Barge (GPS: S34.31.838, E138.03.675), which was created to keep anglers away from the historic *Zanoni* shipwreck, 1 nautical mile to the north. The steel barge is in about 16m of water and fishes best November–February for snapper to 15kg and the occasional large mulloway.

Keep your sounder switched on. The area is littered with sunken boats, officially created artificial reefs, and the decidedly less legal 'drops'. A drop is what the locals call an artificial reef of their own making. It could be car bodies, piles of wood (including old boats) or refrigerators. These reefs are so good at attracting snapper that some commercial fishermen have been known to hire prawn trawlers to catch the 'drops' in their nets and move them to new locations.

King George whiting average 30–40cm, and are caught closer to shore in about 4–6m of water. Look for sandy bottom interspersed with weed or seagrass beds. You will catch squid over the same grounds. Some anglers prefer to wade the shallows and fish for **silver whiting**, which make ideal snapper bait.

There are half a dozen boat ramps further down the coast, including an excellent all-weather boat ramp at Stansbury and jetties at Stansbury and Edithburgh. The next pier suitable for fishing is at Port Vincent.

MARION BAY

To get here from Adelaide, follow the directions to Ardrossan but you keep going south through Curramulka, Minlaton and Warooka before arriving at Marion Bay, almost at the foot of the peninsula. Holiday homes, sandy beaches and a small pier popular with anglers dominate this small hamlet on the shores of Investigator Strait.

ACCOMMODATION: There is a caravan park, tavern and motel and many of the houses are available for rent.
For more information visit
www.marionbay.com.au

Situated at the bottom of the Yorke Peninsula, Marion Bay is angler central and offers access to spectacular offshore and beach fishing. Southern beaches from Marion Bay east to Troubridge, such as Butlers, provide top fishing with **mulloway** up to 36kg, and **school** and **gummy sharks** topping 20kg.

Anglers wanting to catch big **King George whiting** should head to Foul Bay. Launch at Marion Bay and run east along the coast for 10–15km. SA rules when it comes to whiting. Victorian researchers have carried out surveys in the hope of finding spawning grounds for King George whiting in Victoria, to no avail. They are in SA and Foul Bay is a hotspot. You will catch them to 60cm or bigger in winter.

Greg Jenkins, researcher at Victoria's Marine Science Laboratories at Queenscliff, says whiting spawn in SA in 20–40m of water over limestone ground and, when they hatch, the 3mm long larvae drift eastwards to Victoria. 'For the first 3–5 months of their lives, whiting larvae are at the mercy of currents and winds, drifting from their open coastal spawning grounds west of Cape Otway into Victoria's large central coast bays and inlets. Our research suggests that the wind cycle is influencing the number of very young whiting arriving to settle in Victoria's central coast bays, which subsequently affects catches a few years later. Wind and weather affect larval drift, and in a given year, we are able to predict whiting seasons a couple of years ahead based on wind correlation.'

Foul Bay isn't the only place in SA where you will consistently hook adult whiting, but it is as good a place as I have fished. The average size is what Victorians call 'kidney slappers' of 50cm and about a kilogram. The average King George whiting caught in Port Phillip is nearer to 33cm. King George whiting can live for 15 years, reach a maximum length of 72cm and weigh up to 2.5g.

While fishing here, I found myself in the middle of a seahorse migration. These small creatures were so dense that occasionally one would hook its curly tail on to a line.

West of Marion Bay on the southern shore, in Innes National Park, are Jollys Beach, Stenhouse Bay and Cable Bay. These are highly regarded, particularly Stenhouse Bay, which really turns on when the **mullet** are schooling. **Australian salmon**, King George whiting, **tommy ruff** and mulloway are some of the popular species caught.

I fished off Marion Bay with local charter boat skipper, Herbie Glacken. Our target species was **Samson fish**.

Herbie didn't want to give much away about his prime spots, as history has shown that as soon as a top Samson reef is publicised, the fishing doesn't last. A well-known SA charter boat is reputed to have cleaned out at least one area of this species by anchoring up and taking huge catches.

We motored out of Marion Bay and the run down to the reefs where we started fishing took nearly two hours at 20 knots in Herbie's 10m long, tri-hull aluminium boat.

There were four anglers on board and this was a lure-jigging and bait-fishing trip. We dropped on several reefs and pulled **nannygai (red snapper)**, **groper**, **barracouta** and other assorted species. But it wasn't until late in the afternoon that we arrived at Herbie's prime location, Schoolboy Rock. More like a small seamount, Schoolboy Rock rises from about 85m of water to within 40m of the surface. The sonar revealed a ledge at the northern end and a gradual slope at the southern edge.

As he watched the sonar screen, Herbie calculated our drift, allowing for the slight wind and slowing current. As with many areas, a change of tide is often the best time to be around.

We did a couple of drifts over the rock, dropping fresh squid baits or jigging 200g lures. During those drifts, we pulled **blue groper** to 20kg, **blue morwong** to 3kg and nannygai to 4kg. Two of our party were smoked by bigger, more powerful fish.

The first strike resulted in a $30, 200g jig being lost when a snap swivel rated at 200kg straightened. In the second incident, the fish took a squid head and peeled off about 50m of 24kg braid line, dragging it through the rocks until the line caught on a sharp object and parted. Both hook-ups lasted just a few seconds.

Our drift rate was a little fast and Herbie decided it was worth putting the anchor down and holding on the northern ledge where most of the fish were concentrated. He lost the next fish, and then Jim Harris somehow managed to stay connected and steer his fish away from the danger zone.

The fight wasn't over though – another 20 minutes passed before the Samson broached.

Looking similar to yellowtail kingfish except for a slightly blunter head and olive skin tones, Samsons

Above: Ardrossan Pier is long enough to justify the use of trolleys for anglers to cart their equipment
Below: charter skipper Herbie Glacken shows off a sand flathead caught off Marion Bay

are a highly prized sport fish in southern waters. At more than 1.55m long and weighing 35kg, this one was as big as I'd seen.

As if to show the fish had lost none of their fight, the next strike came on Jim's rod and as far as we know, that fish is still running with about 100m of 24kg, multicoloured braid hanging from a 11/0 hook in its jaw. If they were too easy to catch, there wouldn't be any left.

WEST COAST

The west coast of the Yorke Peninsula offers some superb fishing opportunities. In the north it is mainly snapper, calamari squid, salmon and King George whiting, while down south there is surf fishing for salmon and mulloway.

Steve Cooper shows off a 12.5kg snapper caught on cuttlefish in Spencer Gulf

ACCOMMODATION: Whether you want caravan and camping, motel, unit or house, there is plenty of accommodation available.
For more information visit www.yorkepeninsulaaccommodation.com

Head to Innes National Park, at the southern end of Yorke Peninsula, to find two noteworthy places for anglers. The first is Pandalowie Bay where boats can be launched and, north of this, Browns Beach. The latter is well regarded for its winter **salmon** fishing, and the southern end of the beach is a favourite with **mulloway** anglers.

As you work your way north into Spencer Gulf, there are kilometres of beach fishing and boat ramps at most of the coastal towns. Port Hughes near Moonta has a big reputation for its offshore **snapper** fishery. The harbour and boat ramp are well laid out and anglers who fish out of here head for Cape Elizabeth or, on calm days, the Tiparra Reef Lighthouse.

Towns from Port Hughes through to Wallaroo attract crabbers from September–April in the quest for **blue swimmer crabs**.

WALLAROO

Just over an hour's drive from Adelaide, take the A1 Hwy to Port Wakefield, then the Copper Coast Hwy to Wallaroo.

Wallaroo is a snug little township best known for fertiliser and barley, but the same pier used to ship these items dominates the port and comes with a well-earned reputation for producing big snapper.

ACCOMMODATION: Visitors can rent houses, stay in motels or apartments or alternatively use the tourist park for camping and caravanning.
For more information visit www.southaustralia.com/regions/yorke-peninsula.aspx or www.takeabreak.com.au/Wallaroo/YorkePeninsula

The small SA seaport of Wallaroo, north of Moonta, offers an excellent base for anglers wanting to catch big **snapper**, **King George whiting**, **Australian salmon** and **yellowtail kingfish**. Many of the reef systems are close to the port, and the boat-launching facility in the harbour is sheltered. There is plenty of parking for cars and trailers, and the three ramps allow you to launch the largest boats you can legally tow.

Wallaroo pier is a popular fishing destination. On my visit, part of the pier was closed off to angling, but this is open to change.

Never mind: half the pier is better than no pier at all and even up to the halfway mark, anglers catch big snapper. Sometimes when you are in a boat motoring alongside the pier you can spot schools of kingfish swimming between the mussel-encrusted pilings.

I fished for kingfish near the end of the pier from a 5.8m boat. It was all about berley. The berley mix had just started to sink and drift away when the kings showed up, small fish averaging 4–6kg. Even at this smaller size, kingfish have serious pulling power and are great fun on light tackle, using lures or flies. Some of the locals complain about the hordes of kingfish in many parts of Spencer Gulf. Most of them are claimed to be escapees from a fish-farming venture further north.

To the north of the boat harbour is Point Riley, well regarded as a land-based snapper fishing location. A couple of kilometres offshore from this ledge is the Wallaroo Tyre Reef. Water depth is about 20m and the bottom is mud. The reef is a well-known mark for snapper to about 4kg. On the day I fished this reef, most of the snapper were on or just below the SA minimum legal length of 38cm. There is a bag limit of ten small snapper (38–60cm) and a boat limit of 30 fish in this size range. Larger snapper are limited to two per angler or six per boat.

You know there are plenty of snapper in the trail when your bait is taken before it sinks to the bottom. At the reef, snapper were munching on the berley at the surface. Any bait I dropped in was taken, even saltwater flies. The method wasn't rocket science and there was little skill involved. It was simply a matter of putting the rubber-tailed fly in the water and watching the snapper hit it as it sank. After a while, I became a bit blasé – rather than strip the fly in and work it, I waited, and a snapper just hooked itself.

PORT BROUGHTON

From Adelaide, take the A1 Hwy to Port Wakefield, then the Copper Coast Hwy to Wallaroo.

A small town with a big fishery, the town is well known for its snapper fishing and there are charter boats on hand for those people who don't want to take their own boats.

ACCOMMODATION: Every type of accommodation is available.
For more information visit www.stayz.com.au/accommodation/sa/yorke-peninsula/port-broughton

Port Broughton is a favourite destination for anglers wanting to fish from charter boats. The boat ramp in the sheltered harbour is next to a small pier complex and is popular for small fish including **salmon**, **tommy ruff**, **kingfish**, **squid** and **garfish**. The run out of the harbour is in a channel with sandbanks on either side so it is important to stay within the boundaries of the channel.

SA's snapper fishing season closes at midday on 1 November and re-opens at midday on 30 November. The energising effect is enormous. You can usually count in tonnes the weight of big snapper caught over the first couple of days when the snapper season re-opens. In some years when the snapper are slow on opening day, anglers blame the heavy boating traffic, but within a week, you can generally count on some big fish of 9–15kg.

In the lead-up to opening day you will see boats anchored over favourite marks like The Illusions

(GPS: S33 29 041, E137 32 586) between Port Broughton and Whyalla, the Car Bodies (S33.33.100, E137.51.359) off Port Broughton and the Middle Bank (S33.41.730, E137.33.645). These anglers aren't fishing – they are feeding their marks with berley in the hope of attracting the snapper to the area. Many sit on their marks for the final 24 hours up to snapper opening just to maintain their mark and keep feeding out the berley.

PORT AUGUSTA

At the northernmost end of the Yorke Peninsula is the industrial city of Port Augusta. Typical of SA coastal towns, it offers many opportunities for anglers, whether fishing from shore or in a boat.

There are several jetties and three boat ramps, the main ramp located in front of the Augusta Hotel. **Whiting**, **snapper**, **garfish**, **tommy ruff**, sometimes **dolphinfish** and **blue swimmer crabs** are some of the species you can expect to catch, but Port Augusta is best known for the big **yellowtail kingfish** that take up residence in the warm water outlet from the power station, a couple of kilometres south of the city. Best time is June–October.

Methods for Yorke Peninsula

TACKLE Most bait anglers chasing snapper or mulloway use 10kg outfits, sometimes spooling their reel with 15kg or 24kg braid, which is much thinner than monofilament and has less stretch. The advantage of braid line is that it allows you to fish deep water and strong currents with less sinker weight. The popular rig is a running paternoster with a 24kg leader of about 1.5m long and two 4/0 Suicide hooks.

In the surf, when fishing for mulloway or gummy sharks, a running paternoster rig is used and rigging basically the same as you would use for snapper.

If you are chasing whiting, a 3kg outfit will suffice. A running sinker rig is used and hook size should be from about No. 4 Baitholder pattern to a 1/0 Suicide. Anglers chasing silver whiting in the shallows use a fixed paternoster sinker rig with two leaders with No. 6 hooks attached and baited with pipi.

For squid, a baited jig or a prawn imitation will catch them. A handline spool works as well as a rod for the jigs. There are two methods of presentation: first, rig up a baited jig a metre or so below a large bobby cork, cast it out and keep an eye on it while fishing for other species; alternatively, when working prawn jigs, cast out over weed, allow them to sink and then retrieve slowly.

BAIT Snapper bait includes squid, salmon, pilchards, whiting heads and tommy ruff. Whiting will be caught on pipi and squid.

Anglers using crab pots off the piers – rig them up with a bait of fish frame or similar, drop them to the bottom from the pier and lift them every 20–30 minutes to see whether they have attracted crabs.

3 INVESTIGATOR STRAIT

To get to the islands in Investigator Strait you need a boat and I used Herbie Glacken of SA Fishing Adventures, based at Marion Bay.

ACCOMMODATION: Herbie also runs a beachfront two-storey holiday house at Marion Bay and a luxury holiday home on Wedge Island for people who would like to stay there.
For more information visit www.safishingadventures.com.au

WEDGE ISLAND

Wedge Island is one of a number of small islands making up the Gambier Group, about 19 nautical miles west of the southern toe of the Yorke Peninsula. Viewed from the sea it is easy to see how the island got its name with its towering red sandstone cliffs at

SA is famous for its King George whiting like these caught near Wedge Island

the southern end tapering sharply down to sea level at the northern end.

The island is a long way offshore, but its sheltered bay at the northern end is popular among commercial boats taking refuge from the relentless seas rolling in across the Great Australian Bight.

The beach on the north side of the island, set in a bay, is one of the few in this part of the world that does not suffer from piles of dried out ribbon weed. It is also amazingly productive. As soon as we moored, Jim Harris decided the bay was a likely area for squid and cast out a squid jig. On six consecutive casts, he pulled in a **calamari squid** of about 1.5kg. Soon more rods with squid jigs attached were in the water. The squid were hooked constantly, each one destined for use in the morning.

A snapper rod with a squid head on it was put out for bait while dinner was being taken. We weren't even halfway through our meal before the rod bowed and line started ripping out as 20kg of **school shark** took the bait.

There are several patches of reef to the west of Wedge Island and the currents are strong and sometimes require as much as 320g of sinker to take the bait to the seabed. The fishing is hard work but productive, with a range of species including **snapper** bigger than 9kg and **King George whiting** to 55cm.

Thistle Island is north-west of Wedge Island, close to the south-east tip of the Eyre Peninsula. To the east side of the island, a sand and reef bottom creates an excellent area for King George whiting to 60cm, along with **gummy sharks** to 15kg, **flathead** to 2kg and snapper.

When I was here the fishing was constant wherever we went. That's what you get when you fish isolated areas that haven't suffered the excesses of civilisation.

NEPTUNE ISLANDS

The Neptune Islands are best known for their great white shark cage dives.

ACCOMMODATION: The only way out to the Neptune Islands is on a charter vessel, so if you stay overnight you have to be on one of these. Most of these operate from Port Lincoln, which is the nearest port.

Ever wondered where the filming was done for one of those documentaries where divers film great white sharks from the safety of underwater cages? One of the most popular areas for that sort of adventure is around South and North Neptune Islands, about 25 nautical miles north-west of Kangaroo Island.

Fishing the offshore reefs, bays and headlands around these islands is extraordinarily productive. It's hard to drop a bait or lure down without coming up with something. Anglers who fish these waters will tell you, tongue in cheek, that: 'Swimming around the Neptunes is optional.'

The blue morwong is a popular deep-water species caught over offshore reefs

A reef a couple of kilometres south-east of South Neptune is a great spot for jigging. It is deep water and the reef rises from 100m to within 60m of the surface.

Anglers use knife jigs in the 200–300g range and my experience is that the fishing is constant – so long as you have the stamina to keep going.

Nannygai to 3kg are in plague proportions and not at all fussy. They willingly strike lures, as the lures drop or when they are being retrieved. The reef systems also produce **blue groper**, **snapper**, **barracouta**, **samson fish**, **yellowtail kingfish** and **blue morwong (queen snapper)**.

Expect to be nailed at least once by some unstoppable fish that feels like a Volkswagon. Chances are it will be a big Samson or an overgrown groper.

About 15 nautical miles west of the Neptunes is a famous fishing ground known as the Cabbage Patch, where Samson fish and yellowtail kingfish are in good numbers. During season you can expect to run across large schools of **southern bluefin tuna**.

Methods for deep water

TACKLE To fish deepwater reefs you need to work 15–24kg outfits coupled with heavy-duty threadline or overhead reels with high-speed gearing for lures.

LURES Lures for deep jigging start at about $20 each. Green or pink were the most effective colours. When rigging, be aware that unlike normal lures, there is a single hook on a braid line and the leader is attached to the jig on the same ring holding the hook. The reason for the hook placement at the top of the jig is both to avoid snagging and fish that will strike at or near the head.

RIGS When bait fishing for most species, size 4/0–6/0 straight shank hooks and 320g snapper leads are standard. Rig is a double paternoster with 50–70kg breaking strain leaders. If chasing heavyweight predators like Samson fish or yellowtail kingfish, use a single paternoster and hook size ranging from 6/0 O'Shaughnessy to 11/0 Live Bait pattern. Hook size is governed by bait, and the largest hook would be used if putting down a squid head.

Fresh squid was the top bait for all species although fresh barracouta fillets also worked well.

Methods for inshore

TACKLE Most bait anglers chasing snapper use 10kg outfits, sometimes spooling their reel with 15–24kg braid, which is much thinner than monofilament and has less stretch. The advantage of braid line is that it allows you to fish deep water and strong currents with less sinker weight. The popular rig is a running paternoster with a 1.5m/24kg leader and two 4/0 Suicide hooks.

If you are chasing King George whiting, a 3kg outfit will suffice. Use a running sinker rig and hook from about No. 4 Baitholder pattern to a 1/0 Suicide.

For squid, use a baited jig or prawn imitation. A handline spool works as well as a rod for the jigs. There are two methods of presentation: first, rig up a baited jig a metre or so below a large bobby cork, cast it out and keep an eye on it while fishing for other species. Alternatively, cast prawn jigs out over weed, allow them to sink and then retrieve slowly.

BAIT Snapper bait includes squid, salmon, pilchards, whiting heads and tommy ruff. Whiting will be caught using pipi and squid.

4 EYRE PENINSULA

FITZGERALD BAY/POINT LOWLY

Located north of Whyalla, from Adelaide drive to Port Augusta then follow the Lincoln Hwy for 65km south, turn left onto Fitzgerald Bay Rd and after 18km take the left turn to Fitzgerald Bay. Watch out for emus on the road.

Home to a large yellowtail kingfish farming venture, the area produces huge snapper and, from May–August, big numbers of cuttlefish. The world's largest cuttlefish breeding ground is south of Point Lowly in False Bay.

ACCOMMODATION: Most people who fish here stay in Whyalla. But bush camping is available with a free campground. Alternatively, you may prefer to stay in one of two lighthouse cottages at Port Lowly. These are managed by the Whyalla Uniting Church and sleep up to 30 people, and are basic but clean, with good kitchen facilities.
For more information phone (08) 8645 0436 between 10am and 1pm daily.

Snapper fishing has a language all of its own. In Queensland and NSW, anglers talk about small snapper as 'squire'. In Victoria, small snapper are 'pinkies'; in SA, they are known as 'ruggers', with bigger fish called 'cobs'. However, if you want to go to a small area where the biggest snapper are what I call 'hooters', head for Fitzgerald Bay at the top of Spencer Gulf.

The attraction for the 'reds' is a yellowtail kingfish farm. The young kingfish are housed in large, circular floating pens that are anchored to the seafloor. Regular feeding and temperate waters ensure fast growth. Feeding takes place every day, and when the feed pellets are tossed to the fish, much of it falls through the pen's netting to the seafloor. This makes the area around the pens an attractive place for any fish looking for an easy feed.

The biggest snapper that I can verify being caught near the pens weighed in at a cool 19kg. It was a hooter. There is no guarantee of catching snapper this size although if you take the results of Australian Snapper Championships based in Whyalla every Easter as a guide, you are in with a chance. Snapper caught in Fitzgerald Bay usually rank high in the top 20 snapper weighed at each event.

Recreational boats are not allowed to anchor near the pens, but there is no need to be tied up next to the pens. Snapper are always on the move, and the pens are shifted on a regular basis to avoid pollution. It is really a matter of finding a drop or lump on the bottom, dropping the anchor and starting to fish. Some anglers moor as close to the pens as they are allowed and drift baits back, or else cast as far as they can. Still, the snapper are moving about, so chances are they will eventually find your bait.

There is a small bay with a large boat ramp, and this is protected by a breakwater. The marina area is shallow and you need to take care when entering or leaving. Anglers have caught snapper and **kingfish** from the breakwater.

The Point Lowly Lighthouse marks the southern extremity of Fitzgerald Bay. Near the lighthouse is a small community of shacks. These lighthouse cottages are cared for by the Uniting Church, and are available for hire. It is about a 20km run by boat from Whyalla so consider launching in the small harbour that fronts Fitzgerald Bay.

Less than a kilometre off the point, the seabed is marked by gutters, sculpted into wavelike shapes by a strong current known locally as the Lowly Rip. Water depth ranges from about 15m close to shore to 25m about 100m out. Because the tide flow is strong, the best time to fish this water is when Spencer Gulf

Colin Tannahill is all smiles after landing this 18.5kg snapper off Arno Bay

is experiencing its minimal tidal flow each month, an extreme neap tide called a 'dodge'.

I went fishing on the dodge tide, barely a kilometre north of the lighthouse in Spencer Gulf. The sea was calm and it was an hour after sunrise. Our boat, a 7m Nereus run by K&R Fishing Charters, circled slowly as skipper Lawrie Birdseye watched his two sounders, searching for gutters likely to hold big **snapper**.

This was my second trip to Spencer Gulf in four weeks. On my previous visit, I fished with Jim Harris, who was also on board this day. Previously we accounted for plenty of snapper up to 7kg, but nothing in the XXOS class we really wanted.

On this trip, we had left a drop on the Mud Banks, 15km to the north-west, after being harassed by a legion of snapper that barely made the SA legal limit of 38cm. The day before, Lawrie and I fished several drops beginning about 40km south of Whyalla, and again most of the snapper had been small except for one serious fish of about 10kg.

Jim normally fishes the Lowly Rip on the drift, but current was minimal because of the extreme neap tide and Lawrie decided to drop the anchor down the 25m. Our skipper was still organising the berley when Jim brought the first snapper onboard, a 40cm fish.

It took another hour before the first serious snapper came aboard. Jim decided that the only way to get past the pickers was to use big baits. He cubed a salmon of about a kilogram into three baits about 7cm long and 5cm in diameter. We used 170g snapper leads in the (still) strong current with running paternoster rigs. Leaders were 24kg breaking strain and the hooks were size 4/0 Suicides.

Jim dropped his bait to the bottom and proceeded to feed out line, reasoning that somewhere behind the schools of small snapper were some big cobs laying in wait. In one hard-hitting chomp, the salmon was gone; Jim set the hooks, his rod doubled over, and the drag whined as line poured out through the guides. Things were looking up. The tail thumping transmitting through the gelspun braid to the rod tip told the story as the big fish hung deep, using its deep flank to hold in the current and take line.

Well away to our south, there was a huge steam cloud rising from the Whyalla steelworks. Like the molten metal coming from the blast furnace, Jim's fish poured out of the green abyss, the sun's rays reflecting on the snapper's deep flanks just below the surface, turning them the colour of molten steel.

Eleven kilograms of prime snapper were still kicking on the floor when my rod took off. Following Jim's lead, I was also using big bait – a cube of snook about 15cm long. It was smaller in diameter than the salmon, and I reasoned it was probably better suited to 4/0 hooks. A few minutes later there was colour, Lawrie produced the net and a 12kg snapper was landed.

Rob North owns the charter boat and we had prearranged to pick him up at the Point Lowly Marina. By the time we had to pick him up, we had caught more than half a dozen snapper in excess of 10kg and, while it can be hard to leave a solid bite, a deal is a deal. But in the 30 minutes that it took to pick Rob up and return, nothing changed. He caught the next fish, about 11.5kg within 20 minutes of our putting the baits back out. By the end of the session, everyone had caught big snapper, 14 in all, ranging from about 10–15kg.

The southern side of Point Lowly is the northern end of False Bay. I fished here with Lawrie, chasing **cuttlefish** for bait.

False Bay is a declared marine park for giant Australian cuttlefish – the largest known spawning aggregation of the giant Australian cuttlefish – and we were just outside the northern boundary. The SA Government imposed the cuttlefish protection zone to safeguard these creatures from the ravages of commercial and amateur fishers. It's easy to see why – even outside the park boundaries the cuttlefish are numerous, hungry and eager to attack jigs.

An estimated 41,000 cuttlefish migrate to the bay every year to spawn, with the breeding season running from March–September.

Anglers who are serious about their fishing always take the time and trouble to source their own bait. Same day fresh bait should always be your first choice.

As Lawrie moved the boat in close to the rocky point that is Point Lowly, the water was calm but not as clear as I have seen it on other trips. Allowing for tide and wind, Lawrie positioned the 7m Nerius close to the shore and we began the drift.

As soon as we began drifting we put squid jigs out and allowed them to sink. Below us, in water just 1–2m deep, the seabed was dotted with boulders. When the water is clear, you can drift over these shallow rock areas and spot cuttlefish lying between the small boulders. As soon as this happens, toss a jig out and work it across the cuttlefish's line of vision. Like any form of sight fishing, the method is fascinating. There are few experiences in angling that get the juices flowing as well as being able to see your intended catch before you offer a lure or bait.

Lawrie, a former commercial fisherman, said that in the days when commercial operators worked False Bay, they employed the same methods and caught these creatures by the tonne: 'We used to wear wet weather gear and would still go home smelly and covered in black ink,' he recalled.

These creatures are the largest cuttlefish species in the world, and have a maximum-recorded body length (excluding head and tentacles) of 52cm and a weight of more than 6kg.

The ones we caught this day were mainly smaller specimens that Lawrie said were females.

Unlike squid, cuttlefish are pretty, changing colours to suit their environment and they seem to glow when hooked. As they rise to the surface, their body shape looks like a cross between squid and an octopus. Like squid, the cuttlefish are allowed to expel their ink before being lifted inboard. In less than an hour, we had enough for several days' solid snapper fishing.

WHYALLA

Whyalla is about four-and-a-half hours drive west of Adelaide. Take the A1 Hwy to Port Augusta, then left onto the Eyre Hwy and then left again onto the Lincoln Hwy and straight through to the Steel City.

Red ingots may run from the steel furnaces, but Spencer Gulf produces its own red ingots in the form of big snapper. Whyalla has built a tourism industry around its fishing and offers a magnificent harbour, boat ramp and fish cleaning facilities to rival any Australian destination.

Whyalla Harbour offers a safe haven for boats

ACCOMMODATION: Every type of accommodation is available from motels and caravan parks to hotels. **For more information visit www.whyalla.com**

Whyalla is **snapper** central for anglers. Every Easter the Australian Snapper Championships are based here and the top ten snapper weighed in are always over 10kg.

As you would expect with a destination where fishing is the major part of tourism, boating facilities are excellent.

Whyalla Marina is a sheltered harbour with a four-lane boat ramp protected from the vagaries of weather by breakwaters. Anglers often fish from the breakwaters and catch snapper, **squid**, **salmon** and **yellowtail kingfish**. A jetty outside the southern end of the harbour is popular with anglers looking for catches of **Australian herring (tommy ruff)**, **garfish**, **silver** or **yellowfin whiting**, squid and **blue swimmer crabs**. Wheelchair access to the jetty is available via a concrete path from the carpark. A large fish-cleaning bench is located near the boat ramp.

Most anglers fish from boats and sometimes travel long distances into Spencer Gulf in search of big reds. Many of the reefs are artificial and the Gulf is littered with drops. Some better known marks include the Whyalla Tyre Reef (GPS: S33.05.772, E137.36.349), the Leighton (S33.09.638, E137.38.552) and Marecks (S33.05.697, E137.36.387).

Whyalla isn't just about snapper. There are a few surprises in store. Even in the marina you can come across sights you will rarely see in the wild. Like the events that unfolded on the first day of my first visit here.

It was about 1.30pm when we returned to the marina. The 20km or so run to port from the Leighton at 25 knots was quick and relatively comfortable. In the harbour entrance Lawrie slowed the boat and three dolphins, two males and a female, swam alongside. As the boat cruised slowly, the dolphins left the water and hit down with a splash, letting us know they were there. Lawrie tossed a small fish to each of the males, crossed to the starboard side, inserted a tommy ruff into his mouth – tail first – then leaned over the side of the boat. Right on cue, as if it was rehearsed, the female dolphin rose out of the water, almost kissing Lawrie on the nose to take the fish from his mouth.

South of Whyalla on the Cowell Hwy is a small community of fishermen at a place called Murinini, between Plank and Shoalwater points. The seabed off here is littered with drops, and the area produces excellent numbers of large snapper.

I was fishing out of here one day on a hot bite of snapper when we had an encounter with a great white shark. Fishing nearby in another boat, Jim Harris called: 'Get your camera ready, there's a 12-footer cruising around the boat.' Jim was holding a large snapper head, a fish that probably would have topped 8kg had it not been bitten clean through just behind the pectoral fin, blood and bone trailing off the lifeless skull. As he talked, Jim pointed at the side of the boat, his arm following the shark as it circled, then vanished into the depths.

We knew that a few great white sharks were about. Some friends had three of them around their boat and one was a big female estimated to be about 6m long with a bulk comparable to a champion bull. And that was a concern. We were on a good drop and about the last thing you want around the place is Jaws looking for a feed of reds – unless of course you happen to be holding on to a camera!

Jim had no sooner stopped talking when the shark came rushing into the side of our boat and took hold of a snapper of about 9kg. It was a rare opportunity. Leaning over the side, I started snapping photos – and then realised where I was. At first, the shark had the snapper pushing in towards the side of our boat, then it swung around and started coming towards the fool leaning over the boat with the camera ... then the line broke!

For anglers who want to fish these waters and don't fancy the 60–70km run from Whyalla, the best bet is the seaside town of Cowell, which sits on the sheltered waters of Franklin Harbour. This 48sqkm natural harbour supports an array of fish including whiting, snapper, **snook**, tommy ruff, **flathead**, garfish and squid. Blue swimmer crabs are also caught night and day in the shallows. Boat-launching facilities are excellent, or alternatively you may prefer to launch your boat at Lucky Bay.

Arno Bay

Further south is Arno Bay, another area for jumbo-sized snapper. A small seaport and grain town, Arno Bay is situated between Port Neill and Cowell. During a particularly productive window in 2008, three snapper over 17kg were caught offshore. In what must be the best snapper double-header ever, two snapper weighing in at 20kg and 17.6kg were caught on the same trip in early May. Two weeks later, a third jumbo snapper, this time weighing 18.5kg, was caught by Colin Tannahill. Colin, who is based in Sydney and works for fishing tackle company Shimano, was fishing about 25km offshore with local charter boat skipper Grant Fennell. Conditions were rough, with 2m seas, whitecaps and 20-knot winds. It was late in the afternoon when the garfish bait was taken, and it took 20 minutes before Colin saw colour.

'When I saw the snapper in the water I knew it was huge and it took two of us to lift it onboard because its tail was hanging out of the net,' Colin recalled. 'I couldn't wait to weigh it and I said to

The blue swimmer crab is keenly sought after for its table qualities

Fish cleaning facilities getting a work-out at Whyalla

the guys: "I am finally going to be a member of the 30lb club." But when the scales went past 18kg I said: "Forget the 30lb club, I am going into the 40lb snapper club!"' The club probably has no more than six members. Colin's fish was 1.08m long, 35cm deep and 24cm thick.

Colin has been fishing Spencer Gulf for about 10 years, usually off Whyalla. In December 2011 he went to Arno Bay for the first time in company with two Melbourne anglers, Brendan Wing and Warren Carter. In 16 hours on the water using soft plastic lures (Squidgy Flick Baits, Stealth Prawns and Shads) they caught more than 50 snapper of 6–9kg.

COFFIN BAY

Take the A1 Hwy to Port Augusta, then left onto the Eyre Hwy/National Hwy A1, passing through Iron Knob, Kimba to Kyancutta onto Tod Hwy B90 (signposted Port Lincoln) then right onto Flinders Hwy and left onto Coffin Bay Rd.

Situated on the lower Eyre Peninsula on the shores of Port Douglas Bay, Coffin Bay is a beautiful, idyllic destination surrounded by national and conservation parks with an abundance of flora and fauna. The exposed jagged cliffs, sand dunes, long white beaches and wild seas contrast starkly with the sheltered, tranquil waters of the bays. It has some of the best fishing for yellowtail kingfish, snapper and salmon available anywhere.

ACCOMMODATION: Ranges from motels, apartments, holiday homes and caravan parks.
For more information visit
www.coffinbay.net

When it comes to big bruisers, **yellowtail kingfish** are up near the top of the list. Fishing with live bait set under a balloon, you watch as the balloon starts to move across the surface of the water, a sign of nervous baitfish below trying to escape the jaws of a predator. Suddenly the bait is inhaled and the balloon breaks free of the line to drift away. Meanwhile, the ratchet on your reel signifies the fish is running away with the bait, so you push the lever drag setting up and set the hook, and then hang on as 20kg or so of yellowtail kingfish steams off.

The experience is awesome. Your adrenalin rushes so fast, your arms shake and you wonder whether you have the stamina to outlast the fish. As a metre or so of kingfish nears the surface you spy the yellow, crescent-shaped tail and marvel at the band that appears mask-like across its eyes.

Yellowtail kingfish are a serious opponent. In deep water, they will run straight down and drag your line through reef. Hook a big one on a pier and you can count on it running straight through the pilings beneath your feet.

SA boasts the biggest kingfish in the country, with anglers catching them up to 48kg. One of the few areas where big yellowtail kingfish are in good numbers, and the terrain favours the angler, is Coffin Bay. The township is a favourite destination among

Coffin Bay is home to monstrous yellowtail kingfish like this 30kg plus specimen

anglers in the know. Those with the know-how catch kingfish, **squid**, **garfish**, **silver trevally**, **snook**, big **snapper** and kidney-thumping **King George whiting**.

Kingfish have been caught at various times, but the spring tides that occur over the new and full moon periods are most productive. There are several hotspots for the kings, but it depends on weather as to where you can fish.

The entrance to Kellidie Bay, about 2km from the Coffin Bay boat ramp, is popular. The water depth is 3–5m and there is a sandy channel that connects the two bays. Sandbars surround the stretch so you won't hit reefs as easily as in other areas, and it is very well sheltered when the wind is blowing from the west.

Other hotspots are Crinalin Point, at the north-west extremity of the township, and the rock ledge that divides Kellidie Bay from Coffin Bay, which is most popular when a northerly is blowing.

The wharf produces most species, but hooking and landing are two entirely different processes: big kingfish are rarely landed from the pier due to the close proximity of boat moorings, but you will catch **snapper**, **tommy rough** and silver trevally.

Methods for Eyre Peninsula

TACKLE In these waters, where the snapper are big and you may have current to contend with, you should be looking at a minimum of 10kg outfits. My preference is to work 15kg braid lines because they are thinner and require less sinker weight to hold the bottom when the tide is running. In most areas, current isn't a major issue and you can get away with 56–85g (2–3oz) sinkers. If you fish the Lowly Rip, then even on a dodge tide you will need 170g (6oz) snapper leads. Use a threadline or overhead reel, and make sure it will hold a minimum 250m of line and has a smooth drag system. The rod needs to be medium to fast taper, and have a lot of lifting power in the butt.

If you are chasing King George or silver whiting, a 3kg outfit will suffice. A running sinker rig is used and hook size should be from about No. 4 Baitholder pattern to a 1/0 Suicide. Anglers chasing silver whiting in the shallows use a fixed paternoster sinker rig with two leaders with No. 6 hooks attached and baited with pipi.

For yellow-tailed kingfish, minimum tackle requirements are a 15kg gamefishing outfit. Full roller guides are not necessary but the reel should be a quality lever drag reel such as the Penn International or Shimano Tiagra. Spool your reel with 24kg braid and use a 50kg wind-on leader.

RIGS The snapper rig is a running paternoster, with a leader to the sinker of about 1.5m, and the leader to the bait about half that. Use 24kg breaking strain leader to the bait. Use two hooks, 4/0–6/0 Suicide pattern, and have the second hook snelled to the leader to suit the bait length.

BAIT Most baits work for snapper, but to get past the pickers, use big baits. For example, a 1kg salmon is ideally cubed into three baits about 7cm long. The head of the fish is the best bait. Other baits that produce snapper here include kingfish, whiting, squid and cuttlefish. If you want smaller snapper, use small baits like pilchards. Berley trails work well. Use a berley cage with a trigger-release door on the bottom so that you can lower it to the seabed before releasing the berley. This will keep the trail, and the fish, close.

For kingfish, bridle rig live baitfish using an 8/0–10/0 Circle hook. Popular live baits for kings include squid, salmon, garfish, slimy mackerel, yellowtail scad and pike. Live squid are best rigged on a twin 'J' hook rig, snelled far enough apart so that the bottom hook is pinned through the collar of the squid body, and the top hook is hooked lightly in the apex. When live baiting at Coffin Bay, it is necessary to suspend the bait a couple of metres or so under a small balloon. This keeps the bait in the strike zone at all times, particularly at tide changes when the fish hunt at their peak.

Calamari squid are caught for bait and the table

5 GREAT AUSTRALIAN BIGHT

CEDUNA

Ceduna is situated on the far west coast of SA, on the shoreline of Murat Bay at the east end of the Great Australian Bight. The main Ceduna beach begins at the base of Cape Thevenard and runs due north for 1.5km, flanked by 10m high bluffs.

ACCOMMODATION: On my visit to Ceduna, I stayed at Ceduna Foreshore Caravan Park on the beachfront. There are alternative parks and the town has hotel and motel accommodation. Accommodation at Fowlers Bay includes motel style cabins, caravan and campsites.
For more information visit
www.cedunatourism.com.au
www.fowlersbay.com/accommodation.htm

Ceduna has two boat ramps and a 400m long jetty near the town centre. The best of the ramps is Puckridge, in the lee of Cape Thevenard. Ceduna, Thevenard and Denial Bay are popular fishing destinations.

The long jetty at Ceduna runs out over dense seagrass beds and is a noted **squid** fishing platform, and also produces **whiting**, **snook**, **salmon** and **Australian herring**. At the end of the jetty, anglers fish for larger fare, including **snapper** and **mulloway**. A friend who fished here saw several large **yellowtail kingfish** hunting. He caught a small **salmon**, put it out under a balloon, and soon hooked up; that fish is still running.

Murat Bay is safe water for small vessels. Species caught include **silver whiting**,

leatherjackets, snook, garfish, tommy ruffs, King George whiting, salmon, trevally, mullet, mulloway, sweep and a range of sharks including school, gummy and bronze whalers. Offshore anglers go in search of all of the above plus snapper, yellowtail kingfish, Samson fish and southern bluefin tuna. Kings and Samson fish are best in March and April, while bluefin run from late in December to April. Winter is the best time for King George whiting and salmon. Two favourite baits used at Ceduna are squid and a bivalve shellfish called razorfish.

Denial Bay has a breakwall but most anglers head farther west to Davenport Creek, about 40km west of Ceduna. Note though that a 4WD is required to reach the boat ramp on Davenport Creek. To get there, drive out on Denial Bay Rd, about 22km west of Ceduna, then turn south-west onto Nadia Rd and continue to campground, another 19km along a dirt road. There is a designated camping area inland on the banks of the creek, with no facilities except pit toilets. Access is quite easy as the sand is firm throughout most of the dune tracks and easy to traverse with reduced tyre pressure. The beach gets treacherous heading east from the beach entry as it

Above: Denial Bay jetty produces squid, snook and whiting
Below: Beaches at Fowlers Bay and Yalata are popular for anglers seeking mulloway, salmon and sharks

Ceduna jetty is a favourite with anglers as it offers plenty in the way of variety

is rather narrow, sloping and soft, however the rest of the beach is wide and firm. **Mulloway**, **salmon**, **whiting** and **snapper** are some of the species caught off the beach.

Fowlers Bay is further west again. If you want to fish the beaches, you will again need a 4WD. On most of these west coast beaches, drivers need to be cautious at the eastern ends. There is **salmon**, **mullet**, **whiting** and **mulloway** for those who are patient. Fowlers Bay jetty is popular for its big **squid**, **Australian herring** and **snook**. Scotts Bay is close to Fowlers; this is one of the best **salmon** beaches in SA.

YALATA

Next stop along the Eyre Hwy, about an hour west of Fowlers Bay is Yalata, an Indigenous Protected Area (IPA), where the Yalata Anangu People live. It is an extremely remote area and the closest phones are at least 70km away and there is no mobile coverage from the beaches. Note that no alcohol or firearms can be brought into Yalata.

Yalata's beaches are regarded by all who have fished here as the best and most consistent **mulloway** waters in Australia.

ACCOMMODATION: Yalata IPA provides some of the best natural dune camping areas available. Camping is only permissible in designated campsites, and a permit is required. Vehicles can enter the beach at Granites, Bob's Kitchen and Hilton. The other campsites are close enough to the gutters for people to walk. Information relating to camping permits and areas can be obtained by ringing **(08) 8625 6201**. For more information visit www.yalata.org.au

It isn't just big **mulloway** in Yalata. When the **salmon** run the schools are measured by the hectare; and you will encounter big **snapper** and plenty of **sharks**. It is a wild, remote area with dingos and snakes. The roads are sandy, but have sharp, shale along the edges and these will penetrate tyres deflated for beach running, so be sure to carry a couple of spare tyres.

Many anglers head this way to fish in the summer months but the heat can be oppressive

Anglers camp in the sand dunes at Yalata

up to about 40°C. The most consistent months for weather are October and November, and Ceduna locals who fish here say the New Moon period offers the best fishing.

There are several designated beaches for fishing. The Hilton, Bob's Kitchen and Jaxsons are best reached via Red Gate Track. This track runs onto Coombra Dune Track, which commences 17km west of Yalata Roadhouse.

Granites Beach is not difficult to get to, and is reached via Coombra Track. The track from the turn-off on the Eyre Hwy runs for about 20km, and then some easy sand work to a campsite, a couple of minutes from the Granites beach.

Methods for Yalata

TACKLE One thing about fishing at Yalata is that any of the species you may encounter, whether it's mulloway, snapper, salmon or sharks, chances are they're going to be big, so high-quality gear is a must. There is no point spending money and going to all the trouble of travelling to Yalata only to cut corners on fishing gear. Two surf-fishing outfits are needed: one as your main one and another for catching live bait with. An optional third outfit can be used for lure casting. For the main surf fishing outfit, you will need a rod between 3.5–4m long, capable of casting 85–200g sinkers. The rod needs low-down grunt to fight a mulloway of up to 35g. Size 6000 threadline reels are recommended. A light outfit is essential to catch bait so go for a 2.3m light to medium spin rod with a 3000 size reel loaded with 7kg braid. Bait jigs are ideal, and use a 20g metal slice with a treble hook instead of a sinker. This gives you the flexibility of casting lures or bait fishing.

SURF RIGS There are two types of rigs used: The first is a simple two-hook paternoster rig, ideal for presenting cut baits. The second is a running paternoster, with a single 80lb dropper connected to a 6/0 Suicide hook.

BAIT Live bait is best, if you can catch them. Australian herring, salmon and yelloweye mullet make excellent baits. Due to the remoteness of these west coast beaches, take plenty of bait in case it is difficult to catch fresh bait. Fresh frozen squid, octopus, and fish fillet baits work well. If you hook a salmon, fillet the fish and put the fillet on straight away. Salmon fillets are excellent for mulloway and snapper.

WESTERN AUSTRALIA

Steve's

FAVOURITE DESTINATIONS FOR WESTERN AUSTRALIA

If WA were a retail outlet you would call it a one-stop shop. The coastline is huge. In the temperate waters of the south, anglers do well fishing for the likes of snapper, salmon, tailor and mulloway. As you travel north the species become more tropical. In the Kimberley region barramundi is the most sought-after species, while offshore you are as likely to hook a Spanish mackerel or sailfish, as you are a marlin.

Some offshore reef systems have been declared off limits to anglers, and hot spots like Shark Bay have strict regulations to limit the catch and number of people allowed to fish. Despite the size of the state, the WA fisheries people are intent on preserving fish stocks, which is good news for anglers.

ACCOMMODATION

Western Australia's accommodation options are as diverse as its geography, from beachside penthouses, to renovated country pubs or charming chalets. **For more information visit www.westernaustralia.com**

Sunset in the Kimberley is a sight few anglers ever forget

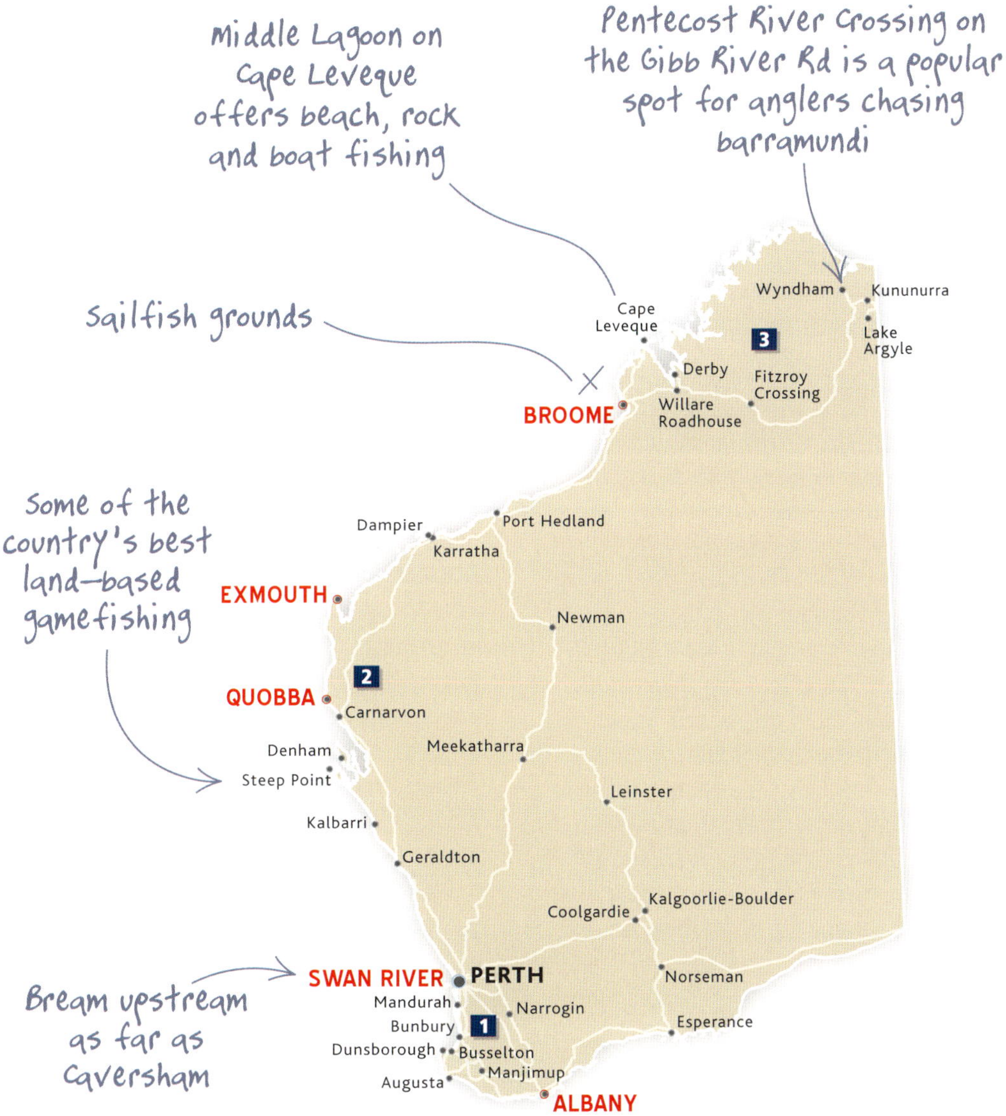

Middle Lagoon on Cape Leveque offers beach, rock and boat fishing
Pentecost River Crossing on the Gibb River Rd is a popular spot for anglers chasing barramundi
Sailfish grounds
Some of the country's best land-based gamefishing
Bream upstream as far as Caversham
Cape Leveque
Wyndham
Kununurra
Lake Argyle
3
Derby
Fitzroy Crossing
Willare Roadhouse
BROOME
Dampier
Port Hedland
Karratha
EXMOUTH
Newman
2
QUOBBA
Carnarvon
Denham
Meekatharra
Steep Point
Leinster
Kalbarri
Geraldton
Coolgardie
Kalgoorlie-Boulder
SWAN RIVER
PERTH
Norseman
Mandurah
Narrogin
Bunbury
1
Esperance
Dunsborough
Busselton
Augusta
Manjimup
ALBANY

1 THE SOUTH-WEST

ESPERANCE

What is most striking about Esperance is the huge expanse of clean, white beach available for fishing. Beach fishing is popular and given the amount of coastline and great looking water, deciding where to fish is a daunting task. Every bay, beach and headland has possibilities. Some beaches are only accessible by 4WD, and if in doubt, seek local tackle store advice. Common beach captures include salmon, tailor, herring, flathead, mulloway and whiting.

ACCOMMODATION: For more information visit www.visitesperance.com

On the town foreshore is the Tanker jetty. It was closed for repair when I was there (although it is now re-open), but locals told me that **squid**, **herring**, **garfish**, **tailor** and **snook** were among the usual catch.

Close to town beaches accessible by 2WD include Salmon, Fourth, Nine Mile, Ten Mile and Eleven Mile Beaches. Fourteen Mile Beach, and further west, Roses and Shelly Beaches, require a 4WD. These beaches offer both beach and rock opportunities. Rock fishing produces **sweep**, **rock cod**, **wrasse**, **queen** and **pink snapper**, **leatherjacket** and **groper**.

East of Esperance, Bandy Creek boat harbour is worth a visit for **bream**. It is a small estuary system, and the boat harbour has clear water. It is used by local commercial fishing boats, and has a public boat ramp. The harbour and the river are separated by a small dam with pipes that allow water to flow back and forth with the tides, without silting up the harbour. It offers anglers the chance to sight cast to feeding schools of bream in the shallows of the river, or prospect the rock walls of the harbour. The biggest bream tend to hang in the deeper water of the harbour.

Other beaches to the east include Cape Le Grande, which requires a 4WD, and access is via Wylie Bay Rd. Cape Le Grande National Park, 56km by road from Esperance, can be reached with a 2WD. There are two good campsites, water and toilets. The area offers beach and rock fishing.

Offshore anglers will find boat launching facilities in Esperance at the foreshore ramp, and on the western side of Bandy Creek boat harbour. Common species caught from boats include snapper, **nannygai**, **swallowtail**, **blue morwong**, **samson fish**, snook, herring, **whiting**, tailor, **mulloway**, squid and **gummy sharks**.

ALBANY

From Perth, head south onto Albany Hwy (State Route 30) for almost five hours. It's a long run but like most places in WA it is worth the effort.

This bustling city of more than 30,000 is most often associated with the nearby Cheynes Beach whaling station. For anglers though, Albany has much to offer from offshore and beach to bays.

ACCOMMODATION: There are more than enough motel rooms, apartments and caravan parks to cater for any taste.
For more information visit www.amazingalbany.com.au

Albany is most famous for being the home of the last Australian whaling station. But talk to tackle store owner Jim Allen and you soon realise there is more to Albany than whales – like a **salmon** run where the fish average 5–6kg and are up to 10kg!

Top salmon spots include the Sand Patch, Cable Beach and the Salmon Holes. Some of these take some effort to reach, in particular the Salmon Holes and the Sand Patch. A WA friend, Mark Griffin, returned from the Sand Patch with a wonderful anecdote: 'The Sand Patch is well known for its salmon and the 506 steps you need to climb at the

The sheltered inlet at the mouth of the Waychinicup River, located 40km east of Albany, is popular with anglers fishing from kayaks and canoes

end of the day. When you are really tired [climbing the stairs] and start to lower your gaze, you can still see under the staircase traces of the old trail anglers used to climb. One old angler told me that blokes would start climbing with half a dozen big greenbacks and drop them one by one as they became more and more exhausted. He reckoned it all got a bit fragrant towards the end of the season.'

There are multiple bays around Albany. In Oyster Harbour, Princess Royal Harbour and King George Sound you can expect to catch **King George whiting**, **herring**, **silver trevally** and salmon. Middleton Beach produces salmon, **tailor**, herring, whiting, **leatherjacket** and silver trevally. The King and Kalgan rivers that flow into Oyster Harbour will produce **bream**.

Anglers fishing offshore do not need to travel far to find productive reef systems. Coral reefs at the back of Michelmas and Breaksea islands are productive for **snapper**, **blue morwong**, **dhufish**, **Samson fish**, **yellowtail kingfish** and, for those willing to fish close to the rocks, **blue groper**. The Continental Shelf is about 26-miles out, but **yellowfin tuna** are often caught in close to King George Sound.

Boat ramps are located at Emu Point in Oyster Harbour and Princess Royal Harbour. Small boats can be launched at the Elizabeth St ramp and there is beach launching at Parry Beach and off Murray Rd in Frenchman Bay. Some anglers launch their boats with tractors from Cheynes Beach.

Another spot that can produce a few nice fish is Waychinicup, about 40km east of Albany. The Waychinicup River widens into a beautiful inlet surrounded by granite hills and enters the sea

Salmon Holes at Albany is renowned for the size and quality of its salmon

through a narrow opening. The inlet is sheltered from the worst of the sea and wind. Expect whiting, **flathead**, trevally and leatherjacket. There is no defined boat ramp, so kayaks, canoes or small tinnies that you can manhandle easily are best.

DUNSBOROUGH

To get to Dunsborough follow the coast road (A1) south for about three hours, passing through Bunbury and Busselton before arriving at Dunsborough.

It is a neat little seaside resort town that overlooks the crystal clear waters of Geographe Bay. A popular family destination, isolation is one reason why it fishes so well.

ACCOMMODATION: Includes resorts and beach cottages and caravan park.
For more information visit
www.westernaustralia.com

Dunsborough offers beach, rock and boat fishing. Local fishing store operator Damien Lane says the rock ledges produce **salmon** in autumn and winter, **Samson fish**, **herring**, **snapper** and **mulloway**. Some of the more popular ledges include Wyadup Rocks south of Yallingup and Torpedo Rocks, 10km north of Yallingup. Sugarloaf Rock, south of Cape Naturaliste, is popular but dangerous when a sea is running. Fish caught here include salmon, **silver trevally**, snapper and Samson fish.

Beach fishing with easy access is available at Eagle Bay and Bunker Bay on the east side of Cape Naturaliste, and these beaches offer shelter from the prevailing south-westerlies. The west side of the cape, north of Sugarloaf Rock, is popular when the wind is blowing offshore. Salmon, **tarwhine**, mulloway, **King George whiting**, **tailor** and herring comprise the bulk of the catch.

Blue crabs are caught at the Dunsborough boat ramp. Offshore anglers fishing places such as Four Mile Reef can expect to hook **dhufish**, Samson fish, **yellowtail kingfish**, **queen snapper (blue morwong)**, **baldchin groper** and **harlequin fish**.

PERTH

Perth is usually the first stop for east coast anglers who prefer to fly than spend a week in a car. For

The Swan River in Perth ranks as one of Australia's most productive big city waters

many anglers, Perth is the first and only stop. That the fishing is good enough to attract and hold anglers says a lot for this western capital, especially given the quality of fishing available north and south of the city. Perth has a diverse range of fishing options that should not be overlooked, after all anglers can catch species including bream and mulloway within the city limits.

And there are some anglers who like the idea of being able to fish close to civilization. There is nothing wrong with being able to come ashore for a freshly brewed coffee; it's a common practice in ports like Sydney Harbour.

ACCOMMODATION: Perth has everything from 5-star hotels to unpowered campsites.
For more information visit
www.westernaustralia.com

The Swan River produces many species, including **bream**, **mulloway**, **herring**, **tailor**, **tarwhine**, **silver trevally**, **Samson fish** and **flathead**. This is a year-round fishery for the much sought bream. In summer the bream run upstream as far as Caversham in the Swan Valley. In winter the best fishing is in the estuary, and the jetty piles downstream of the Causeway, Freshwater Bay and Mossman Bay. Huge numbers of toadfish mean that fishing with soft plastic lures is an expensive exercise. Most anglers prefer to fish bait or work hard-body lures and hope to avoid the toadfish. The Canning River also fishes well for bream.

The Leeuwin boat ramp, just upriver from Fremantle, is a good area for fly-fishing according to Mark Griffin, who explained that the river has a large flat on the eastern side, which allows for good saltwater fly-fishing on the flats and over the drop-off.

Mark found a successful method was to cast a Crazy Charlie fly upriver to deeper water and allow the tide to drag the fly along the side of the channel before starting a slow jerky retrieve. As the fly is brought up and over the edge of the channel into the shallower water it consistently produced flathead and even **flounder**.

In describing this spot, Mark warned me to watch for dolphins. 'That dorsal fin can cause momentary heart failure when wading,' he said.

'One surfaced less than a rod-length from me and I was convinced a bull shark was about to end my fishing days.'

Mulloway are in the Swan River most of the year and favourite locations for them are Canning, Narrows and Causeway bridges. Riverside Dr, near the old brewery building, is another area where mulloway are often caught.

Early summer sees tailor along the beaches and in the Swan and Canning rivers. Big tailor run in winter and are caught in the estuary, but more so from the beaches. North and south moles at Fremantle are popular in summer with anglers chasing **oriental bonito**. In June and July, when the nor-westerlies blow, **snapper** to 8kg can be caught. **Salmon** schools run in large numbers March–May and these fish are caught from the beaches and the moles at Fremantle.

Cockburn Sound, south of Perth, is an extraordinary snapper fishery that fishes best September–December. A few years back I spoke to Lou Rummer, who fishes for snapper in and just outside Cockburn Sound. The Sound is about 5km wide and 9km long, and Lou said that at any one time there could be up to 200 tonnes of snapper weighing 2–17kg in the area. Snapper are caught in the Sound most of the year, but there is a closed season to protect the breeding fish from mid-September until the end of October. Top spots include Southwest Rocks, Barber Poles, D-9, Pinnacles and Sulphur Bay. Reef systems on the west side of Garden Island also carry good numbers.

A favourite with anglers heading offshore from Perth are the six Fish Attracting Devices (FADs) put in place during the summer. The FADs range from about 100m deep out to 200m and can be more than 50km offshore. The most common species attracted to these devices is **dolphinfish** and these often appear in huge numbers. Details on the locations of the FADs, including GPS marks, are available on the Perth Game Fishing Club website: www.pgfc.com.au.

Methods for the South-West

TACKLE In southern estuaries, such as Swan River, use 3–4kg threadline outfits for smaller species such as bream and silver trevally, and 8–10kg outfits for mulloway. Use small bibbed minnows and soft plastic lures for bream and flathead, and bigger versions of these lures for mulloway. Tailor will take metal lures.

2 MID-WEST COAST

KALBARRI

Located 590km north of Perth, Kalbarri is an open and friendly town. It is popular with holidaymakers which causes the local population to swell so it is advisable to book accommodation in advance.

ACCOMMODATION: Kalbarri has an extensive array of accommodation and hotel options from resorts and villas to caravan and holiday parks. From Kalbarri to Broome is almost 2000km and there aren't that many towns along the way so it pays to plan your trip and work out where you intend staying overnight or for longer periods.
For more information visit
www.kalbarri.org.au or www.discoverwest.com.au

The Murchison River at Kalbarri, about six hours' drive north of Perth, produces a variety of fish including **bream** to 52cm. 'We also catch small **mulloway** in the river, **yellowfin whiting**, **blue manna** and **green mud crabs**, the odd **mangrove jack**, **Moses perch** and **giant herring**,' said local angler Dean Robbins. There are two jetties in the river, one of which is public, and as you drive upriver, you'll find many isolated spots. Mulloway to 25kg have been caught from the public jetty.

The main boat ramp is in town and the main fishing beaches are south of Kalbarri. Chinaman

Beach at the mouth of the Murchison produces mulloway, **tailor** to 8kg and sometimes **snapper**. On the north side of the Murchison at Oyster Reef Beach, anglers use quad bikes to drive along the beach and fish for big mulloway, tailor and snapper. Dean said the best beach fishing with easy access was Wittecarra Beach to Red Bluff, where big tailor and mulloway are caught.

Take Red Bluff Rd south from Kalbarri and you come to a spot called Blue Holes. Just north of here, anglers fish for tailor with poppers and chrome slices. At Red Bluff, anglers fish for **yellowfin**, **longtail** and **mackerel tuna**, **mackerel** and tailor. The gorges and rock ledges south of Red Bluff offer good fishing for snapper and tailor.

Offshore species include tuna, **Spanish mackerel**, **dhufish**, **baldchin groper**, **coral trout**, **norwest snapper**, **cobia**, **Samson fish**, **yellowtail kingfish**, **amberjack**, **red throat**, and **spangled** and **red emperor.**

SHARK BAY

The drive north to Shark Bay takes about ten hours from Perth, but the fishing lure is so strong here that many an east-coast angler has driven across from Sydney or Melbourne.

Feeding dolphins at Monkey Mia made Shark Bay famous, but the area also happens to be regarded by many as Australia's premier snapper fishery even if there is a lottery for the privilege.

ACCOMMODATION: Camping, motels, villas and resort-style accommodation are available.
For more information visit www.sharkbay.asn.au/sharkbay-accommodation

Most anglers head for the old pearling town of Denham, the population centre for Shark Bay.

Shark Bay was once touted as the hottest **snapper** fishery in Australia and anglers used to come here in droves for them. However, fishing

A West Australian dhufish that was caught by noted angler, Emma George

pressure took its toll and WA Fisheries stepped in to impose strict regulations. These days to catch snapper you need to enter a lottery run by WA Fisheries to gain a couple of tags that allow you to hook two snapper, and then only one a day. Catch and release still remains an option.

But there are many other species worth chasing here. Boat anglers catch **groper**, **cod**, **mackerel** and **coral trout**.

Bluebone groper can be caught along with **norwest snapper** from the rocks, and shore-based anglers catch **whiting** and **flathead** from the beach where fishing is permitted.

STEEP POINT

Vehicle access to Steep Point can be difficult and a high clearance 4WD is required. It is about 185km by road from the North West Coastal Hwy to Steep Point; the first 41km is sealed, followed by 114km of a formed but unsealed road and the last 30km of the trip is over soft sand so drivers need to reduce tyre pressures to get through. Entry fees apply for everyone. Entry fee (per visit) is $12 per car (up to 12 people). This was accurate at the time of print, but is subject to change.

The home of land-based gamefishing in the west, the greater area surrounding Steep Point, including Shelter Bay and False Entrance is known as Edel Land and has been purchased by the state government for conservation purposes.

ACCOMMODATION: Camping is controlled by a permit system and sites must be booked in advance. A camping permit is required for all overnight stays. Facilities are very basic and you will therefore need to be self-sufficient. No fresh water, food, fuel or other supplies are available in the area. There are pit toilets and a small number of bins at Steep Point and Shelter Bay.
For more information visit
www.sharkbay.org/steeppoint.aspx

One of the most highly regarded destinations for land-based gamefishing, anglers fishing here catch huge **mackerel**, **trevally**, **tuna** and even **sailfish** from the rugged cliffs. It is a specialised sport requiring unique techniques and tackle. Baits are floated several hundred metres offshore using helium balloons. Special gaffs are used to haul fish up the cliffs.

Boat-based fishing is popular around Steep Point and many people launch from Shelter Bay to fish inside South Passage or outside along the Zuytdorp Cliffs and Dirk Hartog Island. Fish caught here include **Spanish mackerel**, **tailor** to 6kg, **sailfish**, tuna, **cobia**, **mulloway**, **snapper** and **bluebone.** Beach-based anglers catch **whiting**, tailor, **flathead** and trevally in Francois Peron National Park and other areas around Peron Peninsula.

CARNARVON

Carnarvon is about 900km north of Perth on the North West Coastal Hwy. Well signposted, the town is between Shark Bay to the south and Exmouth to the north.

Fishing is a popular pastime in Carnarvon, and there are great spots to suit all methods: rock, beach, estuary and pier. Offshore, Carnarvon has it all, including sunken wrecks, reefs and islands.

ACCOMMODATION: There are several large caravan parks, hotels, motels, apartments and backpacker accommodation. Camping is restricted to designated areas but I came across a large contingent of campers at New Beach, about a 40-minute drive south.
For more information visit
www.carnarvon.org.au

Carnarvon is hard to miss: it looks like a green oasis amid a great, yellow sand desert landscape of broad flat plains that stretch for hundreds of kilometres to the north, south and east, an inhospitable place where the only vegetation is mulga and spinifex. Drive around Carnarvon though and you come across green and lush market gardens. It is an amazing visual transformation. More so when you learn that these irrigated paddocks source water from bores below the dry riverbed of the Gascoyne River.

On the ocean, water clarity is excellent. Even on rough days with an onshore wind blowing, anglers can see well into the water, and like Hervey Bay on the East Coast, there is a mix of tropical and temperate species to be caught. Common species caught include **mulloway**, **tailor**, **snapper**, **bream**, **mackerel**, **tuna** and **shark**. Between May and August, **blue manna crabs** are on the menu, and in May/June an annual fishing competition called Carnarfin is held.

The most popular fishing spot in town is The One Mile Jetty, on Babbage Island at the mouth of the Gascoyne River estuary. The jetty runs out into the Indian Ocean, and unlike similar claims around the country, this jetty is actually one mile long. For those who don't wish to make the long walk, there is a train service, which is easy when you are carrying a truckload of tackle. The end section of the jetty spans a deep channel, and about half way along the jetty on the northern side is a purpose-built angling platform.

The jetty is high, so a long handled gaff or net is needed. Boat anglers often tie off from the end

of the jetty and send down a **pilchard** (mulie) for a mulloway. The jetty produces variety and you can expect to hook tailor, snapper, **Spanish mackerel** and even tuna. On my visit, anglers did well on **dart** and tailor, and they were fishing close to the beach.

Boat ramps are located at Launching Point on the way to One Mile Jetty, and Pelican Point on the west side of the Fascine. On the east side of the Fascine is a marina along Harbour Dr. Follow Harbour Dr and you will come to Small Boat. Although it is the home of the commercial fishing fleet, it also has a boat ramp suited to large offshore vessels.

South of Carnarvon are fishing and crabbing spots including Oyster and Uendoo Creeks, New Beach, Bush Bay and Gladstone. **Mangrove jacks** are caught in the mangrove areas of the Gascoyne River estuary and at Oyster Creek.

Beach fishing is a favourite, as is the large estuary system. Expect to encounter tailor, mulloway, mangrove jack and **queenfish** in the estuary, and mulloway, tailor and sometimes even Spanish mackerel off the beach.

The offshore scene is dominated by the collection of tyres at the *Lady Joyce* wreck about 15 nautical miles from the town's excellent boat

Beach fishing at Carnarvon; anglers who fish here can expect tailor, mulloway and sharks to name a few species

It can be a long walk back to the carpark from the end of the jetty at Carnarvon

Beach fishing near the Krait Memorial at Exmouth

ramp. Catches here include snapper, **emperor**, tailor, **pike**, bream, mulloway, **cobia**, Spanish mackerel and sharks. The Coral Patch is further away but locals say the fishing is better than at *Lady Joyce* as the reef has less fishing pressure.

QUOBBA

Head north from Carnarvon for about 30km and you come to a turnoff called Blowholes Rd. Follow this for about 45km, and about a kilometre or so past the lighthouse will bring you out at Point Quobba.

This is the start of a rugged, cliff-lined, coastline that incorporates Quobba Station, a working pastoral station where the outback meets the sea. Quobba is on the southern end of the Ningaloo Reef Marine Park and stretches along the Indian Ocean. Quobba offers land-based gamefishing.

ACCOMMODATION: Camping is available at Quobba Station and near Point Quobba, but there is no freshwater; make sure you take plenty of water with you.
For more information visit
www.quobba.com.au

The rock ledges are a Mecca for land-based game anglers, although note that rock fishing is dangerous, and should not be attempted without seeking local knowledge. The rock ledges are high so rope gaffs are necessary in most areas. Many of the ledges at Quobba are marked with small plaques in memory of anglers who died fishing there, so take care.

The rock ledges at The Blowholes is a popular area, as are many access points along the dusty track called Gnaraloo Rd. Some other well-known ledges include Garths Rock, named after the late saltwater fly fishing pioneer Max Garth, Red Bluff and Cape Cuvier.

The attractions for land-based game anglers include **Spanish mackerel**, **cobia**, **tuna**, **sailfish** and various **shark** species. Other species caught in the area are **Norwest** and **pink snapper**, **baldchin groper**, **queenfish**, **tailor** and **trevally**.

Anglers chasing game fish send out baits, usually **tailor**, under balloons or employ high-speed spinning or popper techniques. Several beaches along the coastline offer a less dangerous option for species including **mulloway**, tailor, trevally, **snapper** and **squid**. **Bonefish** are also reported in these waters.

EXMOUTH

Situated about 1200km north of Perth, Exmouth is an angler's paradise and Australia's only known bonefish fishery. The Continental Shelf is only kilometres offshore and Ningaloo Reef runs 250km along the coastline of the region and forms a giant lagoon with kilometres of shallow sand flats.

ACCOMMODATION: Exmouth has two caravan parks, and another caravan park is located at the top of Northwest Cape, near Vlamingh Head lighthouse. The town has motel, apartment and backpacker accommodation. A few people I ran into were doing some illegal beach camping.
For more information visit
www.exmouthwa.com.au

Saltwater fly aficionados claim these are the least fished **bonefish** in the world. Other fish caught on the flats include several **trevallies**: **golden**, **giant**, **blue** and **gold spot**, and there are **queenfish**, **spangled emperor**, **milkfish**, **giant herring**, **tarpon**, **cobia**, **sweetlips** and **permit**. Ningaloo Reef is recognised as a premier gamefishing destination and produces **black** and **blue marlin**, **dolphinfish**, **Spanish mackerel**, **sailfish** and various **tunas**.

Check out the rules regarding the Ningaloo Marine Park as there are Sanctuary Zones where fishing is prohibited, but never mind as there are many other areas in the park where the fishing is superb. The WA Department of Environment and Conservation puts out free pamphlets that mark fishing areas, and there are signs on beaches marking the zones.

Land-based fishing is a popular recreational pastime as there are many different species to be caught. Beach fishing often produces surprising reef species, while fishing in Exmouth Gulf turns up a variety of estuarine species including **mud crabs** and **squid**. Sought after offshore species include **norwest snapper**, **bluebone**, **coral trout** and **red emperor**.

There are three boat ramps. Exmouth boat harbour, 2km south of the town, has concrete ramps within the sheltered wall of the marina. Bundegi Beach boat ramp is 12km north, and there's another at Tantabiddi, about 35km from Exmouth town (just north of the Cape Range National Park). Other small boat launching areas are available from campsites in the park, though these are generally only accessible to 4WD vehicles.

Offshore anglers leave a sheltered harbour at Exmouth marina to go in search of marlin, sailfish, tuna, GTs and mackerel. Inshore you will come across small boats fishing the sheltered waters of Exmouth Gulf, or bobbing just outside Ningaloo Reef on the Indian Ocean side.

The beaches are extensive, easy to access and many can be driven along in 4WD vehicles. Expect to encounter queenfish, mackerel, trevally, cobia, **barracuda**, **dart**, **yellowfin bream**, squid and **sharks**. Sometimes you come across saltwater fly fishers wading out casting flies for trevally, permit and bonefish.

A favourite place and a squid hot spot is Learmonth jetty, about 30km east of Exmouth, near the airport. A concrete structure with a rock wall extending half its length, the jetty faces into Exmouth Gulf, and does not appear to be anything other than

Beaching a hammerhead shark near the Learmonth jetty

a small fish platform; the sort you run across around most of southern Australia. The water surrounding the jetty is not deep, maybe 2–3m, but it is clear at the top and bottom of the tides. However, the tropical waters of Exmouth Gulf hold an abundant fish population, and what is caught from this jetty may surprise.

Most anglers fish with bait or cast lures, and just about everyone has a squid jig or two in their tackle boxes. I saw anglers driving along the beaches with squid jigs attached to rods that were poking out of car windows.

Standing on Learmonth jetty, the **squid** were easy to spot. Unlike the southern varieties, these West Australian squid swim past in small schools, and they travel faster than their southern relatives. When you learn something of the area, you understand why: survival is about being on the move. Any sea creatures that stop, risk becoming a meal.

Anglers use cast nets to catch small baitfish

On this day, fellow travelling angler, Queenslander Rod Kirby, was on the jetty. Rod multi-tasks when fishing: bait, spin and squid rods were all set up.

Anglers have different techniques when squidding. My preference is to set a squid jig below a 'Dink' float. Dink floats are Canadian and consist of polystyrene 10–15cm long and about 20mm in diameter. The leader is passed through the float and the jig is set below at the required distance. Because these floats are so buoyant, any ripple on the water makes the float bob; this movement imparts action to the squid jig below.

Rod prefers the traditional cast and retrieve technique. Either way, it made no difference as both methods produced squid.

On both sides of the jetty, the shallow beach is lined with weed beds. Time after time, and always on the northern side, we spotted squid hunting along the seaward side of the weed. At the end of the weed, the squid turned and swam diagonally to the jetty. On every occasion, the cephalopods stayed a bit wide, about 30m or so, and it was a matter of judging where they were heading, and casting a jig accordingly.

Once hooked, squid belch clouds of ink. The combination of ink and a struggling squid alerts other squid, and they hang around to see what is happening. Excited by the action, these squid become easy pickings when presented with another jig. I was assured by several anglers that the fishing was slow. That may have been so, but it was still fun, and it gave me incentive to return in the hope of experiencing a hot bite. And that's what happened on my next visit.

On this day on the jetty, a couple of anglers caught a metre-long queenfish on a lure. It was filleted for bait, and the frame hung over the side of the jetty in the water where it acted as berley to attract sharks. There are many sharks in these waters. The first hook-up was a **whaler shark** of about 2.5m long. After a 15-minute fight, the shark bit through the trace and was gone. Soon after, another shark took a bait. This time it was a **hammerhead** about 2m long. After a 20-minute battle, the shark was beached, photographed and released to fight another day.

In conversation with the boys, they told of catching 3m long **tiger sharks** from the jetty. When the wind is offshore, the boys rig their baits to float out under a balloon. However, the wind was onshore on this day, so the boys were tossing baits out by hand: about 30m at most.

Other popular land-based fishing locations on the east side include Lighthouse Bay, Exmouth marina and Bundegi jetty. The marina holds bream and **mangrove jack**. Anglers fish the rock wall for trevally, queenfish, tuna and mackerel using live bait and lures.

Anglers at Bundegi jetty, and the beach near the top of Cape Range, fish in similar vein to Learmonth jetty, but there are also dart and whiting caught. The area is noted for its early morning squid fishing when the tide is high. Close to the Naval pier there are some big GTs to about 25kg that can be caught on poppers, but the pier is off-limits, and there is a restriction zone around the pier.

Beach access is available from Bundegi south past Learmonth to at least Heron Point. It is easier to take dirt roads off the main road to gain access. If you value your vehicle, creeks and drain run-offs are not to be driven through. Remember to deflate your tyres and check the tides if you intend driving along the beach. The soft areas are above high-tide marks, whereas nearer the water the beach is firmer, most of the time. Deep wheel ruts along the beach south of Learmonth suggest there are soft patches lower down.

Fly and lure fishers look out for drains and wade out to fish these areas as they can hold permit, bonefish, queenfish and trevally. As you drive along the main road from the highway to Exmouth, you cross many of these drains. Access to the beach where the drains enter the Gulf is often a matter of taking the nearest dirt road and following your nose. If the track has tyre marks, chances are you are in with a good chance of beach access.

On the west side of the Cape, and despite the Marine Park status of Ningaloo Reef that runs along this side, some great fishing options are available.

At the top of the Cape, anglers take the Mildura Wreck Rd north from Vlamingh Head to access the beach. The oyster ledges at the northern tip of the Cape can be reached by 2WD by this road, then walking along the beach to your right until you reach the ledges. At high tide, this is one of the prime locations to encounter the massive GTs that Exmouth is famous for. Be warned though, when a GT is nudging 20kg, your chances of stopping it are minimal. Queenfish are also caught here on surface poppers, along with mackerel and cobia. As for bait fishing, expect to hook spangled emperor, bluebone, dart and whiting.

Some anglers fish close to the wreck of the steamship *Mildura*, which is visible on the edge of the reef. A couple of anglers I was with floated baits out under balloons near the *Mildura*, only to hook up and be busted up by big **GTs**. The top-end beaches and ledges are best fished on the rising to high tide.

Driving south along Yardie Creek Rd, you will come across many Sanctuary Purpose Zones where fishing is allowed.

The Tantabiddi boat ramp complex and beach is popular for all forms of recreation activity. Whiting and **flathead** are common captures. The north end of Osprey Sanctuary Zone, the southern end of Lakeside Sanctuary Zone at Varanus, Trealla and Tulki Beaches, and Sandy Bay are three areas where the elusive, and highly regarded, bonefish are caught by fly fishers. Most fishing areas hold small GTs, queenfish and mackerel, while the reef entrances, such as at Coral Bay, attract sailfish, mackerel and GTs.

The area, in particular Exmouth Gulf, is well-suited to car toppers. The waters are sheltered, the beaches firm so small boats can be beach-launched near where you want to fish.

Emma George caught this GT on a popper cast off Dampier

DAMPIER

Dampier is a two-day drive from Perth. Billed as the gateway to the famous Dampier Archipelago, the town lies on King Bay, 1558km from Perth (and still 850km south of Broome) on WA's Coral Coast. Dampier was built in 1965 as a port and processing centre for Hamersley Irons mines. Most of the focus these days is on Karratha, about 12km away.

ACCOMMODATION: There are hotels and motels, caravan parks and backpacker accommodation. For more information visit www.westernaustralia.com

The Dampier Archipelago is a maze of 42 islands off the coast of Dampier, within reach of small boats. **Marlin**, **sailfish**, **Spanish mackerel**, **yellowfin**, **longtail** and **mackerel tuna**, **giant** and **golden trevally**, and **queenfish** are all caught, while bottom species include **coral trout**, **red emperor**, **scarlet sea perch**, **spangled emperor**, **black jewfish**, **norwest snapper** and **bluebone**.

Former Olympian and world-record pole-vaulter Emma George and husband Ashley spent nearly three years at Karratha. When I spoke to Emma she told me the family fishing boats included a Haines Signature 702C, which she and her husband used for offshore fishing, and a 4.55m Polycraft centre console for estuaries. 'We were keeping with tradition in that there are more boats than people in Karratha,' Emma said. 'Most of our fishing was offshore, where we would sight-fish for **GTs (giant trevally)**, casting poppers to schools or casting small lures to **tuna** schools. There are heaps of **tuna** – **mackerel**, **yellowfin** and **longtail** – and spinning for the tuna is great but the **sharks** are a problem. Some days we would troll and on others we would live bait for **mackerel**, catching **yellowtail scad** baits around the pilings in the harbour, and then putting the bait out under a balloon.'

Emma said she and Ashley often used to spin for mackerel with metal jigs and she had seen these broken in half by fish that were up to 30kg.

A four-lane boat ramp is available at Hampton Harbour in Dampier, with another ramp suitable for small to medium boats at Withnell Bay, north of Dampier on the Burrup Peninsula. There is a concrete ramp at Back Beach in Nickol Bay. Like many northern locations, the area endures extreme tides and there are many submerged rocks, so seek local knowledge before launching.

Most visitors stay at the adjoining town of Karratha where there are ample facilities. Fields Creek in Nickol Bay produces good catches of **barramundi** to a metre or so, **threadfin salmon** and **trevally**. The creeks fish well October–March and should be accessed on neap tides as they are shallow – a deep hole in these creeks is about 4m. Sometimes it can be a matter of staying fishing until there is enough water to get out again. There is little structure in the creeks and trolling in about 1–2m deep or live baiting with small mullet is the best method. South-west of Dampier, the Maitland River produces **tarpon**, barramundi and trevally, while further down the coast near James Point is the Fortescue River, which produces **black jewfish**, barramundi and threadfin salmon.

Wildflowers are another part of the environment at Burrup

Methods for Mid-West Coast

TACKLE Boating anglers working offshore chasing game fish troll or jig using outfits from about 15kg or heavier depending on the target species. If you are casting poppers to fish such as trevally, then a large threadline with a 6:1 retrieve is fine. Spool the reel with 15–24kg braid line. Take some piano wire trace material, as many fish up that way have sharp teeth.

If you want to troll lures, then skirted jigs produce sailfish offshore, and large bibbed minnows, preferably divers, will produce species such as mackerel and trevally along the reefs. For lure casting, poppers in combination with fast-retrieve reels are a lot of fun when queenfish, mackerel or trevallies are about, and chrome metal jigs do well on most species.

Land-based gamefishing at places like Steep Point and Quobba requires 15kg outfits. The rods are normally 3m (much longer than standard gamefishing rods used from boats).

When bait fishing, lever-drag game reels do well, and for spinning go for a 10kg outfit with a strong, high-speed threadline reel.

BAIT Baits vary with location, but pilchard, prawns, mullet, garfish, herring, squid and whole fish such as tailor will generally produce results.

3 THE KIMBERLEY

The Kimberley region is a unique part of the Australian landscape, as are boab trees, which can grow to 15m high, and have a trunk circumference of 20m. While it is the silhouettes of boabs, with their immense, swollen trunks, that most travellers remember, there is much more to see. In his book *The Rivers and the Sea* author Vic McCristal (Reed, 1974) wrote of the 'height and colour of red escarpments ... mesas and escarpments lie in long, even profiles above the talus ridges and shadowed gorges,' and of bulky old boab trees looming 'like friendly ghosts' around campsites. McCristal's book fired the imagination of a generation of anglers in the mid-1970s. The roads have improved since McCristal's day, however, the landscape remains the same: Wild, unforgiving and magnificent.

ACCOMMODATION: See individual destination entries in this section.
For more information visit
www.derbytourism.com.au
www.broomewa.com
www.kimberleyaustralia.com

ECO BEACH

I first went to Eco Beach in 2000 but a month or so after that visit cyclone Rosita hit the coast and destroyed the resort here. It has been rebuilt and is doing well, and remains a fishing hotspot due to its isolation, being about 130km south of Broome.

ACCOMMODATION: Eco Beach has 'Eco Villas' and 'Eco Tents'.
For more information visit
www.ecobeach.com.au

I fished here before the cyclone with guides Dan O'Sullivan and Greg 'Patches' Fiorenza. These men had built Eco Beach Fishing into an offshore/onshore guiding business that had few peers for what it could offer, both in terms of tuition and piscatorial excitement. The remote location is a bonus.

On consecutive days fishing three-hour sessions, I caught at least half a dozen **barramundi**, **mangrove jack** and **flathead**. One isolated creek, called Jacks Creek, produced barramundi on every cast. They weren't huge fish, but averaging about 3–4kg on light tackle they were a lot of fun.

BROOME

The city of Broome is about 24-hours driving time north of Perth. Unless you are doing a round-Australia trip it is easier to fly in and hire a vehicle. There are many fishing options from charter boats to kayaks.

ACCOMMODATION: Broome is a big, thriving community with every conceivable type of accommodation on offer.
For more information visit
www.broomevisitorcentre.com.au
www.broomewa.com

While pearling in Broome is pushed for its tourism merits, the serious attraction at Broome, at least for anglers, is its fishing.

The city sits on Roebuck Bay and has become the hub in the wheel of angler tourism in north-west Australia. Anglers often board mother ships for several days of live-aboard adventure to remote areas: the Rowley Shoals, more than 260km offshore, or the Kimberley region, one of the world's last great wilderness areas.

You don't need to fork out thousands of dollars to join a mother ship to catch fish at Broome. The place has so much variety on offer I'm surprised so many anglers leave it to go elsewhere. It is possible to fish for **sailfish**, **mackerel**, **trevally** or **tuna** in the morning and then go fishing for **barramundi** in a quiet backwater or chase **blue salmon** on the beach in the afternoon. Much depends on the tide and wind. Spring tides here see the water rise and fall 10m.

The pier at Broome has a walkway along the west side where fishing is allowed

The city built its fishing reputation on the sailfish grounds offshore, and these are usually daytrips. When you can't get out to the sailfish grounds, there is plenty of action bottom bouncing closer in. On one memorable visit the weather cut up so we couldn't get out to the sailfish grounds and I ended up fishing on a 'lump' a couple of kilometres offshore. **Giant trevally**, mackerel and **golden trevally** were mixed in with **spinner whaler sharks**.

Broome also has a large pier on the waterfront that has a well-earned reputation for producing quality fish. Sadly, even though the pier has been extended since I first went there, fishing has been restricted to a walkway that runs alongside the pier until the first bend.

Broome *Advertiser* editor Simon Penn said that even though the fishing area was reduced, anglers still made regular catches of golden trevally, **bluebone**, **coral trout** and **barramundi**.

Dampier and Crab Creek flow into Roebuck Bay and these produce barramundi, **threadfin salmon** and **mangrove jack**.

There are two boat ramps: one at Entrance Point and a second at Town Beach.

One of the most fun ways to fish is catching **blue salmon** off beaches such as the world-famous Cable Beach. Broome's beaches are long, flat white sand beaches with fish stocks that haven't suffered under the bloodfests labelled as competitions. Blue salmon is one of the hardestrunning fish you are likely to catch anywhere. These fish, along with **giant herring** and **permit**, run along the beaches close to shore, so you are able to sight-fish for them with lures or flies.

Situated along Cable Beach are Willie and Barred creeks and these hold **mud crabs**, barramundi, trevally, **queenfish** and mangrove jack. Anglers beach-launch at the southern end of Cable Beach.

CAPE LEVEQUE

Cape Leveque is north of Broome, the turn-off about 10 minutes east on the Great Northern Hwy going to Derby. The road is gravel, wide and graded, for about half the drive before changing back to bitumen. It takes about two hours from the turn-off to the top of the Cape at One Arm Point. Be aware there are many areas of the cape off-limits to visitors and that require a permit to acces. A 4WD is advisable as the side roads can be soft.

Willie Creek and Barred Creek, and the other northern beaches are accessed off Manari Rd, which you reach via a turn-off from the Cape Leveque Rd. Further along Cape Leveque Rd are Middle Lagoon, and the Hunter Creek at Kooljaman Resort/ Cape Leveque.

Remote-area fishing trips can require extreme vehicles for access

Derby pier fishing

The easiest fishing area to access is Middle Lagoon. This sheltered waterway features a campground and cabins. The drive in is on a sand road, and takes about 20 minutes. Beach, rock and boat fishing are available, with boats launched from the beach. Species caught in the lagoon include **golden trevally**, **queenfish**, **threadfin salmon**, **blue salmon** and **reef species**.

WILLARE ROADHOUSE

Between Broome and the Ord River the road crosses a plateau over 500m high. Flanked by the Durack Range with peaks to 900m, to the south is one of the world's largest deserts. Between the Cape Leveque turnoff and Halls Creek, the country opens. Driving from Broome to Derby on the Great Northern Hwy, you cross Willare Bridge on the Fitzroy River before arriving at Willare Roadhouse. The deeper pools near the bridge offer fishing opportunities for **barramundi** and **cherabin**, the latter working well for bait and a feed.

Access to fishing spots along the Fitzroy River is via signposted access roads, and the best source of information about these roads, and access, is Willare Roadhouse: (08) 9191 4775. Many anglers who fish the Fitzroy River prefer to stay at the roadhouse.

Popular fishing spots are Willems Pool, Langi Crossing, and Telegraph Pool. To get to Willems Pool, turn off after you cross the Fitzroy River. There is shady camping and permanent fresh water. The turn-off to Langi Crossing and Telegraph Pool is 140km from Broome. It is a dirt track and you will need a 4WD. Langi is the first pool you will come across; turn right after the second gate and look for the old bridge. The second pool is Telegraph Pool. To get there continue after the second gate without turning off, and follow the track until you see the old telegraph pole and a big pool before turning off. Both pools have permanent saltwater and produce **barramundi**. Boat launching can be a struggle at Telegraph Pool as the sand is soft and the bank steep. These are all on Yeeda Station, and although open to the public, the station owners need to be notified before you arrive on (08) 9191 4766. Camping is allowed for a two-day maximum on the station.

DERBY

Derby in the West Kimberley has Australia's highest tides: a rise and fall of 11.8m. The port has a large wharf and this is a popular fishing destination.

ACCOMMODATION: Derby has a large caravan and camping park, and a couple of motels.
For more information visit
www.derbytourism.com.au

Even though anglers will be found fishing the wharf at any time of tide, the tidal run is so strong that fishing is best pursued near the top or bottom of the tide as the current slows. Fish that are caught from the jetty include **threadfin salmon**, **jewfish**, **golden grunter**, **sharks** and **catfish**. Close to shore, the bank is lined with mangroves, and as the tide drops anglers fish the run-off drains for **barramundi**, or seek out **mud crabs**.

Derby is the gateway to the Buccaneer Archipelago in King Sound. The full range of northern reef species are found including **fingermark bream**, **coral trout**, **mangrove jack**, **bluebone** and **barramundi**. The only way to fish the archipelago is from a boat. Given the enormous tidal range, King Sound is treacherous water, and the safest way to venture to this area is with a local charter boat operator.

The May River, about 40km north-east of Derby on the Gibb River Rd, offers excellent **barramundi** fishing, but you need to contact Meda Station for permission to access areas on the station.

The main river flowing into Derby is the Fitzroy. During the Wet, this river swells to become one of the world's biggest rivers with a 90,000sqkm catchment area. Access to the river mouth is only possible from the south bank due to Noogoora burr quarantine regulations on the north bank.

Geikie Gorge Fitzroy Crossing

FITZROY CROSSING

Driving the Great Northern Hwy from Kununurra, you drive through Halls Creek and then on to Fitzroy Crossing.

For more information visit
www.sdwk.wa.gov.au/business/fitzroycrossingvisitorcentre

As the name suggests, the main watercourse is the Fitzroy River, which produces **barramundi**, **sooty grunter** and **mangrove jack**. The best known attraction is Geikie Gorge, a tourist hotspot. From April–November, private boats and canoes may access the gorge before 7am or after 4.30pm You must notify rangers before launching your boat.

Five Rivers Lookout at Wyndham

Fishing is allowed above and below the gorge. When I visited, nobody could tell me whether I was allowed to fish in the gorge, and given the boating restrictions, I suggest it would be better to fish elsewhere; there are enough options. There are many access points to the Fitzroy River, however, the most popular are further west near the Willare Roadhouse.

WYNDHAM

Wyndham, WA's most northerly town, is about as isolated as any town in Australia can be. It is situated on the southern tidal waters of the Cambridge Gulf where the King, Pentecost, Durack, Forest and Ord rivers meet. To get your bearings, take a drive to Five Rivers Lookout atop Mount Bastian. It overlooks the town and port, tidal marshlands plus the five river mouths.

Wyndham is also the northern gateway to the Gibb River Rd, Kalumburu and Derby. The port has a couple of mooring jetties that are popular with anglers. The best fishing is in the rivers; some of these have already been mentioned.

Pentecost River is a noted waterway for **barramundi**. Pentecost Crossing, where the Gibb River Rd crosses over the Pentecost River, is a popular fishing destination. South-west of Wyndham, it is the freshwater crossing of a small stream at the head of Cambridge Gulf.

KUNUNURRA

Kununurra is an ideal staging post for fishing Lake Argyle and surrounding waters. There are many safe places to fish, but it's wise to call the Kununurra Visitor Centre (*see* below) for the latest road conditions.

ACCOMMODATION: For access to any of the below mentioned places, check with the Kununurra Visitor Centre before leaving: phone **1800 586 868**.
For more information visit www.visitkununurra.com

The most sought after fish is **barramundi**, and all the local waterways have them. Be aware that barramundi have a legal size limit of between 55–80cm for the Lower Ord and Fitzroy River systems. In the Lower Ord and Broome areas, a possession limit of one barramundi per angler applies. Elsewhere in WA a bag limit of two barramundi per person applies.

Some of the better known locations on the Ord River, and these require a 4WD, are:

- Ivanhoe Crossing: a causeway built over the Ord River.
- Buttons Crossing: along Parry Creek Rd, **camping** is permitted.
- Mambi Island: along Parry Creek Rd. There is a boat ramp, and **camping** is permitted. This is a popular base for anglers wanting to spend a few days fishing the Ord.
- Skull Rock: along the Carlton Hill Rd.

For those without 4WD vehicles, the following are easy to access:

- Lake Kununurra: you can fish along the banks of Lilly Creek Lagoon for some **silver cobbler** and **bream**, or head out in a boat further onto Lake Kununurra.
- The Spillway: en route to Lake Argyle from Kununurra, Spillway Creek is noted for producing quality **barramundi** fishing.

LAKE ARGYLE

Lake Argyle, about 70km west of Kununurra, is Australia's largest artificial lake by volume. At maximum flood level, the waters spread out over more than 2,072sqkm, and when this happens Lake Argyle is bigger than Victoria's Port Phillip (1930sqkm).

Part of the Ord River Irrigation Scheme, there are more than 70 islands and, apart from the area of Coolabah Pocket adjacent to the dam wall, the lake is full of dead trees, although these are underwater.

The primary inflow is the Ord River, while the Bow River and many other smaller creeks also flow into the dam. Due to its size, Lake Argyle is a difficult place to know where to start fishing, but there are 26 species of native fish, including **barramundi**, **southern saratoga**, **archer fish**, **forktail catfish**, **mouth almighty**, **long tom**, **bony bream** and **sleepy cod**. The biggest fish in the lake is **silver cobbler** or **shovel nosed catfish**. Regarded as fine table fare, these giant **catfish** can grow to about 1.5m and weigh up to 40kg. As well, the lake is home to an estimated 25,000 freshwater crocodiles.

Methods for the Kimberley

TACKLE In tropical estuaries, baitcasters spooled with 15kg braid with a metre or so of 24kg leader should be employed when casting lures for barramundi, threadfin salmon and trevally. Bait fishers can use 10kg outfits.

Fly-fishers will work eight-weight outfits with shooting heads on the flats and rivers, but go up to 14-weight when fly-fishing offshore for game fish such as sailfish. The favourite fly in the tropics is the Pink Thing, a variation on the Clouser Minnow. Effective flies in the tropics seem to have two things in common: they have some pink colouring and lead eyes that allow them to sink. Fly-fishers who target sailfish use wide-bodied flies about 20cm long, rigged with a second or stinger hook for more effective hook-ups.

NORTHERN TERRITORY

Steve's

FAVOURITE DESTINATIONS FOR NORTHERN TERRITORY

The NT is one big fishing adventure for the dedicated angler, with a heavy emphasis towards barramundi fishing. And rightly so. The barramundi in the Territory have been protected from commercial exploitation to ensure their sustainability. Major beneficiaries of this program are anglers and tourism operators.

Tourism is a major business in the Territory, and fishing makes up a big chunk of the action. Whether you need a fishing guide, want to hire a boat or head out on a charter, it is easy to arrange. But, there is more to the Territory than barramundi; you can also hook into species like black jewfish, mangrove jack, golden trevally, mackerel, coral trout and sailfish. Fishing in the Top End is about rivers, estuaries and offshore; it is about lures, flies and bait. But most of all it is an adventure and, as the advertisement says, 'You'll never never know if you never never go'.

ACCOMMODATION

Finding somewhere to stay in the Territory is as easy as spotting a croc in Kakadu!

For more information visit
www.en.travelnt.com
www.tourismtopend.com

Angler hooks up a small barramundi in a creek in Junction Bay

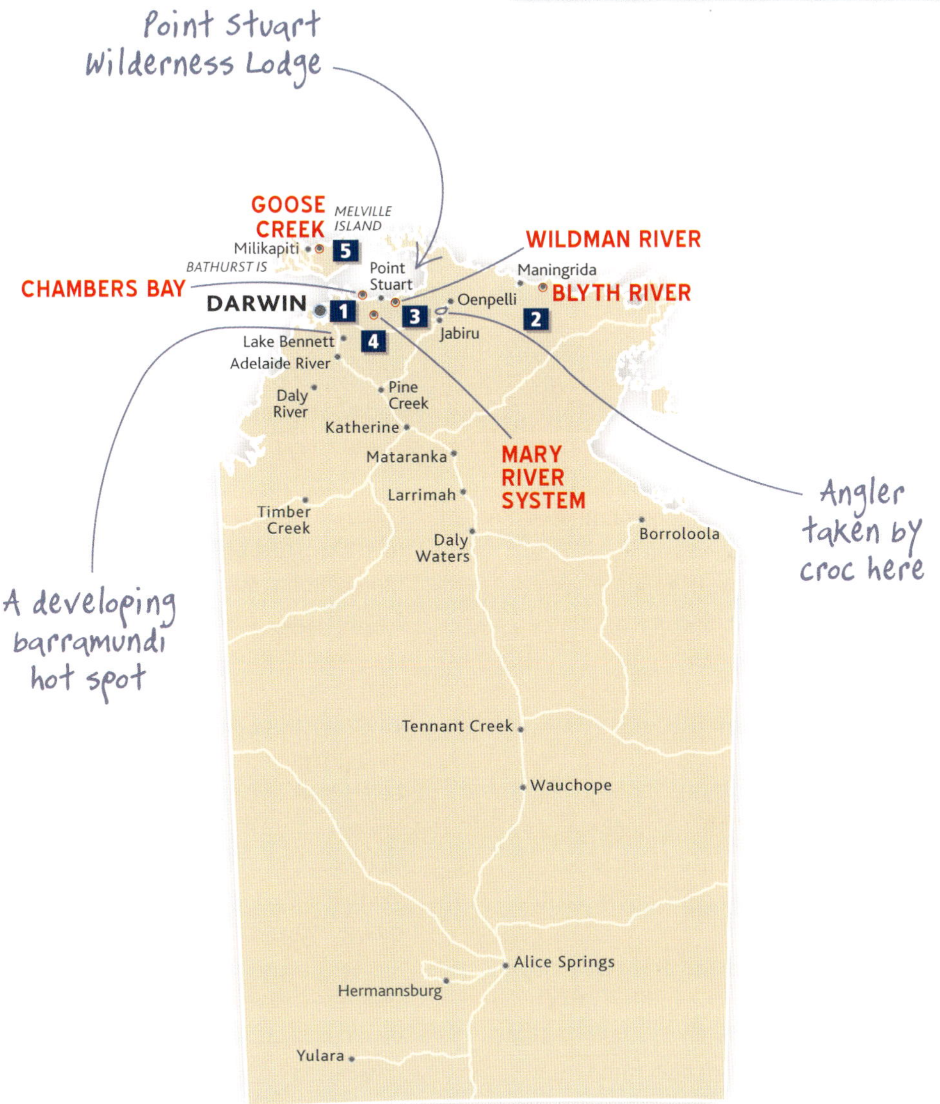

Point Stuart Wilderness Lodge
GOOSE CREEK
MELVILLE ISLAND
Milikapiti
5
BATHURST IS
Point Stuart
WILDMAN RIVER
Maningrida
BLYTH RIVER
CHAMBERS BAY
DARWIN
1
3
Oenpelli
2
Jabiru
Lake Bennett
4
Adelaide River
Daly River
Pine Creek
Katherine
Mataranka
MARY RIVER SYSTEM
Larrimah
Timber Creek
Daly Waters
Borroloola
Angler taken by croc here
A developing barramundi hot spot
Tennant Creek
Wauchope
Alice Springs
Hermannsburg
Yulara

1 AROUND DARWIN

Visitors to the NT either drive or fly. The end of the run-off around March or April is the time for the hottest barramundi bite, but unless you time your arrival right, chances are there will be road closures due to flooding. And remember, due to crocodiles, don't camp next to water, swim or wade; fish from a boat and don't leave it while on the water.

ACCOMMODATION: The Territory is well serviced for visitors.
For more information visit www.northernterritory.visitorsbureau.com.au/accommodation

DARWIN HARBOUR

Darwin Harbour offers anglers quality and variety. To have a fishery this good on your doorstep is the stuff of dreams for anglers.

ACCOMMODATION: Darwin has every type of accommodation available. At the end of the wet season in late March, through to late September, caravan parks are brimming with southerners. The temperature at this time of year averages 30–32°C.
For more information visit www.tourismtopend.com.au

My first fishing trip on the harbour was one of the Territory's most challenging fishing competitions, the annual Barra Bass & Bream Harbourmasters Invitational. The event is held one Sunday in July, and continues to grow.

The day I fished this competition I was with local fishing identity and event organiser, Alex Julius. There were 26 teams comprising 52 anglers. The boats launched at the East Arm boat ramp from 7am with lines in the water at 8am conditions were calm, the water beautiful and the tides, although not ideal, had enough movement to see a lot of **barramundi** caught.

This is a lure and fly competition. Teams must catch both barra and **bream** to score: it is the total combined length of the two species that counts. The hard one to catch is the **pikey bream**. Compared to southern counterparts, pikey bream are not very big, and they don't seem to be around in numbers to be caught on lures. However, going by the results I saw, it seems Darwin anglers can catch bream on lures.

Just to show how challenging this event is, the year I was there only eight teams out of the 26 managed to achieve the double to qualify for the final. Five teams managed a bream but not a barra, and two teams bagged a barra while missing out on bream. This left 11 teams who failed to catch either species. In all, there were 36 barra caught and 26 bream. The winning team landed an 81cm barra and a 30cm bream for a total of 111cm. The boys used 2in Gulp Shrimp lures, and caught a credible 11 barra and two bream.

The competition showed up the variety of fish available. As well as the two target species, competitors caught **golden snapper**, **javelin fish (och och)**, **tarpon**, **golden trevally**, **diamond trevally**, **blue salmon**, **mangrove jack**, **estuary cod**, **flathead**, **Spanish flag**, **catfish**, **blacktip shark**, and **batfish**.

Bait anglers also do well as Darwin Harbour has a lot of huge artificial reefs created by sunken ships. The genesis of these reefs was the Darwin bombing during World War II, which resulted in eight ships being sunk by Japanese warplanes. Cyclone Tracy followed in 1974, and more shipping was sent to the seabed. Most ships have dissolved; the remaining vessels are part salvaged and have become piles of rubble. Nevertheless, these still attract reef dwellers, and several are hot spots for **jewfish**, golden snapper, trevally, sometimes barra, while **sharks** can be a nuisance. Methods employed are the same as those listed for South Gutter below.

An irony of the bombing was that it was a Japanese firm, Fujita Salvage Company, which won

the tender to salvage or cut in half the wrecks in the harbour. The *USAT Meigs*, *British Motorist*, *Zealandia* and *USAT Mauna Loa* were cut in half, but their lower hulls remain. The *Mavie* and *Neptuna* were salvaged.

The value of these artificial reefs wasn't lost on the fisheries departments in other states, and these days artificial reef creation is on the agendas of most state fishery and angling organisations.

Ships sunk:

British Motorist: a tanker, she sank in about 16m of water.
S12.28.967 E130.50.336

USAT Mauna Loa: sank in 17m.
S12.29.815 E130.49.162

USAT Meigs: an ammunition ship, the *Meigs* was the largest ship in the harbour on the day of the bombing and sank in about 18m.
S12.29.269 E130.49.109

Above: **A gun from the destroyer USS *Peary*, which was sunk by Japanese bombers during World War II, is mounted on the Darwin Esplanade overlooking the harbour**
Below: **Coral trout are regarded as one of the finest eating fish in the tropics**

Zealandia: sank in about 18m.
S12.28.883 E130.51.048

USS Peary: drifted as it sank and bottomed in about 30m of water.
S12.28.521 E130.49.788

SOUTH GUTTER

Returning from a barramundi fishing trip in the wilds of Arnhem Land to a reef-fishing session offshore from Darwin is like comparing apples with oranges. Seeing big barra exploding from the water in a mass of spray is an adrenalin-pumping experience, but bottom bouncing is about dropping bait down onto a reef structure and waiting for a bite. It is the essence of Samuel Johnson's famous quote describing fishing as: 'A jerk on one end of a line, waiting for a jerk on the other'.

At least, that's what I expected the first time I fished offshore from Darwin. Steve Compain, who ran Arafura Bluewater Charters, took me out with several other anglers for an evening on his smart, twin-hulled vessel, *Ocean Fox*.

We boarded at Cullen Bay Marina just outside Darwin's CBD and steamed about 30km offshore to our first drop, out from Charles Point. Skipper Chris Highland used the sounder to find structure in about 20m of water. There was no swell, just a chop pushed along by a 15-knot wind.

On that first drop, **golden snapper** were on the chew immediately. Local fishing identity Alex Julius was on board and he described the fish, which were averaging about 8kg, as 'the biggest goldies I've laid eyes on for years'.

When smaller fish started terrorising our baits we moved, this time to the South Gutter some 40km offshore. Chris wanted to hit the gutter at the change of tide, and said that because it was a big tide (7m) the window of opportunity would only last for about 90 minutes.

'The gutter's been fishing well and we should get some **jewfish**,' Chris said.

The skipper was spot on. What ensued was the hottest piece of bottom-bouncing action I've come across in years. It was pure piscatorial mayhem with eight rods buckling on both sides of the boat as **black jewfish (mulloway)** of 6–8kg took the baits.

Steve then decided to try something different. He put a rubber squid imitation down. This lure was fitted with a single hook on a leader at both the head and tail and Steve inserted a red Cyalume light stick into the body of the lure.

Jigging the lure in 1m lifts just above the bottom proved deadly. The jewfish couldn't resist and Steve nailed three fish on consecutive drops. The third fish destroyed the glow stick, but it didn't make any difference. In 45m of water, at night, the jewfish were hot to trot; every jig of the lure resulted in a hook-up. It was a phenomenal session. The biggest fish of the evening was the last, a 15kg jewfish that delivered what looked like the coup de grace to a lure that had paid for itself many times over.

Methods for South Gutter

TACKLE For bottom-bouncing offshore use 10–15kg outfits with a single leader paternoster rig. Attach a 5/0 Suicide hook and a heavy snapper lead to counter the strong current.

BAIT Baits were cocktails: a mixture of mackerel strips, pilchard and bottle squid.

DALY RIVER

The Daly River is a two-and-a-half hour drive south of Darwin. To get there, follow the Stuart Hwy to Adelaide River township, turn right and drive for about another hour. Public boat ramp access is available at the crossing and downstream near Woolianna. Banyan Farm has a private boat ramp and mooring facilities. To access the park, turn right at the signpost before you reach Daly River Crossing.

ACCOMMODATION: I stayed at Banyan Farm Caravan Park, a neat, clean facility with all necessary amenities. As with many NT caravan parks, this one is set up to cover all tastes, from caravans to backpackers. Fuel was available about 5km down the road.

For more information visit www.banyanfarm.com.au

The Daly River is one of the most popular **barramundi** fishing destinations for Darwin anglers. The river is rightly famous for its spectacular run-off fishing at the end of the wet season, but produces barramundi year round. Some experienced NT anglers rate the Daly as the Territory's premier barramundi river. In these days of cheap airfares, I've met interstate anglers who have bought a boat and left it at the Daly, making fortnightly visits.

The river has snags, sandbars, S-bends, creeks and rock bars spread over 40km from the Daly River crossing to where it flows into Anson Bay. The lower reaches are riddled with sandbars so you need to take care.

On my most recent visit, I fished with Dave Shepherd from Port Stephens and Roger Enriquez from Melbourne. We towed a hire boat from Darwin for the week's fishing.

We camped beside a group of three anglers who fish competitions together as 'Diesel & Dust'. These locals pointed us upriver to a small creek called Tommys Creek. It's about 400m below Mango Farm.

The creek is accessible from land, at least by the locals. When we arrived, half a dozen land-based anglers were casting lures and bait into the narrow creek, and among the snags at the mouth. As we watched, one angler pulled a barramundi of about 70cm long, and another couple of fish were lost in the heavy terrain.

Downstream about 50m was a large snag about 20m off the bank. As we drifted over it, we saw good numbers of barra on the sounder. We anchored off it but found fishing difficult, because the snag was fresh from the recent floods, and there were many small branches to negotiate.

Roger worked a soft plastic lure, while Dave and I cast hard-bodied minnows. Dave selected a Barra Classic in the bleeding rose colour, which is a red head with a bright green body. My choice was a Super Barra in pink and silver.

As it turned out, Dave achieved the magical hook-up. He cast to the outer edge of the snag, allowed his lure to drift to the timber with the current, wound down a few turns to get his lure into the timber, and started to retrieve. He had barely wound more than half a dozen turns when 92cm of barramundi inhaled his lure and started to dance across the surface. The fight was tough and close, and Dave had to work the fish hard to keep it out of the timber. After a few minutes, Roger netted the silver slab in the fish-friendly Environet. I took photographs and Dave duly released the fish unharmed.

We had no more luck that day, but other anglers who fished the area did well during the week. There are many small run-offs and creeks along the Daly, and all of them produce barramundi.

Roxsean (Rocky) Edwards shows off a metre plus barra caught in the Daly River

Methods for Daly River

LURES Most anglers in the Daly work lures to about 15cm long, mainly floating/diving minnow types and soft plastics. Successful techniques include casting and trolling. Soft plastics are often taken as they sink and can be worked ultra slowly along the bottom in a slow lift-and-drop action. As with many species, the golden rule of lure presentation is that you cannot wind slow enough for barramundi. Casting anglers work their lures slowly and with an erratic retrieve.

BAIT When bait fishing for barramundi with live mullet and cherabin (giant freshwater shrimp which can be up to 20cm long) hooks from 4/0–6/0 are employed, depending on bait size. Live prawns or popeye mullet set under a float make excellent baits when allowed to drift back into a snag or over a rock bar. Barra will sometimes crush and kill bait without taking it in, so it pays to be alert. If this is happening, the fish may have felt line pressure too early and need longer to take the bait.

MANTON DAM

Manton Dam is located about 75km south of Darwin on the Stuart Hwy. Access hours are restricted and there is no camping.

ACCOMMODATION: The best option for accommodation is to stay in Darwin.
For more information visit www.territorydiscoveries.com

Queensland has received a lot of publicity about stocking lakes with barramundi, but since the mid-1990s NT Fisheries has been doing similar work. More than 100,000 **barramundi** have been put into Manton Dam, a picturesque, 330ha back-up water supply for Darwin, 75km south of the city.

The dam was completed in 1942 and served as Darwin's water supply until 1972 when larger storage (not open to fishing) was built on the Darwin River.

The stocking program started out as an experiment, with relatively small numbers of barramundi fingerlings. Accounts of an occasional 20kg barramundi being caught and a legion of big ones getting away provided incentive for stocking densities to be intensified. The dam already contained a huge baitfish biomass and an extremely healthy self-supporting **saratoga** population.

Manton Dam's barramundi-seeding statistics now compare favourably with any similar-sized body of water, and there is every reason to anticipate the same prodigious growth rates that barra have exhibited in other similar stocked lakes.

Barramundi stocking trials are in progress at smaller waters, including Lake Bennett (81ha), about 70km south of Darwin, and Lake Todd (125ha) near Pine Creek, a 200km drive south-east of Darwin.

As Manton Dam matures in piscatorial terms, it may take some of the angling pressure off wild barra stocks.

The main beneficiaries will be tourism operators and Top End pilgrims able to get their first real shot at this magnet that draws droves of anglers from the eastern states.

No camping is allowed at the dam. Access is limited to 9am–5pm on weekdays and 8am–7pm on weekends and public holidays. As fishing there develops, you would expect more infrastructure and longer access hours. Based on other barramundi dams, these fish bite better at night and locals will increasingly apply pressure to have the dam open for longer. A safe dusk-to-dawn fishery where one is not risking a croc encounter, to say nothing of the insect bites when the sun goes down over tidal wetlands, is something new for Territorians.

By day, Manton Dam is an aquatic playground. Amenities include a boat ramp, toilets, picnic tables and barbecues, and it is popular with waterskiers and secondary-school students on nature excursions.

Those activities, along with extremely clear water, combine to make the fish wary.

Methods for Manton Dam

TROLLING If you intend trolling, take along an electric motor, or at least a four-stroke, as they are quieter than two-stroke outboards.

TACKLE Clear water can make fishing difficult. If you want to fish braid lines, use fluorocarbon leader. This material, which is harder than monofilament, has a light refractive index close to that of water so that it is invisible to fish. If you want to catch saratoga – and some of them are as big as ironing boards – the basic outfit is a small baitcaster or threadline spooled with 6–10kg braid line. If you are seeking barramundi you will need to up the ante and use a 15kg braid and a 24kg monofilament leader.

LURES Diving and surface minnow lures work well on all species. Flatten the hook barbs for ease of release and have a range of colours including reds, blues, metallic and fluoro colours. The Halco Night Walker surface lure is a favourite for saratoga. Fly-fishers use six–eight-weight outfits with floating lines and employ surface flies like the Dahlberg Diver, suspending flies like the 3D patterns and Lefty Deceivers for saratoga.

2 ARNHEM LAND

The East Alligator River at Cahills Crossing marks the border with Arnhem Land. From Darwin take the Arnhem Land Hwy. The drive takes about three and a half hours. During the Wet this road is often under water, and there are access restrictions for Arnhem Land and a permit is required. Talk to the Northern Land Council or Rangers at Jabiru (phone 1800 645 299) and discuss the best places to camp with the regional permit officer. Alternatively, you could take advantage of a fishing lodge.

ACCOMMODATION: The Arnhemland Barramundi Nature Lodge is the only lodge mentioned in this section. Others have started and then finished. For more information phone the lodge on 08 8983 1544 or visit www.barralodge.com.au

LIVERPOOL RIVER

The Bawinanga Aboriginal Corporation at Maningrida in Arnhem Land is a progressive organisation that maintains control of its greatest asset – its heritage, including the land and the fishing. It constructed a modern fishing lodge, the Arnhemland Barramundi Nature Lodge, and leased it to skilled operators. NT fishing personality Alex Julius partnered with fishing guide Lindsay Mutimer and the Bawinanga Aboriginal Corporation to run the lodge.

The lodge is about 20km out of Maningrida. Supplies to Maningrida come from Darwin by ferry, and a large boat ramp was built on the delta of the Liverpool River to accommodate the ferry.

The Liverpool is several kilometres across at the mouth, and several rivers that feed into it are bigger than most Victorian rivers. The rock bars near the entrance hold big **barramundi**, but tide is everything and the first morning I was there the water was too murky to work lures.

Lindsay decided to take a run upstream to get ahead of the tide and look for clear water. The river is lined with a dense, green fence of mangroves for the first few kilometres. Exposed mudflats have crocodiles, mouths ajar, as they inhale the early morning warmth, and the birdlife ranges from Burdekin ducks and waders to kites and sea-eagles.

After an hour of steady running we slowed and Lindsay edged the boat towards a couple of broken tree stumps, where a small drain fed out from the wetlands behind. The procedure was to cast a lure into the fallen timber, wait a few seconds, then twitch it a couple of times and retrieve. In this scenario,

Above: **Fishing guide Wayne Williams displays a 90cm barramundi caught in the Liverpool River**
Below: **Mud crabs are popular table fare, but watch out for those claws**

speed is nothing and Lindsay said: 'You can't retrieve too slowly for barra'.

Melbourne angler Geoff Guest had the first cast, and the action was instantaneous. Barra don't simply inhale lures, it is more like an explosion followed by a couple of feet of polished pewter erupting from the tannin-coloured water.

The snag wasn't big but we pulled half a dozen barra off it in about the same time it takes to boil a billy; then Lindsay decided to move on. At every likely snag, Lindsay manoeuvred the boat within casting range and the lures hit the water. Some

snags produced more than others, and there was an occasional **mangrove jack** in the mix.

Several kilometres upstream and several hours later, we came across a large creek where the fishing was amazing. Working our way up the creek we came across a stretch lined with watercress and a smaller feed creek. Lindsay pointed to the mouth of the creek and we cast. Geoff pulled ten fish in ten casts.

On another trip with Lindsay, we motored even further upriver. The water level was dropping when Lindsay eased the boat into the bank and tied off. He wanted to try a billabong a few hundred metres from the river. The last time I was in the same area the grass was a metre and a half high. Given the wildlife in this part of the country, particularly crocodiles, wild pigs and buffalo, I wasn't comforted by the thought of walking through long grass. But this time the locals had been practising land management here. All around us on the Maningrida escarpment were small smoke plumes, signs that the countryside was being singed and the grasses reduced.

To get to the billabong we worked our way across churned earth, sure signs that wild pigs had been destroying more of the environment. A couple of large divots, still soft, indicated the presence of water buffalo, but we saw neither pigs nor buffalo. What we did see could have come straight off a postcard. The billabong was picture perfect: lily pads, fallen trees and all of it flanked by short, green grasses. Brolgas, jabirus, Burdekin ducks and a host of other colourful birds were feeding in the shallows. The water looked inviting, it was hot and a swim would have gone down nicely.

Lindsay led the way, telling us to wait while he checked the edges, and decided we would fish on several slight rises along the bank. 'Stay well clear of the water,' he warned. 'Just because you can't see them doesn't mean there aren't any crocs here.' So much for a swim.

There were us anglers, looking at the water, seeking out snags and working out ways of luring the barra out from under the lily pads. Below the surface there was just as likely to be a log with teeth, edging its way along the bottom, looking upwards with one purpose in mind: catching an angler. We stayed on slightly higher ground and avoided walking near the soft, muddy edges.

We were using baitcasters, but deep swimming minnows gave way to surface poppers. The first cast produced a small **tarpon**, the second a barra. Almost every cast was a fish, and most of those fish were barra. We hooked and landed barra at will. It was a matter of cast the popper, let it sit, bloop it a couple of times and wind – if the take took that long! These weren't metre-long fish, but in this picturesque water, the action was exhilarating. It was like fishing on a fish farm, except these fish were wild and the location remote.

The fish were also stunningly attractive – the most colourful barra I've come across. They had deep bronze backs and bright silver bellies so that when they lay side-on, their flanks glowed as if they were gold ingots.

SKIRMISH POINT

Tropical reef systems are cosmic places to wet a line because you just never know what you are going to catch next. My first morning off Skirmish Point, near Maningrida, we drifted about 30m off a series of rock ledges that come out from the shore. A few hundred metres behind us, rock lumps just broke through the surface on the falling tide. We cast popper lures as Lindsay Mutimer steered the boat.

The system was to cast the lure, wait and then give the lure a sharp jerk to disturb the water and make a blooping noise. Cast, wait and bloop. On one of these bloops, about 2m of **barracuda** came steaming out of the water, swallowed the lure then cut through my trace.

It was an exciting morning of spinning and trolling that saw us catch **trevally**, smaller barracuda and **giant herring**. Changing to bait we proceeded to hook **coral trout**, **fingermark bream** and **Moses perch**, among a host of other species. You have to be prepared for anything from **Spanish mackerel** to giant herring.

Skirmish Point defines the eastern extent of the Liverpool River mouth. There are many exposed rocks and small reefs a couple of kilometres offshore, and a vast expanse of sand flats. The water over the flats is 1–3m deep. For saltwater fly anglers this is nirvana, as the flats are home to the largest population of giant herring in Australia.

On another day, on a nearby reef locally known as Mamba, we hooked **giant trevally** and **golden trevally**. They weren't huge, just good fish in the 3–4kg range. As we trolled over the reef we could see bigger trevally, but the bucket-mouthed monsters were consistently beaten to the lures by their smaller relatives.

North of Skirmish Point is Haul Round Island. Featuring a lighthouse and thousands of nesting terns, the sandy cay has a reef system at its eastern end. Heading back towards the Liverpool River Delta is Entrance Island, called Kabalko Island by the locals. A sign warns against going ashore here, as the western point is classified as a sacred site.

Several kilometres north-west of Entrance Island another small reef juts out of deeper water and waves crash against the rocks creating a wash that attracts all manner of marine life.

Small fish come in to feed in the wash, and bigger fish follow to feed on the smaller fish. It produces lots of surface action for anglers.

CADELL RIVER

I watched an angler step on to a log that jutted out from the bank of the Cadell River. He cast his lure at a set of snags about 20m upstream and proceeded to wind. Directly opposite the log was a mud bank that bore the unmistakable scar of a crocodile slide. I pointed at the mud bank and the angler immediately moved off the log to higher ground – possibly the difference between catching dinner and being dinner.

Driving through Arnhem Land is an amazing experience and features some odd-looking rock formations

I've fished the Cadell a few times in recent years and one particular crocodile is what I remember most. This croc was easily the biggest I have seen in the wild; built like a bullock and at least 4.5m long.

The Cadell feeds into the Liverpool River and the previous day we had fished the junction, where the river is a hundred or so metres wide, its banks covered in dense green mangrove forests. We trolled bibbed minnows and caught **threadfin salmon**, **mangrove jack** and **barramundi**.

This day we were so far upstream that the Cadell was narrow enough to be called a creek. Low-lying mangroves gave way to high banks and grassy plains. Fishing guide Brad Woollams had driven us to this remote stretch below the Maningrida escarpment. I'd been to this area the season before and the change was dramatic. On my last visit, areas were still green and wet, with big numbers of buffalo, pigs, wallabies and birds, including jabirus and brolgas.

This time it was clearly a sunburned country. The ground was rock hard, covered in cracks and potholes that tested the 4WD vehicle's suspension. The only sign of life on the way to the river was a lone boar running through a tree line that surrounded a dry billabong. About the only part of the country that hadn't changed were the hundreds of termite mounds.

At the river we parked the vehicle in the shade and were given a commonsense safety talk by Brad. He told us to stay high on the bank and to avoid walking near soft edges or the edge of the river. Several hours, a few kilometres and several hundred casts later, we were in a sort of comfort zone. We'd caught a few barra and hadn't seen a croc, which was probably why the angler had become lax and stepped on to that log.

The combination of heat, nature and a sense of adventure added up to a day to remember. There are days when you get as much out of the environment as you do catching fish. In visual terms, the fish and the river were stunningly attractive, a walk on the wild side that got the juices flowing.

MANN RIVER

The road from Cahills Crossing on the East Alligator River through to Maningrida in Arnhem Land is impassable during the wet season. Rivers swell and vast areas become floodplains. Water can rise 3m or more in areas where the dirt road crosses rivers. The Wet starts in late November or December, but the run-off continues for several months and this road is not usually fully open before August.

The first river on the road out of Maningrida is the Mann. I wanted to catch **saratoga** and **barramundi**, so fishing guide Brad Woollams said this was the place to head for. 'It's down to a series of freshwater pools and I reckon we'll find some,' he said.

Above: **Fishing the Tomkinson River for barramundi**
Below: **A typical cabin set in natural surrounds at the Arnhemland Barramundi Nature Lodge**

There are no road signs telling you where to go. The well-hidden turn-off is a narrow two-wheeled track into the bush about 4km south of the lodge.

Much of the route seemed circuitous as we drove around one fallen tree after another. Then we came to an open plain. The country had been burnt off, and there were smoke plumes in the distance.

This is an isolated, pristine wilderness. Jabiru and brolga took flight when we arrived at the first clear pool, but a young boar rooting up grass less than 100m away was more inquisitive, taking a couple of minutes before disappearing.

The only people allowed to fish this area are locals and lodge visitors. There are three large pools that Brad said weren't billabongs. 'A billabong is a pool that has branched off the river and becomes separated as the river flow has declined,' he explained. 'These pools are the river which has simply dried up due to the lack of runoff.'

We used bibbed minnow lures designed to run down to about 2m. The first pool proved a dud so we moved to the next.

This water was not as big and was separated from the first by about 100m of riverbed sand.

This time the action was on from the first cast. This lily-fringed water was deeper and had more snags around the shoreline that offered cover for the saratoga and barramundi. My first fish was a saratoga, the next a freshwater barramundi that was almost black it had been in here for so long.

When the fishing slowed, we had lunch and moved on to the last pool of the three, which turned out to be the best of the lot. There were plenty of strikes, missed hook-ups and a few landed fish.

Glen Booth with a threadfin salmon

JUNCTION BAY

A week before cyclone Monica passed over Maningrida in April 2006, I flew back to Victoria from the NT. I'd been fishing in Arnhem Land for a week. My memories consisted of dense green, mangrove-lined rivers, casting bibbed minnow lures into small drains, run-offs, eddies, and hooking into barramundi. A year later, I couldn't resist going back to the same waters, this time fishing with one of the territory's best guides, Lance Butler. Lance started out as a fishing guide at Townsville more than 21 years ago. Since then, he had plied his trade out of most of the Top End hot spots including Bathurst and Croaker islands, Seven Spirit Bay and the Coburg Peninsula.

We left the Maningrida boat ramp at 7am to make a 30km run west to Junction Bay. The wind was up as we passed Rolling Bay and the 6m Stabi Craft was taking a pounding as Lance steered us around hidden reefs and sandbars. The north had experienced a huge Wet season that had resulted in massive flooding and Lance decided to take the opportunity to do some exploring. 'The run-off has been huge and it has opened up several small creeks in Junction Bay that I didn't even know existed until they burst through to the sea,' Lance explained.

The first stop was along the western shore of Junction Bay, but the creek mouth was too shallow for our boat. However, the sight of a barramundi jumping out of the water at the entrance was enough for us to drop the anchor in knee-deep water and wade ashore.

The beach was sandy and showed no sign of crocodiles. Six casts into the small lagoon produced six barramundi and it was time to move.

At the next creek, Lance manoeuvred the boat inside the mouth before we started fishing. The tell-tale slide of a crocodile encouraged us to stay in the boat this time. As the **mullet** came downriver with the tide, the **barra** followed them and the action was non stop.

Several small creeks later and we were at Number One Creek on the eastern shore of the bay. The so-called creek opens up into a huge river system. Before us was a scene of devastation. Cyclone Monica had ripped thousands of trees out of the ground, and those that managed to hang on were denuded of leaves. It was like something after a bushfire, without the black scarring on the trunks. The backdrop of lush green mangroves was gone, replaced by a stark landscape of bare trees that, in some areas, looked as if they had been harvested and piled into massive windrows. Lance said he had never seen this level of destruction anywhere.

Despite the destruction, the fishing was excellent. We travelled for more than 15km upriver, casting lures into small run-offs and creek junctions, or at snags that lined the watercourse. We caught more than 30 barra and left them biting.

BLYTH RIVER

The Blyth River estuary is about 30km east of Maningrida. Six anglers and three guides in three boats made the run. The wind was slight, blowing from the north across the Arafura Sea and the run along the coast took about 90 minutes. It was low tide when we began to track through the mudflats and sandbars that dot the river entrance.

The estuary is large, a kilometre or more wide, and teems with wildlife. On the exposed mudflats a logjam of crocodiles was soaking up the sun; above us sea-eagles, whistling kites and ospreys glided on updrafts.

Lindsay Mutimer took us well inside the river to 'AJs Bar', a rock bar that had never failed since he took over the lodge with Alex Julius. We hadn't even put our lures in the water when we heard yelling up ahead: one angler had hooked up and nearly a metre of **barramundi** came rocketing out of the water, head-shaking to toss the lure. It was an adrenalin-pumping start to a memorable morning's fishing.

Our lures, Barra Classic 120s, went in and tracked along at about 3m deep as we started trolling, our speed a little better than walking pace. Lindsay eyed the echo sounder and warned us as we came over the rock bars where the barramundi would be waiting. My rod buckled, line poured off the reel and hissed through the water as another shimmering metre of barramundi, gills flared and body twisting, shot from the water like a Polaris missile. The other boats were also hooked up.

For the next three hours we trolled the same stretch of water, and all the time the barramundi were on the chew.

No fish came in easy. Sometimes only one boat would get a hook-up, and missed strikes or lost fish were an ongoing part of the action. At least 20 fish were lost when they managed to toss a lure or, in a couple of instances, cut the 24kg leader material either on the reef or with the spur-like cutter on their gill covers.

This was a session to remember. The tally was 33 barramundi up to 99cm long. The smallest fish was 79cm, and 30 of the barramundi topped 90cm.

On another trip to the Blyth with Lance Butler, I fished well upstream in the fresh water. The first

Lance Butler unhooks a small barramundi caught in a tributary creek in Junction Bay

Above: Steve Cooper with a 93cm barramundi caught in the Blyth River
Below: A blue salmon that took a lure intended for barramundi

stop was a small cut with fresh water draining into it off the high bank. The cut was 5m wide and about 10m long and a fallen tree partly blocked the left hand side of the entrance. As he positioned the boat outside the cutting, Lance said: 'Cast your lures as far up the cut as you can, either next to the snag or along the colour change in the water.'

The first cast brought a barra of about 60cm. Several similar-sized fish quickly followed before the action stopped. Lance fired up the motor and moved upstream until we arrived at a small creek, flanked on one side of the mouth by a small, grass-covered island and on the other with low-lying bushes. This spot proved frenetic. A barramundi would strike on nearly every cast.

These fish were about the same size as those we caught earlier and Lance explained they were average sizes for the freshwater reaches of the river.

Several more creek stops later we arrived at a cluster of boulders set out from a small waterfall that was running hard. The fishing was more difficult due to the rocky terrain, but we had success before Lance took the boat into the creek at the base of the waterfall. After lunch, as we moved away from the creek, we spotted a large water buffalo peering at us through the scrub.

Methods for Arnhem Land

TACKLE You will need a baitcaster, spooled with 15kg braided line with a 24kg hard-wearing monofilament leader attached.

LURES Lures include Barra Classic 120s and 10-plus, and RMG Scorpions. All barbs were flattened on the hooks for easy release. Colours varied from fluoro yellows, silver with red stripes to blue and silver combinations.

3 KAKADU

It's an angler's dream to live in the middle of Kakadu National Park, on the doorstep of the famous Alligator Rivers, magnificent Yellow Waters, with plenty of healthy swamps and waterholes in between. It's home to the iconic barramundi, and there are many salt and freshwater locations.

Kakadu is three hours' drive south-east of Darwin on the Arnhem Land Hwy. A permit is required to stay here, and this can be obtained at Jabiru, or at any Park Ranger Station. It is $25 for all interstate and international visitors aged 16 years and over. All NT residents and children under 16 will be exempt.

ACCOMMODATION: Kakadu is built around tourism, and caters well for all forms of accommodation. The visitor can camp at powered and unpowered sites, stay in cabins or motel rooms.
For more information visit:
www.kakadu.com.au
www.parksaustralia.gov.au/kakadu/plan-your-trip/where-to-stay.html

SOUTH ALLIGATOR RIVER

Adventure is what the NT is about. Be prepared to go home with more than fishing memories. The flora and fauna are full of unexpected excitement too. In this raw environment, anything that swims, walks or flies – including anglers – has the potential to be a meal for something else.

One of the most popular areas for anglers is the South Alligator River in Kakadu National Park. Kakadu covers more than 20,000sqkm and is a vast network of floodplains interwoven by drains, creeks and rivers, and teems with myriad birds and crocodiles.

Anglers trolling for barramundi along the South Alligator River

During the wet season, from about December–February, monsoonal rains sweep down from the north and the floodplains vanish under an inland sea. Sometime in March or April, the water begins pouring off the plains. This run-off is a trigger that brings **barramundi** and other fish like **threadfin salmon**, **mangrove jack** and **longtom** on the bite.

The only boat ramp on the South Alligator River is downstream of the Arnhem Hwy bridge, about 45km west of Jabiru. Like all ramps in this part of the world, this one is long; its tidal range exceeds 3m.

I fished here with Shannon Summerton of Kakadu Fishing Tours in a 6m, flat-bottomed boat powered by a 130-horsepower four-stroke outboard. Our method was trolling bibbed minnow lures close to the riverbanks and over rock bars for barramundi.

When the fishing slowed in the main river, we motored up Nourlangie Creek to a rock bar, with the tide falling. This narrow waterway is highly regarded for its barramundi fishing. We were on the downstream side of the rock bar and another boat was upstream of the rocks. The water was still pouring out, almost roaring, but the level had fallen so that neither boat could cross the bar.

Above: Cahills Crossing on the East Alligator River is popular with anglers
Below: This is why you never put your arms in the water – this crocodile surfaced next to the boat and was trying to take a lure

As the tide was nearing the end of its cycle Shannon said: 'Listen to what happens.' At the very end of the tide, as the flow stopped, an abrupt silence lasted for a minute or so. It was as if someone turned a tap off. Then the gurgling started again as water began pouring back into the creek.

As we fished, a 2.5m crocodile hunted nearby. The croc swam with one leg outstretched and its claws visible out of the water, working its way along the bank and an eddy. Shannon explained that whenever a fish such as a **mullet** touched its leg, the croc would swing its head in the hope of catching it.

We caught a few barra and returned to the South Alligator, heading upstream. We'd often see 'logs' swimming across the river, sunning along the banks and one large croc worked its way up a small tributary, the head and tail of a shark protruding from its jaws.

The river changed from a wide expanse lined with exposed mudflats to one where wetland grasses camouflaged the riverbank. Crocodiles and mud gave way to jabirus, Burdekin ducks and lush, swampy wetlands.

Upstream, a clearly marked area defines where boats are not allowed to enter, but there is enough fishing water for this not to be a problem.

Like most anglers, we spent most of the day trolling.

At the top of the river an angler hooked up and his barra leapt out of the water close to our boat. He was worrying about his boat drifting into the edge of the river, and then fiddled around too long trying to organise his net. We knew he was going to lose that fish: it was just a matter of time.

EAST ALLIGATOR RIVER

One of the prime rivers in Kakadu is the East Alligator, which is at the eastern boundary of Kakadu. Access to the East Alligator is at Cahills Crossing. Turn left on to the Oenpelli road about 5km before Jabiru. The road crosses Magela Creek and you can't get past here until water levels are low enough. Cahills Crossing is underwater at high tide anyway.

A concrete boat ramp about 100m upstream of the crossing has cleaning facilities. Another ramp, also with fish-cleaning facilities, is a similar distance below the crossing. Some anglers fish all the way down to where the river flows into Van Diemen Gulf, but downstream navigation can be hazardous due to rock bars so, at the very least, seek local advice before attempting any downstream boating trip.

Cahills Crossing is popular with shore-based anglers. Most fish from the relative safety of rock walls on the west side of the river. Some adventurous souls have been known to stand in water and fish from the crossing. But crocodiles bank up along here and when the **barramundi** are on the bite, some people lose the plot. A few years ago an angler was taken here.

I was fishing with Shannon Summerton and after launching his boat we headed upstream, barely travelling 100m from the ramp before our first stop. Shannon manoeuvred the boat to sit just off a bunch of snags and we started casting our bibbed minnow lures into the timber. The first hook-up came on the second cast of the morning – not a bad start to the day.

I had fished the South Alligator River the day before, and the two waters are very different in appearance. Whereas the South Alligator features an extensive system of grassed floodplains and mangrove-lined mudflats, the East Alligator is lined with gums, sandy stretches and rocks.

We motored upstream trolling lures. At any likely looking snag, Shannon slowed down and we cast into the timber. Along one 100m stretch, we caught barramundi on every pass. Shannon showed me photographs of a client with a 30kg barramundi caught here.

The pièce de résistance was when we ventured into a magnificent gorge that ran parallel with the river, locally called the Rock Hole. Entry is via a tight, narrow creek and we had to push timber and scrub out of the way to get the boat through. Once inside the gorge, a new world of high cliffs lining one side and dense trees on the other opened up, and the water was deep and still.

We caught about 50 barra that day, mostly 50–60cm: not big by barra standards but a lot of fun. Shannon said that as the run-off receded, the smaller barra slowed down and a higher proportion of bigger fish could be caught.

Methods for Kakadu

TECHNIQUES In areas where fallen trees had created snags or creeks flowed into the river, we cast lures into the sunken timber or close to the banks.

In deeper water areas, particularly over rock bars, trolling is the preferred method. You might put 50 casts into a spot and on cast number 51 catch a fish. It is the same with trolling; you just have to keep working because the barra will be there.

TACKLE Baitcaster outfits are standard but a good threadline outfit will still work okay. Spool your reel with 15kg breaking-strain braid and have a couple of metres of 24kg monofilament leader joined at the terminal end. Shannon uses clips to attach his bibbed lures.

LURES In this country, you are constantly changing colours, sizes or picking lures that operate at different depths to suit the terrain. Preferred lures are large bibbed minnows including Halco Scorpion, Mad Mullet and Barra Classic.

Large soft plastic shads like the Tsunamis are becoming more common among the anglers who prefer to spin.

Rod Mackenzie caught this large jewfish in Chambers Bay

4 MARY RIVER SYSTEM

CHAMBERS BAY

The Mary River system is about three hours' drive east of Darwin. The Arnhem Land Hwy is the only road to the Mary River System. Turn left on the Point Stuart Rd about 5km past the Bark Hut Roadside Cafe and Caravan Park.

The Mary River breaks up into a system of billabongs and creeks that would be called rivers in southern Australia.

Two of the largest waterways are Sampan and Tommycut creeks, which flow out of the famous Corroboree Billabong. These waters are reputed to hold the biggest crocodiles in the Territory, which was why I felt uncomfortable when standing up to my thighs in water at the Shady Camp boat ramp in the predawn grey. I wasn't concerned about the crocodile cruising the water less than 100m away. I was uneasy about what I couldn't see ... knowing there was an even bigger croc hanging about the place, somewhere. I saw it the day before.

I was with Dean McFarlane who runs Point Stuart Wilderness Lodge. Heavy rains had turned the Mary River system into a gigantic floodplain and the boat ramp was under a couple of metres of water, so we were forced to launch the 6m tinnie from the road, which was why I was standing nervously in water.

A few other boats had already launched. We took off down Sampan Creek as Dean decided we would fish some of the creek mouths in Chambers Bay. He said **barramundi** line up at these creeks to feed on **mullet** and **prawns** as they come downstream. To get there we had to cross into Tommycut Creek and run down to the mouth before motoring east along Chambers Bay, a run that took the better part of an hour.

Small creeks were draining into the bay and we first tied off the boat at Marsh Creek and started casting lures. Dean's father, Rod, hooked a big barramundi, but the treble hooks pulled free as the fish ran under the boat. We hooked another couple of barra, and an angler on another boat, anchored less than 50m behind us, hooked a metre-long fish.

Leaving Marsh Creek, we worked back along the coast to a small creek, not much bigger than a drain, where the water at the mouth was alive with **popeye mullet**. Barramundi were feeding on the frenzied mullet on the surface.

The action was so intense that as we slowly motored towards the creek mouth, a barra came out of the water headlong into the side of the boat!

Offshore in Chambers Bay, isolated reef systems hold solid populations of **mulloway** and **golden snapper**. The fish are prolific, so long as you know where to drop a line.

Dean found a likely reef and we dropped our baits straight to the bottom about 6m below, and then wound up about 30cm to avoid the sinker snagging on the seabed. The first indication was a tap-tap on the line, then the 15kg rod buckled over and the reel drag system howled as a metre-long slab of silvery scales scoffed bait and scarpered.

These mulloway ran hard and long, and when brought close to the boat they always made a dive for the anchor rope, or the prop on the outboard. Nevertheless, coming across so many mulloway in the middle of the day in relatively shallow water was an experience bordering on surreal.

At the height of the hot bite, another boat came over and dropped anchor no more than 25m away. I thought the action a little rude. Dean seemed unconcerned – the boat driver was a friend of his, another local fishing guide. As the chatter ran across the water between the boats, one of the anglers dropped his bait over the side. He was using shark fillet, a bait popular with northern mulloway anglers. I would never have thought of using shark fillet, but if I did, I would take the skin off before putting it on the hook, unlike this angler. But it proved effective, and he soon had a 15kg mulloway flapping onboard.

With the tide getting low, we headed back up Tommycut Creek and then crossed into Sampan Creek via a small channel that is a narrow, overgrown series of S-bends a couple of kilometres long. The temperature was about 40°C and a breeze was appreciated.

We arrived at Sampan Creek and made a sharp right turn upstream towards Shady Camp, about 30km as the crow flies from Chambers Bay. We were hot and thirsty when a mirage floated before us: a boat decked out with umbrellas labelled 'Peters Ice Cream'. It was Darwin-based fishing guide Dean Blackler, who had anchored close to the bank out from a small drain.

As we pulled up, we saw his crew hard at it, with barramundi coming in on almost every cast. The fish averaged 50–60cm and the action was consistent. As we watched, Melbourne angler Murray Smallhorn cast his soft plastic lure to a line of discoloured water at the mouth of the drain, the line indicating the demarcation between the fresh drain water and the saline river water. Barramundi sat on this line, feeding on small fish and crustaceans being washed off the floodplain. Murray's lure sank; he gave it a slight lift and hooked up a 5.5kg barramundi.

SHADY CAMP

This barrage separates fresh and salt water and is a famous land-based fishing spot. It consists of a free camping area with a reasonably clean toilet block. There is no worry about dogs and cats getting into rubbish bins: the crocodiles take care of that.

There is a boat ramp above the barrage, but boats wanting to go downstream launch across the riverbank – a sometimes scary exercise given the crocodile population. Some mad anglers fish from the barrage when the water is flowing strongly across it.

In the freshwater reaches the **barramundi** are not as big, but there is the added bonus of **saratoga**, especially for those who fish well upstream at Corroboree Billabong.

TOMMYCUT GRAVEYARD

After seeing so many healthy wetlands in the Territory, Tommycut Graveyard is a shock to the system. In the 1970s this was a thriving freshwater wetland system similar to Kakadu. However, it was all but destroyed by saltwater intrusion. Monsoonal rainforests, pandanus and tall paperbarks have gone; all that is left are the lifeless trunks of paperbarks and ever-expanding mangrove trees.

I fished here with Dean McFarlane and Victorian fishing writer, Rod Mackenzie. Motoring a few kilometres downstream of the shortcut in Tommycut Creek, Dean made a left turn into a small, mangrove-lined creek and drove his boat upstream against the fast-flowing water for several kilometres. We fished the creek with moderate success until lunchtime when Dean decided we should move further upstream. The

Above: A jabiru stalks its prey in the Tommycut Graveyard on the Mary River System
Below: A small barramundi was eating above its weight when it swallowed this lure

tide was low and when we could go no further he nosed the boat into the bank and tied off.

We then stepped ashore and walked a couple of hundred metres across crusty clay to a barrage constructed in an attempt to halt saltwater flow into the Graveyard.

'What about crocodiles?' I asked.

'Shouldn't be a problem,' Dean assured me. 'Anyway, the water is so clear and shallow you should be able to see them.'

Casting soft plastic paddle-tail lures with our baitcaster outfits brought immediate success. The technique was to let the lure sink to the bottom and then retrieve slowly using a slight lift and drop technique. **Barramundi** take the lures on the lift, drop and on the bottom. There was plenty of action as barramundi up to about 70cm schooled along a deeper section of what remained of the barrage.

Barra are a 'boof and bite' fish. They engulf their prey with a huge intake of water, and then forcefully expel the water through their gills with a loud 'boofing' noise that has been likened to the sound of a shotgun fired up a drainpipe. Inexperienced Victorian anglers could be excused for thinking it's opening day for duck season.

After an hour or so, we walked a short distance to another breech where water was flowing into a creek. Dean and Rod opted to fish from a knob of rock about 10m off the bank. The water on one side was about 3m deep and they reasoned it should hold a few barra.

I stayed on the bank with the camera where I was joined by a couple of local anglers who told me they fished here regularly. The first question they asked was: 'Seen any crocs yet?'

'No,' I replied. 'Do you see a few crocs up here?'

'There are plenty of crocs up here old mate,' the older angler said, 'so keep your eyes open.'

I moved back from the water to slightly higher ground. Meanwhile, Dean and Rod continued catching barra, this time standing knee-deep in heavily grassed water and casting their lures into channels among the dead timber.

Next morning conditions were different. The tide had pushed up and several metres of water covered most of the ground we walked over to get to the barrage.

Another fishing guide, Dan Noujock, made the most of this opportunity, and took his boat up the creek to fish with his bow nudging the barrage wall. A small section of the barrage – where we had fished the day before – was about 10cm above water and a large feral pig was stranded on it. As Dan and his crew fished, a big crocodile came spearing out of the water, took the pig in its jaws and went into a death roll. Amid spraying water and a short, high-pitched squeal, the pig disappeared. It pays to stay alert.

WILDMAN RIVER

In an untamed land, the name Wildman River is enough to stir the cockles of any adventure-loving angler. Being told the river is inaccessible by road and that it will take about two hours fast running in a boat to get there only adds to the anticipation.

It was my last day fishing in the Mary River System and I was once again with Dean and his father Rod. It was dark when we launched Dean's boat at Shady Camp. This time the river was so low that we had to wade to put the boat in – not the most comfortable feeling given the many pairs of red eyes that glowed in the beams of the car headlights. The trip was slow for the first couple of kilometres as we strained our eyes looking for sandbars. The poor light conditions made observation tricky. Several times, what we thought were sandbars turned out to be crocodiles so big their backs were humped like camels.

After travelling downriver for 30 minutes, we entered Chambers Bay. To avoid the shallow mudflats, Dean motored several kilometres offshore before turning east to run along the coast past Point Stuart and then into Finke Bay.

An hour later we entered the mouth of Wildman River. This is a big river: there are no

Point Stuart Wilderness Lodge owner Dean McFarlane caught this 76cm barramundi on a soft plastic lure

Attempting to toss the lure, this 17kg barramundi goes airborne in Wildman River

mudflats or breaks in the mangrove-lined banks, and the vegetation is so tall and thick it can be claustrophobic, despite the water being 150m wide.

About 20km upriver, we came to a junction. Another boat had come in ahead of us and the crew were already catching **barramundi** on nearly every cast. We dropped the anchor a little upriver of their boat. Dean said to cast the lures as close to the snags and overhanging mangroves as possible. The first barra came on the first cast, and soon we were enjoying triple hook-ups of 65–80cm fish.

Loud cheers came from the other boat and I turned to see a huge burst of spray as a metre-plus barra went skyrocketing out of the tannin-coloured water. Melbourne angler Chris Memery had hit the jackpot, hooking into one of the bigger fish Dean had assured us were there. The whopper took off around the boat and headed for the safety of the mangroves, but Chris managed to turn it with centimetres to spare. The barra then put on more aerobatics and head-shaking as it attempted to throw the lure, but the hooks held firm and eventually Dan netted it. It was 16.3kg and 1.1m long. After photographs it was released to fight another day.

Barely 10 minutes passed and I hooked a barra that was a tad shorter, but weighing in a kilogram heavier at 17.23kg.

A few more casts and Rod hooked a big fish, but he was too close to the mangroves and he couldn't stop it before it dragged his lure and line down through the mangrove roots, snapping the 24kg braid. The mangrove was shaking as the fish tried to free itself.

There was no breeze where we fished and after several hours sweating in the 40°C heat, our hands were so slippery that holding the rods and fighting fish was difficult. Nevertheless, we persisted. It isn't that often that you come across a barra bite so hot with fish of that quality.

SWIM CREEK

After a long, hot day fishing for barramundi, the bar and dining area at Point Stuart Wilderness Lodge, just north of Mary River National Park, is a magnet for anglers. Thirsts are quenched, meals eaten and fish tales are the order of the day.

On this evening in early May, the bar was crowded when a couple of locals walked in carrying a bucket full of **red claw** and a small saltwater crocodile. They'd almost stood on the croc and the guys decided to 'bring it in to show the tourists' before returning it. The small crocodile didn't raise an eyebrow, but word of the red claw haul had the bar buzzing ... among the locals at any rate.

Red claw is the northern Australian equivalent of the southern Australian yabby. The northern species has red-tipped pincers, but there is little other obvious differences. In some parts of Queensland, red claw are also known as crawchies.

We southerners thought little of the red claw catch because, ho-hum, well they were only yabbies. The locals had other ideas. In freshwater streams in northern Australia, red claws migrate upstream to breed. This migration doesn't sound like a big deal until you find out it occurs just once a year, and lasts no more than a couple of weeks. Red claw usually weigh around 300g, although they have been recorded at 600g.

I've never been into Opera nets for yabbies. In my experience, true sport comes from tying a piece of red meat to the end of a bit of string. The yabby can then be lured to the surface and a hand-net placed underneath to catch it.

The red claws were being caught at the Swim Creek crossing, about 5km from the lodge on Point Stuart Rd. I was told if I wanted to catch a few, all I would need would be a torch and a bucket. No net was required. I was intrigued.

Water was pouring downstream over a causeway below the bridge. About a dozen other red claw hunters were already at the crossing, including three who had made the long drive from Darwin for an evening session. The method was simple: all you had to do was walk around a small barrage shining your torch into the water. When you spotted one, you reached down and took hold of it with your hand, being careful to avoid the pincers.

Given the large population of crocodiles in the area, standing in a stream in the middle of the night isn't something you'd expect to be a popular pastime. Nevertheless, anticipation of the taste of red claw seems to overcome any fear of the crocs. Moreover, everyone was downstream of the causeway and nobody ventured into the calmer, upstream pool. It was a large, dark pool about the size of a house block and surrounded by heavy vegetation. I was assured it would hold plenty of crocodiles.

The red claw hunters working the fast-flowing water had difficulty staying upright. How a red claw was able to scramble upstream against that fast-flowing water is a mystery. Most of the catchers stayed in ankle-deep water and some worked around trees where they could steady themselves. The more adventurous were downstream in dark spooky pools, out of the current. Every so often, the beam of a torch would pan along the darker areas of the water, checking for the telltale red eyes of a lurking crocodile.

In less than an hour, we caught half a bucket of red claw, and then it was back to camp where the catch was placed in the cool room. Lowering the body temperature of the yabbies is like putting them to sleep. Then they can humanely be boiled for about a minute, after which they are shelled and devoured.

Methods for Mary River System

TACKLE Barramundi anglers casting lures prefer baitcaster outfits. These are easy to master and offer better casting control and improved fish-fighting ability. The standard baitcaster rods suit lines of 8–10kg, although most anglers prefer to spool their reels with 24kg breaking strain braid, as it is less likely to wear through on the snags. If you choose to do this, remember to set the drag on your reel to suit the rod, not the line. Attach a couple of metres of 24kg breaking strain abrasion-resistant monofilament to the end of the braid as a leader.

LURES Casting at snags is more fun than trolling. Barra lures tend to be up to 15cm long, mainly floating/diving minnow types in a range of colours because it sometimes comes down to what colour is going to work on a given day. When casting bibbed minnows, try to get your lure right in among the timber or along a colour change and retrieve slowly with a hesitant twitch and pause technique. Don't cast to a different spot if you don't get a hit. Sometimes you have to keep plugging away in the same spot until the fish 'turn on'.

Shad-tail soft plastics were more effective in the 75–100mm sizes. The technique is to let the lure sink to the bottom and then retrieve slowly using a slight lift and drop technique. Flatten the hook barbs on your lures to ensure you can release unwanted fish unharmed.

Reef fishing

RIGS The rig was a two-leader paternoster with 6/0 circle hooks, each with a half pilchard attached. These were dropped straight to the bottom, and then wound off the bottom about 30cm to avoid the sinker snagging on the seabed.

5 TIWI ISLANDS

MELVILLE ISLAND

As you would expect with an island that is isolated from the mainland, the fishing on Melville Island is super. To get to the island there is a regular ferry service from Darwin, however, the easiest and quickest way is to take one of the commuter flights to the island. Melville Island is about 30-minutes flying time north of Darwin.

ACCOMMODATION: On Melville and Bathurst Islands there are three lodges that are the only available accommodation for anglers. These are Melville Island Lodge, overlooking Snake Bay, the remote Johnston River Camp, and Bathurst Island Lodge, which opened in 2013 on the site of the old Barra Base. The lodge is neat, new and offers up all the services anglers have come to expect. It is situated on the west coast of Bathurst Island, close to Capes Helvetius and Fourcroy. All three lodges are operated by the Tiwi Islands Adventures (TIA), a subsidiary company of the Tiwi Land Council.
For more information visit
www.tiwiadventures.com.au

SNAKE BAY

Melville Island is Australia's second largest island, after Tasmania, with an airstrip that is better than many you come across in more heavily populated rural towns in southern Australia.

Milikapiti is a small township on the northern edge of Melville Island, abutting Snake Bay. Set back on a bluff overlooking the bay is Melville Island Lodge, a neat, completely refurbished lodge that fulfils a dream for its owner Mike Baxter.

Mike came to the lodge year after year and promised himself that if he made it big in business, and the lodge came on the market, he would buy it. Not only did he buy the lodge, he rebuilt the place and added a large concrete parking area for boats.

He told me this while we fished in Snake Bay, casting lures to snags along the shoreline, or in some of the many small, no-name tidal creeks that line the bay and the Tjipripu River. The tide was falling and as we mooched along up these creeks we could hear **barramundi** 'boofing' as they fed. The barra were feeding on tiny jelly prawns washing out of the small creeks and drains and our lures were oversized – a size 12 nymph pattern fly would have been best.

Nevertheless, we caught a few barra and mangrove jack. Mike cracked the best of the day, a barra about 78cm, but even he admitted the fishing was tough.

When the barra aren't cooperating, it can pay to go after some of northern Australia's other bottom-dwelling species. At the lodge I met Queensland brothers Vic and Alex Solaga who, after hooking some barra to 88cm and realising the fishing was slow, opted to go offshore looking for **mulloway**, **trevally** and **sharks**. There are extensive reef systems just outside Snake Bay so you don't need to travel far. The largest system is called Saunders Patch, just a couple of kilometres offshore.

Vic and Alex are not the loudest anglers, so when asked how they went, their response was quiet and low-key. Had the brothers sat around the dining table boasting of the day's events, some of us might have taken more notice.

Methinks Vic and Alex have been around the fishing traps a while, because when I caught up with them three days later, they were in the middle of Saunders Patch, and Vic was doing battle with a big **lemon shark**. Alex was at the bow of the boat, bait down, waiting for another **black jew (mulloway)**. The brothers had been catching them to about 9kg, along with golden trevally, giant trevally, **golden snapper** and **coral trout**.

GOOSE CREEK

Some waters achieve almost iconic status in the fishing world due to publicity they receive following successful visits by people in the fishing media. One of these waters is Andranagoo Creek, more commonly called Goose Creek, about an hour's boat ride west of Milikapiti.

Melville Island in December is a hot place. Thunderstorms are brewing all around us and in the distance heavy rain is pelting down on Goose Creek. This is the start of the wet season, when monsoonal rains dump so much water that rivers flood – turning low lying areas into inland seas. It's also one of the hottest times of the year. The build-up to the Wet brings on the barramundi, but the humidity takes its toll on anglers who need to drink fluids constantly to avoid dehydration.

I am in a boat with Mick Chick, our fishing guide, Mark Pettini, captain of English County Cricket Club Essex, and Shepparton tackle shop owner, Steve 'Trelly' Threlfall. We are in a narrow creek, lined on each bank by a dense forest of tall, evergreen mangrove trees, their gnarled roots forming an impenetrable jumble of sticks. There is no breeze

Above: **This manta ray swam into the shallows on Melville Island**
Below: **This buffalo was wading in Goose Creek to take the weight off a broken leg**

Above: Goose Creek is one of the most revered small waters in Australia for both barramundi and saratoga
Below: Crocodiles are a way of life across the Top End

here, the only wind coming from anglers waving rods as they cast soft plastic lures into snags. The fishing is steady. We are hooking mangrove jack, barramundi and golden snapper. In the true spirit of reporting, I ask Mick for the name of the creek.

'Baxters Creek,' is the response.

'Who was Baxter?' I ask.

'Mike Baxter,' he replies.

I should have known better – Mike Baxter owns Melville Island Lodge and in typical guide-speak, when you ask for the name of a small water that has no name, it is invariably called after the lodge owner. To be fair to Mick, this creek is one of possibly several hundred unnamed creeks that run off the Johnston River. We fish other small offshoots, and each one is called Baxters, number one, number two and so on.

On this day we have fished long and hard, and caught plenty. Our fish count stops before lunch, and by my reckoning is well past 50. As we cast our lures into the timber there is a simultaneous 'boof' and splash less than 100m away, followed by frenzied mullet tail skipping across the surface as an escape is made. The 'boofing' noise is a tell-tale sign of a barramundi and the size of the fleeing mullet suggests a big fish. A few minutes later and we are casting our lures into the waterlogged tree branches where the bust up occurred. My lure, a soft plastic, barely hits the water when it is inhaled and almost a metre of silver barramundi shoots out of the water. The fish jumps repeatedly, its gills flared and red gill rakers clearly visible as it tail walks and shakes its head in an effort to toss the hook. It is a nice fish, measuring 87cm before being returned.

On another trip after about 45 minutes motoring along the coast, guide Chris Chilton slowed the boat and began sounding an area known as 'Goose Creek Bommie'. He said we were over a small reef system that can produce a variety of fish ranging from **black jew** to **trevally**.

I was fishing with Steve Threlfall, a tackle shop proprietor all the way from Shepparton in Victoria. Fish showed on the sounder as arches, and there were enough arches for us to tie on large soft plastic lures and start jigging. A few small reef fish were followed by golden trevally. As the first trevally was brought to the boat, Steve dropped his lure down to another accompanying it, and immediately hooked up. After this, the action slowed so we moved into Goose Creek.

A few hundred metres inside Goose Creek, a water-buffalo was standing in a creek on our right. They are normally flighty and getting close enough for a photograph is difficult, but not this time. When the buffalo did finally move it struggled to get out of the water, revealing a broken right foreleg. It was a death sentence. Chris said he would inform the local ranger who would put the animal out of its misery, 'if the crocs don't get it first'.

Our run upstream was a stop-start affair as Chris constantly put the boat into a new position and we cast lures to snags along the bank. Goose Creek is famous both for its **saratoga** and **barramundi**. Our intention was to go up the creek as far as we could in search of toga. As we slowly worked upstream, the salt marsh and mangroves gave way to lily pads and reeds. It was easy to see why this water is regarded as one of the Territory's most picturesque waterways. In one stretch, there was a strong smell where a huge colony of flying-foxes was roosting.

The scenery was magnificent, but Chris said the water level was still too high for saratoga. We caught 37 barramundi in the day, but that was described as a 'slow' day, leaving me wondering what a fast day would be like.

JESSIE RIVER

The run from Milikapiti to Lethbridge Bay at the entrance to Jessie River is about 40km, or a little over an hour. The Jessie is a big river and the rock bar near the mouth is famous for producing **barramundi** and **black jew (mulloway)**. Not this day, though. After a few trolls over the rock bar with lures, we headed upstream.

Our run was stop-start as we fished snags and creek mouths along the way. The tide was falling and barramundi were feeding on jelly prawns washing out of the small creeks and drains into the river. At almost every stop, we cast lures into snags and hooked up on barramundi. The fishing was steady but not spectacular.

Several kilometres upstream, we hit the jackpot: a rich vein of silver seemed to be hanging on a single black stick of timber that protruded from the water. In fact, the stick was a branch, part of what remained of a long-dead mangrove tree that now lay parallel with the riverbank.

Steve 'Trelly' Threlfall cast his lure, which plopped on the water alongside the stick. He gave the lure a couple of twitches and started to wind: boof, splash! A barra about 70cm long struck. One cast, one fish is good, but Steve enjoyed a run of 12 barra on consecutive casts. Perhaps the secret lay in the sarong he was wearing; many northern anglers wear sarongs because, they claim, the wraparound skirts help them stay cool when fishing. Hmmmm.

A metre long barra in the net on the Johnson River

We must have caught 50 **barramundi** off that snag and, as we moved closer to free a lure, we saw why. Beneath the arched roots of the mangrove trees, it was like peak-hour traffic in Melbourne. Hundreds of barramundi lay nose-to-tail. I dangled a gold lure near some and got an immediate strike.

In another creek, we came across schools of **mangrove jack**. They were so aggressive that they were shouldering each other out of the way to get to the lure.

After lunch, we crossed the river to another large creek mouth. First cast raised a fish about a metre long that didn't take the lure. Several casts later and the treble hooks held on to an 86cm fish, followed by a few barra in the 70cm range and another of 82m.

JOHNSTON RIVER

Johnston River camp, run by Melville Island Lodge, is a remote, wilderness retreat 40km upstream. It's a special place that gives anglers access to waters that would otherwise be unreachable on day trips. It's remote, but has several air-conditioned containers, beds, showers, hot meals and cold drinks. It was refreshing at the end of a long day on the water to sit around and chat in a wilderness environment with few discomforts. Most importantly, it offers quick access to an awesome, fish-rich environment.

Our best barra of the day measured 87cm. But the day had begun miserably, with the **barramundi** refusing to cooperate. After we had tried every colour, type and shape of bibbed minnow lure on board, Trelly brought out several packets of soft plastic lures – Berkley Gulp stick baits. We had already tried another well-known brand of soft plastic lures without success, so I didn't hold much hope.

The mangroves are large and overhanging near the creek entrance and Mick held the boat out from a likely looking small cove riddled with dead timber. Trelly cast his 'Nuclear Chicken' Gulp into the dead timber, allowed it to sink to the bottom then tightened his line and lifted his rod tip to jump the lure off the bottom about 30cm. As the lure sank again, a **mangrove jack** slammed it. Trelly hooked the fish and as he fought it to the boat, a school of jacks followed.

A second cast hooked a **golden snapper**, by which time Mark and I were exchanging our bibbed minnows for quarter-ounce jig heads with Gulp lures. What followed was pleasant chaos; multiple hook-ups were the norm as jacks, snapper, **cod** and barramundi were caught; a contrast to the tedium earlier in the day.

For four days straight, we started each morning casting minnow lures into snags. This was successful because it seems there was always a hot bite first up. When the fishing slowed, after an hour or so, we converted to soft plastics and stayed with them for the rest of the day. The list of species grew to include **barracuda** and **Queensland groper**. It was a consistently hot bite during a particularly slow period. Anglers on another boat were equally frustrated,

English professional cricketer Mark Pettini caught this giant cod while fishing Trevally Alley

but when they learned what we were doing, they followed suit and their catch rate shot up.

TREVALLY ALLEY

Many a fishing spot, often no more than a dot on a chart, has earned its name based on the species caught. So it is with Trevally Alley. No more than a reef system, between Melville Island Lodge and Goose Creek, it is a convenient stop-over to catch a different range of fish to those being encountered in the estuary systems.

ACCOMMODATION: The only available accommodation is at Melville Island Lodge. Comfortable and clean with excellent meals and fishing guides, the lodge is highly recommended. For more information visit www.melvillelodge.com.au

The wind had been blowing across the Timor Sea from the northeast for several days, creating a swell and soiling the normally clear waters. On the third day of my visit to Melville Island the wind started to abate; on the fourth morning there was no wind. It was an opportunity to head offshore and our guide Scotty Mathews decided we should make for a reef system called Trevally Alley.

After spending the first few days fishing creeks and inlets for **barramundi**, some offshore action was a welcome change. The baitcaster outfits we had been using gave way to tackle more in keeping with southern snapper – overhead outfits spooled with 15kg breaking strain braid. The rig was a single leader paternoster, with the bait close to the snapper

An unwanted fish, estuary cod are tough competitors and give a good account of themselves when hooked

lead. Bait was queenfish and barracuda caught the previous day in Snake Bay.

The other angler on board the 6m boat this day was Andrew Rutyna from the Sunshine Coast in Queensland. Our first stop was about 15km offshore and before dropping anchor Scotty sounded around until he found a patch of reef loaded with scaly booty.

As soon as our baits hit bottom, bites came thick and fast. They weren't trevally but tricky **snapper** aka spangled emperor or northwest snapper. Tricky snapper fight well enough but are not on Scotty's list of preferred table species so they were landed, unhooked and returned in good health.

Andrew's third hook-up of the morning bent his rod almost double, and as he braced himself against the side of the boat line poured off his reel. We knew Andrew had hooked something bigger and it turned out to be an **estuary cod** that Scotty netted and lifted into the boat to remove the 6/0 Suicide hook. On deck something unusual happened, a pair of parasites, some sort of sea lice that look the same as those found in the throats of silver trevally, crawled out from the cod's nostrils. 'All the cod we catch have these parasites living in their nostrils,' Scotty said. It was something different.

When the action on this part of the reef slowed, Scotty lifted the anchor and moved the boat to another section. Soon there were **coral trout** and **golden snapper**, table quality fish much sought after by NT anglers. In between the quality fish and the unwanted species there were **sharks**. Small black-tipped reef sharks for the most part, but sometimes a strike, hard run and bite-off came from a toothy that was a bit bigger.

The fishing action was consistent all morning but despite the name, Trevally Alley, we caught no trevally, nor any black jew (mulloway), the species Scotty wanted to put us on to. I have fished these reefs before and can vouch for both species and I can only put their non-appearance down to water quality soured by a season of consistent onshore winds.

By lunchtime with a rising swell and an increasing hot wind blowing we headed inshore for more sheltered estuary waters.

BATHURST ISLAND

Bathurst Island Lodge is a 30-minute flight from Darwin airport. Visitors are met at the end of the dirt runway and ferried by boat to the lodge. Upon arrival, the boats pull into a trailered platform with seats; visitors transfer to the trailer, which is then towed up over the sand courtesy of a Deutz tractor. It's a different way to start a fishing trip.

At least that was how it was for Bob Hart, Rod Harrison and I, as our fishing guide, Kelly Mills, drove the boat a kilometre or so up Second Creek for a four-day trip. The channel ran along the east side, and there was an indentation between two points where eddies, caused by the current, gouged out the soil.

Bob took the outside, and I went for the inside running; we were both using Barra Classic 120 lures. On the first run, my lure was snaffled and, after a few minutes' tug of war, a lumpy old cod was netted and released. Kelly returned to the start of the run, and again, Bob stayed with the outside while I went with the inside. This time Harro cast his lure inside mine, and ran it on shorter string. Harro was using a green Classic F18 Manta Ray lure, and the boat covered about 50m before Harro hooked up, the water erupted and a **silver slab** came spearing out.

After four days, Harro's **barra** was a bonus. We had been building our barra numbers and increasing sizes. Bob had a hot casting session in the morning, landing several barra that went from just legal to 78cm. Harro's barra, measuring 92cm from nose to tail, was the best of the trip. The slab of silver was duly netted, photographed and released, and then we went back to trolling for the remaining half hour of our trip.

If only it were that good every day. We had spent our time at the lodge, and although we had good tides, the scarcity of big barra was no different to what was being experienced on the mainland. On a positive note, we and the other lodge visitors, caught plenty of fish on most days.

My favourite session was on the second day, fishing for jewfish near some buoys that mark a defunct aquaculture farm, and within sight of the lodge dining area. Earlier in the day Bob caught a GT, and a decision was made to keep it for bait. Kelly must have had the jewfish in mind.

It was nearing the top of the tide when Kelly tied off on one of the buoys and we rigged and cast our baits. The first jewfish was about 12kg, and I was happy with that. Bob and Harro were hooking **catfish**, and I was happy about that, too. My second bite was a **shark**, and it's still running as far as I know. My third bite was a slightly smaller jewfish. Yes, the action was a bit lopsided, but I didn't mind. Jewfish fight well and, according to the people at the dinner table, they eat well.

Methods for Melville Island

TACKLE When fishing for barramundi and mangrove jack, or jigging the reefs with soft plastics, we used baitcaster outfits, the reels spooled with 15kg breaking strain braid with about a metre of 24kg leader. Lures were 10–12cm bibbed minnows and 75mm soft plastics.

Bottom-bouncing outfits were overhead reels spooled with 15kg braid on a light game rod. Bottom rigs were similar to those employed down south, comprising single leader paternoster rigs with a 6/0 Suicide pattern hook.

QUEENSLAND

Queensland is an enormous state offering diverse opportunities for anglers who like to travel because there are good roads to isolated regions. An angler could spend a lifetime exploring Queensland, and still feel as though there is so much more fishing to be experienced.

All preferences are catered for. There are jungle perch for discerning fly-fishers, and the world's biggest black marlin for those who prefer a blue-water adventure. There are fat yellowbelly to be caught in the muddy rivers of Queensland's Channel Country, and you'll find Australia's biggest barramundi in dams from the Atherton Tablelands south to Gladstone. Saltwater fly-fishers can wade through the flats of Hervey Bay for golden trevally, while surf fishers can fish for tailor on Fraser Island.

ACCOMMODATION

Queensland's accommodation options are as varied as its beaches, from exotic safari lodges to beachside units.

For more information visit www.queenslandholidays.com.au

Borumba Dam on the Sunshine Coast is famous for its saratoga, Australian bass, yellowbelly and silver perch

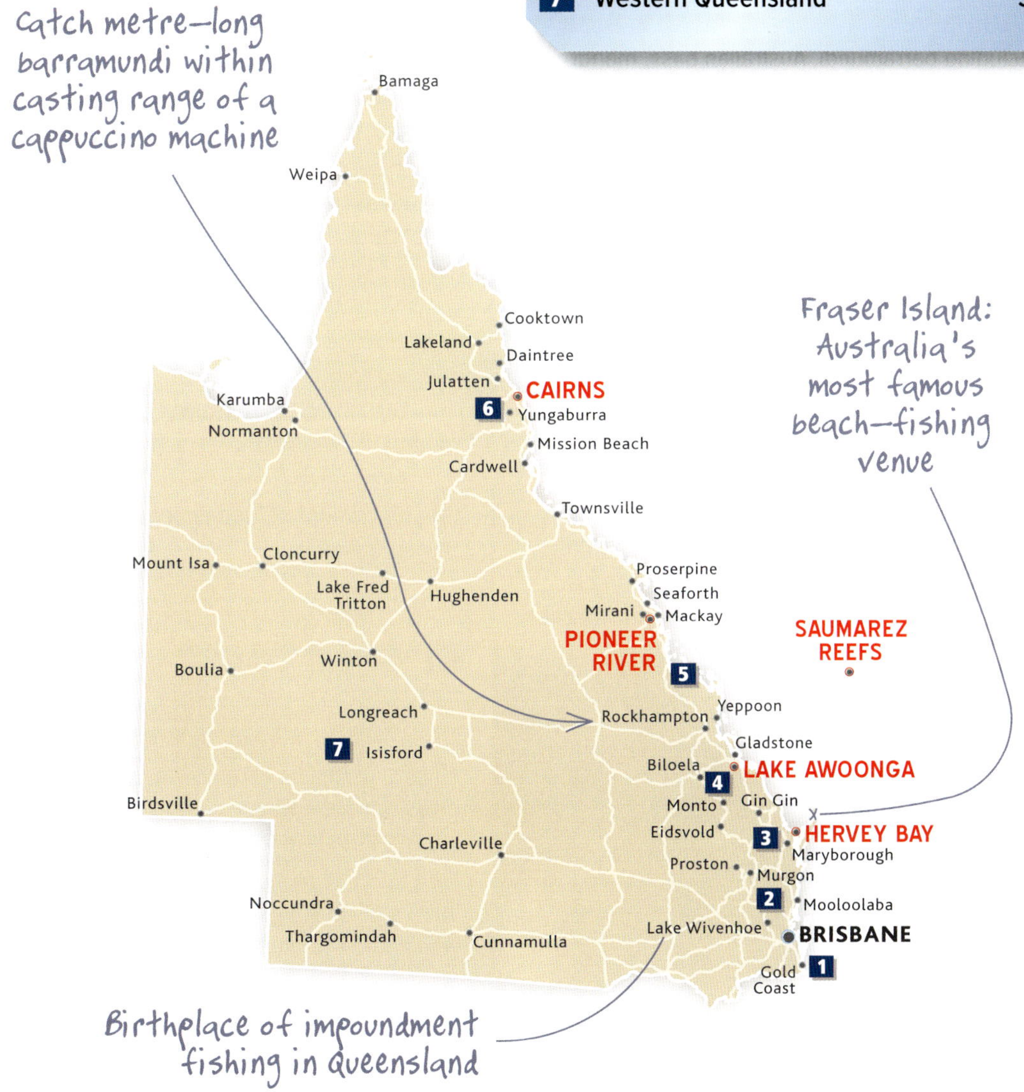
Catch metre-long barramundi within casting range of a cappuccino machine
Fraser Island: Australia's most famous beach-fishing venue
Birthplace of impoundment fishing in Queensland
Bamaga
Weipa
Cooktown
Lakeland
Daintree
Julatten
CAIRNS
6
Yungaburra
Karumba
Normanton
Mission Beach
Cardwell
Townsville
Mount Isa
Cloncurry
Lake Fred Tritton
Hughenden
Proserpine
Seaforth
Mirani
Mackay
PIONEER RIVER
5
SAUMAREZ REEFS
Boulia
Winton
Longreach
Yeppoon
Rockhampton
Gladstone
7
Isisford
Biloela
4
LAKE AWOONGA
Birdsville
Monto
Gin Gin
Eidsvold
3
HERVEY BAY
Maryborough
Charleville
Proston
Murgon
2
Mooloolaba
Noccundra
Thargomindah
Cunnamulla
Lake Wivenhoe
BRISBANE
Gold Coast
1

STOCKED IMPOUNDMENT PERMIT SCHEME

Queensland's Stocked Impoundment Permit Scheme (SIPS) has been a huge success for the angling community. The scheme raises funds for stocking groups in the state to enable them to buy native fish fingerlings and for other activities, all aimed at enhancing the fishery. There are more than 30 dams involved in the scheme and hundreds of thousands of fish including barramundi, Australian bass, mangrove jack and golden perch have been paid for and stocked into waters that previously offered little in the way of piscine excitement.

Any angler 18 years or older requires a permit to fish in any of the dams listed as part of SIPS by Queensland's Primary industries and fisheries department. The angling permit only applies to people using fishing line and is not required if you happen to be using permitted traps to catch the likes of red claw. Permits are issued to an individual, but the permit cover the angler's partner (married or de facto) so long as the partner is nominated on the permit.

An annual permit costs $35, which allows the holder to fish in any of the dams involved in the scheme. These are available at Australia Post offices throughout Queensland, at some fishing supply stores, and from the websites listed below. There is a 10 per cent discount for holders of particular concession cards. A weekly permit costs $7 and again covers all SIPS dams. Paying for a permit means you are contributing to the cost of restocking the state's dams and helping to sustain fish stocks.

Dams like Awoonga, Callide, Lenthall's, Monduran, Prosperine, Tinaroo and Wivenhoe have been immensely successful and developed legendary status among the angling fraternity for their quality fishing. Stocking fish in dams does more than create a fishery; it brings with it a tourism boom.

In southern Queensland there is the Bass to Barra Trail that takes in seven dams from Murgon to Gladstone and, between them, these waters are stocked with a Who's Who of tropical freshwater sport fish including Australian bass, **sooty grunter**, golden perch (yellowbelly), **saratoga**, mangrove jack and barramundi.

See: **www.smartservice.qld.gov.au/services/permits/fishing/apply**

Alternatively, they can be purchased online via the Department of Primary Industries: **www.dpi.qld.gov.au/fishweb**

Freshwater Point boat ramp

1 GOLD COAST

There is much more to the Gold Coast than surf, sand and meter maids. Anglers have a range of exciting prospects from which to choose. The estuary systems are marvellous, and offshore anglers catch more than their share of mackerel, marlin and tuna. If you are into beach fishing then expect to hook tailor, bream, whiting and sometimes even mulloway.

ACCOMMODATION: All accommodation options are available.

For more information visit www.visitgoldcoast.com

NERANG RIVER

The Gold Coast's river and canal system offer anglers many opportunities in sheltered waters. Although not planned as a fishery, this largest of Australia's manmade estuarine systems is a bonanza for anglers.

I first fished here many years ago with Kevin Ballantine. On that trip, we caught **bream**, **trevally**, and **mangrove jack** using bait, lure, and fly-fishing methods. Originally from Melbourne, Kevin thought the fishing fantastic as he had been catching **mulloway** in the seaway, and **big flathead** on the sand flats and channels of the Broadwater at Southport.

More recently, I fished in company with Chris Cleaver and a couple of Shimano Fishing Tackle executives, Yuzo Shimano and Kenji Komada from Osaka. Chris is one of Australia's top tournament anglers, and works for Shimano Australia.

The run down the Nerang River to the Seaway at Southport from the boat ramp at Freshwater Point takes about an hour. It's not the distance as much as the 6-knot speed limit that slows boaters, and that was a pity when I was there as the boat was a 5.8m long Skeeter Bass Boat with a 150HP Evinrude outboard on the stern, and is capable of 105km/hr.

The Gold Coast is a maze of canals where locals catch a variety of species including mulloway, **yellowfin bream**, mangrove jacks and **dusky flathead**. Chris found large schools of bream the day before on some flats near the Seaway entrance, so this was our destination. The sky was clear and there was little wind; the day before had been overcast and blowing a gale.

If you have not been near the Broadwater on a sunny Sunday, it is worth a look. Here jet skis play dodgems with million dollar cruisers and kayakers paddle down channels oblivious to everything. On either side of this frothy chaos, are anglers fishing from boats and breakwalls.

Chris motored past the Seaway and took us to some sand flats off Crab Island in Runaway Bay. The seabed consisted of sand interspersed with weed in water so clear you could easily count the nipper holes, and even see footprints where anglers had pumped nippers on the low tide.

Fishing at Southport in the Nerang River

As we drifted slowly across the sand flats, soft plastic lures were cast and jigged ultra-slowly in the hope of attracting a bream or flathead. Yuzo struck first with a small flathead; soon several more small flathead and a few yellowfin bream were landed. The fish were small and not what we were after. Clear water and sunshine are not a good mix for spooky fish like bream. We fished these flats for about an hour and reluctantly headed for deeper water, fishing near the Seaway then further upstream under a bridge where small **queenfish** annoyed our lures.

Our final destination was off the Southport School where Chris assured us there was a reef. The water was deeper and not as clean as near the Seaway and Chris was confident we could pull something decent. The first fish aboard was a bream, and there were a few of them. Then Chris hooked into a bigger fish; a flathead that followed his Devil Vibe lure up from the bottom before taking it near the surface beside the boat.

Chris had a clear look at the flathead and called it for 70 or 80cm. He was using a 2kg line and as flathead are well-endowed with small, sharp teeth, Chris wasn't sure his fine leader would go the distance. It was a case of being patient and handling the fish gently. If Chris put too much pressure on the flathead, it might turn and dive, dragging his fine leader material across its teeth. Slowly and surely he brought the flathead to the boat, and after a couple of short directional changes, the fish swam into a small Environet handled by Kenji. It was a good net shot given that the flathead was too big for the small net.

2 AROUND BRISBANE

MOOLOOLABA

A Sunshine Coast holiday hot spot built on tourism, it nevertheless has some great fishing available both offshore and inland. Offshore game fishers chase tuna, mackerel and even marlin, while bottom bouncers concentrate on species like pearl perch, red emperor, snapper and coral trout. Beaches produce tailor and flathead and the estuaries have trevally, flathead and bream.

ACCOMMODATION: All accommodation options are available.
For more information visit
www.mooloolabatourism.com.au

The normal association with the Sunshine Coast is sun and surf: the region doesn't have a big reputation for fishing. It should. It has enough piscatorial opportunities to cater for all fishing tastes. Offshore there are game fish such as **marlin**, **sailfish** and **tuna**.

The surf fishes well for **tailor** and **flathead**, and the estuaries are fine waters for **trevally**, flathead and **bream**. Inland within a couple of hours drive you can catch **Australian bass**, **saratoga** and even **barramundi**.

It's 6am on the Mooloolaba waterfront behind Kawana Waters Hotel. The temperature is mild enough to be wearing shorts and a shirt. All is quiet amid the moored boats except for the eager anglers sitting around the stern of the 12m game boat *Cervantes*, who are washing down freshly toasted raisin bread with coffee.

The crew was waiting for a couple of anglers to arrive before the charter took me and the other customers offshore for a morning of bottom bouncing over the nearby reefs. The holidaying customers were from as far away as Bendigo, Casino and Townsville.

It took about 15 minutes to reach the harbour entrance; then the *Cervantes* was pointed east and the V8 Caterpillar engines were opened up. When asked where we were heading and why, skipper Allan Harvey said he was undecided. 'It's hard to tell where the fish will be some days,' he said.

Our first stop was after about 40 minutes steaming. Baitfish showed on the sounder and where there is baitfish, bigger fish are sure to follow. Tackle was pure Queensland – indestructible Alvey centre-pin reels. The lines were baited with squid, dropped to the bottom and it wasn't long before all manner of reef fish started coming inboard: **red emperor**, **Moses perch**, **coral trout** and **parrotfish**. There were a few **snapper** too; small fish called **squire** locally.

Some Queenslanders I know would walk barefoot across broken glass to have a shot at some serious reef fish – particularly red reef fish. Here we were several miles offshore – an area where during the summer **marlin**, **sailfish**, **mackerel** and **tuna** abound – and yet most Queenslanders would sooner bottom bounce.

After an hour or so, Allan moved closer inshore, and the fishing was even better. Along with most of the previously mentioned fish were some **pearl perch**, which are highly prized for their taste. The patrons were happy, and so was the skipper.

LAKE WIVENHOE

Lake Wivenhoe is about an hour's drive north-west from Brisbane via the Brisbane Valley Hwy. It is a monster of a dam with more than 460km of shoreline and holds twice as much water as Sydney Harbour.

Only non-fuel powered boats are allowed. A permit is required for camping, fishing and boating. Mainly an Australian bass and yellowbelly water, it has also been stocked at times with silver perch, Murray cod and saratoga. Sometimes you may hook a rare lungfish.

ACCOMMODATION: Camping is permitted at 'Captain Logan Camp' and Lumley Hill: booking is essential at peak times and a camping fee applies. Toilets, barbecues, a public telephone, hot showers, playground, picnic tables, drinking water, limited firewood and a kiosk are provided.
For more information visit www.queenslandholidays.com.au

Above: Rod Harrison caught this Australian bass in Lake Wivenhoe
Below: Gary Fitzgerald with a lungfish caught in Lake Wivenhoe

Impoundment fishing for native species in southern Queensland has enjoyed phenomenal growth and it all began at Lake Wivenhoe. Wivenhoe has a surface area of about 108sqkm and an average depth of 11m. This dam and the Brisbane River below offer superb fishing for anglers wanting to catch **Australian bass** and **yellowbelly**.

Wivenhoe was completed in 1983. More than one million native fish have been liberated there, and the lake regularly produces 4kg-plus trophy bass (May–September) and big, pot-bellied yellowbelly (September–May).

Lungfish were translocated to the Brisbane River in 1890 when it was thought they were on the verge of extinction. These creatures thrived in the river, and continue to do so in the dam. Anglers sometimes catch them, but lungfish are fully protected and must be released.

In recent years **tilapia**, **banded grunter** and **redclaw crayfish** have found their way into Wivenhoe. Tilapia, a declared noxious fish that rates as the Queensland carp, has become popular with anglers due to its table qualities.

Redclaw, originally native to the Gulf of Carpenteria drainage system, have multiplied to form the basis of a recreational activity that sees many folk expending more time and effort pursuing them than fish. Locals will argue that redclaw is the most scrumptious of all freshwater crayfish.

Anglers who prefer to fish rivers will find the narrow confines of the Brisbane River below Wivenhoe a viable alternative. Boat access is at Twin Bridges, about 6km below the dam. In stark contrast to Wivenhoe, the river is almost claustrophobic, flanked by bottlebrush, casuarina and melaleuca trees. Beneath the surface, small fish and crustaceans provide food for the likes of **Mary River cod** (Murray cod), Australian bass, yellowbelly and tilapia.

The fishing technique on the lake is mainly trolling, working lures near weed beds, rocky points

The long jetty at Urangan is a favourite fishing destination for locals and visitor alike who catch a range of fish from whiting to tuna

and drop-offs. River fishing is about working snags, drifting slowly while casting lures towards bank indentations, beneath low-lying, shady overhanging trees and to fallen trees. Start the retrieve as soon as the lure starts to disappear. If you let the lure sink too far you will hook on a snag and may lose the lure.

Boating on Wivenhoe is restricted to electric, paddle or sail. If you are running an electric, it pays to take extra deep-cycle batteries to ensure that you make it home. During the summer, the afternoon south-easterly breeze can turn the surface of the lake into white caps.

Boating access is restricted from daylight till dark, with all access gates locked at night. A south-east Queensland water boat permit is required for all trailer boats. Popular fishing spots include those known as Platypus Cliffs, Hamon Cove, Tulungra Inlet and Billies Bay.

Methods for Mooloolaba and Lake Wivenhoe

TACKLE Baitcasting and threadline outfits, with the reels spooled with 6kg braid line, are popular for trolling and bait fishing. A 15kg monofilament leader is standard for bass, as they have gill cutters.

LURES Lure fishers casting at snags will find spinnerbait lures a better option than bibbed minnows, as the former are less likely to snag on a branch. Soft plastic lures are popular for bass, as are Jackals and metal Vibes.

BAIT Worms will account for the likes of yellowbelly, tilapia and even bass. Use a No. 10 to 2/0 medium shank hook. You can fish on the bottom with a running sinker rig, or else flip an unweighted bait into the snags, let it sink and wait for the strike.

3 HERVEY BAY AND SURROUNDS

HERVEY BAY

Hervey Bay is about 290km north of Brisbane. Take the National Hwy to Gympie, then drive on Route 57 to Maryborough, and on to Hervey Bay.

Tropical and temperate water-species, big game to surf – there isn't much that you cannot catch at Hervey Bay. And just to cap it off, much of the area is protected by the 123km long Fraser Island, the world's biggest sand island. The fishing is diverse and includes a mix of tropical and temperate species. Marlin, mackerel, tuna and giant trevally are some of the game fish that inhabit the region. But many anglers prefer to fish the beaches for tailor, the estuaries for flathead and the channel edges for whiting or squid.

ACCOMMODATION: All sorts of accommodation are available. On Fraser Island many anglers camp, others stay at Kingfisher Resort. On the mainland at Urangan the accommodation on offer covers all tastes.
For more information visit
www.discoverherveybay.com

Hervey Bay and Fraser Island are inseparably linked to each other and to fishing. Variety and quality of species is a true measure of a fishing destination and here you can catch **longtails (northern bluefin tuna)**,

The flats of Hervey Bay are home to large schools of golden trevally, like this one caught by Rod Mackenzie

mackerel tuna, **giant trevally**, **queenfish**, **threadfin salmon**, **sailfish** and **marlin**. Inshore reefs offer a fair selection of edible species, including **coral trout** and **emperor**, while the estuaries have **mangrove jack** and **barramundi**.

Hervey Bay is the name of the township and also the bay between Fraser Island and the mainland. A favourite land-based destination in town is Urangan Pier, which fishes well for **whiting**, particularly in the peak spring period. Baitfish – **hardyhead**s, **garfish** and **herring** – school under the pier, attracting pelagic fish including mackerel and tuna. The outer end of the pier is in deep water and anglers bait up with live herring to fish for queenfish, **school** and **Spanish mackerel**, **trevally** and tuna. Whiting anglers use local bloodworms and nippers.

Land-based anglers can also catch whiting and **bream** from Shelly Beach, the Urangan Steps, just west of the Urangan Pier, and the Great Sandy Strait Marina walls.

Boating anglers are well catered for with protected boat-launching facilities in the Great Sandy Strait Marina, at the end of Boat Harbour Dr in Urangan. It is a boating angler's paradise with large and small islands, tidal flats, mangrove creeks, reefs and sand flats. Care needs to be taken, especially at low tide, as the northern entrance to Great Sandy Strait has shallows, reefs and sandbanks. Strong winds can cause dangerous sea conditions, especially if the wind is against the strong tidal flow.

The first island out from the marina is tiny Round Island, between Urangan and Big Woody Island. The reef here produces **parrotfish**, **snapper**, **squid** and **sweetlip**. On the east side of the island, anglers catch whiting, bream and **flathead**.

Big Woody Island is popular and it has many reefs on the north-east side, including one called The Graves that can produce snapper, sweetlip, **morwong**, **mulloway** and parrotfish.

About 2km to the east of The Graves is an artificial reef. Pelagic species including northern bluefin and mackerel tuna, mackerel and trevally are caught along and outside the reefs.

Between Big Woody Island and Fraser Island is Little Woody Island, with reefs on its western side, a rocky area at its northern tip and a long reef vein to the south. The eastern side, which is made up of mangrove and sandbanks, attracts flathead, trevally, whiting and bream. A number of holes and ledges around Little Woody Island are also worth exploring.

Little Woody offers exciting sight-fishing for anglers working lures or flies. On my first visit I waded with local fly-fishing guide Sid Boshammer on a broad sand flat at the northern end of the island. Our quarry was **golden trevally**. These fish can be seen on the flats with their tails protruding out of the water as they suck crabs and invertebrates from the sand.

The wind was gusting to 20-knots from the south-east, making sight-fishing and fly-casting difficult. Sid said I would have a maximum of two back casts to get a shot in. Anymore and the fish would move on.

When a trevally school came towards us, I fired away a cast to place the fly in front of the feeding fish, and then they were gone. One minute the school was 50m in front and in seconds it reappeared 100m behind. It was fast, frustrating and exhilarating.

My fly shot was lucky. The 300m screaming run and 43-minute fight that ensued was extraordinary. We ended up catching a few golden trevally to about 8kg.

There are many **sharks** in these waters. We were about 300m or so away from the boat when I saw a shark gliding through the water along the edge of the drop-off that marked the line between the shallow sand flats and the deeper channel. It was a dark, heavyset creature a bit more than 2m long and it followed us as we moved along. Spooky.

There are also stingrays everywhere. They range from pancake size through to king-size blankets. As I walked I slid my feet on the bottom to scare them away. Touching a ray's flap with a foot will make it take flight; stand on it and the barbs in its tail are likely to react.

Golden trevally have large lips used for sucking nippers

At the northern end of Hervey Bay, past Fraser Island, is an area called the Breaksea Spit. On my first visit I went out with local guide Geoff Taylor on his 11.5m fly-bridge catamaran. Geoff runs live-aboard charters, which is just as well as it takes more than eight hours steaming from Urangan to get to Breaksea Spit. However, the sailing time is worth it. We sailed north past the Pelican Bank and Moon Point, across Platypus Bay to Rooney Point at the north-west end of Fraser Island, where we camped before taking the final leg.

The Breaksea Spit is a vast expanse of sandbars, reefs, gutters and seamounts. It is a junction for tropical and temperate currents. Combined with an undulating seabed and wind, these conditions create a recipe for turbulence, and a predator's paradise.

The spit attracts such a variety of species that you never really know what you will catch. There are at least four species of **trevally – giant**, **golden**, **white** and **turrum**. It's the same with tuna and mackerel, while marlin, **sailfish** and **dolphinfish** are also caught. On the bottom you can pull snapper and then hook something more exotic like a big **mangrove jack**, **strawberry cod**, **coronation trout**, **Moses perch**, **blue** and **brown Maori cod**, **Venus tusk fish**, **gold spot wrasse**, **saddlebacks** or **jobfish**. Other likely captures include **bonefish**, **barracuda**, **amberjack** and **cobia**, not to mention just about every shark known to inhabit east coast waters.

On calm sunny days, the water can be so clear it is like peering into an aquarium as you look through the water column and watch fish taking bait. Use a berley trail and drift and you will be amazed at the quantity of fish that rise to the feed.

On the downside is the fickle weather. Even a little wind can make Breaksea Spit dangerous. On a wild day it can be gut-wrenching. Those same sandbars, reefs and strong currents that are

These anglers are hunting for beach worms on Fraser Island

attractive to the fish create conditions that make the seas stand up dangerously.

When the weather cuts up rough, there are better options inside the bar, like the wreck of the 84m *Chin-Chow* that sank near Fraser Island on her maiden voyage early last century. It's a known GT (giant trevally), amberjack and cobia haunt that holds **whaler sharks** to about 2.5m and attracts schools of mackerel tuna and bluefin. Or come back to Rooney Point, well known for producing marlin, sailfish, mackerel and tuna.

The style of fishing is anything from fly- and gamefishing to bottom bouncing. On one trip we caught turrum, giant trevally and Spanish mackerel to 20kg on lure and fly, but it was the bottom bouncing that was the most exciting. We hooked a couple of dozen big fish, but only the large skull and lips of one solitary fish was landed. Sharks accounted for a few, but most of the fish were simply too big and they dragged our lines through reef and rock.

FRASER ISLAND

The only vehicles allowed on Fraser Island are 4WD vehicles. Vehicle barges operate daily from Hervey Bay to Moon Point, Wangoolba Creek or Kingfisher Bay. Alternatively you can catch a barge from Rainbow Beach (Inskip Point) to Hook Point on the southern tip of the island. Permits are required. Contact Queensland Parks & Wildlife Services: www.nprsr.qld.gov.au/parks/fraser/about.html.

ACCOMMODATION: Staying on Fraser Island, the visitor has the option of camping, beach house or lodge accommodation.
For more information visit www.visitfrasercoast.com/destinations/fraser-island/accommodation/

The world's biggest sand island, Fraser Island is 123km long and has become Australia's most famous beach-fishing venue, albeit one that also offers rock- and offshore fishing. The list of inshore species includes **tailor**, **sharks**, **whiting**, **flathead**, **swallowtail**, **trevally** and **bream**. Offshore anglers can also expect to add **marlin**, **cobia**, **sailfish**, **coral trout**, **red emperor** and **snapper** to this list.

Most beach fishing takes place on the eastern or ocean side of the island along the northern half of Seventy Five Mile Beach. From July to November, these beaches are best known for their tailor fishing, while for most of the year anglers can expect to hook bream, whiting, **dart**, **mulloway** and flathead. The best fishing is in gutters with north and south entrances, and the best gutters are generally found from the *Maheno* shipwreck to Indian Head at the north end of Seventy Five Mile Beach. Rock fishers do well at Poyungan Rocks, Yidney Rocks, Indian Head, Middle Rocks, Waddy Point and Ngkala Rocks.

Sandy Cape, at the far northern end of Fraser Island, fishes well for whiting, bream, flathead, dart and tailor. A large part of the north end of Fraser Island has been closed to 4WD traffic, as part of the land management of the Great Sandy National Park. The restricted area is from Wathumba Creek on the west coast around to the Sandy Cape lighthouse.

Surf fishers soak up the warm afterglow of the sun during a late afternoon session on Fraser Island

Boats can be launched at Waddy Point on the east side, where there is a large gutter that makes launching and retrieving a boat easier and safer. Most boating anglers head offshore looking for reefs or the Gardner Bank, which is about 20km further east.

On the western side of the island, the main areas are Wathumba, Coongul and Moon creeks. There is no surf on this side of the island. Many creeks cross the beaches facing the Great Sandy Strait but there is limited vehicle access, and 4WD vehicles are banned from passing further north than Wathumba Creek. There are good campsites beside Wathumba, Awinya and Bowarrady creeks and plenty of **yabby** patches for bait.

Hawks Nest Beach, on the north side of Moon Point, fishes well for **sand whiting**. Pelican Bank is worth casting surface poppers around for **giant** and **golden trevally**. If you go ashore, keep an eye on the tide. Boat anglers fish reefs and banks including Pinnacle, Moon Ledge and Sammys around Moon Point for **sweetlip**, **parrotfish** and snapper, the latter best where there is granulated, dark-brown rock known locally as 'coffee rock'.

Other places to wet a line include Moon Creek, Bridge Creek, Bridge Gutter and Christies Gutter, where you can expect to catch whiting, bream and flathead.

East of Little Woody Island, some of the best land-based fishing spots are Bogimbah Creek, which has **mangrove jack** and **cod**, and Urang Creek, with whiting, bream and flathead.

Kingfisher Bay Resort and Village, south of Big Woody Island, offers good fishing for bream, whiting, trevally, flathead and sometimes **barramundi** and **golden trevally** around the jetty. South of the resort is Mackenzie's jetty, which also provides good fishing for whiting, bream, flathead and tailor.

Methods for Hervey Bay and Fraser Island

TACKLE For bottom bouncing or lure trolling use 15kg outfits. On the reefs, 24kg leader is the minimum, and if you are trolling for mackerel or wahoo, use piano-wire leader. Threadline reels are the best option for light-tackle spinning and most anglers use gamefishing outfits for trolling and sometimes bottom bouncing. This is a popular area for blue-water fly-fishing, and 10–14kg weight outfits with sinking lines are suited to most species.

Beach anglers chasing tailor and similar species prefer the Alvey sidecast reel with a 5m rod.

LURES Beach anglers do well working small lures for flathead, and you will also find plenty of options for lures on the west side of Fraser Island in the creeks. Take plenty of surface poppers, big minnows and skirted jigs. Small baitfish patterns such as Lazer lures do well on mackerel tuna; and have plenty of soft plastic lures at hand.

Fly-fishers work big flies including Deep Clouser minnows, 3Ds and wide-bodied and baitfish patterns.

RIGS Bottom-bouncing rigs are fixed sinker and leader paternoster style – common everywhere. Hook size is about 6/0 for reef fishing. The size of the hook is determined by the size of the bait. Most Queensland anglers working whole fish or fillets for bait tend not to thread their hooks through the bait, but instead hook it through one end of the bait. Beach anglers chasing tailor use ganged hooks and rig up whole pilchards, which they cast and retrieve. For other species such as whiting, a running sinker rig with a hook size No. 4–2/0 is suitable.

BAIT On the beaches, worms and pipis can be caught for bait. The western side of Fraser Island also has yabby or nipper banks, which can be pumped.

If you are bottom bouncing offshore, top baits include squid and fish fillets.

LAKE LENTHALL

Lake Lenthall or Lenthalls Dam – it goes by both names – is Brisbane's closest barramundi lake, about 40 minutes from Hervey Bay. To get there from Brisbane, take the turnoff west from the Bruce Hwy about 20km north of Maryborough.

A Stocked Impoundment Permit is required to fish here, as with many Queensland impoundments (*see* page 322). Stocked Impoundment Permits are available at the roadhouse on the Bruce Hwy a few kilometres north of the turnoff, or fishing supply stores in Hervey Bay and Maryborough.

Allan Greig with a mangrove jack caught on an offshore reef

ACCOMMODATION: There is no accommodation at the lake but surrounding towns like Maryborough and Hervey Bay are geared up for tourism and cater to all needs.

For more information visit www.discoverherveybay.com

Anyone who has read about the **barramundi** boom in Queensland's impoundments will know about lakes like Awoonga, Faust and Callide. But there are many, less known waters that also offer excellent fishing, and one of these is Lake Lenthall, situated at the head of the Burrum River. Lenthall is a relatively shallow, picturesque 400ha dammed water.

Each year, the Fraser Coast Fish Stocking Association, with financial assistance from Wide Bay Water Corporation, stocks Lenthall with fingerlings. Since 1984, more than 450,000 fish have been released, including barramundi, **Australian bass**, **yellowbelly (golden perch)**, **silver perch** and a few **saratoga**. The stocking of saratoga was minimal and has ceased due to environmental concerns. Barramundi stocking has proven excellent with fish growing up to 12kg in three years.

The dam is proving so productive that Hervey Bay fishing guide Paul Dolan has turned fly-fishing for barramundi into a specialty and said he rarely misses.

There's a picnic area with barbecue facilities, a shelter with tables, a public toilet and a boat ramp. You'll find that a boat is a necessity because rainforest grows right to the water's edge, where there is a fringe of lily pads.

The dam is the main water source providing drinking water for Hervey Bay, so to ensure the water is not contaminated by oil, fuel or soil from bank erosion caused by boat wash, there is a speed limit of 4-knots and motor size is limited to six-horsepower.

This white trevally was caught fly-fishing on the Breaksea Spit

Methods for Lake Lenthall

TACKLE Anglers chasing bass and perch tend to have 5–10kg baitcaster or threadline outfits for trolling and bait fishing. Bass have gill cutters so a 15kg monofilament leader is standard.

In recent times, enough anglers have been burned by big barramundi that there is a swing to heavier, 15kg outfits with 24kg breaking strain leaders.

Fly-fishers have started to visit the lake more regularly and some excellent captures of barramundi to 15kg have been taken on ten- and 12-weight outfits.

BAIT Worms will account for the likes of yellowbelly, silver perch and even bass. Use No. 10–2/0 medium-shank hooks. You can fish on the bottom with a running sinker rig, or else flip an unweighted bait into the snags, let it sink and wait for the hot strike.

LURES The fishing technique with lures is mainly trolling or casting near weed beds, rocky points and drop-offs. Fly-fishers tend to work the same areas using intermediate lines for barramundi.

For bass and perch, Halco Nightwalkers work well in the predawn light. During the day, bibbed minnow lures and spinnerbait lures are a better option. Soft plastic lures are also popular. Large bibbed minnows will work on barramundi. Popular lures include Halco Scorpion, Barra Classic, B-52 and Predatek Sand Viper.

The top fly used in Lake Lenthall is the DK Dancer, developed by Paul Dolan and Lionel Kemp. Other productive flies for bass and barramundi include the Whistler, Clouser and Deceiver.

4 BASS TO BARRA TRAIL

The Bass to Barra Trail is a link-up of seven impoundments in the Gladstone, Bundaberg and Capricorn Regions, north of Brisbane. It commences in the south at Lake Barambah, about 15km south-east of Murgon, and finishes at Lake Callide, about 20km east of Bileola.

If you had to spend the rest of your days travelling and fishing the same route and the same waterways then the Bass to Barra Trail waters should be at the top of your list. These lakes offer some of the most consistent quality fishing with easy access available in this country. Fish you are likely to catch include barramundi, bass, saratoga and yellowbelly.

ACCOMMODATION: Most of the lakes have camping grounds in some form while others, like Lake Awoonga, are close enough to major towns to offer even more comfort whether it be B&B or classy motel with full restaurant facilities.

For more information visit www.queenslandholidays.com.au

The angling dollar is an ever-expanding business in Queensland. The closure of much of the Great Barrier Reef to fishing has been counter-balanced by the success of impoundment fish stocking in creating opportunities for regional tourism, in particular stocked lakes.

Whenever bacon sizzles in the pan and the aroma wafts through the air, I am reminded of morning campfires on riverbanks. Bacon is the smell of a fishing trip, and it was no different that morning in New Zealand Bay on Lake Awoonga. It was dawn and my fishing companion Bob Hart was doing one of his favourite things off the water – cooking. Only this time he was on the water, in a houseboat that was moored to a stump on the shore of the lake. Outside the cabin, the lake was calm and grey, the sun still hidden behind low-lying clouds that shrouded the ranges of Castle Tower National Park.

We were in need of a serious breakfast. During the night, Bob and I had left the houseboat and fished a small, shallow bay less than 200m away. It was a hot **barramundi** session. The fish were averaging about 8kg, small by Awoonga's lofty standards but there was the occasional lure-tossing monster thrown into the mix.

Our *modus operandi* was to drift and cast our minnow lures inshore to the edge of the weed bank. The lure was allowed to sit for a few seconds, the slack line was taken up and then the lure was retrieved slowly in a stop, start motion. A hook-up was a spectacular, adrenalin-pumping event. Wind slowly and stop, then twitch the lure with the rod and wind some more. Sometimes we only managed to crank the handle half a turn before, wham! The rod would bow, line would pour off the reel and we were hooked up. When these barra take lures in the shallows they go ballistic, blasting out of the water like a Polaris missile. Given the benefit of hindsight, we should have anchored the houseboat in the bay and fished from it, rather than work around the shoreline in the tender.

This was my first houseboat experience, and one that made a lot of sense given the amount of boating traffic on the lake nowadays. Awoonga is so popular that there are long queues at the main boat ramp at Ironbark Gully and some anglers prefer to leave their boats in the water in a sheltered bay below the caravan park.

A houseboat is a good option to avoid the queues; it can save a 30-minute drive to and from Gladstone each day as well. Moreover, there are countless bays and inlets around the lake where a houseboat can be parked in total isolation. Houseboats are a common sight on big waters like the Murray River or Lake Eildon in Victoria, and most anglers hire them to use as a base, preferring to fish from smaller boats or tenders. Even though houseboats are not regarded as fishing boats, there are enough tales of **trout** and **Murray cod** being caught on lures trolled behind these boats to suggest that the fish don't know this. Another advantage is that when you tie up for the night you can sit on the rear deck with your lines in the water.

Everything you want is available in your home on water: cooking, bed, shower, toilet and importantly, shelter. Anyone looking to hire a houseboat should make certain to have two important items. One is a cook, (someone like Bob is ideal) the other a small boat or tender to fish from. Oh, and remember the bacon.

Houseboat fishing is just one option that has come out of an imaginative marketing exercise that saw tourism people in the Gladstone, Bundaberg and Capricorn regions join forces and develop a concept for anglers called the 'Bass to Barra Trail'. The trail promotion aimed to lure anglers who would otherwise travel several thousand kilometres further to Australia's tropical north.

An ace drawcard is that the barramundi in these southern Queensland impoundments waters are consistently bigger than those caught in the wilds of northern Australia. In Lake Awoonga for instance, the average size of the barramundi ranges from 10kg to a whopping 15kg. The biggest barra caught in this lake has weighed in at more than 29kg. At Callide Dam, the barra average nearer 10kg, but there are still a few monsters left over from early stockings that have been known to spool anglers. In other waters, fish like **bass** attain weights in excess of 3kg.

The Bass to Barra Trail incorporates seven impoundments and, between them, these waters are stocked with a Who's Who of tropical freshwater sport fish including **Australian bass**, **sooty grunter**, **golden perch (yellowbelly)**, **saratoga**, **mangrove jack** and **barramundi**.

Don't be confused by different names for the same waters. Lake Monduran is also called Fred Haig Dam, but the latter name refers to the dam structure, not the waterway. It's the same at Bjelke Petersen Dam, which is actually Lake Barambah. Then there is the town of Biloela in the Banana Shire in Queensland, about halfway between Gladstone and Rockhampton, and the location of Lake Callide. The Banana Shire is named after a famous bullock, not a bent fruit, and Biloela is pronounced bilo-wela.

BJELKE PETERSEN DAM

Also known as Lake Barambah, this 2150ha water is about 15km south-east of Murgon. Bjelke Petersen is regarded as one of the state's best big bass waters, but also has yellowbelly, silver perch and saratoga. It is relatively shallow for a dam, the shoreline is fringed with weed beds and the back of the dam features snags. A Stocked Impoundment Permit is required (*see* page 322).

ACCOMMODATION: Accommodation is available at Murgon, while at the lake camping is permitted at Yallakool Tourist Park. The dam has two boat ramps, one near the dam wall and another below the camping area.

LAKE BOONDOOMA

Situated to the west of Bjelke Petersen Dam and on the Boyne River, the lake is about 15km from Proston. Since its construction in 1983, a variety of species have been stocked here including **Australian bass**, **silver perch**, **yellowbelly**, **saratoga**, **Murray cod** and **barramundi**. **Bass**, **silver perch** and **yellowbelly** dominate the angling, with **barramundi** and **Murray cod** stocking proving unsuccessful.

A Stocked Impoundment Permit (*see* page 322), available at the campground, is required to fish here. Fishing is banned in the Boyne River from 200m upstream to 400m downstream of the Boondooma Dam wall. The Lake Boondooma Camping and Recreation Area is a modern camping ground with self-contained cabins and a caravan park on the lake foreshore. A boat ramp facility is located in the recreation area, along with a hire boat business.

The shining centerpiece of the Bass to Barra Trail: the barramundi; this fish is being held by Lake Awoonga fishing guide, John Mitchell

WURUMA DAM

Situated 35km north of Eidsvold, this 1775ha little known water contains **Australian bass**, **barramundi**, **saratoga**, **silver perch**, **yellowbelly** and **sleepy cod**. A Stocked Impoundment Permit is required (*see* page 322). There is a large bush campground north of the dam wall with basic facilities including cold showers, toilets and picnic shelters. There is a single lane concrete ramp and the only boating restrictions are to stay at least 200m away from the dam wall.

LAKE MONDURAN

Monduran is situated near Gin Gin, a four-hour drive north of Brisbane on the Bruce Hwy. It's a vast waterway that at first glance appears narrow. However, it has a surface area of 5342ha and a holding capacity of 585,900ML of water, which is about 1.6 times that of Sydney Harbour. Boat anglers can drive upstream for 35km, and the lake has more than 384km of shoreline.

A Stocked Impoundment Permit is required (*see* page 322).

ACCOMMODATION: The barra tourism boom has seen the lake facilities expand rapidly and it now has an approximately 4ha modern campground with powered sites with all amenities including hot showers, camp kitchens, laundries, stainless steel fish cleaning table, barbecues, and fireplaces. Moreover, if camping isn't your go, there are air-conditioned, self-contained cabins, including one disabled-friendly unit. The cabins sit on a hill overlooking the lake and have large decks out the front so you can sit back and enjoy the view. Another option is a three bedroom self-contained holiday house.

Most importantly, all the accommodation options are within 500m of one of the two boat ramps and basic supplies including ice, gas, tackle, boat hire, fishing permits and cold drinks are available. The lake has no motor restrictions on it and is open to fishing 24-hours a day, while the maximum length of stay in any one period is three months.
For more information visit
www.lakem.com.au

Above: Dawn on Lake Awoonga
Below: Catfish are a problem in some of the Bass to Barra Trail lakes

Until December 2010, the International Game Fishing Association all tackle world record for **barramundi** was 37.85kg (83lb 7oz), caught by David Powell in September 1999, while fishing Lake Tinarro in North Queensland. That record was smashed on 12 December 2010 at Lake Monduran in southern Queensland by Denis Harrold who caught a barramundi that weighed 44.64kg (98lb 6oz). The fish was 135cm long and had a girth to rival a porker, a whopping 107cm. What's more, Denis caught his trophy while fishing from a kayak. Those are staggering weights for barramundi, a size unheard of in the wild rivers of the Top End.

The fishing attracts most visitors to the lake and this is due to the success of the barramundi and **bass** stocking. Barra over the magic metre mark and weighing about 18kg are being caught, and the average size of the barra in Monduran is 90cm or about 10kg. As for the bass, they are up to 50cm and there are plenty of them.

An area of the lake called 'Bass Strait' is a favourite. The Strait is a north–south running ledge or drop-off. It is west of the main boat ramp and is marked by a couple of trees protruding out of the water.

CANIA DAM

Located close to Monto, Cania Dam holds yellowbelly, silver perch and Australian bass to 3kg. Cania's real drawcard is the **saratoga**. Initially stocked with only 200 individuals, the saratoga have bred to a population where they are quite easily targeted and caught.

The lake features postcard surroundings of sandstone escarpments and cliff faces, and an abundance of wildlife. A dual lane boat ramp, between the dam wall and the spillway at the southern end of the dam can be used even when the lake is down to half. When water levels are lower than this, many anglers drive down a track toward the dam wall and launch. There are no boating restrictions at Cania Dam but you will require a Stocked Impoundment Permit (*see* page 322).

LAKE AWOONGA

The jewel in the crown of the Bass to Barra Trail, Lake Awoonga is Queensland's premier barramundi impoundment. Situated just 28km south of Gladstone, and just 6km off the Bruce Hwy, it is also the only water that does not require anglers to buy a Stocked Impoundment Permit.

ACCOMMODATION: Facilities include cabins and powered sites, camping, licensed restaurant, kiosk, picnic facilities, tackle, hire boats and houseboats for hire. The main boat ramp is at Ironbark Gully.
For more information visit
www.lakeawoonga.net.au
www.gladstoneregion.info/accommodation

Clean waters, the result of a largely undisturbed watershed, contains **barramundi**, **mangrove jack**, **forktail catfish**, **redclaw**, **sooty grunter**, **saratoga**, **sleepy cod**, **golden**, **mullet**, **bream**, and **silver perch**.

It is a truly magnificent stretch of water – 5000ha of lake surrounded by bush, featuring rivers and feeder streams set against the backdrop of Castle Tower National Park. The lake serves the domestic, industrial and recreational needs of the Gladstone region and features extensive and beautifully maintained facilities.

Unlike many barramundi waters, there is no closed season for barramundi, although from 1 November to 1 February there is a bag limit of one **barra** in possession. Minimum size limits of 58cm apply year round and the bag limit for the remainder of the year is five, although only one fish over 120cm is allowed.

Stocking in the lake began in January 1996 and since then millions of barramundi supplement by **sea mullet**, **yellowfin bream**, mangrove jack and even **saratoga** have been liberated. Barramundi achieve exceptional growth rates in this waterway. The fish are about 50mm long when liberated, but grow at an astonishing 3kg a year. Legal size for **barra** is 58cm; in Awoonga, this translates to a fish between 12 and 14 months old. An average Awoonga barra is about 94–96cm long and weighs about 15–16kg.

I have visited Awoonga several times and fished with various anglers including local ranger Gary Wode, fish breeder Andrew Hamilton, houseboat operator Ross Peace and fishing guides Rod Harrison

Steve Cooper with a good 15kg barramundi caught in Lake Awoonga

and John Mitchell. Each angler had a different perspective on how and where to hook barra.

On my first visit, the barra were working best in the evenings, feeding in about a metre of water among the light timber lining the many coves and bays along the southern shore. On other visits, the fish have been hanging deep, working the shallow grass area at the back of the lake or attacking baitfish in New Zealand Bay. I have cast and trolled lures and know that fly-fishers also do well. In fact, it doesn't seem to matter that much how you fish, just so long as your lure or bait is in the water.

LAKE CALLIDE

Built on upper Callide Creek, a Dawson River tributary 20km east of Biloela, this lake has a primary function of supplying cooling waters for the nearby coal burning power station that's part of the Boyne Island complex.

A Stocked Impoundment Permit is required (*see* page 322).

ACCOMMODATION: Many anglers camp around the lake, not always legally. There are caravan parks and motels in Biloela (pronounced BIL-O-WELA) so there is no excuse for this.

For more information visit www.outbacknow.com.au

Red claw are a delicacy and are caught in many southern lakes

Lake Callide has been stocked with **barramundi**, **saratoga**, **sleepy cod**, **yellowbelly** and **silver perch** and has become an outstanding barramundi fishery. Due to its consistency, anglers focus mostly around the perimeter of an aerator that has been installed as a measure against blue-green algae. The lake produces barramundi to 26kg and yellowbelly to 5.4kg. The lake also has a huge population of **redclaw** (the Queensland yabby) as well as species like sleepy cod, **dewfish** (**eel-tailed catfish**) and freshwater **long tom**. Forage species include **bony bream** and **stripey grunter**. The dam has excellent facilities including toilet block, picnic tables, barbecues and tap water. When I was at Callide, boats were being launched from the southern shore, a steep rocky ramp along the western shore being out of favour with boaters.

I fished the lake with local angler Norm Crouch. We didn't catch any big barramundi but we did manage to hook a few oversize yellowbelly. The lake is a year-round fishery, and Norm says: 'Barramundi bite best during the warmer months of the year from late September to early April and yellowbelly fill the void during the colder months.'

Unlike most waters, this one seems to lack names for its bays and points. Most anglers use their depth sounders to find rock and channels, like the old creek bed that runs along the southern shore. Top spots include the bay to the east of the disused quarry on the southern shore, and another bay directly across the lake from the quarry. Structure such as old stands of timber is scarce, the best of it is found at the back of the lake where the creek runs in. An aerator pipe running into the lake from the power station is a major fish attractor, but there is a no-fish zone around the aerator. Many anglers fish the lake at night, and you don't have to be Einstein to know where many of the boats will be found.

Methods for Bass to Barra Trail

TACKLE The style of fishing is up to the individual. Fishing magazines generally

Small dogtooth tuna caught trolling near Saumarez Reefs

promote lure fishing in Queensland lakes and impoundments, giving little credence to bait. However, the reality is that bait fishing, especially for yellowbelly, and to a lesser extent barra, is alive and well in Queensland.

A problem with using different outfits for different fish in this water is that you might not hook what you expect. With this in mind you should consider fishing heavy for everything. After all, it is not much fun fishing for yellowbelly with a 3kg outfit and hooking a 25kg barramundi.

Anglers fishing for barra with lures prefer baitcaster outfits. Bait anglers tend to lean towards threadline outfits as these give the option of casting small lures and lightweight baits. Recommended line is 15kg breaking strain braid for both species. If you are specifically after barra, use a hardwearing 24kg monofilament leader, for bass 8kg leader will suffice.

BAIT Top baits include live shrimp for yellowbelly; stripey grunter and **catfish** will attract barra. Hook size is controlled by bait size. When bait fishing with shrimp, use a hook size about No. 2, medium shank and keep the bait off the bottom. A 6/0–7/0 straight shank hook set under a float at about 2m deep is the preferred rig for live baiting for barramundi.

LURES Trolling lures is popular but some of these lakes offer areas that are ideal for spinning from shore. Some effective barra lures include Gold Bombers; B-52s, Sand Vipers, Halco Poltergeists, Scorpions and Lazer Pros. Soft plastic lures are also popular. As for the **bass**, trolling small, bibbed minnow lures such as the Viper, or alternatively casting soft plastic lures or Vibes into the sunken timber while on the drift seems to work best. Spinnerbaits work well when cast into the snags and retrieved slowly.

5 GLADSTONE TO MACKAY

ACCOMMODATION: Every type of accommodation is on offer, including caravan parks, camping, hotel and motel.
For more information visit www.queenslandholidays.com.au

SAUMAREZ REEFS

Gladstone is home to a fleet of long-range charter boats. Several specialise in fishing and diving expeditions to remote areas of the Coral Sea.

I travelled out of Gladstone on a fishing and diving trip on the *Kanimbla,* which is about 30m long and weighs 60 tonnes. It has a cruising speed of 10-knots. There is above- and below-deck accommodation, a cook and, some would say best of all, beer on tap.

Four lines were trailing lures from the stern of the *Kanimbla.* We were steaming along at 9-knots, 350km north-east of Gladstone.

The fishing was hot, the boat was rolling and its stereo system was blaring Black Sabbath.

On board were 14 Americans, mainly from Alaska or with close ties to Alaskan tour leader Russell Knight, an Anchorage-based taxidermist. Our destination was a 48km strip of coral and rock called Saumarez Reefs.

The Dawson River is well known for its saratoga

We'd left port at about noon the previous day and arrived at about 9am, but nobody was in a hurry to drop the anchor. The 15- and 24kg outfits were trolling lures, mainly big-skirted jigs, and Halco Tremblers. The action had been non-stop for over an hour with **yellowfin tuna** to about 17kg, **wahoo**, **barracuda** and **jobfish**.

With the reef in sight, the *Kanimbla's* skipper Bruce Stobo started circling a seamount inside the reef. The starboard outer rod doubled over and line was melting off the reel as Idaho diamond dealer, Dan Clark, stepped in for his turn. This fish was bigger than anything hooked so far that morning – including the 15kg remains of a wahoo attacked by an oceanic **whaler shark**. Dan worked hard and the sweat poured off him as the big **dogtooth tuna** made long, deep supercharged dives.

The battle raged for 10 minutes on the 15kg game gear before the tuna finally breached the surface, belly up. A fish of about 40kg, it rolled slightly and the treble hooks fell out. That's fishing.

Other than trolling when on the move, fishing was via twin-hulled 4.2m dories stored on the top deck. All of the small boats were equipped with full safety equipment plus radios to stay in contact with the mother ship. Each day the dories would head out to fish, inside or outside the reef depending on the weather. There was lure trolling for tuna and **mackerel**, saltwater fly-fishing for tuna and **trevally**, and bottom bouncing for the likes of **red emperor**, **coral trout** and **sweetlip**. Restrictions were simple: be back at the boat at the designated times for lunch and tea.

There was no shortage of fish, and the fishing wasn't restricted to daylight. At night, after the evening meal, there were **sharks** to be caught, attracted to the boat by the fish-cleaning. The biggest sharks were never landed. Carolyn Ray fought a monster for about an hour only to have the hook pull. Or so we thought. When she wound her line in, there was a whaler shark of about 20kg on the end, its body savaged by teeth marks. We surmised that the small shark had taken her bait, was subsequently swallowed by a bigger shark, and somewhere along the way she had pulled the smaller shark out of the bigger one.

The *Kanimbla* made regular shifts along the reef to offer a diversity of options. On every leg, the lures were out. The water was warm, cobalt blue and covered with shearwaters chasing schools of pelagic fish like tuna. **Sailfish** and **marlin** followed the lures and either failed to hook-up or simply turned away. Whaler sharks were less discerning, attacking lures regardless of whether they had a fish on the end.

Long-range charter fishing is a lot of fun. You get to fish remote waters that don't have the same fishing pressures of inshore waters. If you get the opportunity to go, take it.

DAWSON RIVER

Moura is a two-hour drive west of Gladstone. Better known for its prime cattle production and huge coalmines, the township and the nearby Dawson River is not exactly number one on most people's list of top fishing spots.

The Dawson River at Moura is more like an extended lake. The river has been dammed, causing the water to back up, flooding forests that once marked the course of the riverbank. At first sight it looks a lot like some of the Victorian swamps that were turned into lakes. A maze of dead eucalypts provides cover for **barramundi**, **yellowbelly** and **saratoga**.

My guides for the day, Craig Nowland and Ken Blyton, were heavily involved in the local Apex

Fish Stocking Group, which raised funds to buy yellowbelly and barramundi. Craig said that in a four-year period the group had put in more than 61,000 barramundi and 50,000 yellowbelly.

'A two-year-old barramundi in this river is between 65- and 75cm long,' Ken said. 'The fish tend to grow to a certain size and then head downstream to the salt water. One of our barramundi was caught between Rockhampton and Gladstone, and several have been caught in the Fitzroy River at Rockhampton.'

What makes this fish-stocking exercise so enlightening is that the people are proud that the fish they buy and release are moving downstream to benefit other anglers. 'Fish-stocking groups on the Mackenzie River are doing the same thing,' Craig said. The Mackenzie River flows into the Dawson downstream of Moura, and the Dawson subsequently flows into the Fitzroy River, which passes through Rockhampton on its way to the sea.

I fished the river with Ken, while Craig and a few other group members took their boats off in different directions. Several anglers were using crawchies (yabbies) to fish for yellowbelly; others preferred lures. I'd come from Lake Awoonga, where I'd fished for barramundi, so I told Ken I wanted to fish for saratoga. He didn't think that would be a problem.

Saratoga is a territorial species and you can see them as they swim near the surface patrolling their beat. They are unusual in that they have an upturned mouth. The female fish incubate their eggs in their mouths until they hatch. For about three days after hatching, the fry flee to their mothers' mouths for safety.

Saratoga fishing requires finesse. If you spook a saratoga, move along the river to the next likely area. We were casting lures into calm, shaded areas where we could see the saratoga working. As we worked our way through the channel lined with dead trees, Ken would manoeuvre the boat from one shaded shore to another looking for saratoga. There were plenty, but they kept getting spooked. On about our third location we managed to pin the first fish, a handy little specimen that took a Halco Laser lure and then fought well with some out-of-water acrobatics.

The best lure presentation was an ultra-slow, jerky retrieve featuring long pauses and slight twitches. This was particularly effective near snags and weed banks as the fish often waited in ambush in these areas.

At 10.15am it was time to head for shore because, as Ken said, 'the ladies are coming down for morning tea'. Morning tea turned out to be fresh, hot scones and assorted cakes as well as the usual coffee and tea. Then we were back on water for a couple of hours for a look at the dam's fish trap before returning to shore for lunch. This was an even bigger spread of food and included some of the juiciest steaks and homemade sausages I've eaten. You cannot beat country hospitality.

Prawns are a favourite bait for barramundi in the Fitzroy River at Rockhampton

The cast net is used to catch baitfish and prawns in the Fitzroy River

FITZROY RIVER

Great fishing rivers flow through some of our best known cities: the Yarra in Melbourne, the Swan in Perth and the Derwent in Hobart, to name a few. One of the best city rivers I have come across is the Fitzroy, which runs through Rockhampton. Australia has very few waterways where you can catch metre-plus **barramundi** within casting range of a cappuccino machine. In terms of consistency in numbers and size, the Fitzroy is up with the best, and certainly better than most. Some Queensland friends tell me the Fitzroy consistently produces the biggest wild barramundi in Australia.

My first visit to the Fitzroy River took place early one October, just before the staging of the annual Rocky Barra Bounty, a tag-and-release barramundi fishing competition. The competition is based on the most metres of barramundi tagged, to ensure minimum impact on fish stocks.

I fished with a couple of local anglers, Mitch Lester and Neville Hewitt, who had each won the competition, or been involved in the winning teams. We fished downstream for about 10km, casting lures around rock bars, snags and even an old factory pump house, without success.

Later in the day, we came back near the city and it was here that the barramundi proved more cooperative, especially near the main road bridge close to the city centre, where fish to about 75cm were caught.

We were fishing our way upstream of the bridges, towards the saltwater barrage, when we spotted a chap floating in a large polystyrene packing box about the size required for a television set. He reached a small rock about 10m off the riverbank, stepped out of his polystyrene dinghy and proceeded to fish from the rock.

'Brave fellow,' Mitch observed. 'There are some mighty big crocs in this river. A few months back a croc attacked a racehorse that was being walked in the river.' We hung around for a photo opportunity, but none was forthcoming.

We cast lures and then tried live prawns, which were caught in cast nets. These nets are excellent when it comes to catching live baits such as small fish. The barramundi didn't like our lures as much as the fresh prawns. We worked the prawn baits near structures such as the bridges and rocks in the river and our catch was only limited by the number of prawns in the net.

Waterpark Creek is just half an hour out of Rockhampton and produces plenty of spectacular sport fish including threadfin salmon

Mitch and Neville fished as if we were in the competition, so everything was released. The practice came into vogue during the 1980s and has proven so popular that it has become a national pursuit.

The Rocky Barra Bounty started in 1998 to market Rockhampton as a fishing destination, and Rockhampton became the first city to adopt tag-and-release fishing for competitions. Participating anglers go to a compulsory briefing at the start of the event, where they are taught the correct procedures for catch and release. All entrants receive a fishing pack containing items for use during the competition, including line, lures and hooks, disposable camera, fish ruler, tagging equipment and data-logging forms. Captured fish must be photographed. The fish is then released back into the river and the catch phoned in. Points are awarded based on the combined length of fish caught and released. Kept fish do not count.

As well as promoting Rockhampton, the competition helps researchers compile research data. Concentrating the anglers for two days of fish-tagging provides them with valuable information that would otherwise take a long time to collect.

The final touch is that all profits from the event are used to restock the river with barramundi fingerlings, so the Fitzroy River will continue to provide excellent fishing in the future as well.

WATERPARK CREEK

Corio Bay is north of Rockhampton, at the mouth of Waterpark Creek in Byfield National Park. The highway turnoff is signposted, but it's a case of following well-worn tracks through the bush. My advice is to get some local directions before heading in. To download the map and for more information visit: **www.nprsr.qld.gov.au/parks/byfield/pdf/byfield-area-map.pdf**.

Unlike its namesake Corio Bay at Geelong in Victoria, best known for its snapper and King George whiting, Corio Bay in north Queensland produces **trevally**, **barramundi**, **threadfin salmon** and a host of other tropical species.

I visited there with local guide, Neville Brooks. It was a day of setting pots for **mud crabs**, working lures around mangrove runoffs and casting poppers to rocky headlands in search of roving predators like **mackerel**.

We launched Nev's 5m long punt, powered by a tiller-steer, 60-horsepower four-stroke engine, a few kilometres upstream. It was low tide when we put in and the trip downriver was slowed by the need to navigate shallow sandbars, and to make occasional stops while Nev ran into the mangroves to lay his pots for mud crabs.

Nev showed no fear of crocodiles as he walked along the exposed mud banks to place his pots in gullies that would fill as the tide rose. The pots, which have a piece of fish wired inside, have a long rope with a polystyrene float attached. The rope and float are tossed over the branches of a mangrove. Crocodiles love these floats and I have

The reefs offshore from Yeppoon can produce great results

seen many in the NT with tooth marks. But Nev was more concerned with hornet nests in the mangroves than crocodiles.

As we reached Corio Bay, Nev positioned the boat so we could cast bibbed minnows and soft plastic lures into snags and alongside rock bars, likely areas for barramundi to be waiting in ambush along the sheltered, mangrove-lined shore.

The water was rich with baitfish, the edges glittering with a shimmering mass of **herring**. There were turtles in one of the small coves, and **squid** were easy to catch on jigs. Several of the barramundi we lured refused to stay on the hooks, but we landed a few fish including **estuary cod**. Anglers who fish here regularly also seek out bread-and-butter species like **sand whiting**, **bream** and **grunter**, or the superfast threadfin salmon.

A change of tactics was called for and we began casting metal lures over a partly submerged reef. The fishing was consistent for **giant trevally** or GTs as they are called, but these were juveniles, not the big ones we wanted.

Nev beached the boat near the entrance so we could look over Byfield National Park. It was, he said, the long way to our next destination. Back in the boat, we headed out the mouth of the bay, turned north around a rocky headland and then steamed north for a few kilometres before arriving at an expanse of reef and rock called Corio Heads. This area produces sportfishing delights including **black mulloway**, big GTs, **queenfish**, **cobia** and mackerel.

We rigged up heavy threadline tackle with large surface poppers, and starting casting and retrieving. Popper fishing is great fun. It involves casting the lure and then winding fast to bring the popper to the surface, creating a splash across the water during the retrieve. Nev held the boat out from the wash of the rocks and we cast poppers into the gutters. Fish more than a metre long were here, judging by the dark shadows that followed the lures below the surface, but they weren't hungry enough to strike.

On our return to Corio Bay, Nev collected the crab pots. This time he didn't have to wander over muddy banks as the tide was up and the gullies had filled. The pots held a few mud crabs with nippers big enough to snip a man's thumb.

YEPPOON

Yeppoon, about a 30-minute drive north-east of Rockhampton, is the main port for visitors wanting to go to the Keppel Islands.

ACCOMMODATION: Visitors are catered for with all types of accommodation, from backpacker hostels and caravan parks, through to luxury hotel rooms. **For more information visit www.capricornholidays.com.au/destinations/yeppoon/accommodation**

In the harbour at Rosslyn Bay I met up with fourth-generation cattle producer Richard Wilson and

Red emperor and coral trout are just two of the species caught offshore from Yeppoon

boarded the *Keppeluna*, a 12m twin-hulled fly-bridge cruiser that seemed almost as wide as it was long. Richard had invested more than $40 million on the marina and infrastructure and used the *Keppeluna* for fishing charters, including live-aboard trips and social days. Today was a social day and Richard had a few friends on board, including local fishing specialist Graham Scott. It was 4.30am with a light nor-easterly as we headed out of the marina. Several hours and 88km later we made our first drop on a patch of reef about 50m below.

The first fish to come aboard was a giant **estuary cod** of 20kg. The weight rather than the fight in the fish made for a difficult landing. The cod had a swollen stomach and bulging eyes, a result of the expansion of gases in the swim bladder as it was pulled up from the bottom. Not all deep-water species are affected this way. This was soon followed by good numbers of **hussar**, some of which were despatched and used for bait.

Queenslanders working offshore reefs have a thing about red fish, and **red emperor** is at the top of the list when it comes to eating. It didn't take long before the first red emperor was caught. Queensland regulations put a minimum 55cm on red emperor and we averaged about one legal fish in three. All fish kept for the table must have one pectoral fin clipped, and brought back to port as whole fish.

Other species caught included **red-throated sweetlip** and **frying pan snapper**. The frying pan snapper has the head of a snapper, the tail of a bream and the first dorsal spine is more like a long whisker that extends most of the way along its back.

As soon as this reef system slowed, we moved to another mark, and then another. Sometimes we motored for more than 30 minutes to get to the next small rock jutting above the ocean floor.

That is how the fishing went for most of the day, interspersed with sightings of olive sea snakes, whales and dolphins, and feeds of Moreton Bay bugs and prawns.

On our return journey, our deckie Don, who has spent much of his working life on charter boats working offshore reefs, wanted to try an old shipwreck where birds were working baitfish. Some anglers dropped baits, but a few of us started jigging with large, chrome lures. The first fish on a lure was a **white trevally**, followed by **amberjack** to about 10kg and **mackerel tuna**. Meanwhile, the bait anglers were hooking emperor, sweetlip, hussar, **coral trout** and a **shark** of about 1.2m that tangled several lines.

Anyone deciding to head to Queensland should experience reef-fishing. Offshore reef-fishing charters are available in most ports from the Gold Coast to Cairns. The species vary as you go north. In southern Queensland, you are likely to hook snapper and pearl perch, but as the water warms further up the coast, the species change to tropical varieties.

SEAFORTH

Seaforth is about an hour's drive north of Mackay, depending on cane harvester traffic. The small seaside resort is remarkable in that it hasn't yet been overrun by developers, although that is changing according to my guide, Arthur Lovern.

ACCOMMODATION: Seaforth has a caravan park, but there is plenty of accommodation in the area. For more information visit www.mackayregion.com/accommodation

The good news is that fish are aplenty and you don't have to travel 20–30 miles offshore to find them. On this day, we fished a drop-off on the north-west corner of Low Island, reached within a half-hour run.

Arthur gave me a small popper to cast, and used the auxiliary electric motor to hold his 4.2m boat steady in the slight wind and chop. On the first cast, **queenfish** rose to the lure, busting the surface all around it but missing the treble hooks. This went on for half a dozen casts until one of the silver missiles latched onto the lure in a spectacular strike that saw the fish doing somersaults about a metre out of the water. Queenfish are a great sport fish, performing with long, fast runs and plenty of jumps. Once one fish is hooked, the rest of the school hang around, giving other anglers an opportunity to cast and hook up.

We were using 5kg threadline and baitcaster outfits, and hooking fish up to a metre in length. It was light-tackle sportfishing at its best.

After half an hour or so, the queenfish action slowed. Arthur tied on a bibbed minnow and started working the lure over the drop-off. His technique was to cast, wind quickly to take the lure down and then slowly work it back with a gentle twitch and wind action. The technique proved too much for a school of **golden trevally**. These tough fighters were more cautious than the queenfish, but there was sustained action for about an hour.

Arthur said he knew of similar drop-offs offering solid fishing action on all these islands. He promotes catch-and-release fishing, which explains why the drop-offs are still fishing well more than 20 years after he moved to Seaforth from Sydney.

Low Island is one of a pair of islands – the other being High Island – north of the Newry Islands National Park. We had launched Arthur's boat at Point Newry, in Victor Creek, and followed the channel out between Acacia and Mausoleum islands.

Newry Island was once home to Annette Kellerman, the mermaid in Hollywood silent movies in the 1920s. Camping is permitted on the island, although you need a permit from Queensland National Parks. See: www.nprsr.qld.gov.au/parks/newry-islands/camping.

About a kilometre east is Outer Newry Island. Anglers can fish here, but are restricted to one line and one hook per person. To the south is another island, which is off limits to anglers.

Between the Newry islands and High and Low islands is Rabbit Island, along with plenty of reef systems – all in relatively sheltered water less than a 40-minute run from the boat ramp.

Arthur said anglers who come here should bring an Admiralty chart and take care when travelling around the islands at low tide.

Above: Heavy timber at the back of Teemburra Dam is the place to be casting lures for barramundi
Below: Sooty grunter grow to large sizes in Teemburra

Species you can expect to hook on the reefs include **giant trevally**, **mackerel**, **coral trout**, **fingermark** and **red bass**. There are many mangroves around the islands and most hold **barramundi**, **estuary cod**, **threadfin** and **blue salmon**. Even Victor Creek, which is navigable for about 3km at high tide, is worth a look. Dense stands of mangroves line the creek, and it is deep in the lower reaches. Arthur has caught metre-long barramundi, **mangrove jack**, **javelin fish** and **tarpon** there.

TEEMBURRA DAM

Mackay has excellent freshwater options. The most popular venues are the region's dams in the Pioneer Valley – Teemburra, Eungella and Kinchant. Of these, the best known is Teemburra in Eungella National Park, about a 40-minute drive west of Mackay through fields of sugarcane. The dam was constructed in 1997 and when full it has a surface area of 10sqkm and can hold 147,500ML of water.

ACCOMMODATION: For more information visit www.mackayregion.com/accommodation

Teemburra is a maze of inlets and bays with creeks, and there are platypuses almost everywhere you look. The birdlife is also prolific. Sea-eagles nest in tall trees and thousands of swallows feed close to the water, stirring the surface up so much that you think baitfish are jumping.

Barramundi are the most prized northern sport fish and many experienced anglers rate this waterway on a par with Proserpine and Awoonga lakes, and better than Lake Tinaroo. The main reason for the praise is that Teemburra is one of the most heavily stocked impoundments in Queensland. More than a million barramundi and **sooty grunter**, have been introduced since it was built. The barramundi

average about 85cm, but fish to 1.10m have been caught. The sooties are up to 60cm, and when you hook a big one you are just as likely to think it is a barra staying deep.

I fished Teemburra with part-time fishing guide Mick Rethus. He runs a 3.85m punt with bow- and stern-mounted electric motors and a 25-horsepower outboard (the maximum size allowed on the lake).

Mick, who was born in Nhill in western Victoria, met me at what is usually the boat ramp at dawn. This area of Queensland had long been in drought and the ramp finished well short of the water. Mick said that when full, the dam was 45m deep, but during my visit, it was about 20 per cent capacity. He told me this as we were snaking our way around hills and stands of dead trees that he normally motored over.

Timing in fresh water can be more important than in salt water and as far as Mick was concerned, my timing couldn't have been worse. Barramundi can be caught during the colder months, but they are easier to hook when the weather is warmer, which is why you are more likely to latch on to a sooty grunter when it is colder.

It was also the day after the full moon. Generally, the nights leading up to and on the full moon are best if you are fishing between sundown and dawn. For daylight fishing, the days leading up to and on the new moon are better. 'The problem is that on a full moon the barra normally feed at night so I reckon they will have fed up last night and will be lying low during the day,' Mick said. 'I think we'll have a better chance at a sooty.'

Sooty grunter are not the preferred choice of anglers in Lake Proserpine, but they do grow to large sizes and put up a good fight when hooked

Many experienced barramundi anglers fishing in Queensland's lakes also choose their fishing times based on the tides. It sounds silly, but the impoundment barramundi bite better on the change of tide.

Mick was right. We couldn't buy a barramundi, but a few sooties of up to 2.5kg made life interesting.

Our fishing techniques varied from casting large bibbed minnows and soft plastic lures to headlands and around trees, to trolling large bibbed minnow lures over sunken timber and rock bars. The fishing was slow, but what impressed me about sooties is how hard they pull. They are a similar shape to yellowbelly, but their body is heavier and they definitely have more pulling power.

LAKE PROSERPINE

The closed season for barramundi in Queensland runs November–February, but some of the best barra waters are exempt and this includes the fabulous Lake Proserpine, often called Peter Faust Dam, 26km east of Proserpine.

ACCOMMODATION: Lake Proserpine has campground accommodation at Camp Kanga. **For more information visit www.tourismwhitsundays.com.au/destinations/proserpine/attractions/peter-faust-dam**

This 44sqkm lake is one of the jewels in Queensland's fishing crown where, since 1996, **barramundi, sooty grunter**, **sleepy cod** and **saratoga** have been stocked.

A Stocked Impoundment Permit is required. See: **www.smartservice.qld.gov.au/services/permits/fishing/apply**. Permits are also available at tackle outlets and post offices.

Most anglers come to catch barra, which is what you would expect given that it has produced specimens to 30kg. Make no mistake, the barra here are the stuff of piscatorial legends. Nowhere in Australia are so many 'Holy Grail' barramundi being caught, and in water that at best can be described as challenging.

The lake isn't easy to fish. The northern side is littered with stands of dead trees and logs. On completion of the main dam structure, workers set about clearing the main basin, but while letting their chainsaws cool, enough rain pelted down to float the Ark. The result is a snag city.

Inexperienced anglers find the going tough, but the environment suits barramundi. On a big day in the snags, it's common to bang the rod on a branch during a cast. It's also usual to end up securing just one fish in five. Hooked barra may only need to run a rod length to haul you into the sticks. When they're 10kg, you can stop them dead and bring them thrashing to the surface, eyes crossed, jaws dislocated. However, when they're 25kg, the take is explosive, the run supercharged and you have about eight seconds to gain control.

Most of the main basin is as treeless as the Nullarbor. The Dam Wall and the Horse Paddock are deepwater locations suited to trolling. The fish can be the size of Shetland ponies, but among the open spaces, even the most inexperienced fish stay in the saddle. The trend for anglers new to the area – many a bit light-on when it comes to knowing barra – is to join the clusters of boats trolling the main basin. But the higher strike rate in the sticks is commensurate with the challenge. Short rods are better suited than long. Barra can be caught more than once, and can be just as inclined to rush to open water as plunge into the snags.

PIONEER RIVER

Fishing from a canoe is one of the best ways to get close and personal with the environment. Even when the fish are small, catching them from a canoe is both challenging and rewarding.

With that in mind, I jumped at the opportunity to fish the Pioneer River with Mackay fishing guide Arthur Lovern. Arthur knew I was keen to catch 'chimney sweeps' (aka **sooty grunter**), and he said the Pioneer was ideal.

We launched the two-man canoe just out of Mirani, about a 40-minute drive west of Mackay. Even though Teemburra Dam, about 15km south, was down to about 20 per cent capacity, the Pioneer River was as high as Arthur had seen it other than in flood.

Access is easy. Drive over the bridge at Mirani, turn left at the first turn off and follow the track down to the river. Our launching place was just below the rail bridge, a popular area with swimmers.

The river has a good covering of lily pads in shallow areas, and even though the canoe had an electric motor on the stern, we paddled downstream for half a kilometre until we were out of the lilies and the water was deeper.

Arthur said the sooties school under the cover of cluster fig trees. These trees have an orange fruit that grows off the trunk. When the fruit fall into the river, the sooties devour them. We cast our poppers close to the timber and wound them back with a slow, jerky retrieve.

Sooties also hang under snags, particularly those popular with birds, because the fish feed on the bird droppings. We went downstream for about 5km, casting lures at white-stained snags and under the overhanging cover provided by the branches of fig trees. The water was so clear the pebbles could be counted on the riverbed and turtles could be seen swimming beneath the canoe. In the clear areas between lily pads where the comb-crested jacanas were feeding, distinctive double bumps of platypus ruffled the surface. I counted at least 12 in the first hour.

However, there wasn't much to see in the way of fish. We ventured up a small tributary called

Sailfish are one of several high-speed billfish available along the Queensland coast

Macgregor Creek, a water Arthur optimistically said had never failed to produce sooties. It has now.

'Let's go upriver and see if we can catch a few in the pools above the bridge,' Arthur suggested.

The high water hid large boulders that Arthur normally stood on to fish. A couple of times he got out of the canoe to push it through narrow ways over shallow water. He wore shoes to do this, explaining there was a fish in the river called a bullrout that can inflict a serious wound if you stand on it.

Fish life started to improve almost as soon as we passed the bridge. Schools of **bony bream** and **banded grunter** became apparent, and soon we were seeing large schools of sooties.

We trolled our minnow lures along the longer, deep stretches and when at last our first sooty came to the boat we both heaved a sigh of relief. Like any drought, once broken the rest is easy and more sooties joined the party.

Trolling was the easiest way to fish and we trolled small bibbed minnows that dived to a couple of metres. The lures were set about 20m behind the canoe and towed a little slower than walking pace.

We paddled or motored our way several kilometres upriver until a wall of rock barred our progress. At this point, we got out of the canoe and proceeded to fish around the rock pools against a backdrop of running water, eucalypt-lined riverbanks and green mountain ranges, with azure kingfishers, swallows and sea-eagles adding to the experience. In the rock pools and riffles upstream, we cast small poppers across the runs, letting them drift downstream before retrieving. The biggest fish landed probably didn't weigh more than a kilogram, but the fishing was stimulating and the surface strikes in the clear, shallow water were spectacular.

Methods for Gladstone to Mackay

TACKLE
Salt water

Light tackle lure enthusiasts will find 5–8kg outfits adequate for most of the species off Seaforth. When rigging, employ a leader of about 15kg breaking strain and attach a cross lock snap to enable quick lure changes. If mackerel are about, a piano wire leader may be necessary, but shouldn't be employed for most species, particularly if casting rather than trolling lures.

For offshore bottom bouncing, it's worthwhile considering a 15kg outfit.

Many Queenslanders prefer to work the Alvey centre-pin, but large overheads and big threadline reels do well and allow the option of working lures. You will need leader material.

On the reefs, 24kg leader is the minimum. The popular rig is a fixed sinker and leader paternoster style. Use hooks about 6/0, straight shank.

Some Queensland anglers using whole fish or fillets tend not to thread their hooks through the bait but place the hook at one end of the bait. Top baits include hussars, squid and pilchards, although the latter do not last long.

Fresh water

In Pioneer River, 5kg baitcaster outfits spooled with gelspun line and rigged with a 5kg breaking strain leader were ideal.

The lures were 20–30mm surface poppers and deeper running bibbed minnows.

In the dams and the Fitzroy River, we used baitcaster outfits spooled with 15kg breaking strain braid and a metre or so of 15–24kg leader.

Most anglers prefer to work lures up to 15cm long, mainly floating/diving minnow types and soft plastics. Successful techniques include casting and trolling. Soft plastic prawn and baitfish imitations, 50–75mm long and hard-bodied lures of similar size proved effective. Soft plastics are often taken as they sink. If this is not successful, the lure should be worked slowly along the bottom in a slow, lift and drop action.

Prawn baits were hooked with a 4/0 hook through the tail and a running sinker that ran down the line to the eye of the hook.

For saratoga and yellowbelly in the Dawson River, the standard outfit was a small baitcaster or threadline reel spooled with 6–10kg braid line.

Bait fishers work similar tackle, and use size 2/0–4/0 hooks set on a running sinker or paternoster rig with a small amount of lead. In the Dawson River, bait used was yabbies, but scrubworms would have to be on the menu for yellowbelly.

Diving and surface minnow lures work well on all species. Flatten the hook barbs for ease of release and have a range of colours including red, blues, metallic and fluoros. The Halco Night Walker surface lure is a favourite for saratoga.

Fly-fishers use 6–8kg weight outfits with floating lines. Surface flies like the Dahlberg Diver are excellent for the saratoga but, like barramundi and yellowbelly, saratoga will also inhale Clouser Minnows, 3D patterns and Lefty Deceivers.

6 FAR NORTH QUEENSLAND

CAIRNS

Cairns is billed by the locals as the international gamefishing capital of the world. I agree, at least as far as black marlin are concerned. But there is far more to fishing North Queensland than marlin and once you go it's hard not to return again and again ...

ACCOMMODATION: I've slept in five-star hotels, and under the stars on boats and beaches. There are so many ways to enjoy the tropical north that it is up to individual choice.

For more information visit www.queenslandholidays.com.au

Cairns is the home of black marlin, and to chase big marlin you need a well-equipped game boat

Many international game anglers regard Cairns as the game fish capital of the world, with plenty of big **black marlin** – the Holy Grail of gamefishing. Granders or Julies, call them what you will, these huge female marlin are the biggest and the best on offer. From September to December, anglers arrive from all over the world to battle with blacks in excess of 500kg.

This is a big deal, and can cost big bucks. At the peak of the black marlin season, anglers arrive willing to spend $2500 or more a day to catch the world's biggest fish. The high rollers not only charter game boats, they also stay at sea on live-aboard mother ships, which can double the cost of the trip. Add airfares and incidentals and you are talking bills that look like telephone numbers – especially when you consider that some anglers will stay around for a month.

However, other anglers fish Cairns on a budget by sharing charters and staying in budget accommodation. In this way, the cost shared by five or six anglers fishing for marlin for a week is about the same as staying at a lodge in the NT and fishing for barramundi.

It still isn't cheap, but it is certainly an adventure to remember.

The marlin boom in Cairns began on 25 September 1966. Crewman Richard Obach was fishing with Captain George Bransford on his gamefishing vessel *Sea Baby* when he caught a world-record 1064lb (483kg) marlin off Euston Reef on 37kg tackle.

Jack Erskine watches a marlin powering away from him

Nowhere else in the world can anglers lay claim to the number of 1000lb (game fishers still talk imperial measurements) blacks caught off Cairns. Little wonder the black marlin fishing developed into a multi-million-dollar-a-year business.

The experience is great. I once did a stint there as an observer in a major gamefishing tournament. The event was serious, with big dollar prizes and dedicated competitors. Strict rules applied and observers were put on game boats to ensure no one misinterpreted them. For example, at one tournament, an angler caught a ripper marlin but under the tournament rules, the leader used to catch the marlin had to be handed in to verify it was legal. A deckhand's decision to toss the leader over the side on the way back to port cost the angler $32,000 in prize money. I wouldn't have liked to be the deckie.

However, Cairns has more than big marlin. There are plenty of exciting sport fish options for anglers who want to chase serious fish on light tackle, including saltwater fly. Most of the action takes place 30–45km offshore, inside the Great Barrier Reef and near the reef openings. The most sought-after fish are juvenile black marlin and **sailfish** to about 50kg, **Spanish mackerel** and **tuna**.

On a three-day live-aboard expedition I fished with Cairns-based tackle guru Jack Erskine off Cairns. His 'job' was to field test new reels from the Penn stable.

On this day, the south-easterly wind was blowing 10–15 knots and the sea had a moderate chop. 'Helluva job, but someone's gotta do it,' Jack smiled.

Skipper Ross Finlayson reduced speed on the *Sea Baby IV* to about 8-knots and signalled for deckhand Glen Campbell to feed out teasers and baits.

The spread consisted of two skipping garfish, spring-rigged with skirts over their heads and

Big black marlin is what the game fishers come to Cairns to catch

10/0 hooks; a swimming mullet and a Boone daisy chain teaser consisting of five plastic squid and a small **Watsons tuna** rigged to skip behind.

We were several kilometres west of Pixie Reef, about 20 nautical miles north-east of Cairns. These waters inside the Great Barrier Reef are famous for marlin, sailfish, mackerel and tuna.

In the game chair rod-holder was a 12kg threadline outfit and from the end of the rod, a leader ran down to a plastic container where a small baitfish, rigged and ready, swum. Everyone watched the lures, waiting and wishing for a sailfish or marlin to rise. Within an hour a small black marlin moved in on one garfish. Laurie spotted it and Ross gave urgent instructions to haul in the baits.

'You ready Jack?' he called. By now we could all see the slim, streamlined shape of the marlin eyeing off the lures and baits, moving left and right across the stern. The beaky was undecided. Jack took up the rod, dropped the live baitfish into the wake and free-spooled line, relying on Ross's keen eyes to tell him when the bait was in front of the marlin. Live bait is the trigger that pulls a marlin out of its indecision.

'He's got it!' yelled Ross. 'Let him take some line Jack ... more line, more ... now give it to him!'

At that, Jack flipped the bail arm over, waited for the line to tighten and set the hook. He did this to perfection. Admittedly, Jack's had plenty of practice, having caught more than 400 marlin and sailfish on light tackle.

Not a heave-and-reef angler, Jack kept the rod low and maintained control. It might have been a smallish specimen, about 25kg, but the runs and jumps were magic. Line sizzled through the guides and the drag system purred under each shortening run. Small marlin are a sweet option on light tackle. After 10 minutes the fish was alongside and Glen took hold of the bill and lifted the marlin inboard where the hook was removed, the fish held up for photos and released. Lift to release took less than a minute. This was sight fishing at its best.

We raised three more marlin that day; the biggest about 50kg. We didn't catch it, though it managed to eat two baits.

The method is called switch baiting. If a marlin rises, hopefully it will take the bait and become hooked, but if the fish is looking at the baits and not taking them, live bait is fed out while the other baits and lures are brought in.

Despite the consistent availability of this sort of action, both Ross and Laurie are frustrated. 'It seems almost impossible to get the message across,' Ross said. 'People come for the big blacks in October and November, but Cairns has a lot more to offer than big marlin, and if it's just the horses you want, you can still catch them in September and December.'

The Daintree River has much to offer light tackle sport fishers

Ross said the heavy tackle black marlin season runs from September to December along the outer edge of the Great Barrier Reef from Cairns to Lizard Island. The best results often come in the afternoon, from about 2pm onwards. Depending on the location and the degree of difficulty getting back into the anchorage, most boats fish through to as late as 6.30pm.

Laurie said when he was skippering *Sea Baby* he offered clients cheaper rates to fish earlier in the season, but they didn't want it. 'They don't know what they are missing out on,' Ross said.

He was right; the action over the three days we spent offshore 'out of season' was constant. On our first day we did a fair bit of trolling. About an hour before the tide change, Ross manoeuvred *Sea Baby* onto a seamount and we started laying a cube trail. Soon we were hooking up on **scaly** and Spanish mackerel, and the occasional bottom fish like **red bass**. That wasn't quite as exciting as the two sailfish that were hooked earlier that day while trolling an area known as Onyx Reef.

The mackerel action seemed to continue for as long as baits were fed out. Mackerel take off like express trains and line fairly sings as it cuts through the water. Fortunately these fish are tasty, which is just as well because there is no way of removing a hook from the razor-lined jaws of a frisky mackerel. In between there were longtail and mackerel tuna, a never-ending procession of high-speed, light-tackle sport fish that many punters who come to Cairns seem to overlook.

Methods for Cairns

TECHNIQUES This is predominantly a bait fishery with two rods usually trolled from the outriggers and up to four rods trolled using lures. Top baits include scad, bonito, scaly mackerel, Spanish mackerel, yellowfin tuna, queenfish and rainbow runner. Baits can be up to 15kg, although the preferred size is about 1–2.5kg for swimming scads, and 4–6kg for skip baits. Baits are trolled just under and on the surface at 5–6 knots.

Blue marlin offer an exciting alternative to the blacks, coming on as the black marlin season closes. Top months are January–April, and again most of the action is from Cairns to Lizard Island. Most blues are caught trolling lures. Main bait species for the blues are skipjack and yellowfin tuna.

For sportfishing enthusiasts, December–February and May–September are the most productive months, although blue-water fishing off

Cairns is generally excellent year round. The winter months (May–September) are best for Spanish mackerel and juvenile black marlin (up to 50kg). The warmer months (October–March) provide good fishing for **wahoo**, big Spanish mackerel, sailfish and black marlin to 100kg.

Methods include lures, live baits and natural dead baits. Preferred lures range from bibless minnows to minnow style bibbed lures for mackerel tuna, Spanish mackerel and other species. Marlin and sailfish prefer lures of the pusher style. Live baits used are yakkas, trevally, pilchards, pinkies and gobbers. The more prominent dead baits are mullet and garfish (ballyhoo).

Anglers who want to jig or work poppers will find the best action is in May–January and takes place along the Great Barrier Reef where anglers jig the offshore shoals, reef edges and the Continental Shelf. It is a lucky dip of species that includes yellowfin and dogtooth tuna, wahoo, Spanish mackerel, **amberjack**, **GTs**, **coral trout** and **mangrove jack**.

TACKLE Large-capacity spinning reels and short fast taper rods about 2.1–2.3m need to be spooled with 25–35kg braid. Jigs are 70–250g in many different styles and colours.

Popper fishing tackle consists of stiff 2.2–2.4m spinning rods and large capacity reels. The best line to use is 20–30kg braid. Large surface poppers, which give a 'blooping splashy' action and skipping fast-retrieve style poppers are popular.

TRINITY INLET

Cairns, nestled on Trinity Inlet, and its region offers more than gamefishing. South of the city are rivers like the Russell and Mulgrave; to the north are the Daintree and Mowbray rivers. Anglers heading inland will find opportunities like the famous Lake Tinaroo on the Atherton Tablelands.

One of the wonderful aspects of Cairns is that you don't need to travel far to find exciting fishing. Take Trinity Inlet. This mangrove-lined estuary is just a couple of minutes drive away from the Cairns CBD and, in its 90km of waterway, you can catch a diverse range of fish species.

I fished the inlet with Robert Anderson and Nathan Ruth, as diverse a pair of anglers as you are likely to meet. Cool, calm and methodical, Robert is a retired wool broker from Corowa who split his time between a house at Kurrimine Beach, south of Cairns, and Melbourne. Nathan worked at Tackle World, and was one of that up-and-coming group of young anglers blessed with an uncanny ability to drop a lure on a 5c piece hidden under a mangrove root.

Trinity Inlet is primarily a huge tidal basin with several creeks but no major river flowing in. It offers almost year-round action and is a prime fish-breeding and nursery area, one reason why larger predators are consistently caught here.

We launched Robert's 4.35m Quintrex Hornet at the ramp upstream of the shipyards. Within 5 minutes of starting the 50-horsepower outboard, we were fishing.

Robert proved a capable guide. We started by casting small hard-bodied and soft plastic lures around the mangrove roots, into small run-offs and across snags. The results were slow, although Nathan managed to hook a **barramundi** of about 60cm, which subsequently tossed the lure.

Nathan said the small creeks fished better when the tide was rising because the fish head up the creeks and drains after baitfish and prawns. In other areas where I have fished barramundi, anglers prefer to fish creeks when the tide is running out. Casting lures into small drains, creek mouths and among snags isn't difficult – provided you are accurate. The lure rarely travels more than 15m, often much less. Precision is the key to avoid hooking up on timber, so do your casting practice.

Our best results were to come from trolling the rock bars. The inlet has a large population of **mangrove jack**, an aggressive red fish that seems to fight well above its weight. We caught them to 1.4kg.

Nathan had a few spots that he liked working the lures and, on each one, mangrove jacks were waiting for the lure to come across their line of vision – or so it seemed. The fishing was consistent, the jacks and small **giant trevally (GT)** were plentiful, all within cooee of the city centre.

Baitfish and prawns abound in the inlet and locals use cast nets to catch their bait.

Prime species in this water include **flathead**, **long tom** and **fingermark**. During the cooler months, GT, **queenfish**, **estuary cod**, **flathead**, **bream** and **grunter** are more prolific.

RUSSELL HEADS

Russell Heads is the junction and estuary system of the Russell and Mulgrave rivers, south of Cairns. Access was via the boat ramp at Deeral, 45km south of Cairns on the Mulgrave River. The boat ramp is accessible on all tides, and has toilet facilities.

I was fishing with Kieran Livingstone who had a Cairns Custom Craft aluminium, a solid boat ideal for river and estuary work.

As with many boat ramps in northern Australia, this one had the 'Beware of Crocodiles' warning posted. Kieran walked down the ramp and pointed a torch beam into the undercut bank – just to make sure. He explained that recently the local ranger had taken his Jack Russell for a walk. As usual, he tossed a stick into the river and the little yapper went in after it. As his dog came scooting out of the water, stick firmly in its mouth, about 4m of crocodile came sliding in behind it on the ramp. Motoring downriver, I couldn't help but notice the rope swings hanging from trees ...

Munbah fishing guide Les Gibson

Russell Heads was slow at first. We worked around the edges, casting to banks and snags. There were no barramundi, but we caught a few **bream** and **cod**. After an hour or so of this a school of **queenfish** arrived and the action turned on. We were casting small poppers and saltwater flies at the marauding fish that were hunting along a sandbar. Queenfish are a pretty species with classic trevally lines but are skinny and don't weigh much. While there wasn't a fish under about a metre in length, those we caught were 7–10kg.

The wind blew, rain fell and the fishing action was relentless for more than three hours. A school of **wolf herring** entered the estuary and was hunting with, and being hunted by, the queenfish. Wolf herring are a fierce-looking fish and have a thick coating of slime. About 35–40cm long and shaped like a barracuda, the herring have two front fangs that come out of the top jaw parallel with the body.

When a hook-up comes, the queenfish invariably leap out of the water several times in between making long dashes for freedom. Sometimes the fish take a nose-down approach and all you see is their tails churning up the surface. Kieran said this was a common behaviour locals described as 'the washing machine'.

JULATTEN

Fishing is where you find it, and sometimes you find it in unlikely places. Julatten is situated midway between Port Douglas and Lake Tinaroo on the Mossman–Mt Molloy Rd. At Julatten, I came across a couple of people fishing in a pond. I pulled over to check out the action. The place was called

Dawn on the beach at Munbah

Barramundi Gardens and comprised 5.6ha with six commercial aquaculture ponds and a tourist pond set up to hook passing anglers. Mick Petersen ran the park and was charging visitors $25 an hour, including tackle. The fish in his ponds averaged about 3–4kg and offered a nice break on a long drive. 'There is no pressure for anglers to keep their catch,' Mick said, 'but if they do, the **barra** will cost them $10 a kilo.'

Anglers are supplied with threadline outfits and soft plastic lures. Despite being pond water where the fish are fed regularly, they were not so easy to catch.

Mick said what made this fish farm different to others was the barramundi strain. He took me into his breeding shed and proudly showed off a tub full of 15kg barramundi that were as white as snow, but had blue eyes so they were not albinos. 'I'll bet you've never seen anything like this before?' he asked. 'No one wants to breed this strain of barra so I thought I'd do it anyway.'

MUNBAH

Munbah is midway between Cape Bedford and Cape Flattery, an hour's drive north of Cooktown.

It's predawn and Les Gibson walks down to the creek and stops. He is on his way to push some boats out into deeper water as the tide is falling rapidly. Following Les are three journalists. He stops at the creek, turns to the group, and says: 'I can smell a croc; there's one up the creek somewhere.'

Wary, the journalists watch Les as he crosses the knee-deep creek and continues out across the sand flats to the boats. Shortly after, the water downstream stirs and about 3m of saltwater crocodile heads out to sea. It's an experience: not seeing the croc so much as being told there is a croc about when you can't see it. Les said crocodiles sometimes went up the creek with the salt water and left as the tide ebbed. 'We don't have a problem with them because we understand their habits and know what we can do and how to avoid them,' Les said.

Unlike Martin Luther King Jr, Les didn't have a dream, but he did have a vision. He wanted to start fishing charters in remote areas just north of Cooktown in North Queensland. When I was there, Les was well on the way to achieving that objective.

He wasn't one of your $600-a-day suburban fishing guides who only know as much about the bush and rivers as they can see on a map. A member of the Guugu Yimidhirr tribe, Les lived at the Hope Vale Aboriginal Community. Short and wiry, he grew up in the bush and was keen to start up fishing charters that linked Aboriginal bushcraft with modern angling techniques.

To kick-start his business, Les has established a **camp** on the beach at Munbah, midway between Cape Bedford and Cape Flattery. The only way in is by travelling several kilometres along a beach at low tide.

The camp was what I call five-star bush accommodation: a corrugated iron building, floor, single beds, and a couple of outside toilets, inside cooking facilities and an outside barbecue area. The fishing included the beach and the McIvor River for **barramundi** and **mangrove jack**. The area has extensive sand flats with large nipper beds that attract **golden trevally** and perhaps even **oyster crackers**.

The beach, famous for its 37 different colours of sand, has gutters and sandbars, attractive to **giant**

Above: Lake Tinaroo on the Atherton Tablelands is one of Queensland's most productive barramundi waters
Below: Julatten fish farm gives visitors an opportuntity to catch barramundi

trevally, **queenfish**, **giant** and **oxeye herring**, **sand whiting** and the ever-present small **sharks**. You can drive the beach until you spot a school of fish, get out of the vehicle, and start fishing.

Les was running two aluminium boats of 4.2m and 5m and we fished Conical Rock, a few kilometres offshore. Most of the fishing was bottom bouncing for the likes of **coral trout** and **red throat**, but there were giant trevally around the bommies as well as **barracuda**. Further out were the Three Islands, where Les said big schools of pelagic fish such as **mackerel** and trevally run past.

Methods for Trinity Inlet to Munbah

TACKLE In Trinity Inlet we used baitcaster and threadline outfits. Threadlines are often better suited to casting light, soft plastic lures. Regardless of what outfit style you choose, spool your reel with 15kg breaking strain braid and add a metre or so of 15–24kg leader. If you expect big barra, opt for heavier leader. Soft plastic prawn and baitfish imitations, 50–75mm long, and hard-bodied lures of similar size proved effective.

LAKE TINAROO

Lake Tinaroo is built across the Barron River Gorge in the Atherton Tablelands; about two-hours' drive from Cairns via Gordonvale and Yungaburra.

The lake was the first of Queensland's impoundments stocked with **barramundi**.

ACCOMMODATION: There is ample accommodation, with caravan parks at Yungaburra and at Tinaroo. Both parks are near boat-launching facilities, and the latter has been refurbished and offers more facilities.

For more information visit www.tablelands.org/laketinaroo

In 1989, barramundi fingerlings bred from brood barramundi captured near Cairns and grown out at the Department of Primary Industries research station at nearby Walkamin were released into the lake. These liberated fish demonstrated a remarkably fast growth rate due to the amount of feed available. The growth pills were **bony bream** that had been seeded into the water years before the barramundi release. Subsequently, the lake has produced world-record barramundi topping 39.9kg. Local fisheries officers claim to have electro-fished even bigger ones.

The best fishing happens around dusk and through the night, if the barra are cooperating. For some reason the fish can shut down and stop feeding for days on end. These mood swings have been put down to altitude and the cooler water temperatures.

Don't forget to pack a coat. It can get very cold in the Tablelands; don't be fooled by the coastal weather forecasts.

Methods for Lake Tinaroo

TACKLE Trolling, lure casting and fly-fishing are all common here, but bait fishing's popularity has waned due to the successes achieved with lures.

Most anglers fish with lures and use baitcaster outfits and, to a lesser extent, threadline outfits. The lines are mainly 15–24kg breaking strain braids.

Leaders are essential because of the heavy terrain that the barramundi like to hide in, and their gill cutters. The minimum size is a 24kg hard-wearing monofilament about a metre long, although anglers with bigger fish in their sights often opt for heavier, 37kg leader material.

BAIT Bony bream are about the only available bait, and these should be fished live under a float with a 6/0 Suicide hook set about 3mm deep in front of the first dorsal spine.

LURES Top-water trolling from the surface to about 4m down is the preferred method for most anglers except near the dam wall where deeper running lures are preferred. Barramundi are ambush predators and they hang in structure waiting for their meals to swim past. To that end, lures need to be worked near timber and rock for the best results. Lure casters and fly-fishers tend to work many of the same areas, casting their lures or flies into the snags. One angler I met had done well fly-fishing along the shallow shore areas to the west of the boat ramp at Yungaburra.

Most standard barra lures are employed. Some of the more popular types include Halco Scorpions, Halco Lazer Pros, Predatek Vipers, Barra Classics and B-52s.

7 WESTERN QUEENSLAND

LAKE FRED TRITTON

Lake Fred Tritton is at Richmond in western Queensland. It is about a 550km drive from Townsville, via Charters Towers on National Hwy A6.

Australians love the coastline, but there are also many outback gems waiting to be discovered. Lake Fred Tritton is one of these. An oasis in the middle of somewhere, it is worth a trip just to see what enterprising rural folk are capable of creating, and once you get away from the cities and rub shoulders with rural Australians, there is no turning back.

A Stocked Impoundment Permit is required (*see* page 322.)

ACCOMMODATION: The Richmond Lakeview Caravan Park is a clean, friendly outback park and overlooks Lake Fred Tritton. There is motel accommodation in Richmond, which is situated halfway between Townsville and Mount Isa.
For more information visit www.richmond.qld.gov.au

Fishing Lake Fred Tritton as the sun sets

Not all Stocked Impoundment Permit Scheme (SIPS) waters are part of grandiose tourism schemes. Other, isolated waters have also benefited from stocking. Among the more remote is Lake Fred Tritton. Unless you have travelled through the Gulf Country chances are you won't have heard of this lake, which is after all, a small water in a huge expanse of outback Australia. A friend of mine dubbed this water the 'little lake on the prairie' and I reckon he was right. Lake Fred Tritton is only 1.2km in circumference and averages about 4m deep with a central trench that drops down to 6m. And, even though the lake is on a prairie, it does have some exciting fishing to offer anglers travelling the Overlanders Way and in need of some piscatorial pleasure.

One hundred millions years ago, or thereabouts, a vast inland water covered this area. Called the Eromanga Sea, it was home to a creature called a kronosaurus, a sort of dinosaur fish estimated to be about 10m long with a 2.4m long skull filled with huge conical teeth. Nowadays the only sign of an inland sea is Lake Fred Tritton and while it doesn't have dinosaurs, it does have **Karumba strain barramundi**, sooty grunter, **sleepy cod** and **yellowfin perch** – a kind of oversize glassfish. The best of Tritton's barra are nearing trophy fish sizes – the magic metre mark!

Every March an annual fishing competition conducted by the Richmond Fish Stocking Group is held. In 2011, George Fortune, secretary of the neighbouring Mount Isa stocking group travelled 400km to attend and upon arrival, decided to test the water by casting a fizzer (lure) from the boat ramp. It was blasted by a feisty 88cm barra that left George figuring he'd used up all his good luck given that the competition wasn't scheduled to start until 7am the following day.

The voluntary fish stocking associations throughout the state exemplify a deep community spirit. The turnout for the competition must have included every kid in town. Like many similar events in Queensland towns with a nearby lake, event sponsorships come from community minded local businesses. The people power to organise and run things comes free. Fish stocking groups are voluntary organisations and proceeds go towards fingerling purchases from private hatcheries.

The Fred Tritton competition was catch and release and the oval shaped lake facilitated the transport of catches to a central weigh station, from there the fish were carried 30m to the water and released. A steady stream of bucket carrying kids kept things moving at the weight station with their sleepy cod and yellowfin perch.

A stroll around the lake during the competition revealed a variety of fishing techniques. Live baitfish suspended under a float, dead bait on the bottom, lure casting from the bank, even a bloke fly-fishing and a number of boats quietly mooching their lures around using electric motors.

As the clock wound down to Sunday's midday final weigh-in, things were looking good for Mark Norman. His barra, caught, weighed and released the previous morning, survived several close calls. George Fortune and his mate had mooched close to a buoyed area where kids were swimming. Slow trolling minnow lures on the electric motor, and with just minutes to go, George hooked the winning fish.

Bigger barra are to be had in the upper Flinders River, about 10km from town. There are a number of notable holes close enough to town also for an early morning cast or an arvo fish after work. The big rains of recent years have re-filled the upper reaches and allowed barra to migrate extraordinary distances upstream. At a guess, over 500km from the Flinders mouth near Normanton.

Methods for Lake Fred Tritton

TACKLE At Lake Fred Tritton, methods are the same as for other stocked dams. Anglers fishing for **barra** with lures prefer baitcaster outfits. Bait anglers tend to lean towards threadline outfits as these give the option of casting small lures and lightweight baits. Recommended line is 15kg breaking strain braid for both species. If you are specifically after barra, use a hard-wearing 24kg monofilament leader.

LURES Trolling lures is popular but some of these lakes offer areas that are ideal for spinning from shore. Some effective barra lures include Gold Bombers; B-52s, Sand Vipers, Halco Poltergeists, Scorpions and Lazer Pros. Soft plastic lures are also popular. Spinnerbaits work well when retrieved slowly.

Yellowbelly are on the bush menu three times a day

CHANNEL COUNTRY

Names like the Barcoo and Diamanitina rivers are not exactly in common usage in Australian cities, but they should be. More anglers need to get out on the road and experience the marvellous fishing that can be had from waters that appear magically out of nowhere in the middle of vast spinifex grass plains.

ACCOMMODATION: This is truly the land of the SKI (Spending the Kids Inheritance) army. Caravans and motorhomes are on most of the roads. But there is alternative accommodation available for those who don't want to stay in a caravan park.
For more information visit www.queenslandholidays.com.au

There are not many places where you need to hide behind a tree to put a bait on a hook – but fishing in western Queensland's Channel Country has about come to this following recent floods. The rivers and waterholes are full of fish and providing anglers with a once in a lifetime opportunity to experience the marvels of Outback Australia.

In her poem *My Country*, Dorothea Mackellar wrote of her love of a sunburnt country and a wide brown land:

Of ragged mountain ranges,
Of droughts and flooding rains.

Mackellar could have been writing about the Channel Country. The 'once in 100 year flood' has passed, but travellers – thousands of them, caravans in tow – continue to enjoy the benefits the excess water has produced, turning this black-soil spinifex grass country into an inland sea bigger than some small European countries.

A friend of mine, Bob Hart, who grew up on a property called Spring Leigh in the 'Flooded Country' on the Barcoo River, about 97km north of the Channel Country, told of experiencing a big flood about 55 years ago.

'It was amazing. **Yellowbelly** suddenly appeared from nowhere and were in every waterhole along the Barcoo,' he said. 'In those days it was legal to put frogs on hooks and we would catch small frogs and use them. As soon as the frog landed on the water it would be eaten; my father used to say it was the time when you stood behind a tree to put your bait on a hook.

'There weren't many freezers around in those days so you shared the fish around. The interesting thing about those yellowbelly was that most had a layer of fat between the skin and the muscle. To this day I cannot explain why,' Bob said.

Fast forward to 2010 and the summer downpours caused another 'once in 100 year flood' breaking the longest outback drought in living memory, turning dry, dusty creek beds into rivers stretching beyond the horizon. In what is a timeless ritual of nature, the dormant food chain exploded as the water run-off linked dry waterholes and spread across black soil plains.

Yellowbelly and other fish that languished in a purgatory of evaporating holes lower in the system were rejuvenated. The flood acted as a stimulus that urged these fish to migrate to the uppermost extremities of the system, and breed. Making the fish population explosion happen was an incalculable biomass of bony bream.

Winton is known as the place where Banjo Paterson penned *Waltzing Matilda* in 1895, while staying at Dagworth Station. Matilda is a euphemism for the one blanket bedroll lumped through the outback by the swagmen of the era. Well, fishing in Matilda Country is on in a big way with places most anglers have never heard of back on the radar.

Hot spots include Old Cork Station on the Diamantina River south-west of Winton; Isisford south of Longreach; and further south there is Noccundra and Thyangra on the Bulloo River, south-west of Thargomindah.

The Channel Country is twice the size of Victoria, the roads are graded and the shires keen on fishing tourism. Add the huge numbers of fish that have come on the bite and you have an anglers' dream. A campfire of Gidgee coals a few steps from the Diamantina River on the Old Cork Station with yellowbelly fillets in the pan and a billy simmering on the edge of the fire is a comfort that makes bearable the icy wind blowing from the Simpson Desert.

About 400km to the east, the Barcoo River at Isisford is running clear and frozen prawns and spinnerbait lures are doing well, not just of yellowbelly but also **Barcoo grunter** and **Welsh's grunter**. Other species include **eel tailed catfish** and **spangled perch**; a fish able to thrive in sulphur-smelling bore drains uncomfortably warm to paddle in.

An oddity up this way is Murray cod but don't count on catching any. Native fish guru Rod Harrison says a few entered the Lake Eyre system via overflowing stock and mining dams and were caught in Cooper Creek at Innamincka and the Thompson River at Longreach.

Methods for Channel Country

In the Channel Country, southern anglers will be shocked at the water colour in some waterholes. Outback waters at best are milky. At worst, they are the colour of a strong espresso, and almost thick enough to plough. The fish don't seem worried as they rely as much on sound and vibration as sight when hunting – and importantly for the fish, muddy water shields a predator's approach.

Anglers, however, can turn this to their advantage by giving baits an on-going tea-bag jiggle. Subtle movement, hands-down, beats an inert bait.

TACKLE Tackle is a 4kg threadline outfit, or even a basic handline rigged with a 3/0–4/0 Suicide hook and a running sinker to the bait, or a paternoster rig. Float fishing is also popular. Queensland regulations limit hooks to one per line and a maximum of four lines that are required to be within reach at any one time. There is a bag/possession limit of ten yellowbelly.

Dawn on the Diamantina River finds this angler with a prawn bait ready to start fishing for yellowbelly

BAIT Popular baits include frozen prawns, which are sold almost everywhere. Keen anglers catch shrimp and yabbies in collapsible traps. These baits offer a natural presentation with a better hook exposure. Believe it or not, but some anglers achieve a better hook-up rate by attaching crustaceans with a drop of super glue.

LURES Double bladed spinnerbaits with a stinger hook configuration do well and, if need be, the angler can add a small portion of bait to the lure without losing action.

TASMANIA

Steve's FAVOURITE DESTINATIONS FOR TASMANIA

When you head to Tasmania you can fly or take the ferry across Bass Strait with your own vehicle. The latter makes sense because you can carry more fishing tackle. This island has such an amazing offering of fishing opportunities that it should be on every angler's 'must-do' list.

Tasmania hosts salmon in the surf, big black bream in its estuaries, enormous southern bluefin tuna, marlin and mako sharks, and in the north are waters that produce snapper. Despite this range of quality fishing opportunities, the island is best known for its freshwater lakes and rivers that produce superb brown and rainbow trout. In fact, Tasmania is regarded as having the best trout fishing available in Australia, and this in turn attracts many fly-fishers.

ACCOMMODATION

The Apple Island relies heavily on tourism and there are plenty of places to stay.

For more information visit www.discovertasmania.com

Anglers who fish the Derwent River can choose between big trout or big bream, it's that style of river

Egg Lagoon
KING ISLAND
Currie
Naracoopa
Grassy
Year-round fishing well worth the effort
Palana
FLINDERS ISLAND
Emita
Whitemark
Lady Barron
CAPE BARREN ISLAND
Stanley
Marrawah
Arthur River
Wynyard
Burnie
Penguin
George Town
Bridport
Devonport
2
Waratah
Sheffield
ST HELENS
Launceston
Deloraine
GREAT LAKE
St Marys
Zeehan
LITTLE PINE LAGOON
Miena
Bicheno
Strahan
ARTHURS LAKE
Swansea
Coles Bay
Bradys Lake
Great Oyster Bay
1
Strathgordon
Salmon Ponds
Bagdad
Even novices will have success here
New Norfolk
HOBART
Museum of trout fishing
Eaglehawk Neck
Port Esperance
Port Arthur
Adventure Bay
Southport
BRUNY ISLAND
D'Entrecasteaux Channel

1 FRESHWATER TRAIL

THE SPRINGS

This place is private water situated west of Hobart and about 20 minutes drive from the CBD. The Springs isn't marked on any maps and the only way to fish here is by contacting Ken Orr on ken@orrsometassietrout.com.au.

ACCOMMODATION: As the Springs is located in the suburbs of Hobart, the visitor has a huge array of accommodation options available. My visits have been mainly apartment or motel stays and I have found the best way to get competitive rates is to use one of the online vendors.
For more information visit
www.wotif.com

Visitors to Hobart who are short on time can get a **trout** fix less than 20 minutes drive from the CBD at an exclusive fishery called The Springs. It is a year-round fishery and is restricted to a maximum of two anglers and one guide, Shannon Orr. This water is so well-hidden that the short drive from Hobart, through bush-block suburbia on the outskirts of the city, gives no inkling of the 10ha lake's existence. It's nestled in a crater-like clearing surrounded by tall eucalypts.

One of the huge rainbow trout brood stock on show at the Salmon Ponds

It was pelting rain when I arrived. We stopped the car and Shannon got out, walked to the dam wall and started fly-fishing. He was using a six-weight fly rod and had tied on a Woolly Bugger Mark 2, a searching pattern fly used when the fish are not feeding on the surface. Shannon worked a fly rod as if it was an extension of his arm. The green fly line formed a tight arc on the back cast, followed by a smooth follow through. There were no ripples in the fly line and the leader straightened out to allow the fly to plop gently onto the water.

The dam wall was slippery, but Shannon wasn't fazed. On his third cast, he hooked-up and a plump **rainbow trout** of a couple of kilograms was soon at his feet, ready for release. Less than a minute later, Shannon repeated the exercise with a twin of the first fish.

Anglers can walk and wade the shore, or fish from kayaks and dinghies. Either way, there are fish enough for everyone. The trout are mainly **browns** up to 2kg with many 500g trout still growing. They were sourced from wild-bred stock from the Great Lake spawning run.

We moved away from the dam wall to a cleared area along the southern shore. Here the water was shallow and there was watercress for trout to move through while feeding on invertebrates. Shannon cast and hooked-up, catching a brown trout of about 1kg. It was returned and he waited for more trout to move into the feeding lane.

The lake has a cleared area for barbecues and during the clearing operation around the shoreline, small groins were established to give anglers better sight fishing opportunities.

The Springs offers half- or full-day fishing with motel-to-lake connections and fly-fishing tutorials for beginners. If you have tried to teach yourself fly-fishing you will realise the value of a day spent with a competent fly-fisher.

The birthplace of all of Australia and New Zealand's brown trout, the Salmon Ponds at New Norfolk features an angling museum as well as displays of various trout species

SALMON PONDS AND MUSEUM OF TROUT FISHING

To get there take the Lyell Hwy from Hobart. At New Norfolk, continue onto Glenora Rd. It takes about 45 minutes to drive from Hobart.

ACCOMMODATION: Accommodation is available at New Norfolk but most visitors prefer to stay in Hobart.

For more information visit www.tasmania.visitorsbureau.com.au

Most Australian trout anglers regard Tasmania as the nation's premier **trout** destination. It's like Tasmania was purpose-designed for trout, with hundreds of lakes and a cooler climate. Mother Nature didn't seed the waters, but the early settlers saw to this. If you have an interest in the history of trout fishing in the antipodes, spare half a day and go to the Salmon Ponds. Every **brown trout** caught in Australia – and New Zealand for that matter – can trace its roots back to the Salmon Ponds.

The facility is located 10 minutes from New Norfolk, less than an hour's drive from Hobart, and includes a Museum of Trout Fishing and an Anglers Hall of Fame.

Since the late 1880s, the Salmon Ponds – the oldest trout hatchery in the Southern Hemisphere – has been a favourite picnic spot for Tasmanian families and a popular place to take visitors. It has been operating since 1864, when a shipment of Atlantic salmon eggs, and a small number of brown trout eggs arrived. The concept was to grow the salmon, release them into Tasmania's rivers where they would go to sea and return, as happens in Europe and North America. The salmon were grown, released into the rivers and that was the last anyone saw of them. Meanwhile, the brown trout did exceptionally well and became the foundation stocks for brown trout in Australia and New Zealand.

The ponds are set within an English garden setting. Surrounded by a hawthorn hedge, the manicured lawns are interspersed by imported English trees, some of them more than 140 years old.

This angler was successfully working a soft plastic lure for brown trout in an inflow canal on Bronte Lagoon

Each of the six ponds contains different salmonids: **rainbow trout**, **Atlantic salmon**, **tiger trout**, **albino rainbow trout** and brown trout. Displays explain the annual cycle of fish-breeding activities.

The albino rainbow trout is a rarity bred at the Salmon Ponds for decorative purposes. Someone suggested replacing the koi carp at Government House in Hobart with the albinos; the governor liked the idea and the trout went in.

A display based on the original trout hatchery is set up in a building next to the brook trout pond and opposite the Museum of Trout Fishing. Anglers with an interest in the history of their sport will appreciate the collection of memorabilia in the museum, which is housed in the cottage built for the first superintendent of the Salmon Ponds in 1865. Every room is filled with antique fishing equipment, showing changes in fishing reels, rods, flies, lures and accessories.

Visitors to the Salmon Ponds pay an entry fee, unless they have purchased a full Tasmanian freshwater fishing licence.

There is opportunity to feed the trout with pelletised food, something I always do when I visit a hatchery or trout farm. If you want a feed yourself, try the Wily Trout Cafe, a licensed restaurant at the entry gate that offers a diverse range of food and drink.

Behind the barbecue areas at the back of the facility is the River Plenty, where several fishing platforms are set up for disabled people. This is a wild river and the trout are free to roam, so I didn't expect to see much. But I walked onto the platform and tossed a few fish pellets into the river and trout – some of them better than 2kg – came thundering out of the water.

CENTRAL HIGHLAND LAKES

Most of these lakes are accessible from the Highland Lakes Rd, which feeds off the Midland Hwy about 55km north of Hobart. Once on the Highland Lakes Rd you will find directions to Arthurs Lake and Great Lake well signposted. To go to Little Pine Lagoon and Bronte System, turn left onto Marlborough Hwy near Miena.

ACCOMMODATION: Lodge and hotel accommodation is available, but lodgings can be tight when the trout season is on in earnest.
For more information visit www.centralhighlands.tas.gov.au

Trout anglers probably already know that Tasmania's Central Highland lakes are among the best in the world. Many offer fly-fishers an opportunity to sight fish for tailing trout around the lake margins. Fly-fishing doesn't get any better than that.

The Bronte system consists of four main lakes: Bronte Lagoon, Bradys Lake, Lake Binney and Tungatinah Lagoon.

The fishing is dominated by naturally spawned **brown trout** with lesser numbers of **rainbow trout** in Bronte Lagoon and Bradys Lake. Tasmania's Inland Fisheries Service has also stocked **Atlantic salmon** and **brook trout** in the lakes.

All waters in the system provide good opportunities to sight fish wearing polaroid sunglasses. Use beetle falls during summer, particularly on the western shore of Bradys Lake.

BRONTE LAGOON

One of the best known **trout** fisheries in Australia, Bronte Lagoon is easy to access from the Marlborough Hwy and is fringed with significant areas of tussocks and grassland. Anglers **camp** on the western shore near the boat ramp. There is another launching area suited for small boats where the main canal feeds the lake. When I was here there were only two anglers, and they were fishing the canal. One had been flicking small, soft plastic lures in the canal and along the lake margins, and had caught some brown trout, keeping a pair and releasing the rest. The bag limit is 12 for **brown** or **rainbow trout**, and five for brook trout.

Fly-fishers do well here early in the season with tailing trout, especially along the southern shore from Fly Corner to Woodwards Bay. During the summer, dry fly-fishing can come into its own with mayfly hatches, black spinners and gum beetle falls along the western shore. Trolling and spinning are popular.

LITTLE PINE LAGOON

It is only when you see those tailing trout working along the shallow, tussock-lined waters that you realise why so many fly-fishers put Little Pine Lagoon on their 'bucket list' of must-fish destinations. To get here, turn left onto Marlborough Hwy near Miena.

ACCOMMODATION: Lodge and hotel accommodation is available, but lodgings can be tight when the trout season is on in earnest.
For more information visit www.centralhighlands.tas.gov.au

Little Pine Lagoon is not much to look at, but is highly regarded by fly-fishers for its springtime tailing **trout** and summer dun hatches. Some anglers rate it Tasmania's premier fly-fishing water.

Boats can be launched on the east side near the Monpeelyate Canal. Car parking is available below the dam wall where there is a walkway across the Little Pine River so anglers can fly-fish the grassy promenade and western shore.

The origins of every brown trout on mainland Australia or in New Zealand can be traced back to Tasmania

GREAT LAKE

ACCOMMODATION: Lodge and hotel accommodation is available, but lodgings can be tight when the trout season is on in earnest.
For more information visit www.centralhighlands.tas.gov.au

A year-round **trout** fishery, Great Lake is one of Tasmania's best known waters and a thriving centre for holiday homes. **Brown trout** were first released here in 1870 and they still dominate the fishery with an average weight of about 1.5kg. **Rainbow trout** are fewer and account for less than 25 per cent of the trout catch.

To protect rainbow trout stocks, Tasmanian fisheries increased the minimum size to 40cm and put a bag limit of three a day.

Great Lake is a popular boating venue and there are boat ramps at Swan Bay, Haddens Bay, Tods Corner and Cramps Bay. A low water ramp has also been constructed at Boundary Bay.

Boats are launched elsewhere around the lake but this can be difficult when the lake level is low.

ARTHURS LAKE

Arthurs Lake is the most popular brown trout fishing water in the Central Highlands with more than 10,000 angler visitors a year and an estimated catch rate of 2.5 trout per angler. The lake was created by damming the Upper Lake River and is used as a water storage facility by the Tasmanian Hydro Electricity Commission. Situated 5km north of the Lake Hwy intersection, there are campgrounds at Pump House Bay and Jonah Bay, which are supervised by the Department of Parks and Wildlife. There is no power but both camp areas have toilets and cooking areas. Boat ramps are located at Pump House Bay, Arthurs Dam and Jonah Bay.

ACCOMMODATION: Lodge and hotel accommodation is available, but lodgings can be tight when the trout season is on in earnest.
For more information visit www.centralhighlands.tas.gov.au

Tasmanians claim that 'even novices can catch trout in Arthurs Lake'. This probably explains why this waterway is Tasmania's most popular trout fishery, hosting more anglers than any other water in the state.

Arthurs Lake is a **brown trout** fishery and all methods are employed. Every year, it's reported trout in excess of 4kg and up to 7.5kg have been caught here. Numerous boat ramps are available and camping areas are located at Pumphouse Bay and Jonah Bay.

LAKE RIVER

This river is south of Launceston, north of Hobart. I travelled from Hobart through Bagdad and Campbelltown on the Midland Hwy. Seek permission before venturing onto private property.

ACCOMMODATION: The nearest accommodation is in Launceston, with all styles available.
For more information visit www.discovertasmania.com

'Tasmania is in drought, we simply don't have enough water,' said my guide Roger Butler as we departed Hobart for Lake River, which joins the Macquarie River south of Launceston.

Roger was president of the Trout Guides and Lodges Tasmania, an organisation that looks after fishing guides and lodges. A big, amiable man, he sports a flock of white hair along with a white beard. All that separated him from being a twin to Santa Claus was a pillow.

It was hard to believe that this state, with several thousand lakes, was in drought; even harder when we arrived at our destination and I saw a river that was running high and fast. Water was coming down from the Central Highlands, flowing out of

Above: Roger Butler working a nymph fly in Lake River, between Launceston and Hobart
Below: Eyeball trout

Woods Lake and down the escarpment into Lake River. Even the paddocks we drove across were soggy, but Roger said this was due to recent rainfall.

Lake River is a meadow stream, flanked by flat pasture, grassy basins and backwater lagoons, but on my visit the water was so high and discoloured it was difficult to spot the weed beds and channels it is known for. And the wind was blowing consistently enough to make fly-casting difficult.

We carried four-weight fly rods, donned waders and set off to walk a couple of kilometres downstream. Roger was concerned that conditions were against us and it would be difficult to catch **trout**. Still, he was willing to have a go. Our rigs comprised a dark brown copper beadhead nymph set about 60cm beneath a fluoro material indicator. Roger preferred copper to brass beads, as they were 'more subtle'.

Lake River is rich in insect life. For proof, Roger pulled a sodden branch from the river to show the amount of mudeyes living in the timber.

Several hours of casting later, we arrived at a backwater. Roger worked this water square metre by square metre. He had two chances; both times the trout managed to get off the hook. That's fishing.

Back at the car, Roger was at a loss. He said Lake River was one of his most consistent waters, but conditions were against us. We had lunch and he decided we would go to Currawong Lakes between Lake Leake and Tooms Lake in the east coast highlands, a bit over an hour's drive away.

Currawong Lakes is a trout fishery and game park, set on 12sqkm and comes complete with fully appointed two- and four-bedroom cabins that can accommodate up to 20 visitors. There are three lakes and these are stocked with trophy-sized **rainbow** and **brown trout**. Fishing is year round and you don't need a fishing licence.

Ken Orr (left) and Ian Cook (right) with a sample of the trophy-sized trout available at Twin Lakes

Roger said there were prolific insect hatches and the fishing was usually excellent. An hour and a half after leaving Lake River we were casting flies into crystal clear water in the bottom lake. I cast, hooked-up and the trout was gone. It was one of those days. A trout was working near the mouth of an inlet channel and Roger began to stalk the fish. He had changed his fly to a dark brown emerger pattern. Presenting the fly wasn't easy, the wind was blowing about 20-knots and the only cover was a small island at the mouth of the channel. Roger persisted, but this trout wasn't cooperating.

We stopped fishing when it was too dark to see our flies. At the end, we didn't bag out on trout, but thankfully fly-fishing isn't just about the fish. It is also about the experience, the challenge of presenting a bogus offering of fur and feathers and trying to fool Mr Speckles into believing it is food.

TWIN LAKES

Twin Lakes is just under one hour's drive east of Hobart. To get there drive to Sorell, about 25km, then follow the Tasman Hwy for 36km then turn right onto Nugent Rd.

ACCOMMODATION: A house is available to rent on site.
For more information visit
www.twinlakes.com.au

I always thought the title of John Gierach's entertaining book, *Where the Trout are all as Long as your Leg* was a little far-fetched, until I realised it related to a time when he was five years old. I am a little older than that now but, having fished in Tasmania, I can claim to have been to the land of giant trout. The fish may not be as long as your leg, but you know you are into some serious fishing when you watch fly-fishing guide Ken Orr tie on a 10kg tippet because 'you will have no hope without heavy leader'. Ken is a fly-fishing guide with 30 years experience and an international reputation, and runs his own lodge at Bradys Lake.

The giant trout are on a 12sqkm property called Twin Lakes. It is a private fishery that consists, as the name suggests, of two lakes. My hosts at Twin Lakes were Rose and Ian Cook who moved to Australia from Devon, England. It was a major shift when you consider that Rose comes from a family who had lived in the same house for more than 900 years, and Ian was a former gamekeeper in Cornwall and Devon.

The lakes are 2ha and 1.6ha in size, and the top lake has a fully furnished house complete with spa set back from the shore. When full, this lake spreads out across the pasture, giving anglers the opportunity to sight-fish for tailing trout. The lower lake has **brown** and **rainbow trout** and small numbers of **Atlantic salmon**. Both lakes feature a productive ecosystem with good hatches of duns and mudeyes.

On my visit, the wind was swirling from west to south with gusts to about 20-knots. We went to the dam wall at the southern end of the bottom lake. The wind was blowing in from behind us, which made fly-casting difficult. It didn't worry Ian who was using a six-weight outfit and casting straight and true with a tight arc on his back cast.

The first hook-up came within 15 minutes of starting. The bend in Ian's rod and the blur from his fly reel as the fish peeled line indicated a big fish.

It was several minutes before Ken was able to net the fish, a beautifully coloured rainbow trout that weighed 5.2kg on the net scales.

Unlike some hatchery rainbow trout dispensed in lakes, these fish showed plenty of fight and came with the hallmark rose cheeks and pink flash along their flanks that divides the cream belly and green back.

With the trout in the net, Ken placed it in a revival tank fed with an oxygen bottle to ensure the fish made a quick recovery before being put back into the lake. Like most private fisheries, this one is about catch and release. The next fish to fall to a fly was an Atlantic salmon. Ian said the salmon had come in with a batch of trout, so he thought he would put them into the lake to see what happened.

Ian walked along the western shore of the lake and promptly hooked another rainbow, a twin of the one still recovering in the holding tank. When the second trout came in, another was following. Ken removed the trout from the net, realised it was egg bound and proceeded to strip the fish of its eggs by running his thumb and forefinger along the fish's belly. Removing the roe ensures the trout will not become egg-bound and die.

The week before I arrived, a group of fly-fishers at the lakes caught rainbow trout to 9kg and brown trout to 6.2kg. These are enormous weights for trout in any water. Ian explained that the average size of the trout in the lakes was 5.5kg, and most of them are five–six years old, but they have a lifespan of eight–ten years in this environment. All the trout came from wild stocks sourced from places like Great Lake and reared by Tasmanian Inland Fisheries. The fish are released into the lakes at 250–300g. As you might expect, the trout are well educated in the ways of fly-fishers.

Methods for Freshwater Trail

TACKLE Fly-fishers work five- and six-weight outfits, although a few were working outfits down to two-weight for finer presentations. Weight-forward floating lines are the most popular, with leader length of 3–4m. Tippet size is up to the individual, but can be gossamer-thin 1–2kg breaking strain for the small flies.

LURES For trolling, use bibbed minnows, bladed lures, soft plastics and winged lures (Tassie Devils, Loftys). In the lakes, downrigger trolling deep diving lures is popular.

BAIT Brown trout are the dominant species in Tasmania, but there are rainbow trout in some waters, with lesser numbers of Atlantic salmon and **brook trout**. All can be caught on bait (where allowed) such as wattle grubs, worms and mudeyes, using light threadline outfits spooled with 2–3kg lines. Hook size varies with bait: a No. 6 is a big hook, and for mudeyes, you will find No. 12 a better size. The method is to either fish under a bubble float and drift the bait into deeper holes, or put a couple of pieces of split shot on the line to take the bait deeper, again casting upstream and allowing it to be washed into holes where larger fish are likely to wait.

FLIES Match the fly to suit activity: midge and gum beetle patterns, exciter flies and gold beadhead nymphs in brown or black. Popular flies include Highland Dun, Black Spinner, Red Spinner, Emerger patterns and green nymphs. Fly-fishers – as well as walking the shoreline and fishing with polaroid sunglasses on the margins – often use boats to work wind lanes on still mornings.

Many Tasmanian estuaries harbour large populations of black bream

2 SALT WATER

Note: You do not need a licence for saltwater fishing in Tasmanian salt water, however, a sea fishing licence is required to fish for abalone, rock lobster and scallops or with a graball, mullet and beach seine net.

HUON VALLEY AND BRUNY

The drive south along the Huon coast from Hobart to Gordon takes about an hour. To get there follow the Southern Outlet (A6) to the Kingston Bypass then follow the signs to the Channel Hwy (B68).

The D'Entrecasteaux Channel encompasses the waters between Bruny Island and the south-east Tasmanian mainland, and is regarded as a fishing hot spot. The channel extends between the estuaries of the Derwent and Huon rivers.

As a 'recreational only' fishery, there is no commercial fishing pressure, and as a result reliable catches are almost assured. Anglers can expect to catch **flathead**, **cod**, and **gummy sharks** in the channel all year. Species that visit these waters on a seasonal basis include **Australian salmon**, **barracouta**, **mackerel**, **warehou** and **squid**.

Access to the Channel is good with many areas accessible from the shore. Plenty of small boat ramps are scattered along its length. Shore-based anglers do well at places like Port Esperance, which features deep shelving waters accessible at Dover from headlands and jetties. Flathead is the dominant species, but anglers also hook into Australian salmon, barracouta, **silver trevally** and sometimes **sea-run brown trout**.

Southport jetty produces barracouta, squid, flathead, mackerel and **leatherjackets**. The Lune River is popular, and this water can produce brown trout to 6kg, flathead, Australian salmon and **bream**.

Three places that suit shore-based angling are Gordon, Woodbridge and Kettering, as they offer good structure. Gordon is noted for its squid runs.

Brendan Wing (centre) caught this big southern bluefin tuna offshore from Eaglehawke Neck

Woodbridge jetty fishes in similar vein for squid and other species mentioned. The Bruny Island ferry departs from Kettering, but the bay fishes well.

Atlantic salmon are farmed along the south-east coast and escapees are often caught by anglers. What are called 'break-outs' of Atlantic salmon are common, and are caused by damage to the nets by seals, storms and even human error. The salmon average about 3–4kg. Atlantic Salmon fight well and make for a tasty meal.

Top spots for Atlantic salmon include the open water adjacent to the sea pens in the D'Entrecasteaux Channel, and in sheltered areas such as Port Esperance, where these fish can be caught from shore.

EAGLEHAWK NECK

To get here, take the A3 Hwy out of Hobart, and then swing onto the Arthur Hwy. The drive takes about an hour and a half, depending on time of day and traffic.

Heading north of Hobart, Eaglehawk Neck on the way to Port Arthur, is noted for its offshore fishing for big, **southern bluefin tuna**. As well, offshore anglers can hook **yellowfin tuna**, **mako sharks**, **albacore** and sometimes **striped marlin**.

The game fish season runs from about January–August. Bluefin are best from about April–July.The amazing feature of game fishing in these waters is that the fishing grounds are close, ranging from inshore out to the Continental shelf, only 8NM east of the Hippolite Rocks. Other species you can catch include **striped trumpeter**, **barracouta** and **Australian salmon**.

The jetty in Pirates Bay, near the Blowhole, produces **mackerel** and **flathead**, and anglers fishing from shore in Eaglehawk Bay catch flathead and salmon.

GREAT OYSTER BAY

The drive from Hobart to Swansea takes about two hours on the A3 Hwy. Great Oyster Bay is surrounded by the west coast of Freycinet National Park, Nine

Mile Beach in the north and the historic township of Swansea to the west.

The most common capture is flathead, but squid are also on the menu, along with wrasse and sometimes whiting.

ACCOMMODATION: Swansea has a holiday park, motels, B&Bs and cottages to rent.
For more information visit
www.visitswanseatasmania.com.au

There are beaches, rocky headlands and piers to fish from. The Swansea jetty is popular, and species caught include **flounder**, **garfish**, **flathead**, **whiting** and **mullet**. The Swan River, north of Swansea, is popular for both shore and boat fishing for **bream**, which average about 1kg, and fish in excess of 2kg are caught. Best access to fishing spots on the Swan River is along Dolphin Sands Rd. Crabs, prawns, pretty fish and nippers all make good bait. The lower reaches of the river produce garfish and **leatherjackets**.

Nine Mile Beach, and several other beaches and rocky outcrops that flank the northern and western sides of Great Oyster Bay, offer good fishing.

Coles Bay

FREYCINET NATIONAL PARK

Coles Bay is a 45-minute drive from Swansea at the northern edge of the Freycinet National Park in Great Oyster Bay, and the turn-off is a few kilometres north of Swansea.

Coles Bay is a popular fishing area, producing flathead, silver trevally, Australian salmon, mackerel, cod, gummy sharks, squid, rock lobster, and bream. Offshore anglers catch striped trumpeter, albacore, and southern bluefin tuna.

ACCOMMODATION: Coles Bay offers a holiday park, cottages and houses to rent, as well as the luxurious Saffire if you really need to indulge.
For more information visit
www.discovertasmania.com.au
www.wineglassbay.com

The waters around Coles Bay are deep and clear. The main pier at Coles Bay often has good numbers of **squid**, and these are caught on jigs with the best results coming at night. **Australian salmon**, **longfin pike** and **mackerel** are also caught from this jetty. Coles Bay is protected from the open sea, and the channel that runs behind the coastal strip of Nine Mile Beach produces **bream**, **flathead**, **flounder** and **salmon**. Bream are common in the creeks and rivers along this coast, and move downstream to the entrances after heavy rain. There is a spot behind Nine Mile Beach called Moulting Lagoon that holds good numbers of bream along with **baitfish** and **shrimp**.

ST HELENS

From Launceston, the drive takes more than two hours to reach St Helens. Head south on the Midland Hwy for about 50km, then turn left on to Esk Hwy to St Marys, then continue on the Tasman Hwy to St Helens.

Entrance to Moulting Lagoon

ACCOMMODATION: A tourist centre, visitors can choose from caravan parks, motels, units and cottages.
For more information visit www.discovertasmania.com

Most mainlanders once regarded Tasmania's east coast seaport of St Helens as a gamefishing destination, and little else. Anglers came here to head offshore in search of **marlin**, **tuna** and **sharks**. However, the phenomenal growth in light-tackle lure fishing, in particular soft plastics, in recent years has seen Georges Bay at St Helens become a hotspot for smaller species including **bream**, **trevally**, **salmon**, **flathead**, **yellowtail kingfish** and **mullet**.

There are two reasons why St Helens is a productive game fish destination: the close access to deep water, with the 100m line about 5km offshore; and the East Australian Current, which runs down the east coast. Bait and jig anglers will appreciate the reef systems closer to shore that rise to within 6m of the surface and offer holding areas for baitfish schools.

Land-based anglers have beach and jetty fishing options. Five boat ramps service the area, including two that give direct access to the ocean, thereby eliminating the need to cross the bar. Georges Bay is so well regarded that the Australian Bream Tournament series holds events here, and in 2009 Tasmanian Steve Steer won the event and his biggest bream was 1.84kg. The average weight of more than 300 bream weighed in was 730g. Steve headed to the mouth and fished the flats near the outer oyster racks, and was fishing water so shallow that his electric motor was hitting the bottom. The technique was long casts followed by a slow retrieve, punctuated with twitches.

STANLEY

The drive from Devonport to Stanley on the north-west coast is about two hours along the Bass Hwy. It is a scenic drive so time your departure to go in daylight.

Stanley is best known for its run of **blue warehou** or **trevalla**, also known as **snotty trevalla** from the Stanley Wharf.

The trevalla run from about December to April, and when this happens anglers stand shoulder to shoulder and multiple hook ups can see 20 anglers hooked up at the same time. As well as trevalla, **Australian salmon**, **barracouta**, **mullet**, **leatherjacket**, **squid** and sometimes **yellowtail kingfish** are caught. Stanley is surrounded by the

Arthur River on Tasmania's wild west coast

East and Western Inlets where anglers can hook Australian salmon, **flounder**, **barracouta**, **pike**, **gummy sharks** and **flathead**.

ARTHUR RIVER

Drive down the west coast and you come across Arthur River, a small, coastal holiday village on the banks of the Arthur River, about 61km from Smithton. The area is pristine wilderness, surrounded by dense forests with giant tree ferns, blackwood, myrtles, and celery top pine.

Arthur River is famous for producing big, sea-run brown trout.

ACCOMMODATION: There is canoe and boat hire available, and Parks and Wildlife operate three campgrounds: Manuka, Peppermint and Prickly Wattle.

For more information visit www.arthurriver.com.au/page3/arthurriver

Nelson Bay, at the mouth of the river, is accessible by car and is popular with anglers who catch good numbers of **Australian salmon**. These fish appear in late spring and stay until the first major floods push them out to sea in the autumn.

An excellent boat ramp is situated on the southern side of the river, and to find it travelling from the north, take the first left on the southern side of the bridge. The estuary is safe for small boats, but seek local advice before attempting to cross the bar into the ocean as a number of boats have come to grief. The river is navigable for about 18km upstream from the township.

A right turn will take you down to a rocky headland at the rivermouth, also popular with anglers.

The beach on the northern side of the river allows shore-based anglers easy access; the turn-off is on the northern side of the bridge. The sand is hard and easy to drive on.

Trolling for **trout** in the upper reaches of the river can produce fish to 5kg; the peak time is during the whitebait runs.

The beaches and rocky headlands can produce salmon to 6kg, **gummy sharks** and **sweep**. Top spots include Sandy Cape, Sandy Cape Beach, Arthurs Beach, Browns Hole, Netley Bay and Sinking Rock, noted for its **yellowtail kingfish**. The easiest fishing is when the wind is blowing from the east, which settles the seas.

Methods for Arthur River

TACKLE In the surf, bait fishing using bluebait or pilchard in conjunction with surf poppers is the standard method. However, in the estuary, spinning with chrome metal lures, and saltwater fly fishing produce results on salmon.

LURES Trolling with lures and flies will produce salmon and trout. When the salmon are running, they will strike most lures.

FLINDERS ISLAND

Visitors to Flinders Island find the easiest and quickest way to get there is by plane. Flinders Island is halfway across Bass Strait. Air travel to the island is limited but it's worth the effort. Commuter flights are limited, so often it is a matter of taking a charter. Whatever the cost, the visit is worth the effort and you can expect to hook salmon and flathead from the shore, while offshore tuna, sharks and marlin are caught.

ACCOMMODATION: There is accommodation ranging from farm stays to motel and camping. It depends on what you are after.
For more information visit www.visitflindersisland.com.au

Most anglers who visit the island and sample the fishing return full of praise for the place.

Flinders Island is the largest of the 52 islands that comprise the Furneaux Group that runs from the southern tip of Wilsons Promontory to the north-east tip of the Tasmanian mainland. When you can't get offshore at Flinders, kilometres of pristine beaches produce excellent fishing, especially for **Australian salmon** that reach better than 3kg.

Local fishing tour operator Jim Luddington (Flinders Island Adventures) runs a 10m twin-hulled vessel called *Strait Lady* out of the port of Lady Barron. The boat is well set up for fishing, a stable platform with plenty of room for anglers.

Fishing off Flinders Island is a year-round proposition. Game fish such as **yellowfin tuna**, **marlin** and **albacore** run from about December through to about April. Anytime from March through to May sees **southern bluefin** tuna migrating past the islands. For most of the year anglers can expect to catch **salmon**, **flathead** to 2.5kg and **snapper** to 5.5kg around the islands. Offshore bottom bouncing in deep water is popular for the likes of **trumpeter** and **trevalla**.

Before I went to Flinders Island a friend said: 'It's a great place for fishing, pristine waters and magic scenery, but they bottle the wind down that way.' On the first day of a three-day trip the wind roared up from the Southern Ocean, at times blowing hard enough to pluck the feathers from the wild turkeys that roam the island. But with all those beaches it didn't matter.

Jim and I fished a few different areas, beach and offshore. Sea conditions prevented a run into the Tasman Sea for tuna, so instead Jim opted to fish in the lee of Gull Island where there was a good chance of catching **snook (shortfinned pike)** on fly rods. Snook look similar to barracouta; the snout is a bit longer and the colouring is olive on the back to white on the belly, whereas couta can be almost black on the back, but the wolf-like teeth and teddy-bear eyes are similar.

Jim Xyga shows off a fine pair of black bream caught on lures in Tasmania.

You won't suffer a heart attack fishing for snook; this fish is not built for speed or hard, diving lunges. But the good thing about these fish is that they hunt in packs, so once you find them, you will catch a few. At Gull Island the *Strait Lady* was positioned to take advantage of the wind and allowed to drift across a small bay close to a rock with a good wash.

The flies, Lefty Deceiver and Closer Minnows in yellow, blue and white, were laid out onto the water, allowed to sink and then stripped back with a slow, hesitant retrieve.

It was a case of hook-up, catch and release. The snook session went for as long as we wanted it to. After a couple of hours, Jim opted for a change of venue and species. 'I reckon we should go up to the Pot Boil and fish for **school sharks** and **gummies**,' he suggested. 'It might be a bit rugged, but it's fishable.'

The Pot Boil is an awesome stretch of water and on the shallow sandbars to the east, west and south of us, waves were lifting and crashing. The wind was blowing about 25-knots, and pushing the tide. When the tide changed to flood the fishing would become difficult as the waves stood up against the wind.

It was like fishing in the Port Phillip Heads rip on the ebb tide; a roller-coaster with pressure waves pushing the boat in different directions. The first drift over 24m of water produced a 3.6kg **yank flathead**, known locally as **Castlenau's flathead**. The next drift raised a 17kg school shark that threatened to empty the reel several times. The final drift produced a 6kg gummy shark and we lost another school shark at the net while we fiddled around taking photos. By then our window of opportunity was over and it was time to think of a change before the 3m tide churned up the sea and the pot started to boil over.

'I say we head in and make tracks for Red Bluff,' Jim said. 'The wind will be behind us and there could be a few salmon on the beach if we time our arrival right.'

At Red Bluff the beach stretches away to the south to Sellars Point. Just one bait was in the water and a 2kg salmon came ashore for Jim. We caught three more salmon about the same size in three consecutive casts, but the fishing didn't last. Heavy freshwater run-off slowly worked its way south along the beach and the salmon moved to more saline grounds.

Methods for Salt Water

TACKLE

Offshore

Most anglers work 15–24kg outfits. Marlin fishing is about trolling live baits such as slimy mackerel or small tuna at about 2km/hr. Lures and fish rigged up as skip baits are trolled at higher speeds of about 8–10km/hr. Teasers are used to attract fish. These include daisy chains of plastic squid, 'birds' or large flashing reflectors such as the Witchdoctor or Reflector Bonito. Yellowfin tuna can be caught trolling, cubing or live baiting.

Bottom fishing requires 8–10kg outfits and paternoster rigs, either with the sinker fixed or running. If you intend dropping a line in deep water then run a 15kg outfit and spool the reel with 24kg (or heavier) braid as this will reduce the need for a heavy sinker.

Surf, pier and rock

On the beaches, an 8–10kg surf outfit will cover most options, although if you prefer spinning to bait fishing then you can reduce your outfit size to about 4kg. When fishing for salmon use a two-leader paternoster rig with size 3/0–4/0 hooks and bait such as pilchard. Put a soft plastic lure, surf popper or saltwater fly on the top leader and bait on the bottom one.

Estuary

In the estuaries, a 2–3kg threadline outfit will cover most scenarios. Choose a rod with a fast tip action that is light enough to cast small lures or lightly weighted baits. Fly-fishers will find six–eight-weight outfits suitable. An intermediate or slow sink fly line will cover most options. Work 5kg level line leaders straight to the fly.

A No. 4 Baitholder pattern will suit most species and a running sinker rig will account for bottom feeders. For top-water fish, such as garfish, mullet and luderick, use a float rig, and be prepared to downsize your hook to a No. 6 to No. 8.

Trolling and spinning has developed a strong following and anglers can do well using bibbed minnow or soft plastic lures.

Fly-fishers will find small baitfish patterns such as the Lefty Deceiver and Deep Clouser Minnow effective, along with small Pink Things and Crazy Charlies.

In terms of popularity, lure and fly-fishing still rank well behind traditional bait methods. Pipis, mussels, sandworms and garden worms, crab, fish strips and squid will account for most species.

INDEX

PLACE NAMES

Note: *Bold page numbers refer to major descriptions.*

D

E

F

G

H

I

J

K

L

M

N

O

P

Q

R

S

T

U

V

W

Y

Z

FISH SPECIES

Acknowledgements

The publisher would like to acknowledge the following individuals and organisations in the production of this edition:

Editorial manager
Melissa Kayser

Project manager
Alison Proietto

Editor
Alice Barker

Cartography
Bruce McGurty, Emily Maffei

Cover design
Philip Campbell Design

Illustrations
Chris Palatsides

Layout
Megan Ellis

Index
Max McMaster

Pre-press
Splitting Image

Photography credits
Cover
Fishing for tailor on the beach at Carnarvan, WA (Steve Cooper)

Cover pattern
Empty blue ocean and blue sky (EpicStockMedia/Shutterstock.com)

Back cover
Fishing at Lucky Bay, Cape Le Grand National Park, Esperance, WA (©Ozimages/Alamy); Steve Cooper (Raymond Clifford)

All images are © Steve Cooper, except for the following:
Pages 8 (bottom), 11, 117 (bottom), 127 (top), 131, 134 (top), 136 (top), 212, 219, 235 & 244: Rod Mackenzie
Page 22: Phillip Stathis
Pages 24, 26, 86, 95, 325, 348, 360, 361 & 363: Rod Harrison
Pages 43, 44, 45, 46 & 47: Mick Hall
Pages 89 (bottom), 90 & 271: Mark Griffin
Pages 91, 105, 146, 152, 158, 190 & 380: Cam Whittam
Pages 110 & 164: Sing Ling
Pages 132, 155 & 157: Dominic Domagala
Pages 174 & 375: Brendan Wing
Page 188: Gary Fitzgerald
Pages 266, 273, 280 & 281: Emma George
Pages 329 & 330: Alex Julius

Explore Australia Publishing Pty Ltd
Ground Floor, Building 1, 658 Church Street,
Richmond, VIC 3121

Explore Australia Publishing Pty Ltd is a division of Hardie Grant Publishing Pty Ltd

hardie grant publishing
Published by Explore Australia Publishing Pty Ltd, 2014

A Cataloguing-in-Publication entry is available from the catalogue of the National Library of Australia at www.nla.gov.au

ISBN-13 9781741174700

10 9 8 7 6 5 4 3 2 1

Printed and bound in China by 1010 Printing International Ltd

Publisher's note: Every effort has been made to ensure that the information in this book is accurate at the time of going to press. The publisher welcomes information and suggestions for correction or improvement. Email: info@exploreaustralia.net.au

www.exploreaustralia.net.au
Follow us on Twitter: @ExploreAus
Find us on Facebook: www.facebook.com/exploreaustralia